Almost Citizens

Almost Citizens lays out the tragic story of how the United States denied Puerto Ricans full citizenship following annexation of the island in 1898. As America became an overseas empire, a handful of remarkable Puerto Ricans debated with U.S. legislators, presidents, judges, and others over who was a citizen and what citizenship meant. This struggle caused a fundamental shift in constitutional jurisprudence: away from the post-Civil War regime of citizenship, rights, and statehood and toward doctrines that accommodated racist imperial governance. Erman's gripping account shows how, in the wake of the Spanish–American War, administrators, lawmakers, and presidents, together with judges, deployed creativity and ambiguity to transform constitutional law and interpretation over a quarter century of debate and litigation. The result is a history in which the United States and Latin America, Reconstruction and empire, and law and bureaucracy intertwine.

Sam Erman is Associate Professor at the University of Southern California Gould School of Law.

See the Studies in Legal History series website at http://studiesinlegalhistory.org/

Studies in Legal History

Editors

Sarah Barringer Gordon, University of Pennsylvania
Holly Brewer, University of Maryland, College Park
Michael Lobban, London School of Economics and Political Science
Reuel Schiller, University of California, Hastings College of the Law

Other books in the series

Jessica K. Lowe, *Murder in the Shenandoah: Making Law Sovereign in Revolutionary Virginia*

Martha S. Jones, *Birthright Citizens: A History of Race and Rights in Antebellum America*

Cynthia Nicoletti, *Secession on Trial: The Treason Prosecution of Jefferson Davis*

Edward James Kolla, *Sovereignty, International Law, and the French Revolution*

Assaf Likhovski, *Tax Law and Social Norms in Mandatory Palestine and Israel*

Robert W. Gordon, *Taming the Past: Essays on Law and History and History in Law*

Paul Garfinkel, *Criminal Law in Liberal and Fascist Italy*

Michelle A. McKinley, *Fractional Freedoms: Slavery, Intimacy, and Legal Mobilization in Colonial Lima, 1600–1700*

Mitra Sharafi, *Law and Identity in Colonial South Asia: Parsi Legal Culture, 1772–1947*

Karen M. Tani, *States of Dependency: Welfare, Rights, and American Governance, 1935–1972*

Stefan Jurasinski, *The Old English Penitentials and Anglo-Saxon Law*

Felice Batlan, *Women and Justice for the Poor: A History of Legal Aid, 1863–1945*

Sophia Z. Lee, *The Workplace Constitution from the New Deal to the New Right*

Michael A. Livingston, *The Fascists and the Jews of Italy: Mussolini's Race Laws, 1938–1943*

Almost Citizens

Puerto Rico, the U.S. Constitution, and Empire

SAM ERMAN
University of Southern California

CAMBRIDGE
UNIVERSITY PRESS

CAMBRIDGE
UNIVERSITY PRESS

University Printing House, Cambridge CB2 8BS, United Kingdom

One Liberty Plaza, 20th Floor, New York, NY 10006, USA

477 Williamstown Road, Port Melbourne, VIC 3207, Australia

314-321, 3rd Floor, Plot 3, Splendor Forum, Jasola District Centre, New Delhi - 110025, India

79 Anson Road, #06-04/06, Singapore 079906

Cambridge University Press is part of the University of Cambridge.

It furthers the University's mission by disseminating knowledge in the pursuit of education, learning and research at the highest international levels of excellence.

www.cambridge.org
Information on this title: www.cambridge.org/9781108401494
DOI: 10.1017/9781108233866

© Sam Erman 2019

First published 2019
First paperback edition 2019

A catalogue record for this publication is available from the British Library

Library of Congress Cataloging in Publication data
NAMES: Erman, Sam.
TITLE: Almost citizens : Puerto Rico, the U.S. Constitution, and empire / Sam Erman, University of Southern California.
DESCRIPTION: Cambridge, United Kingdom ; New York, NY, USA : Cambridge University Press, 2018. | Series: Studies in legal history | Based on author's thesis (doctoral – University of Michigan, 2010), issued under title: Puerto Rico and the Promise of United States Citizenship : Struggles around Status in a New Empire, 1898–1917. | Includes bibliographical references and index.
IDENTIFIERS: LCCN 2018035531 | ISBN 9781108415491 (hardback)
SUBJECTS: LCSH: Citizenship – United States. | Puerto Ricans – Legal status, laws, etc. – United States. | Puerto Rico – International status. | Puerto Rico – Politics and government – 1898–1952. | BISAC: HISTORY / United States / 20th Century.
Classification: LCC KF4720.P83 E76 2018 | DDC 342.7308/3097295–dc23
LC record available at https://lccn.loc.gov/2018035531

ISBN 978-1-108-41549-1 Hardback
ISBN 978-1-108-40149-4 Paperback

For Joo

Contents

Figures

Acknowledgments

Rebecca Scott made me a historian. She inspired, mentored, corrected, and encouraged me for nearly a decade as a graduate student. Her voice, literal and imagined, guides me still.

Other voices also made signal contributions to this project. Martha Jones encouraged me to put the legacies of Reconstruction at the center of my work. Daniel Ernst awoke my passion for analyzing agencies and institutions. Jesse Hoffnung-Garskof kept me rooted in the experiences of the people I study. Susanna Blumenthal knew when to nudge, when to cheer, and when to nudge again. Judge José Cabranes, Laura Gómez, Jeff Lehman, and Sandy Levinson all also offered valuable assistance.

I received my JD and PhD from the University of Michigan. Having expressed my gratitude to many people there in my dissertation and in print, I enthusiastically incorporate those acknowledgments here.[1] My debts have grown in the interim. I trust that my Wolverine bondholders, whether old or new, know how profoundly appreciative I am.

I could not ask for a better professional home than my current one, the University of Southern California's Gould School of Law. Among many friends, mentors, critics, and boosters who gave of their time as I wrote this book, Ariela Gross deserves special mention. Brilliant, generous, accomplished, and wise, she lit my way with her insight and camaraderie. Rebecca Brown, David Cruz, Dan Klerman, Daria Roithmayr, Hillary Schor, and Nomi Stolzenberg read and advised to my great benefit. My deans, vice deans, academic deans, and the institution they run were unflaggingly generous in providing me the time and resources to complete this project. I am grateful to my fellow junior colleagues, including those now in the senior ranks. I am also grateful to our library faculty. Traces of their skill, precision, and energy marble this book. I have benefited from the excellent work of too many research assistants to list and from members of the greater USC community, particularly Jessica Marglin, Nayan Shah, and Diana Williams.

My other professional home is the American Society for Legal History and the community of scholars who constitute it. To work among such warm, constructive, welcoming, inspiring, and incisive colleagues is a gift. I owe particular thanks to Greg Ablavsky, Clara Altman, Kevin Arlyck, Bethany Berger, Mary Sarah Bilder, Michael Churgin, Deborah Dinner, Willie Forbath, Bob Gordon, Dan Hulsebosch, Kelly Kennington, Jeremy Kessler, Jed Kroncke, Sophia Lee, Maeva Marcus, Serena Mayeri, Michelle McKinley, Bill Nelson, Kunal Parker, Nick Parrillo, Polly Price, Intisar Rabb, Gautham Rao, Lucy Salyer, Logan Sawyer, Veta Schlimgen, Mitra Sharafi, Daniel Sharfstein, Brad Snyder, Clyde Spillenger, Karen Tani, Kate Unterman, Laura Weinrib, Barbara Welke, John Witt, and many others.

I have been blessed with amazing editors. For the society's book series, Sally Gordon is an editor like no other. She gets her hands dirty and grapples with prose throughout the writing and revising process. Her example, advice, vision, and edits have elevated my work. Reuel Schiller joined Sally as the series' coeditor late in my writing process, yet his keen editorial eye was invaluable. Grey Osterud and Pamela Haag helped me bring the word on the page ever closer to the story in my head. At Cambridge University Press, Debbie Gershenowitz was an enthusiastic, organized, and forward-looking quarterback; Julie Hagen was a meticulous and sensitive copyeditor; and Julie Hrischeva attentively shepherded the book through to production.

I have been fortunate to work as a law clerk for three judges I admire enormously. Judge Merrick Garland has more integrity than any person I know. He is a stunningly talented legal practitioner and is utterly dedicated to getting the law right. Justices Anthony Kennedy and John Paul Stevens are legal trailblazers and profoundly decent individuals. I aspire to honor the example of all three men. I am also grateful for my dazzlingly talented coclerks, whose assistance and support I cherish.

Archives are the lifeblood of historical scholarship. In the physical world, I worked with excellent collections and archivists at the Universidad de Puerto Rico, the Archivo General de Puerto Rico, the National Archives, the Library of Congress, Hunter College's Center for Puerto Rican Studies, the New York Public Library, the Centro de Investigación y Desarrollo de la Cultura Cubana Juan Marinello, the Centro de Estudios Martianos, and the Biblioteca Nacional José Martí, among others. José M. Encarnación, Pedro Juan Hernández, Sra. Merche Hicón, Edwin Meléndez, Jose H. Morales Cardona, Evelyn Sola, and the entire staff at the Universidad de Puerto Rico's Centro de Investigaciones Históricas in Río Piedras welcomed me into their archives and ensured that my research there was a success. Online, I used databases compiled by Proquest, Readex, the Library of Congress, Ancestry.com, Family Search, Gale, and many others. To my great benefit, the U.S. Supreme Court library assisted me beyond all reasonable expectation.

These many resources came alive in new ways after Belinda Torres-Mary introduced herself to me as the great-granddaughter of Isabel Gonzalez, an individual who figures prominently in the chapters that follow. A crack genealogist with whom I was lucky enough to collaborate, she put me in contact with her parents, told me family lore, swapped research finds with me, and joined me in brainstorming. The book is richer for her participation. Although genealogists and academic historians use the past in somewhat different ways, Torres-Mary and I shared a connection to Gonzalez, a passion for research, and a commitment to listening to the sources. Through Torres-Mary, I gained a deeper appreciation of my obligation to do right by the people about whom I write. I am hopeful that the Isabel Gonzalez portrayed in these pages is one that Torres-Mary and her relations recognize.

Financial and institutional support is crucial to historical scholarship. I owe a special debt to William Jentes, whose named scholarship accelerated my studies at a formative moment. I am grateful to the Smithsonian Institution's Latino Studies Fellowship, which funded my work and my year in residence at the National Museum of American History. I am also grateful to the Raoul Berger–Mark DeWolfe Howe Legal History Fellowship for funding my research and year in residence at Harvard Law School. At Harvard, particular thanks are due to Mike Klarman, Kenneth Mack, Bruce Mann, Jed Shugerman, and Mark Tushnet. Georgetown University Law Center and the Universidad de Puerto Rico's Recinto de Río Piedras both provided me homes away from home. In Río Piedras, Juan José Baldrich, Gonzalo Córdova, Astrid Cubano Iguina, and Lanny Thompson were invaluable interlocutors.

One of the pleasures of writing this book has been the opportunity to contribute to national conversations. Kris Collins, Linda Kerber, Nathan Perl-Rosenthal, Christina Ponsa, Gilien Silsby, and Neil Weare have been companions and instructors in this endeavor.

Family and friends sustained me throughout the process of bringing this book about. I am thankful to the Corcoran and Ermann clans and to my in-laws, whose combined support and encouragement were wonderful and unstinting. Rebecca Batiste, Brian Corcoran, Casey Corcoran, David Corcoran, Sue Dollinger, Lynn Ermann, Allan Ermann, Kay Lee, Kevin Lee, Sue Lee, Jonathan Ragle, Kate Toews, and Elaine Tung all contributed time, wisdom, or resources that benefited the book. My oldest and dearest friend is Greg Walton. To speak of his many contributions to the book is to miss the point. He has contributed much to the making of me, and it is that for which I am most grateful. Rabia Belt is also like family. She inspires me, truly.

I have extravagantly good parents. Low on the list of their gifts to me, but of relevance here, they introduced me to the world of ideas, to the aspiration to do good, to the joys of collegiality, to the rewards of mentoring and being mentored, and to the hard-won satisfactions of writing and editing. For this and so much else, I am grateful.

Eli, Ella, and Lola are the bright, shining center of my world. I love them and am proud of them beyond all measure. I thank them for their patience and forgiveness when I worked late or became cross because writing was hard. And

I am grateful for their advance reviews of the book. Eli judged it impressive that I typed so much, but also odd. Lola approved of a book with stories, but declared that fairy tales would have been better. Ella simply yelled: "Boring!"

Listing Julia Lee's many contributions to this volume would be a fool's errand, especially because they are not the wellspring of my greatest gratitude. My pulse still quickens each time she enters the room because she encouraged my water balloon zipline, rode the *guagua* with me all summer, embodies lawyering for a better world, cuts our whole family's hair, is as quick to silliness and joy as our children, and betters my world in a million other ways. She is my great and perpetual benediction. Her love, companionship, humor, warmth, wisdom, faith, goodness, and generosity fill my life with meaning, happiness, and passion. It is my astounding luck to have a lifetime to spend with her.

Far too many others have had a hand in this book to attempt to list them all. The errors that remain are mine alone.

Abbreviations

1880 Census, ED _	Tenth Census of the United States, 1880, DC NARA, Record Group 29, Microfilm Publication T9, Brooklyn, Kings County, NY, [Enumeration District (ED __)]; available at Ancestry.com
1892 Census, _	New York State Education Department, Office of Cultural Education, 1892 New York State Census, Albany, New York State Library, [district]; available at Ancestry.com
1900 Census, ED _	Twelfth Census of the United States, 1900, DC NARA, Record Group 29, Microfilm Publication T623, Brooklyn, Kings County, NY, [Enumeration District (ED __)]; available at Ancestry.com
1904 Census _/_	New York, State Census, 1904, Population Schedules, New York State Archives, Albany, [Election District], [Enumeration District]; available at Ancestry.com
1910 Census _/_/_/_	Department of Commerce and Labor – Bureau of the Census, Thirteenth Census of the United States: 1910 – Population, FHL microfilm 1375016, DC NARA Record Group 29, Microfilm Publication T624, [Supervisor's District], [Enumeration District], [Ward or Assembly District of city], [sheet], [place]; available at Ancestry.com
1915 Census _/_/_	New York State Archives, Albany, State Population Census Schedules, 1915, [Election District], [Assembly District], [place], [page]; available at Ancestry.com

1920 Census _/_/_/_/_	Fourteenth Census of the United States, 1920, DC NARA, Record Group 29, [state or territory], [city], [neighborhood], microfilm publication T625, [Enumeration District], [sheet]; available at Ancestry.com
1930 Census _/_/_/_/_	Fifteenth Census of the United States, 1930, DC NARA, Record Group 29, Microfilm Publication T626, [city], [county], [state], [Enumeration District], [sheet]; available at Ancestry.com
AG/DE/SPR/COS	Archivo General de Puerto Rico, Fondo del Departamento de Estado, Sección del Secretario de Puerto Rico, Serie del Correspondencia Oficina del Secretaria
AG/OG/CG/_/_	Archivo General de Puerto Rico, Fondo del Oficina de Gobernador, Serie Correspondencia General, [caja (box)], [cartapacio (folder)]
CDO:_	El Centro de Documentación Obrera Santiago Iglesias Pantín, Microfilm Collection, [roll]
CIHCAM_/_/_	Centro de Investigaciones Históricas, Colección Ángel M. Mergal, [caja (box)], [cartapacio (folder)], [documento (document)]
CIHCAM _/L_	Centro de Investigaciones Históricas, Colección Ángel M. Mergal, [caja (box)], [libro (book) (L __)]
CPMN	Colección Puertorriqueña, Microfilm, Newspapers, Biblioteca de la Universidad de Puerto Rico, Recinto de Río Piedras
DC NARA	District of Columbia Branch, National Archives and Records Administration
46/_/_/_	Record Group 46, [box,] [Senate file number], [folder]
85/_/_~_/_/_	Record Group 85, [entry,] [volume number out of total number of volumes], [page], [number]
233/_/_	Record Group 233, [box], [folder]
MD NARA 350/_/_	Maryland Branch, National Archives and Records Administration, Record Group 350, [series], [file]
NYCMA _/_/_	New York City Municipal Archives, [place], [reference ID], [GS film number]
NY NARA	New York Branch, National Archives and Records Administration
21/_/_/_	Record Group 21, [journal for the District Court for the District of __], [city], [volume]
M_/_/_	Microfilm series [M__], [roll], [frame]; available at Ancestry.com

PCLVANY _/_   Passenger and Crew Lists of Vessels Arriving at New York, NY, 1897–1957, ARC ID: 3887372, DC NARA, Record Group 85, [microfilm publication], [NARA roll]; available at Ancestry.com

SGL _/_   Samuel Gompers Letterbooks, 1883–1924, Library of Congress, [volume], [page]

Introduction

This book tells the story of "almost citizens" – the people of Puerto Rico who were deemed neither citizens nor aliens, and who lived in a land deemed neither foreign nor domestic. For them, citizenship functioned like terrain during war. It was a prize to be won and a field of battle whose strategic value shifted as the fight developed. This book follows the debates about the U.S. Constitution that swirled about them. It tends to the voices of federal judges and elected officials but also follows Puerto Rican politicians, labor organizers, litigants, lawyers, administrators of government agencies, and journalists in Puerto Rico and on the mainland. People in all of these groups had a view of what citizenship should look like, and the idea of citizenship took shape and changed only as they advanced their sometimes competing concepts in the media, in law, and through bureaucratic maneuvers.[1]

The story begins at the very end of the nineteenth century as annexation of the islands that comprise Puerto Rico, Hawai'i, Guam, American Samoa, and the Philippines was bringing millions of people of African, Asian, and indigenous Pacific Island descent under U.S. control. Would these people become U.S. citizens, and if so, what would that citizenship mean? Citizenship at this time did not always or automatically guarantee full rights to participate in public life. Although women were undoubtedly citizens, for example, only four states accorded them suffrage on an equal basis with men. Southern states were driving African American citizens from the ballot box and the public sphere. Among many other examples, Mexican American and Chinese American children were often required to attend segregated schools.[2] Most of those whose rights were thus constrained were nonetheless deemed "Americans." And with the exception of Indians born into recognized tribes, all Americans were also U.S. citizens.

If there was ambiguity about the meaning of citizenship, there was much less ambiguity about whether citizenship would have to be conferred to the people of these annexed territories. The Civil War and the Thirteenth, Fourteenth, and Fifteenth Amendments had transformed the Constitution and dramatically moved the racially heterogeneous United States toward rights, membership, and equality. I term this new constitutional regime the Reconstruction Constitution. It introduced near-universal citizenship, expanded rights, and eventual statehood. Specifically, all Americans other than Indians, regardless of race, were citizens. All citizens within U.S. sovereignty had full constitutional rights that for men potentially included voting rights. All U.S. lands other than the District of Columbia were or would become states.[3]

For more than three decades these provisions of the Reconstruction Constitution essentially put a halt to the territorial acquisitions that fueled U.S. empire. Before the Civil War, the United States was ever expanding, annexing lands and then killing, displacing, subordinating, or assimilating those already living there. By 1860, U.S. international borders spanned the continent. But from shortly after the Civil War until 1898, the prospect of having to acknowledge so many nonwhite persons as citizens, coupled with expectations that they would hold some key rights and that the annexed lands they occupied would one day become states, had kept the United States government from expanding its borders as an imperial strategy. To annex was to accept the fact under the Reconstruction Constitution that the resident population could one day wield decisive votes in the Electoral College, Congress, and proposals to amend the Constitution. Sharing the widespread racism of their day, most U.S. officials preferred no annexation of lands that held overwhelmingly nonwhite populations to their potential inclusion and participation in national governance.

Beginning in 1898, however, the constitutional legacies of Reconstruction that acted as a restraint on imperial annexation began to unwind. What rights the Reconstruction Constitution guaranteed or acknowledged, and who could or must enforce them, had been hotly debated from the outset. But whatever limits and protections this constitution had applied initially, they narrowed considerably during the late nineteenth century. Declines were steepest for African Americans, a tragedy that has been thoroughly and skillfully told by other historians.[4] This study sits alongside that body of work and recounts the decline of the Reconstruction Constitution along a different dimension: as a durable and consequential constraint on that archetypal imperial form, annexation.

Three decades later the Reconstruction Constitution no longer impeded expansion of U.S. empire's borders. No single, dramatic decision marked the descent of this tradition at odds with unrestrained colonialism, or the triumph of the new imperial doctrine of "territorial nonincorporation." The shift came haltingly, laid out across a quarter century in a string of so-called *Insular Cases*.[5] Aware of the change under way – the movement from a constraining constitutional view of imperial governance of newly acquired lands to a much more flexible vision – Congress was emboldened. It asserted the power to extend or withhold statehood, citizenship, and rights in whatever combinations it chose.[6] Congress devised three novel, hybrid categories: lands that were neither foreign nor domestic, nonindigenous people who were neither citizens nor aliens, and domestic citizens who had less than full constitutional rights. The defining trait among the triad was – and still is – uncertainty about their scope and meaning.

Citizenship proved to be a slippery and adaptable concept. As constitutional interpretations changed, U.S. officials and many Puerto Ricans put citizenship to new uses, seizing on its ambiguity and conceptual instability. Initially, islanders and federal officials regularly presented views of citizenship consistent with the Reconstruction Constitution. They envisioned it as an achievable – perhaps inevitable – gateway to rights, belonging, and self-government. As the Reconstruction Constitution declined as a restraint on empire, much of the rhetoric was reversed; citizenship was all but meaningless, a "perfectly empty gift" or even a dishonorable badge of colonial status. Yet, as some perceptive observers realized, citizenship retained vibrancy, even in the context of empire. It was a font of rights, a basis for claims, a means of exclusion, and a powerful symbol of membership.[7]

Almost Citizens expands our understanding of the decline of Reconstruction by considering how the legacy of the Civil War affected empire, and how Reconstruction and its legacies reverberated through imperial ambitions and designs. For example, some accounts of the decline of Northern whites as a resource in the struggle for African American rights point to the imperial turn as a final nail in the coffin. War with Spain and the ensuing expansion in 1898 and 1899 kindled nationalizing and racist impulses that tempered Northern opposition to Southern white supremacy. Cross-sectional reconciliation among whites followed, to African Americans' detriment.[8]

Another body of work, and a growing one, has demonstrated the long half-life of the post–Civil War settlement. Well into the twentieth century, jurists, white supremacists, and African Americans continued to shape and be shaped by Reconstruction's legacies. Some legal doctrines that impeded racial discrimination survived a decade beyond the Supreme Court's approval of segregation in *Plessy v. Ferguson* (1896). Implementation of black disfranchisement and Jim Crow was not complete until the second decade of the twentieth century. The most influential white-supremacist accounts of post–Civil War federal efforts to reconstruct the South appeared in fiction, film, monuments, and academic history long after the 1890s. Conversely, African Americans' own resistance to the solidifying racial caste system never ceased.[9]

In the same vein, these chapters show that well into the twentieth century, fights over the past of Reconstruction and the future of empire were inextricably intertwined.[10] The aftermath of the Civil War provided both Republicans and Democrats with reasons to oppose the imperial turn. Republicans were the party of emancipation. After giving meaning to freedom by sanctifying the Reconstruction Constitution, they had to some extent been constrained by its dictates, even at the cost of preventing otherwise desired annexations. At least formally, the party remained committed to African American voting rights, a stand at odds with colonial rule. Democrats denounced Reconstruction as a period of federal tyranny and black misrule. They celebrated its overthrow, which brought them to power throughout the former Confederacy. As members of the party of white supremacy, they abhorred the prospect of statehood, citizenship, and rights for nonwhite residents of the Philippines. And because Democratic dominance in the South remained tenuous, the prospect of national Republicans wielding federal power as colonial masters was also an outrage. Better not to annex such lands than to enter the imperial morass.

The War of 1898 shattered this uneasy truce. Following annexation, Puerto Rican political leaders strategically played on aspects of each party's vision of the Civil War and its aftermath to try to blunt colonial strands in U.S. law and policy. Some appealed to Republicans by casting themselves as racial equals who had struggled for such liberal-democratic ideals as emancipation. Others, courting Democrats, declared that empire was itself a parallel to Reconstruction. Colonial rule in Puerto Rico replicated federal occupation of the South after the Civil War. Democrats must redeem Puerto Rico into home rule.

At the same time, both Republicans and Democrats had reasons to reconcile Reconstruction and empire. Those reasons were rooted in racisms so ingrained among U.S. officials that they could not imagine a world structured otherwise. For the increasing numbers of Republican leaders who drew from the failure of Reconstruction the lesson that racially inferior peoples could not be entrusted with self-government, the methods of white-supremacist Southern Democrats had great appeal. Those Republicans favored imperial governance outside the strictures of the Reconstruction Constitution. Democrats spread Jim Crow and disfranchisement throughout the former Confederacy before they returned to national power in 1913. Thereafter, with their stranglehold on Southern politics all but unbreakable, they increasingly saw empire less as a threat to white-supremacist policies than as a new field for their implementation.

Citizenship occupies a powerful middle ground between officialdom and the populace. As a circulating idea that was also an official category, citizenship provided a language that spanned both domains. Essentially contested and unsettled, it could be customized to a variety of purposes. This book, in its approach, pursues a key goal for scholars of citizenship: it illuminates how modestly situated individuals, powerful actors, and large structural forces all interacted to bring about historical change.[11] Three remarkable Puerto Ricans who sought full citizenship from the United States will be our guides through the shifting political and constitutional landscape; together they illustrate the breadth and versatility of citizenship and its uses. Each initially pursued anticolonial constitutional change when the island was ruled by Spain. Federico Degetau y González was a member of Puerto Rico's liberal cosmopolitan elite. Like many of his peers, he sought to mitigate Spanish imperial rule, not to end it. He favored either full integration of Puerto Rico into the Spanish polity as a coequal province, or broad autonomy for Puerto Rico to order its affairs without interference from its Spanish sovereign. Domingo Collazo had more revolutionary aspirations. A typesetter and journalist who emigrated to New York in 1889, he aimed to end Spanish rule in Puerto Rico. He would have preferred to accomplish that by insurrection, but if need be he would accept U.S. annexation. Santiago Iglesias rejected the primacy that Degetau and Collazo gave to the question of whether Spanish, U.S., or island authorities should govern Puerto Rico. His priority was a far-reaching social revolution that would transfer resources and power from island elites to members of the laboring classes. Citizenship and alterations in the government were instrumental, and secondary, to the achievement of this goal.[12]

As these chapters show, Degetau, Collazo, Iglesias, and many others used claims to citizenship and claims based on citizenship to harness governmental power. U.S. officials deployed it to co-opt people and justify coercing them. Cabinet members, judges, elected officials, and perhaps especially midlevel administrators all played prominent, complex, and intertwined roles, inspired by their own ambitions and goals.[13] Where U.S. rule extended, collisions between popular and official visions of citizenship reliably followed.

From the July 1898 arrival of U.S. troops until the first islandwide elections under U.S. rule in late 1900, the law and politics of United States–Puerto Rico relations resembled a tropical storm system. Alliances, legal analyses, and political strategies spawned complex, unstable, and interconnected formations prone to dramatic changes in speed and direction. Initially, leading Puerto Ricans and U.S. officials envisioned a future subject to the Reconstruction Constitution. Puerto Ricans would receive citizenship and rights, and Puerto Rico would eventually become a state. But then Republican president William McKinley determined to annex the Philippines, whose people U.S. lawmakers broadly agreed were too numerous and racially "unfit" for citizenship and statehood.[14]

Indeed, race was all but annealed to citizenship, and both were conjoined with a Court that pursued empire-friendly ambiguity rather than clear defenses or repudiations of the Reconstruction Constitution. This dynamic, of judicial evasion and a powerful undertow of race and racism, recurs in all of the chapters that follow. By late 1900, U.S. War Department administrators and other key nonjudicial officials had set a course toward imperial governance of Puerto Rico and the Philippines. To speak of U.S. empire during these years was to reference these new insular policies, not the long history of continental subjugation.[15] The officials' approach appeared to require renunciation of ideals of Reconstruction, as Democrats demanded and Republicans seemed ready to concede. Degetau, Iglesias, and other Puerto Rican leaders charted alternate routes toward more liberal formulations, but prevailing conditions favored imperialism.

With the turn toward empire gathering strength, other federal officials hid from the storm, neither hindering the effort nor providing it with explicit constitutional validation. The Supreme Court exemplified this pattern of empire-friendly ambiguity in its 1901 *Insular Cases* decisions, none of which settled islanders' citizenship status or prospects for statehood. The most important of the cases, *Downes v. Bidwell*, had no majority opinion. Justice Edward Douglass White's influential concurrence proposed the new territorial nonincorporation doctrine. But he stopped short of identifying what rights it would or would not guarantee.

Nonetheless, empire rooted in racial hierarchy along the lines set by the War Department seemed at least temporarily safe. By 1901, Degetau was Puerto Rico's first nonvoting representative in Washington. Convinced that deep legal and political currents in the United States ran toward inclusion, he pressed Republicans to recognize Puerto Ricans as U.S. citizens. He focused particular efforts on administrators, whom he perceived as potential agents of legal change. His arguments equated the Puerto Rican racial character with that of white gentlemen such as himself. But highlighting paternalist benevolence in this way also focused attention on the islanders of color, whom he proposed to uplift. Rather than risk reversal, administrators evaded Degetau's claims.

Seeking to force the citizenship question that officials had steadfastly dodged, Degetau aligned himself with Isabel Gonzalez and Domingo Collazo in *Gonzales v. Williams* (1904), the test case for Puerto Ricans' citizenship. Shortly after immigration officials excluded Gonzalez as an undesirable alien, Collazo helped his niece launch her suit. Degetau then weighed in on Gonzalez's side as a friend of the Court. To the disappointment of all three, the Court promulgated empire, once again, through ambiguity. The Court held that Puerto Ricans were not subject to immigration laws as aliens – so it found no need to decide whether they were citizens. Doing this signaled the possibility that they were noncitizen nationals instead.

Although colonial governance of Puerto Rico and the Philippines was firmly in place by late 1904, it operated according to conflicting values, which Iglesias, Collazo, and the Bureau of Insular Affairs within the War Department all gambled could be resolved in their favor. The Court had neither rejected the Reconstruction Constitution as a constraint on empire nor expressly embraced the territorial nonincorporation doctrine. U.S. colonial governance was similarly equivocal.

For the overseers of U.S. empire, ambivalence, ambiguity, evasion, and inconsistency had benefits, which they enjoyed from 1904 to 1910. As federal interactions with mainland labor unrest demonstrated, pretending to uplift workers while condoning unchecked labor exploitation was a sustainable approach. In the same way, promoting decentralized and nonsystematic colonialism was a way to soothe Democrats' fear of centralized power while aligning with white supremacy.

Support for U.S. colonial rule over insular territories grew increasingly bipartisan after 1910. With Democrats' white-supremacist government in the South seemingly secure from federal intervention, Democrats united with Republicans in support of federally administered imperial white supremacy. Through 1917, the Supreme Court remained unwilling to adopt or reject the constitutionality of permanent colonies containing noncitizen subjects. It thereby implicitly delegated the issue to nonjudicial officials. Congress used this authority to promote colonialism at home, even as Woodrow Wilson demanded democracy abroad. To mitigate the embarrassment of having permanent noncitizen subjects, Congress legislated. It promised eventual independence to the Philippines, and for Puerto Rico it proposed a collective naturalization that foreclosed independence and brought no new rights.

Even as the Supreme Court confirmed after 1917 that the doctrine of territorial nonincorporation had replaced the Reconstruction Constitution as the dominant legal framework for overseas empire, citizenship retained relevance for Puerto Ricans and colonial officials. Nonincorporation determined rights by the status of a place, not of persons; constitutional rights did not apply in full in unincorporated lands, which would not necessarily become states; both outcomes marked Puerto Rico as subordinate and racially inferior. Nonetheless, Iglesias used citizenship to secure mainland labor's gains for islanders and to promote the American Federation of Labor's assertions of authority abroad. Collazo transformed stateside Puerto Ricans' votes into electoral power in New York City. Colonial officials emphasized the expressive significance of citizenship; to counter rising anticolonial sentiment in Puerto Rico, they touted it as a token of national belonging and equality. By 1926, the Court had declared territorial nonincorporation to be binding doctrine, and citizenship, Constitution, and empire had reached an ambivalent, unstable resting place.

The shift across the first quarter of the twentieth century was dramatic. Key leaders had once doubted that the deliberate U.S. turn toward empire could survive its confrontation with the Reconstruction Constitution. Only through a slow and creative process did administrators, elected officials, and judges together forge new and much more ambiguous doctrines to suit the less democratic and more exclusive contours of imperial power.[16] Key Puerto Ricans struggled mightily against the change, and sometimes they were able to bend it to their own purposes. The pages that follow tell that story.

1898: "The Constitutional Lion in the Path"

In 1897, a half dozen great powers claimed sovereignty over nearly half the planet's land and people, and their empires were expanding. The British Empire alone had grown by fifty million souls and two million square miles since 1891. The eminent U.S. naval strategist Alfred T. Mahan feared that the United States was dangerously secluded in comparison, and sidelined in the global land rush that was under way. He also worried that, in the age of steamships, the Atlantic Ocean no longer adequately protected the United States against European powers.[1]

Mahan judged the most urgent U.S. need to be a foothold in the Greater Antilles archipelago, anchored by the Spanish colonies of Puerto Rico to the east and Cuba to the west. Located off Florida's coast, these islands were maritime access points to the Caribbean Sea, the Gulf of Mexico, and the Mississippi River, as well as to any trans-isthmian canal that might someday connect the Atlantic and Pacific Oceans. Many U.S. leaders had long expected that some or all of Spain's Antillean holdings would come under U.S. sovereignty. Mahan thought it was time to make good on that forecast.[2]

A key obstacle, he wrote, was that "any project of extending the sphere of the United States, by annexation or otherwise, [would be] met by the constitutional lion in the path." In the 1873 *Slaughter-House Cases*, the Supreme Court had declared that "the one pervading purpose" of the Reconstruction amendments was "the freedom of the slave race, the security and firm establishment of that freedom, and the protection of the newly-made freeman and citizen from the oppressions of those who had formerly exercised unlimited dominion over him." The Reconstruction Constitution discouraged overseas empire building by making citizenship, rights, and eventual statehood prerequisites to any annexation. As a result, the pursuit of empire through the extension U.S. borders would mean that people assumed to be racially inferior would have to be brought into the polity and granted citizenship and rights.[3]

Mahan proposed an elegant solution for this obstacle to imperial rule of new acquisitions: slay the lion. The beast was vulnerable, after all, as the last thirty years had demonstrated. The Reconstruction Constitution had not safeguarded African Americans from racial subordination. Nor had it worked well for women, American Indians, territorial residents, or Chinese aliens.[4]

Decades of relentless hostility from Southern white-supremacist Democrats had inflicted serious wounds. But even in 1898 Democrats were still reluctant to provoke constitutional conflict too forthrightly. Moreover, the very act of overseas empire building might inadvertently revive the doctrine. The Spanish Antilles that Mahan wanted to acquire were neither vacant nor inhabited by peoples unfamiliar with Western politics and law. Indeed, their residents were uniquely suited to deploy available legal protections for anti-imperial ends. The vast majority of politically engaged Puerto Ricans resented their second-class status. As residents of the oldest colony in the Americas, Puerto Ricans had been contesting colonial domination for a long time, utilizing Spain's constitutional tradition to do so. Puerto Ricans also drew on radically egalitarian concepts of interracial democracy that had gained visibility during neighboring Cuba's protracted anticolonial war. The people of Puerto Rico knew how to exploit shifting U.S. orientations toward empire and Constitution: they had organized revolutions from U.S. shores, encouraged the United States to pressure Spain on their behalf, exploited any pressure that the United States brought, and sometimes even encouraged the United States to annex Puerto Rico. Far from slaying the lion, U.S. expansion into the Spanish Antilles might well arm it with new allies.

Nevertheless, Mahan reasoned that if determined imperialism and the pursuit of empire now required dismantling the Reconstruction Constitution's constraints on empire, then so be it. However, the Reconstruction Constitution would prove more durable and adaptable than he imagined.

When Mahan set his eyes on the Reconstruction Constitution, the United States was still struggling with the legacy of the Civil War, which had ended thirty-two years earlier. The conflict had abolished slavery, devastated the South, enshrined the sanctity of the Union, remade the national party system, and spawned a more powerful and centralized federal government. Initially, the Republican majority after the war pursued a policy of Reconstruction aimed at recasting the nation as a republic with formal equality among self-governing male citizens. Their far-reaching statutory and constitutional innovations could credibly be argued to guarantee former slaves full, permanent citizenship with expansive "privileges" and "immunities," and equal civil and political rights. Disfranchisement, even if achieved, would cost states federal representation. Radical Republicans were committed to expanding and enforcing the new guarantees. Federal officials would fight racial discrimination, not perpetrate it.[5]

The emancipatory promise of the Civil War and Reconstruction buckled under counterassaults during and after the 1870s. The Supreme Court articulated increasingly cramped interpretations of the Reconstruction

Constitution. Of perhaps greatest interest to federal lawmakers, the Court moved quickly to limit federal racial antidiscrimination enforcement to voting and cases where state officials interfered with civil or political rights, or systematically failed to punish private interference with them. As Republican commitment to African Americans' rights waned in Washington, Southern white-supremacist Democrats unleashed unprecedented domestic terror and voter fraud. This caused the remaining electorates in former Confederate states to "vote" uniformly Democratic in presidential elections after 1876. Republicans' lack of political will to defend equal rights reached a new nadir from 1889 to 1891, when the party won control of the White House and Congress but failed to enact new federal election protections. Republicans also never exercised their constitutional prerogative to reduce federal representation for Southern states that disfranchised African American voters. When Democrats won control of the political branches in 1893, they repealed Reconstruction-era election protection statutes en masse. With some distinct exceptions, elected Republicans on the national level all but abandoned African Americans.[6]

To consolidate the gains of the white-supremacist onslaught, Southern Democrats denigrated Reconstruction, removed African Americans from political life, and enfeebled the Fourteenth and Fifteenth Amendments. They also propounded a false history in which tyrannical Northern radicals imposed on the South governments of incompetent and barbaric blacks, corrupt Northern carpetbaggers, and opportunistic Southern scalawags. The resultant misrule had emptied state coffers and unleashed sexual violence by black men against white women until white Democrats "redeemed" their states with the help of the Ku Klux Klan, or so the story went. "Redemption," the myth concluded, had restored the constitutional balance between the state and federal governments and returned the South to clean government and its proper racial order under white men's rule. In reality, the Redemption political order was unstable and was challenged from 1892 to 1896 by the Populist Party's uneasy coalition of black and white farmers and workers. Only renewed violence and fraud preserved Democratic dominance.[7]

In the 1890s Southern Democrats sought permanent power via Jim Crow laws and African American disfranchisement. This constitutionally dubious scheme required Supreme Court acquiescence. To secure it, Louisiana's Separate Car Act (1890) thinly veiled racial domination and segregation with a requirement of "equal but separate" facilities. Likewise, rather than explicitly disfranchising African Americans, Mississippi granted discretion to local registrars, who then found African Americans wanting. The Supreme Court upheld both schemes.[8]

Clearly, by early 1898 the Reconstruction Constitution was vulnerable. But its specific restraint on empire, which Mahan proposed to demolish, remained fearsome even as the rest of the Reconstruction project crumbled.

The Constitution required statehood for all annexed lands and citizenship with accompanying rights for their populations.[9] That principle was still intact largely because it was an irrelevant part of the constitutional menagerie for white Southern Democrats, who were focused on depriving African Americans of the benefits of Reconstruction.

Somewhat protected by the indifference of white Southern Democrats, the Reconstruction Constitution commitment to inclusive citizenship and eventual statehood was also bolstered by a longer, unbroken, and still influential tradition that all inhabited U.S. lands would eventually become states. The Northwest Ordinance (1787), which predated the Constitution, had influentially promised statehood for the territories it governed. In 1857, the Supreme Court's infamous *Dred Scott v. Sandford* decision crystallized that norm into doctrine by declaring that the Constitution permitted territories to be acquired only as future states, not as perpetual colonies. The Union victory against Southern secession established on the battlefield the proposition of once in, never out, which clearly applied to states seeking to depart unilaterally, but conceivably also bound the federal government and applied to territories. Those two rules would bar any acquired land from later becoming independent through a grant of sovereignty. So eventual statehood became the inevitable consequence of annexation. As one senator explained in 1871, because "divorce is impossible," annexation was an "irrevocable" promise that acquired territory "be admitted in due time as a State."[10]

The other key component of this constitutional regime was the guarantee of rights-rich citizenship for all Americans other than American Indians. After the Thirteenth Amendment ended legal slavery within the United States, the Fourteenth Amendment provided the first constitutional definition of U.S. citizenship: "All persons born or naturalized in the United States, and subject to the jurisdiction thereof, are citizens of the United States and of the state wherein they reside. No state shall make or enforce any law which shall abridge the privileges or immunities of citizens of the United States." Together, these constitutional provisions and interpretations obliterated *Dred Scott*'s notorious deprivation of African American citizenship – but they did not obliterate *Dred Scott*'s bar on perpetual colonies and could be reconciled with it easily enough.

The declaration in the *Slaughter-House Cases* that birth within territories was birth within the United States clarified that all Americans, other than American Indians, were citizens with associated privileges and immunities. However, the rights attached to such citizenship had long been subject to competing lines of authority. One view was that citizenship was highly consequential. *Dred Scott* argued as much when it declared citizenship so substantive and so linked to voting that its extension to African Americans was unthinkable. The Fifteenth Amendment (1870) could be read to work from the same premise, but to opposite ends: it too associated citizenship with suffrage when it barred racial discrimination in voting. The other view was that citizenship conferred few rights inherently. The Court took this approach in the *Slaughter-House Cases* when it all but nullified judicially enforceable privileges and immunities of U.S. citizenship in cases not involving race discrimination. Officials and jurists generally held both views simultaneously. They judged citizenship too valuable to be extended via annexation to people of color, and understood that it brought those who already held it little advantage in court.[11]

The Reconstruction Constitution – fortified by these earlier constitutional interpretations – had occasioned an unprecedented hiatus in annexation. Presidents had repeatedly contemplated annexation, but confronted resistance to its constitutional consequences and stopped short. Before ratification of the Fourteenth Amendment, a U.S. annexation had occurred at least every fifteen years; in 1897, more than thirty years had passed since Alaska was annexed in 1867. Republican President Ulysses S. Grant (1869–1877) promoted the benefits of annexation within the Reconstruction Constitution framework when he sought ratification of treaties to annex the Danish West Indies and the Dominican Republic. Although the West Indians were overwhelmingly of African descent, Secretary of State William Seward declared that the islanders would receive all "liberties and rights of American citizens" and be organized in polities "preparing to be States." Under the Dominican treaty, Dominicans, most of whom were of mixed race, would be immediately protected as U.S. citizens. Their nation would eventually join the Union, perhaps even within a decade.[12] The unspoken corollary was that statehood would bring new privileges such as full participation in U.S. governance, including senators, representatives, presidential electors, and a say on constitutional amendments.

Debates about annexation at this time focused not on whether the rights of citizenship would be extended to alien peoples – that was assumed to be true – but on the desirability of that prospect. For his part, Grant happily envisioned 150,000 citizens of color dominating a state of Dominica that would reinforce and bolster Reconstruction. But as the London *Spectator* observed, many U.S. senators balked at a further "increase of the dark electorate." The prospect of a Dominican vote that would "cancel that of a million whites in the House of Representatives" aroused many senators' "dread of the negro." Equating Americanness and whiteness, one senator objected to any eventual "share in governing us" for Dominicans, who were "wholly incapable to governing themselves." Republican senator Carl Schurz of Missouri feared annexations begetting annexations. He foresaw the addition of "ten or twelve tropical States" whose "ten or twelve millions" of "people of the Latin race mixed with Indian and African blood" would elect senators and representatives capable of tipping "the scale of the destinies of this Republic."[13] The treaties to annex the Danish West Indies and the Dominican Republic never won ratification.

Subsequent attempts to assert U.S. control abroad met with the same kind of resistance from those who feared that annexation would trigger eventual statehood for acquired lands and immediate citizenship for the inferior peoples resident there. In 1893, a group of American businessmen and planters overthrew the Hawaiʻian government and sought U.S. annexation. Stateside opponents complained that such an acquisition was irreversible, a "step into the abyss" that could "never be retraced." The "interference of the Fourteenth Amendment" would pollute citizenship by bringing in Hawaiians who were "incompetent," "incapable of self control," "ignorant, vicious," "degraded," "incongruous," and lacking in "education," "ability," and "mental and moral faculties." If further annexations followed, the result would be a "polyglot House" whose speaker might "recognize 'the gentleman from Patagonia,'" Cuba, Santo Domingo, Korea, Hong Kong, Fiji, Greenland, or, "with fear and trembling, 'the gentleman from the Cannibal Islands,' who will gaze upon you with watering mouth and gleaming teeth."[14]

Proponents of annexation changed tactics. Rather than celebrate the extension of the Reconstruction Constitution to new territories and the peoples present there, they downplayed it. But they did not dispute or deny the consequences of annexation. The proposed treaties remained silent on citizenship, voting rights, and future statehood. Executive-branch advocates of expansion punted those matters to Congress, where lawmakers were not assuaged or reassured. Hawaiʻi remained outside U.S. borders. In 1896 leading Republicans renewed their contention that the benefits from expansion outweighed its costs, but they were stymied once again.[15]

Lack of annexations, however, did not make the United States an anti-imperial paragon. Between 1868 and 1898, U.S. officials projected power abroad, consolidated power at home, and subordinated peoples on both sides of the border. Their actions heeded the Reconstruction Constitution, but circumscribed and limited its reach. In this way, they paved the way for more direct attempts to "slay" it at century's end.

Internationally, the United States traded, defended, postured, and wielded as much influence as before. Only annexations had disappeared from the nation's quiver. In lieu of annexation, the United States deployed workarounds that extended its economic and military interests while leaving foreign sovereignty in place. For instance, the United States negotiated a uniquely favorable trade agreement with the Dominican Republic and gained significant control over its finances after a U.S. syndicate purchased its outstanding debt. In the Danish West Indies, the United States took advantage of the free port, enjoying access to the valuable coaling and naval harbor there on terms equal to those of other great powers. And Hawaiʻi gave the United States preferential access to its ports, trade, and territory. In the words of a U.S. secretary of state, the Hawaiian islands were "practically members of the American *zollverein*" (a form of customs union without political unification that bound together northern German states) and "an outlying district of the State of California." Internationally, the United States claimed the islands within its sphere of influence. Yet formally the kingdom was as "remote from our control as China."[16]

In other cases, U.S. officials rejected the annexation option in lieu of other forms of control. Rather than accept a proposal that Germany, Britain, and the United States each annex different portions of Samoa, the United States insisted on a fractious co-supervision arrangement. The United States protected its citizens' interests in parts of Asia through extraterritoriality agreements that let citizens facing prosecution or civil suits abroad receive adjudication by U.S. officials who applied U.S. law.[17]

In the Western Hemisphere, the United States used trade to assert predominance. A reciprocal agreement between the United States and Spain underlay the U.S. role as the leading market for the Spanish colonies of Puerto Rico and Cuba. The United States also aggressively asserted its Monroe Doctrine rule that no European power would be allowed to expand its footprint in the Americas. This was another way for the United States to broaden control without extending U.S. borders. In 1895, the United States declared itself "practically sovereign on [the] continent" of South America and insisted that Great Britain submit a border dispute with Venezuela to arbitration. This "twenty-inch gun," as the demand became known, signaled a willingness to resort to arms if Britain refused. The British pointed out the inconsistency of asserting "interests" in a country for which a nation "assumes no responsibility" but acceded to U.S. demands all the same.[18]

Through most of the late nineteenth century, then, the United States pursued a variation of imperialism in the American hemisphere unlike many European models because it involved no formal extension of borders. U.S. supremacy and sovereignty in the Americas grew, but U.S. territory and control did not. The U.S. stood down only where the tripwire of the Reconstruction Constitution might get triggered.

Domestically, the U.S. military pursued large-scale warfare to defeat autonomous native nations and expropriate their land. The Reconstruction Constitution accommodated such violence, but at the cost of sacrificing theoretical coherence. Recall that the Fourteenth Amendment extended citizenship to those "born ... in the United States, and subject to the jurisdiction thereof." A major function of the "jurisdiction" requirement was to exclude American Indians from citizenship. The clause analogized tribes to foreign nations; an Indian who owed primary loyalty to a tribe at birth was homologous to a foreign ambassador's child whose primary loyalty at birth was to the ambassador's home country. The analogy might have been somewhat apt in 1868, but not after 1871, when the United States abandoned treaty relations with American Indians in favor of direct congressional rule by statute. *United States v. Kagama* (1886) recognized inherent and plenary federal power over American Indians. By the time of the U.S. Army massacre of Lakota Indians at Wounded Knee in 1890, American Indians' military power no longer posed a credible threat to U.S. dominance. Nonetheless, the Court had held in *Elk v. Wilkins* (1884) that an American Indian could not gain citizenship by forswearing tribal allegiance in favor of U.S. jurisdiction. This ruling left many American Indians with citizenship neither in the United States nor in a foreign country. If those who disassociated from their tribes did not become U.S. citizens, then they had no nationality.[19]

Beginning in the 1880s, the United States swapped one betrayal for another. Federal officials imposed assimilation on American Indians. They dissolved tribal governments, alienated collectively held tribal lands, implemented coercive education programs to extinguish Native American cultures, naturalized Indians en masse, and expanded states' jurisdiction over Indians.[20] Often envisioned as a shield for individuals against federal overreach, citizenship had become the government's sword.

Clearly the Reconstruction Constitution did not prevent the expansion of U.S. power and sovereignty, either domestically or internationally. Nor did it prevent federal officials from establishing broad latitude to act within territories. Quite the opposite: A strong national government grew stronger. Southern white-supremacist Democrats abided such aggrandizement in federal power because they had the least to fear from the federal behemoth when it exercised its powers beyond state borders. In Utah Territory, the Constitution little hindered the federal campaign against Mormon polygamy, which was often condemned as another form of slavery. Before the Civil War, by contrast, *Dred Scott* had protected slaveholders in the territories from federal interference. The promise of eventual statehood did little to impede federal power. As New Mexico passed the half-century mark as a territory, federal lawmakers routinely cited its residents' race and monolingual Spanish when they rejected statehood measures.[21] Inevitable statehood, lawmakers realized, could be indefinitely delayed.

Federal officials' freedom to act was unrestrained by the Reconstruction Constitution in particular lands and territories, as these examples show. It was also unrestrained in cases that involved particular groups of people: namely, aliens within U.S. borders, or U.S. citizens living abroad. Officials enjoyed all but unreviewable discretion if they could convince a court that an action targeted foreign lands or actors. *In re Ross* (1891), for example, upheld the criminal conviction of a U.S. citizen who had been tried by a consular tribunal after being denied a jury trial. In upholding the conviction, the Supreme Court emphasized that the trial had taken place outside the country. The Reconstruction Constitution drew high-stakes lines between Americans and aliens. This was evident in two Supreme Court rulings, *Chae Chan Ping v. United States* (1889) and *Fong Yue Ting v. United States* (1893). Both cases involved virulently anti-Chinese federal statutes that flatly forbade naturalization of Chinese individuals and sharply limited their entry, reentry, and residence in the United States. Decisions in the two cases established an absolute, inherent federal power to bar aliens' entry into the United States and to deport them after they arrived. Contrast these rulings with *United States v. Wong Kim Ark* (1898), which declared the United States-born ethnic-Chinese Wong Kim Ark to be a citizen with the right to reenter the United States.

The Court rejected the race-based claim that Wong's birth to Chinese parents was a form of birth outside the jurisdiction of the United States. Such judicial unwillingness to bend the Reconstruction Constitution to the dictates of racism was just what many opponents of annexation feared and predicted. The crux of the matter was the decision's emphasis on federal power: "Jurisdiction of the nation within its own territory is necessarily exclusive and absolute."[22]

By 1898, all of these shifts in federal power had weakened individual rights and strengthened those of the states. This had occurred across thirty years of official interactions with African Americans, American Indians, people of Chinese descent, and members of other disfavored communities. The change was effected in matters concerning national borders, irregular locales, territories, and U.S. consular courts abroad. Simultaneously, the Supreme Court had sharply delimited the reach of the Reconstruction Constitution. Constitutional rights could abruptly vanish upon crossing U.S. borders, or where an alien rather than a citizen was concerned.

Although the restraints that the Reconstruction Constitution imposed on empire were still standing, the elements of a doctrinal alternative had been fulminating for thirty years. Specifically, federal power was being defined – and transformed – by malleable distinctions between foreign and domestic, alien and citizen. What was missing before 1898 was the impetus to synthesize and then deploy this alternative doctrine.

While the U.S. empire built up to its global debut in 1898, the Spanish Empire that had once been the world's leading power was now fading from the world stage. Its non-American holdings encompassed little beyond the Philippines in the Pacific Ocean and a sliver of the coast and some islands in northwest Africa. In its traditional colonial stronghold of the Americas, Spain had controlled more than half the population as late as 1800, before cessions and independence movements created separate sovereign nations there. By the end of the U.S. Civil War, Puerto Rico and Cuba were both the only island colonies or nations in the Americas that still permitted slavery and Spain's only remaining American possessions. Neither island received full constitutional rights or parliamentary representation from Spain, which officially favored *peninsulares* (Spaniards born in Spain, on the Iberian Peninsula) above *criollos* (the island-born). This unequal colonial relationship fomented discontent and instability. The problem in Cuba was of particular moment to Spain and the United States. The larger and more populous of the Spanish Antilles, its slavery-propelled economy was highly profitable.[23]

In 1868 a decade-long uprising in Cuba began that nourished abolitionist and egalitarian ideologies as well as the military service and leadership aspirations of Antillean Spaniards of color. Cuba's insurrectionary activities, often refracted through Spain or the United States, reached Puerto Rico as well. Lacking Cuba's size, wealth, population, and capacity for insurrection, Puerto Rico was undoubtedly the less important of Spain's Antillean holdings, and rarely the driver of hemispheric events. However, Puerto Rico and Cuba shared colonial disabilities. Like Cubans, Puerto Ricans were second-class Spaniards who lived in a second-class province. They exercised little self-governance and held inferior rights and privileges. Grinding, rural deprivation on both islands enriched imperial Spain.[24]

Spanish forces quickly suppressed a nearly contemporaneous Puerto Rican uprising, but Spain's own 1868 Glorious Revolution ushered in a new liberal Spanish constitution just a year later. To appease and forestall further colonial rebellion without too clearly rewarding and thereby encouraging it, Spain elevated its Antillean holdings to provincial status and reestablished their representation in the Cortes (the national legislature). In 1869, for the first time in a generation, Puerto Rico held an election for *diputados* (representatives) to the Cortes. Although highly restrictive suffrage laws benefited conservative *peninsulares*, liberals still won nearly half the seats. A year later, they formed the Partido Liberal, Puerto Rico's first political party. Soon afterward, conservative *peninsulares* formed a competing party, which came to be known as the Partido Incondicional for its unconditional support of Spanish colonial rule. In 1870, Spain acted to emancipate enslaved children and the elderly, liberalize voting rules, and create new elected posts in the island's government. By this time, leading Liberal politician Román Baldorioty de Castro had taken his seat in the Cortes as a *diputado* from Puerto Rico. Publicly suspected to be of African descent, Baldorioty differed from many Cuban liberals because he and his colleagues sought the immediate end of slavery, albeit with compensation.[25]

Spain's reforms set in motion dynamics that diversified the Partido Liberal alliance along class and racial lines. Under the new rules, voting lists expanded sevenfold. Many of the new voters were artisans whose economic security, social prominence, and education elevated their standing within the working class. Men of color were prominent both in the ranks and in leadership positions. Men of African descent in the trades had a path to upward mobility absent in the more prestigious professions. Allying with the Liberales gave artisans an opportunity to advance a more radical commitment to meritocracy over race hierarchies. Conservatives' disdain, Liberales' support for equality without reference to race, and Baldorioty's suspected African heritage also motivated their choice for an alliance. In 1873, Liberales swept the election in Puerto Rico, Spain declared itself a republic, and Liberales won the abolition of slavery in Puerto Rico. Thus, thirteen years before slavery ended in Cuba, Puerto Rico witnessed the liberation of all 30,000 of its souls still in bondage. Those who remained subject to coercion and deprivation were now formally free.[26]

Under the liberal Spanish government, from 1868 to 1873, workers in Puerto Rico began to organize. Many formed arts associations, mutual aid societies, recreational organizations, study groups, or guilds. They circulated radical labor ideologies with European roots. They opposed authoritarianism alongside elite liberal *criollos*. The *criollos* of the professional, landholding, and commercial classes experienced Spain's liberal interlude as an opportunity to rule at home, participate in metropolitan affairs, and thereby liberalize the empire.[27]

Politically active Puerto Ricans pursued overlapping constitutional strategies. Many favored a program of assimilation, by which they meant full equality between Puerto Ricans and other Spaniards, and between Puerto Rico and other provinces. They wanted Spaniards born or residing in Puerto Rico to enjoy the same access to office, national representation, local democracy, and individual rights as *peninsulares* resident in the metropole. Others favored autonomy – broad self-governance subject only to lightly exercised Spanish sovereignty. National independence appealed to a third group. Still others imagined a workers' revolution on behalf of the backbone of the island's economy: its desperately poor, unorganized, disfranchised agricultural laborers.[28]

Notwithstanding emancipation, most Puerto Rican laborers had little immediate prospect of improving their dire circumstances. More than 85 percent of Puerto Ricans lived outside urban areas, where they depended on wages from work in the coffee, sugar, and tobacco fields. These export-oriented sectors of the economy were being transformed by new technologies and more concentrated land ownership, and conditions for workers were abysmal. Illiteracy rates topped 80 percent, hunger was common, and mortality was high. Laborers wore poor clothing and often owned just one outfit. Their houses were small, windowless, and frequently made of palm fronds or the like. Extensive rural violence and acts of plantation arson demonstrated a will to resist the degradation, but workers faced the ever-present threat of Spanish repression, as well as daunting and numerous structural obstacles. Seasonal agricultural employment meant that plantation workforces were reconstituted annually. The economy's dependence on a small number of export crops meant that a price dip or a hurricane could suddenly leave a sector in disarray and deprive workers of any bargaining power. Illiteracy, inadequate communication and transportation, and geographically dispersed workforces hampered coordination. Common demands were difficult to formulate because workers had diverse employment situations that variously included formal wages, room and board, access to land, seasonal opportunities, or more enduring client–patron ties. Workers' goals also varied. Some sought land ownership, not class solidarity. Others looked to a mythologized past of honorable *hacendado* (estate-owner) patrons who rewarded workers' loyalty with protection.[29]

Spain's liberal turn seemed to augur imminent improvements across the island, certainly for elite liberal assimilationists and perhaps for the rural masses. Those hopes were shattered when a political reaction swept Spain in 1874, and a military coup toppled the Spanish Republic and installed a constitutional monarchy. Puerto Rico and Cuba remained provinces in name only, and by 1880 Spain had suppressed the Cuban uprisings. In Puerto Rico, Spain preserved abolition, but it reduced individual rights and shrank the electorate nearly to 1869 levels. The Partido Incondicional of the *peninsulares* returned to dominance. Liberales would eventually gain some concessions following election boycotts, which were an accepted and established form of protest, but in the meantime the new governor-general of Puerto Rico suppressed Liberales' newspapers and Masonic lodges, stripped them of government posts, and installed loyal Incondicionales in their stead.[30]

By 1886 most Puerto Rican liberals had abandoned the quest for assimilation into the Spanish empire as a coequal province. Instead, they pursued an autonomy that might promote the island's economic growth and break the *peninsulares'* economic stranglehold. The Partido Liberal reorganized into the Partido Autonomista, akin to Cuba's new autonomy party. The Autonomistas demanded that Puerto Ricans receive near-universal manhood suffrage and the same Cortes representation and individual rights as other Spaniards. They wanted local power over banking, budgets, education, public works, tariffs, immigration, and commercial treaties. Baldorioty favored going further and demanding the degree of self-government that Britain afforded Canada. However, given Spanish hostility to the idea, that proposal would require Spain's transformation from a monarchy into a republic. Prioritizing unity, Baldorioty acceded to the more modest platform of the majority and assumed leadership of the new party.[31]

Economic powers were a platform priority for Autonomistas because Spain was neither purchasing all of Puerto Rico's exports nor relieving the island's credit scarcity. That combination of policy choices exacerbated the already entrenched divide between the *peninsulares* and *criollos*. Trade agreements were the foundation of economic health on an island where sugar and coffee were leading industries. The United States bought the bulk of island sugar, while European countries were major coffee consumers. The only credit available to finance modernization and growth came from *peninsular* merchants, whose high interest rates consumed subsequent profits.[32]

While contending with profound inequality, Autonomista leaders seeking the reins of island power also had to overcome issues of representation and race that estranged popular movements and leaders from the political elite. Restrictive suffrage laws favored the Incondicionales, so the Autonomistas could not easily acquire political bona fides through electoral wins. Yet Autonomista leaders were poorly positioned to claim to speak for all the disfranchised. In 1887, many laborers and members of the artisan social sector, which was disproportionately led by men of color, operated outside the Partido Autonomista. They opposed Spanish oppression by forming secret societies and launching boycotts.[33]

Incorrectly suspecting that Autonomistas and militants were part of a unified anti-Spanish conspiracy, the governor and his allies unleashed a brutal crackdown on island liberals and radicals in 1887. This experience, coupled with Baldorioty's death in 1889, permanently eroded Autonomistas' optimistic faith in Spain and their loyalty toward it. For the Incondicionales, the presumed association between Autonomistas and militants only strengthened their claim to racial privilege. They boasted of pure bloodlines, untouched by colonial decay. Elites associated the assertiveness of social "inferiors" with the Haitian revolution and the insurgencies in Cuba from 1868 to 1880, events they equated less with the fight for emancipation and enfranchisement than with racial revenge and barbarism. These prevailing racial and political attitudes left Autonomistas struggling to assuage elites' fears of working-class activism, even as they sought to muster that activism to their cause.[34]

Elite *criollo* Autonomista leaders approached artisans and, to a lesser degree, other workers with a coded compromise. They envisioned Puerto Rican society as a *gran familia*, they said, with themselves at the head. Their aim was to unite an island population among whom more than a third were "mulatto" and more than one-tenth were "black" (as recorded in the 1899 census). The kinship metaphor required no explicit mention of race. It thus sidestepped *criollos'* tenuous claims to pure Spanish whiteness. It also discouraged racially chauvinistic *criollos* from explicit, and offensive, assertions of racial superiority. Conversely, the family imagery highlighted the Liberales' genuine cross-race and cross-class ties of affection and admiration. They offered working men promises of liberal citizenship with access to suffrage, freedom of the press, and jury participation. Like the Cuban revolutionary leader José Martí, they celebrated the unthreatening masculine virtues of self-control, hard work, cordiality, and confraternity. But unlike Martí, they expected assertiveness, leadership, and postures of violence in defense of honor to remain the exclusive province of male elites. According to some Autonomista leaders, the repression of 1887 was a backlash against the ill-considered exuberance of social inferiors. Nonetheless, workers repeatedly asserted themselves. Strikes increased through the early 1890s and won gains in 1895. A labor newspaper was founded. New workers' organizations were formed, and existing ones gained legitimacy.[35]

Revolt was again brewing in the early 1890s when José Martí united anti-Spanish Antilleans behind his proposal to launch an egalitarian, antiracist social revolution. His radical vision of interracial fraternity rested on notions of manly self-restraint and accomplishment. In 1892, Martí founded the Partido Revolucionario Cubano (Cuban Revolutionary Party) on principles of civilian leadership and broad participation. In 1895 the revolution began in Cuba.[36]

As the insurrection in Cuba gathered steam, Autonomista leaders in Puerto Rico remained loyal – and opportunistic – Spaniards. They sought concessions and self-advancement, not independence or martyrdom. Their internal debates centered on whether to prioritize empirewide republicanism or local autonomy. The rising Autonomista leader and newspaper editor Luis Muñoz Rivera negotiated an autonomy pact in 1897 that the Partido Autonomista signed. It required dissolving the party into Spain's monarchical Partido Liberal. When the Spanish Partido Liberal returned to power in 1897 amid growing U.S. pressure to end the bloodletting in Cuba, Spain extended charters of autonomy and greater constitutional and electoral rights to Cuba and Puerto Rico. It was more than Autonomistas or even Baldorioty had sought. Puerto

Ricans received individual liberties, a mostly elected local legislature, near-universal manhood suffrage, and broad authority over domestic policy. The crown retained power to choose judges, the governor-general, and his cabinet-like Council of Secretaries, which it initially used to appointment Muñoz Rivera to the council. In the ensuing election the conservative Incondicionales won just 2 percent of the vote. The Liberales secured a large electoral majority through deft cross-class outreach, control of the administrative machinery of voting, repression of opponents, adroit patronage politics, and by taking credit for the new autonomous regime.[37]

It seemed that paternalistic self-government by elite *criollos* had arrived.

In April 1898 the fates of the United States, asserting itself in a world of empires, imperially decaying Spain, and Spain's Antillean colonies became more tightly bound. With Congress displaying great sympathy for the Cuban insurgency, unvanquished by Spain's brutal tactics, President McKinley offered to purchase Cuba. Spain declined. After a series of mishaps ratcheted up tensions, Congress acted decisively in favor of Cuban independence by authorizing McKinley to use military force, even as it disavowed any intention to annex the island.[38]

When the United States declared war on Spain in mid-April, the governor of Puerto Rico suspended the opening of the legislature. On May 1, U.S. naval forces crushed the Spanish fleet outside Manila, the main harbor in the Philippines. Within two months, U.S. troops were in Cuba, which raised the specter of an imminent invasion of Puerto Rico. Muñoz Rivera and his allies scrambled to convince Spanish officials to convene the legislature, which eventually opened on July 17. Muñoz Rivera became the assembly's president.[39]

In the United States, the unfolding naval war permitted long-thwarted expansionists finally to gain a victory. Emphasizing Hawai'i's naval value, they declared its acquisition to be a military necessity. They thus implied that Hawai'i was worth the constitutional price, whether it be adherence to the Reconstruction Constitution or its violation. In early July, annexation of the Hawaiian islands was complete.[40]

The United States now had a momentous decision to make. It could "stop short" after acquiring Hawai'i, reaffirm the applicability of the Reconstruction Constitution to all newly acquired territories and recognize Hawaiians as citizens of a future state, and forgo further annexations. Alternatively, the United States could sacrifice the Reconstruction Constitution on the altar of empire. This was an urgent matter: the U.S. victory over Spain offered an opportunity to annex the thousands of islands that comprised the bulk of Spain's remaining colonial holdings. Their more than ten million inhabitants, the great majority of whom were people of color, equaled more than 10 percent of the U.S. population. Most lived in colonies that were undergoing pro-independence rebellions with substantial nonwhite leadership.[41] To annex these islands en masse would force a choice: to obey the Reconstruction

Constitution by eventually incorporating large numbers of people of color into the U.S. polity, or to jettison the prevailing constitutional regime in favor of empire.

On the island of Puerto Rico, groups were divided internally over whether annexation by the United States would favorably alter the constitutional and political terms of their struggle. Perhaps the United States would make Puerto Rico an autonomous and assimilated state. Perhaps it would hold it as a perpetual colony. Annexation would foreclose independence, but perhaps independence was unrealistic and the United States' rule and its treatment of workers would be better than Spain's.

Whatever Puerto Rico's diverse opinions on the matter, by mid-1898 annexation seemed increasingly certain to some of the island's political and constitutional leaders, among them the lawyer and politician Federico Degetau, the labor leader Santiago Iglesias, and the printer and journalist Domingo Collazo. These men had honed their leadership skills, aspirations, and constitutional concepts through years of struggle.

Federico Degetau was born in Puerto Rico in 1862. He grew up as a privileged son of an elite family, reared on a mix of cosmopolitanism and liberalism. His parents' library, and the family tree, contained Spanish, German, French, English, and Danish names. Leading liberals gathered in their sitting room. He was named after his uncle, a lawyer active in pro-emancipation circles, yet when he was a child his family had a household slave, named Chalí. After relocating to Spain at the age of twelve, Degetau earned a law degree, led political and intellectual groups, joined the Freemasons, and became a successful lawyer. He gravitated toward liberal-republican leaders and causes. As the protégé of the renowned liberal Puerto Rican leader Román Baldorioty, he promoted such causes as progressive pedagogy, relief for needy children, and the rehabilitation of prostitutes. He also wrote for Madrid's liberal newspaper *El Globo*, held public conferences, and published well-received novels. A republican patriot of means, he declined posts in Spain's monarchical government and purchased an exemption from military obligation. During the government's 1887 crackdown in Puerto Rico, Degetau forcefully entered island politics from Madrid. Aware that newspapers were central to Spanish political culture, he wrote articles in *El Globo* condemning the repression and founded, published, and distributed a Spanish paper, *La Isla*, for the same purpose.[42]

In the 1890s Degetau hitched his political future to Baldorioty's view that Spain's transformation into a republic would offer the best way to facilitate robust autonomy in Puerto Rico. He wanted to reform the existing order on the island, not overthrow it. Degetau dissented when an Autonomista commission on which he served with Luis Muñoz Rivera negotiated a pro-autonomy pact with a monarchical Spanish party. When Autonomistas ratified the agreement in 1897, Degetau broke away from the group and cofounded a competing republican party with José Celso Barbosa, a doctor and newspaper publisher who was the island's most prominent man of color. Both men had deep republican roots. Barbosa's ancestors were in Haiti during the Haitian Revolution that founded the Americas' oldest free-black republic. He attended the University of Michigan when U.S. Republicans still boasted of their antislavery and emancipation credentials. The men's new party nominated Degetau to a rare safe *diputado* seat, which he won in 1898 even though Muñoz Rivera's coalition carried the islandwide vote by a large margin.[43]

Degetau was in Spain, leveraging his extensive political network and sterling reputation to lobby top officials, when winds of war threatened to sweep away liberal autonomy in Puerto Rico and, with it, his own influence with his island's imperial masters. One colleague foresaw Spain treating Puerto Rico like "Isaac sacrificed by his father Abraham," except without a last-minute reprieve. With Spain's claims to Puerto Ricans' loyalty collapsing, Degetau pressed Spanish officials to release Puerto Rican political prisoners. After Spain and the United States sought terms of peace, he left Spain for his property in France, and next contacted the Spanish prime minister and U.S. president. Both men's negotiators met with him. He proposed mandatory U.S.-Spanish arbitration as part of any annexation. Otherwise, he said, future hostilities between the United States and Spain would cause Puerto Ricans to experience a "civil war" between the "narrow, juridical link" they would have to the United States and their "indestructible link of origin" to Spain. Negotiators rejected the proposal, though they did accept Degetau's substantially more modest suggestion to honor Puerto Ricans' Spanish heritage: they agreed that if U.S. annexation of Puerto Rico occurred, the importation of "Spanish scientific, literary and artistic works" into Puerto Rico would not be subject to the usual U.S. tariffs.[44]

Santiago Iglesias was just twenty-four years old when he disembarked at San Juan in 1896, after sailing from Cuba. A son of "modest workers" in Spain, he had trained as a carpenter, participated in republican protests, and studied republican, Marxist, socialist, and anarchist theory. Unlike his contemporary Degetau, he wanted to overthrow island hierarchies and governance, not reform them. He brought to this endeavor a keen eye for the contingencies of status and state power. After being blacklisted by Spanish employers, he migrated to Cuba. There, he found work as a tobacco factory *lector*, reading aloud to workers as they produced the island's renowned cigars. Although authorities had previously banned the job for its associations with political radicalism, Iglesias held the position during the 1895 insurgency when political speech and revolutionary news again were heard from *lectores'* platforms. As secretary of the anarchist-dominated Círculo de Trabajadores (Workers' Circle), Iglesias led strikes, organized meetings, and published a labor newspaper. Decades later, reports circulated that Iglesias had written a revolutionary manifesto for José Martí and received a lieutenancy from famed revolutionary general Máximo Gómez. When Spanish authorities cracked down on anarchists in Havana in 1896, Iglesias evaded arrest by fleeing to San Juan. He took with him a dozen years of experience in labor organizing, revolutionary politics, and newspaper publishing.[45]

As Iglesias poured his energy and charisma into organizing San Juan's workers, his heritage as a Spaniard and a *peninsular* temporarily provided him with legal advantages in Puerto Rico over aliens and *criollos*: "I was frank and spoke in the colony without any kind of reservation," he later recounted; "having been born in Spain was, in a way, a form of security." He launched a labor newspaper that featured anarchist commentary and European labor news, and urged workers to imagine radical transformations of their circumstances. But his impunity evaporated in early 1898 when Luis Muñoz Rivera took high office within the new autonomous government and sought to establish the elite *criollos*' preeminence over workers and *peninsulares*. Island officials fined and briefly jailed Iglesias for his labor organizing and publishing activities. Then Iglesias and his colleagues backed Degetau and José Celso Barbosa against Luis Muñoz Rivera in the 1898 elections. Barbosa, after all, had African ancestry, was a defender of republicanism, and had introduced *el pueblo* (the people) into the island's political discourse. In response, Muñoz Rivera ordered Iglesias's arrest. After being detained, Iglesias remained imprisoned throughout the active hostilities between Spain and the United States.[46]

Domingo Collazo decided early in his career that life as a second-rate Autonomista in Puerto Rico was not good enough. He came to see Spanish rule as the primary obstacle to fuller participation by ambitious artisans like himself in island politics and society. In the 1880s he was a printer, one of the skilled workers officially categorized as a "second-class" Puerto Rican: as such, he was ineligible to vote alongside the smaller group of "first-class" islanders but superior to the racially diverse "third-class" masses. U.S. officials would later call him white, but in Puerto Rico he moved within his city's racially mixed world of printers, a calling generally associated with African heritage. The printing trade offered upward mobility to those with the right education and entrepreneurial spirit. Many printers developed public personae as authors; in print, their African ancestry could go unnoticed. Printers also launched newspapers, produced political theater, cofounded the Partido Autonomista, and published dissent to the repression of 1887. But printers could not overcome the elitism and political hesitancy of Autonomistas. In 1889 Collazo joined a growing flow of Cuban and Puerto Rican workers bound for the United States.[47]

In New York, Collazo worked alongside leading men of color in the Partido Revolucionario Cubano founded by José Martí. Where other Antillean revolutionaries participated in late-1880s Republican politics or mid-1890s populist-Democratic politics in the United States, Collazo spent the years of active fighting in Cuba (1895–1898) organizing, publishing, and propagandizing on behalf of Martí's social revolution. And he focused on extending it to Puerto Rico. Collazo joined two revolutionary clubs dedicated to joint Cuban–Puerto Rican independence. One was led entirely by Antillean men of color. While secretary of the other, he cosigned and distributed a manifesto exhorting Puerto Ricans to reject the "disguised slavery" of "false autonomy" by taking up arms for "absolute emancipation." When prominent Antillean artisans of color founded and led the newspaper *Doctrina de Martí*, Collazo was its administrator. The paper defined itself as an "organ of the working class," advocated "restorative justice" for laborers, and devoted space to the demand that "ethnographic classifications and difference die on the lips of those who esteem themselves Cuban patriots." Citing U.S. racism, the paper opposed annexation. It celebrated what Reconstruction had briefly accomplished and favored uprooting the "horrors" of Cuban slavery. Its banner featured Martí's promise of a "republic with all and for all," and the articles Collazo authored emphasized Puerto Rican independence.[48]

As prospects dimmed for the expansion of the Cuban insurgency to Puerto Rico, Collazo embraced U.S. annexation. With U.S. invasion and annexation all but certain, he adopted the aspirations of the Puerto Rico Section of the Partido Revolucionario Cubano, which prioritized overthrowing Spanish rule and sought U.S. intervention. The section members passed intelligence to U.S. military officials, offered to recruit Puerto Rican troops, penned a pro–United States manifesto for invading troops to distribute, and anticipated being given leading positions in the civilian government that they thought would follow. But U.S. officials preferred invading on their own terms. They rejected the group's manifesto and its promises of "constitutive government" and a future Puerto Rican "state or nation." Instead, they offered to place the head of the Puerto Rico Section of the party on the invading general's staff, not in a civilian leadership role. In lieu of a substantial, militarized Puerto Rican force, they formed a nine-member Puerto Rican Commission, to be led by a former U.S. consul-general to Mexico. Collazo secured one of the positions. Once the invasion began, he and the other commissioners would translate, guide, advise, lead Puerto Ricans' anti-Spanish uprisings, propagandize, advocate for annexation, and hold civilian office.[49]

In late July, Collazo stood alongside U.S. soldiers aboard a ship steaming toward Puerto Rico. As annexation neared, a widely published portrait of Collazo and the commission showed him as a well-heeled, light-skinned gentleman, gathered with the others for war, in an image connoting manliness, patriotism, and belonging (Fig. 1.1). This public persona was substantially more elite than Collazo's lived experiences. The photograph is also evidence of Collazo's early support for U.S. authority.[50]

For his part, Degetau often cast women and fieldworkers as racial, sexual, or class-based others against whom white men asserted their "rightful" place at the head of Puerto Rican society. Yet in reality, Degetau lived alongside, was mentored by, partnered with, and recruited men of color. Like Collazo, Degetau

FIGURE 1.1 The Puerto Rican Commission, photograph from Ángel Rivero, *Crónica de la Guerra Hispanoamericana en Puerto Rico* (Madrid, 1922), 270. Courtesy of HathiTrust. Domingo Collazo (back row, white jacket) was a member of the commission.

was willing to accept Puerto Rico's subjection to an outside sovereign if it advanced his constitutional aspirations. Iglesias joined Collazo and Degetau in taking up privilege, although he primarily used his *peninsular* status to contest capitalistic exploitation. Unlike the other two, Iglesias was willing to abandon constitutionalism altogether to advance his cause. But the dissolution of government was not a realistic option. Iglesias shared with Collazo and Degetau the more pragmatic, immediate priority of making progress, however limited and within whatever regime was to come.

Stateside, whether the Reconstruction Constitution would hold and prevent further annexations remained an open question among U.S. officials. Even if the Reconstruction Constitution did set the terms of new annexations, citizenship, statehood, and constitutional rights would not guarantee robust liberties or full national membership. African Americans, American Indians, women, Chinese aliens, Mormons, and U.S. citizens abroad could all attest to that. The United States also faced questions concerning whether and how to test the issue. In mid-1898, U.S. sovereignty encompassed Hawai'i, U.S. ships held Manila harbor, U.S. troops advanced in Cuba, and U.S. forces steamed toward Puerto Rico.

What Mahan termed the "constitutional lion in the path" of expansion had neither stepped aside nor vanquished U.S. expansionists. A confrontation loomed.

2

The Constitution and the New U.S. Expansion: Debating the Status of the Islands

As U.S. troops overran Puerto Rico, islanders and conquerors alike hailed what they saw as a benevolent constitutional revolution. It was easy to imagine that annexation would bring Puerto Ricans U.S. citizenship, rights, and eventual statehood. Military commanders leading the invasion, as well as many prominent Puerto Ricans, shared this view.[1]

Indeed, after the invasion of Puerto Rico began in late July 1898, U.S. officials shepherded the island's residents toward a presumptive future of U.S. citizenship. This process began while the fighting still raged. Because Spain remained the technical sovereign, fighting for the United States was treason for Puerto Ricans, punishable by execution. Given the United States' military superiority, however, those who served as Spanish troops risked a battlefield "slaughterhouse." U.S. commanders navigated this delicate situation by increasing the service and commitment that they demanded from Puerto Ricans in proportion to growing U.S. power over the island. Initially they paired lofty and vague U.S. promises with modest requests (a strategy that the same military leaders had deployed during the Indian wars of preceding decades). On July 28, for example, General Nelson A. Miles promised "the liberal institutions of our government" to islanders, and demanded only that they refrain from "armed resistance." Two weeks later, with Spanish forces routed, U.S. and Spanish representatives reached an agreement. Spain would leave Manila, Puerto Rico, and Cuba. Puerto Rico and Guam would be ceded to the United States. Spain would relinquish Cuba. And the disposition of the Philippines would await peace negotiations. General Miles had experience with such postbellum occupations, having been a federal official in the South during Reconstruction. At this point, the promises to Puerto Ricans became more specific and the demands more far-reaching. Future military governor Guy Henry declared: "The forty-five states ... unite in vouchsafing to you prosperity and protection as citizens of the American union." Officials within the State Department opined that naturalization inevitably followed annexation under international law. U.S. military authorities required some island officeholders to swear to "bear true faith and allegiance" to the United States, defend its Constitution "against all enemies," and "renounce forever every . . . state or sovereignty . . . particularly the King of Spain."[2] Because this oath extinguished all non-U.S. nationalities, it was traditionally administered only at the moment of naturalization.[3]

The War Department further integrated Puerto Ricans into the U.S. order through the policies it administered, which the president and the Departments of State and Treasury helped to set. The Chinese Exclusion Act barred most Chinese people from immigrating to the United States, and the War Department acknowledged that the act did not provide authority to ban Chinese entry into Puerto Rico. Nevertheless, when rumors arose "that Chinese agents were preparing to flood Puerto Rico" to circumvent the bar, officials began to enforce the ban at Puerto Rican ports, in this case treating Puerto Rico, de facto, as part of the United States. Similarly, they began treating Puerto Rican ports and ships as U.S. ones, applying U.S. laws on immigration, coasting, and trade. However, on the sensitive topic of tariffs, executive branch officials were unwilling, without congressional participation, to cease treating Puerto Rico as "a foreign country within the custom laws." But the assistant secretary of war did solicit an internal legal opinion stating that the cession of Puerto Rico by treaty made it subject to tariff uniformity with the rest of the United States.[4]

Puerto Rico's prospects changed abruptly in late 1898, when President McKinley exercised his prerogative as the military victor and sought annexation of the Philippines. McKinley asserted that Filipinos' inability to govern themselves left them vulnerable to other imperial powers, and that any course of action short of annexation would entail "more serious complications."[5] Although the constitutional implications of McKinley's action were not yet clear, U.S. officials' intentions to exclude the archipelago and its people from the polity soon were. Like most white mainlanders, McKinley argued that island colonials were unpracticed in republican governance and peoples of Asian Pacific descent were racially unassimilable. He also subscribed to the widely held view that tropical climates were unsuitable to white settlers, which alone could make colonies eligible for self-government.[6]

McKinley did not recommend extending the Reconstruction Constitution to Filipinos. But he offered no clear constitutional alternative. Instead, he groped for and improvised solutions in collaboration with William R. Day, who resigned as secretary of state to head McKinley's treaty negotiations with Spain over Puerto Rico, Cuba, Guam, and the Philippines. The men looked for ways to honor the Reconstruction Constitution while minimizing its impact. McKinley proposed provisions to deny U.S. citizenship to "uncivilized" tribal people and to "Mongolians and others not actually subjects of Spain." The first exclusion had appeared in the treaty annexing Alaska, which provided that its "uncivilized native tribes" would have the same status as other Indians; the second had roots in Chinese exclusion, a variant of which formed part of the resolution annexing Hawai'i. Spain recognized the jus soli citizenship rule, that birth within its territory generally made one a Spaniard, so these exceptions meshed with the Fourteenth Amendment, which permitted denials of U.S. citizenship to members of Indian tribes and also to people neither born nor naturalized within the nation.[7]

McKinley ducked questions about the political status of residents of the ceded islands. Instead, he handed off these issues to Congress, with only the Constitution as a backstop.[8] McKinley did not declare the Reconstruction Constitution inapplicable to the Philippines, but he seemed to sense its vulnerability and maintained the prerogative to make such an argument in the future.

Long-simmering conflicts over U.S. imperial expansion came to a boil when McKinley submitted the treaty to annex the Philippines to the Senate for ratification. All sides agreed, however, that the Philippines was different in kind from Hawai'i, Puerto Rico, and Guam. The Philippines was home to a uniquely large, ill-led, "utterly alien," and racially inferior population of "Malays, Tagals, Filipinos, Chinese, Japanese, Negritos, and various more or less barbarous tribes." Opponents of the acquisition of the Philippines organized into a national network dubbed the Anti-Imperialist League. The choice of name reflected the widespread view that the United States had heretofore been innocent of empire, notwithstanding its long history of expansion and domination. On that premise, it would be the acquisition of overseas colonies that would transform the United States into an empire. Democratic senators also mobilized against the treaty, and jurists analyzed the constitutional dangers of expansion.[9] Republicans, by contrast, rallied to the president's defense. Meanwhile, lawmakers and legal scholars clashed over how a nation bound by the Reconstruction Constitution could both acquire the Philippines and exclude the Filipino people.

Drawing on deep wells of white-supremacist ideology, opponents of annexation assumed that acquisition would bring Filipinos U.S. citizenship, full constitutional rights, and eventual statehood. Jurists stressed that principles of public law, the predecessor statute to the Fourteenth Amendment, and the Supreme Court's decision in *United States v. Wong Kim Ark* (1898) all confirmed that nontribal people born within the United States were citizens by virtue of the Fourteenth Amendment. Citizens enjoyed such rights as freedom of movement, equal franchise to whites, opportunities to compete for stateside jobs, and free trade with the mainland. The spirit of the Fourteenth Amendment required universal male suffrage. Portions of the *Dred Scott* decision not repudiated by the Reconstruction amendments – together with other precedents – established that the Bill of Rights operated in U.S. territories and that statehood would follow.[10]

Anti-imperialist Senate Democrats equated annexation with national perdition. Fidelity to the Constitution would pollute the national body politic with millions of racially degraded Filipinos. In the words of two opponents, the Philippines held "a mongrel and semibarbarous population ... inferior to but akin to the negro" and thus permanently "unfit ... for the glorious privileges, franchises, and functions of an American citizen." But if statehood for the Philippines and citizenship for Filipinos were anathema, the alternative was no better: to deny citizenship and statehood would violate the Constitution that Democrats interpreted as a bulwark against tyrannical federal overreach. This claim took breathtaking gall. Men who had fought to preserve slavery and then recreated a system of racial castes after the Civil War now praised equality and consent for all people, regardless of race. Erasing his service in the Confederate Congress, George Graham Vest of Missouri savaged imperialism for replacing "consent of the governed" with the transformation of "millions of human beings" into "mere chattels." Denying U.S. citizenship to any person born "within the jurisdiction of the Government," other than American Indians, would "void" the Fourteenth Amendment and betray a "result of the war crystallized in the Constitution for all time and beyond question." Democratic Senator Donelson Caffery of Louisiana added: "We have no subjects. ... Nationality is the equivalent of citizenship." Confirmation, he claimed, came from the *Slaughter-House Cases* of 1873, which declared that annexation made new "inhabitants of Federal Territories" into "citizens of the United States."[11]

Expansionists responded by claiming that the Constitution gave the United States substantial discretion to stop short of full inclusion. Legal scholar Christopher Columbus Langdell said the Constitution did not require citizenship or full constitutional rights for the inhabitants of annexed territories. The Fourteenth Amendment, Langdell wrote, was aimed at states, not Congress. Its guarantee of citizenship to those "born ... in the United States" required birth in a state, not a territory.[12]

McKinley's Senate allies claimed that the Constitution permitted imperial governance of Filipinos, whose racial inferiority was all but universally conceded in Congress. They rejected the idea that the Revolutionary War or *Dred Scott* barred colonialism. His allies further denied that the Fifteenth Amendment enfranchised all citizens, or that the Declaration of Independence, the Preamble to the Constitution, or even the Civil War stood for self-government and universal suffrage. In the words of Republican senator from Connecticut Orville Platt: "The right of a citizen to vote guaranteed by the fifteenth amendment! Women are citizens; [the illiterate and] minors are citizens; they do not vote." Federal discretion in territories was the norm, the expansionists contended. According to Platt, the Court's Mormon polygamy decisions established that the "'power of Congress over the Territories is general and plenary,'" limited only by "moral obligations." Knute Nelson of Minnesota added that the ongoing territorial status for Arizona and New Mexico demonstrated congressional power over eventual statehood. Indeed, McKinley's allies wanted to emulate British colonialism. In Nelson's words, the Philippines had been "bound hand and foot" in "shackles of Spanish tyranny," whereas British rule had brought "the liberties and blessings of a good government."[13]

White-supremacist Democrats were quick to point out that Republicans who had supported Reconstruction were now enthusiastically supporting an openly racist imperialism. South Carolina congressman John McLaurin condemned their stance as "a glaring inconsistency." Platt and others, he crowed, "most amply vindicated the South" with their stance on the Philippines, which was so "outside of the spirit of the fourteenth and fifteenth amendments of the Constitution."[14]

Republicans struggled to respond to this critique. To varying degrees, they were still committed to the Reconstruction Constitution and presumed that it retained binding authority, yet they were trying to evade or slip its constraints. A January 1899 cartoon from the popular nonpartisan magazine *Puck* captured the divergent impulses (Fig. 2.1).[15] In it, schoolteacher Uncle Sam embodies the McKinley administration as he teaches self-government. The day's lesson echoes Republican senators' embrace of British colonialism: "The consent of the governed is a good thing in theory, but very rare in fact.... By not waiting for their consent [England] has greatly advanced the world's civilization." Visual cues confirm that disparaged races may be denied the Reconstruction Constitution. Displaying post-Reconstruction indifference, Uncle Sam makes no effort to teach the sole African American youth, who is shown happily and servilely washing the classroom windows. The only American Indian pupil, clad in tribal garb, pretends to read an upside-down book. Seated alone at the back of the room, he remains unalterably outside of and inferior to U.S. society, despite federal assimilation policies.[16] Legally validated Chinese exclusion keeps a Chinese youth standing outside the schoolhouse door. For their part, islanders – Filipinos, Hawaiians, Puerto Ricans, and Cubans – loll on a remedial bench. An unbridgeable divide separates them from the light-skinned students, representing antebellum U.S. states and territories, who earnestly study at desks.

Or, perhaps not.

The cartoon's caption reveals that Uncle Sam anticipates a different trajectory for the occupied islands than that followed by African Americans, American Indians, ethnic Chinese, or British colonial subjects. He announces that as he teaches and islanders learn self-government, they will soon resemble the citizens of traditional U.S. territories. An Alaskan, although rendered as a dark-skinned caricature, sits in the "class ahead" with previously acquired states and territories. Nor does the classroom motto make racial inferiority grounds for denying consent to be governed. Instead, it asserts that it is the consent of responsible majorities that legitimizes democracy, whether or not intractable minorities concur: "The Confederate States refused their consent to be governed; but the Union was preserved without their consent."[17]

As the vote to approve the treaty with Spain neared, Democrats, who feared undermining a president in wartime, and Republicans, who feared dividing their party, reached a compromise. A majority of senators united behind a plan to ratify without annexing. Democrat Augustus Bacon of Georgia proposed that the Senate treat the Philippines like Cuba and disclaim any purpose to hold the archipelago permanently or to naturalize its inhabitants. Republican Joseph Foraker of Ohio agreed that there was no support for permanently holding the Philippines.

FIGURE 2.1 Louis Dalrymple, "School Begins," *Puck*, 25 Jan. 1899. Courtesy of Library of Congress Prints and Photographs. The cartoon's caption reads: "Uncle Sam (*to his new class in Civilization*). – Now, children, you've got to learn these lessons whether you want to or not! But just take a look at the class ahead of you, and remember that, in a little while, you will feel as glad to be here as they are!" The blackboard reads: "The consent of the governed is a good thing in theory, but very rare in fact. England has governed her colonies whether they consented or not. By not waiting for their consent she has greatly advanced the world's civilization. The U.S. must govern its new territories with or without their consent until they can govern themselves." Above and to the left of the door are the words: "The Confederate States refused their consent to be governed. But the Union was preserved without their consent." The students on the front bench are labeled Philippines, Hawaii, Porto Rico, and Cuba. Behind them sit California, Texas, Arizona, New Mexico, and Alaska, the darker-skinned student just to the right of the door.

FIGURE 2.1 (cont.)

In early February all but two voting Republicans and a sizeable minority of Democrats approved the treaty, a decision the Senate explicitly stated was "not intended to incorporate the inhabitants of the Philippine Islands into citizenship of the United States, nor ... to permanently annex said islands as an integral part of the territory of the United States."[18]

Harvard government professor Abbott Lawrence Lowell soon provided a constitutional justification for annexation without citizenship. Uniform taxation, trial by jury, and citizenship could be withheld where inhabitants lacked U.S. citizens' "social and political evolution," he proposed. Others accepted his theory, though Lowell himself conceded that its precedents – three cases – were "meagre." The first, *Fleming v. Page* (1850), held that temporarily occupied ports were "part of the United States" vis-à-vis foreign nations, yet "foreign" for purposes of U.S. tariff laws. But the decision did not address whether permanently acquired lands and people could be governed outside the Constitution. *Jones v. United States* (1890) involved a statute empowering the president to declare uninhabited islands rich in guano, which was used as fertilizer, as "appertaining to the United States" and subject to rules for U.S. ships on the high seas. The law envisioned temporary U.S. jurisdiction for the discrete purpose of guano extraction. Yet these islands – barren, uninhabited, and presumptively unsuited to settlement – more closely resembled offshore drilling platforms than conquered civilizations. Because the United States maintain "exclusive jurisdiction" over such islands, *Jones* permitted federal prosecution of crimes committed there. U.S. citizens on the islands, the Court soon added, held only the rights that would accompany them to "countries having no civilized government." The presence or absence of "civilized government" was a key aspect of international law in 1890, the idea being that uncivilized countries were not nations at all but merely the high seas made solid. The third and most recent precedent, *In re Ross* (1891), held that constitutional rights to a jury were inapplicable in U.S. consular courts that were located in Japan by Japanese consent.[19]

Lowell argued that the Supreme Court had already determined that the United States could invade and govern overseas territories without extending the Constitution beyond U.S. borders. He did not provide insight, however, into the central question raised by annexation: Could the nation's borders be extended beyond the reach of the Reconstruction Constitution?

By late 1899, lawmakers and sympathetic jurists had a tentative answer. They identified a middle ground between the anti-imperialists and the expansionists. Congress would determine the status of Puerto Rico and the Philippines when it next legislated for each of them. Because Puerto Rico was slated to be the test case for the Philippines, it would receive its organic act first.

Federal attention returned to the Caribbean. There, Puerto Rican leaders had already begun charting their own responses to the policies with which U.S. officials confronted them.

In Puerto Rico, the labor leader Santiago Iglesias and the politicians (and committed foes) Federico Degetau and Luis Muñoz Rivera adapted their ambitions to the new regime.[20] These practiced colonials studied their new imperial masters. The U.S. invasion had demolished or upended some parts of the political landscape while leaving other parts unscathed. Spanish rule disappeared. So too did island elites' patriotic allegiance to the Spanish mother country. Iglesias later wryly noted that island officials "who had sworn to stay in their posts and there defend and die for the Spanish flag" instead "continued ... enjoying the same positions" after "swearing to respect and defend the American flag." Island politicians were still divided; that had not changed. After U.S. military authorities reconstituted the Council of Secretaries with Muñoz Rivera still at its head, Degetau continued to spar with his old opponent.[21] Both men retained their long-standing commitments, including a reluctance to martyr themselves for the elusive ideal of independence. Iglesias faced ongoing persecution by Muñoz Rivera. But the replacement of Spain with the United States as the object of islanders' hopes and fears did transform the terms of their debate.

Contrary to the adage, Iglesias chose the devil he did not know. He was released from prison when Spain complied with a U.S. request and abandoned its plans to prosecute him. Afterward, U.S. troops told him, "Now you don't have anything to fear; the American flag protects you. ... [C]onsider yourself a free citizen." With Spain vanquished and his nemesis Muñoz Rivera vulnerable, Iglesias immediately tested the troops' promise. Iglesias had a different goal entirely from those of Degetau and Muñoz Rivera: the betterment of workers. He founded the Federación Regional de los Trabajadores de Puerto Rico, which became the dominant labor organization on the island, and established an associated newspaper. Organized San Juan wage earners launched strikes and demanded protection for workers.[22]

Predictably, Muñoz Rivera objected. In Iglesias's later recounting, Muñoz Rivera summoned him for a meeting in late 1898 in which he berated Iglesias, pressured him to leave Puerto Rico, and declared him a "foreigner" with no place in public affairs. When Iglesias publicized the incident, he was charged with criminal slander. He and his allies claimed that the prosecution for slander was "contrary to the laws of the great American Republic." Henry Carroll, whom President McKinley had commissioned to investigate Puerto Rican conditions, criticized the prosecution as representative of "the Spanish method of trial and the Spanish policy toward labor, though it occurred under military rule" by the United States. Iglesias told an assembly of labor representatives, "We are annexationists." A colleague reported that Iglesias spoke "so enthusiastically of freedom, that he was nicknamed by Americans as 'Mr. Liberty.'"[23]

The United States, however, was soon revealed as more devil than savior to organized labor. To the leader of a racially mixed union, U.S. officials were, at best, imperfect allies. On the mainland, federal troops helped break mass strikes; federal officials condoned Jim Crow, African American disfranchisement, and the repression of cross-racial, farmer-laborer Populist politics. When Governor-General Davis made taxpaying or literacy a prerequisite to voting in a round of local elections in Puerto Rico, Iglesias and his colleagues condemned the disfranchisement as slavery and tyranny, contrary to citizenship, and worse than Spanish rule. But even the threat of thousands of literate workingmen boycotting the election did not produce results.[24] Defeated, Iglesias sought a new ally.[25]

Degetau and Muñoz Rivera prepared for the upcoming elections by founding competing political parties, each pursuing the long-standing goal of Puerto Rican autonomy within the new constitutional structure. On 4 July 1899, Degetau's alliance formed the Partido Republicano, which Muñoz Rivera and his supporters' new Partido Federal soon opposed. Because both sides sought U.S. citizenship, full constitutional rights, and eventual statehood, mainlanders sometimes found it difficult to discern their differences and divisions. Yet they differed in their constituencies, potential institutional allies, strategies for securing change, and visions of patriotism. According to their critics, Muñoz Rivera's Federales attracted "the larger property-holding interests and the merchants" and held "the masses of agricultural and industrial workers under political bosses' dominion and control." Translated into terms familiar to mainlanders, Federales displayed a "horror of negro domination" coupled with a fear of widespread voting by "the poorer whites." By contrast, Degetau's Partido Republicano called itself the "popular party of the island" and courted "elements hitherto neglected – the poorer whites and the negroes." The Republicanos' name and the party's founding on the Fourth of July signaled its heritage, aspirations, and patriotism. Its leaders proudly recalled their Spanish-era stand against monarchists and identified openly with the U.S. Republican Party. The impetus for that alliance was twofold. Republicanos had benefited from Muñoz Rivera's falling out with the Republican administration. And afterward, Degetau had secured an appointment as secretary of interior, one of the four top civilian posts on the island. In accepting the job, he swore to "support and defend the Constitution." General Henry soon described him as among the island's most "able and honest men." The alliance was also rooted in Puerto Ricans' understanding of U.S. history. As leading Republicano and man of color José Celso Barbosa recalled, he had faced relatively little racial prejudice during his medical studies at the University of Michigan in the late 1880s. At that time, the Republican Party was more supportive of Reconstruction and African Americans' rights and more focused on its role in achieving emancipation than it had since become. Aligning with Republicans thus meant laying claim to the legacy of emancipation.[26]

Republicanos identified patriotic faith in U.S. institutions and law as the surest path to full inclusion. Degetau's fluent English, knowledge of U.S. law and politics, high standing in the Partido Republicano and the island bar, public and charitable service, and promotion of modern, liberal reforms all made him a logical spokesperson. Degetau espoused a view that resembled the sentimental rhetoric of Republican Civil War victors. Unlike such "monarchical and centralized nations" as Spain, he wrote, in the United States' federal system localism went hand in hand with nationalism. Degetau's logic assumed that mutual love between one's region and the Union arose from the extension of U.S. liberties and institutions to local jurisdictions. He envisioned that these U.S. ideals guaranteed rapid integration of Puerto Rico into the United States: "Puerto Rico will be a Republican Territory today and tomorrow a State of the Union," for otherwise it would "be what the Anglo Saxons call 'a crown colony'" in a United States where "citizenship had been reduced to the monopoly of 74 million oligarchs."[27]

Rather than acknowledge that the likely exclusion of the Philippines from the United States undermined his analysis, Degetau depicted it as an exception that proved the rule and little more than a temporary inconvenience for Puerto Rico. For the moment, federal lawmakers persisted in seeing Puerto Rico as a key test case for governing the Philippines, especially as a matter of constitutional law. But Degetau reasoned that this fleeting association between the two would be severed once the United States recognized Puerto Ricans' readiness for full membership in the Union. After all, Degetau pointed out, "Latins" and Anglo-Saxons were coauthors of democracy. Latin contributions dated to the Roman Empire and included the enshrinement of the individual at "the center of juridical relations," the unification of diverse peoples under common laws, and the invention of separation of powers. Even if Puerto Ricans and mainlanders were not equals, General Miles had promised U.S. liberties to Puerto Rico. To renege on such an obligation, Degetau said, would be to "shamefully" tarnish the nation, its "honor and good name."[28] The Philippines were not really relevant to Puerto Rico, in Degetau's view.

Federales were dismissive of Degetau's idealism and his political views. They emphasized autonomy rather than rights and savaged as an unpatriotic "collaboration" the Republicanos' faith in patience, law, Republicans, and the Union. In their view, Puerto Ricans were facing a political fight for autonomy, against the McKinley administration and its federal overreach. In contrast to Degetau, Muñoz Rivera called for a boycott of George Washington's birthday. He even proposed that Puerto Rico petition to return to Spanish rule, presumably agreeing that such a maneuver "on the eve of a presidential election would undoubtedly be highly injurious to the Republican party" and that a Democratic administration might benefit Puerto Rico. The aim of this belligerence, which was inattentive to legal details, was salutary neglect pending statehood. Although autonomy was not the historical norm for U.S. territories and no territory elected its governor, the Federales demanded "that Porto Rico be ... a Territory ... with all the rights of a State, except" that to vote for congressional representatives.[29]

Muñoz Rivera defended his approach with a portrayal of the Civil War familiar to Democrats. He predicted that mainlanders "will not consent to the enslavement of the whites after spilling so much blood to prevent the enslavement of the blacks." Like Democrats, Muñoz Rivera made white rather than black freedom the measure of post-emancipation struggles and compared himself to the leaders of the American Revolution who "spoke loudly" against British abuses, which they condemned as political slavery. He resembled key Southern Democratic leaders in another way too: the son of a slave owner, he portrayed himself as a father figure ready to guide the unwashed masses as they equipped themselves for freedom.[30]

Both Degetau and Muñoz Rivera failed to predict how profoundly U.S. racism would alter officials' understanding of liberty and citizenship. But citizenship, race, and racism were powerfully interleaved. Puerto Rican leaders and U.S. officials drew disparate conclusions from key, shared premises. Both sets of men were accustomed to racial hierarchies with whiteness on the top and blackness anchored on the bottom. Drawing on their Spanish-era experiences, Degetau, Muñoz Rivera, and, to a lesser degree, Iglesias sought and expected the privileges, protections, and dignity accorded to whiteness. This had been a fragile aspiration even under Spanish rule, given the men's racially mixed constituencies. Many Puerto Ricans persisted in viewing race as a continuum on which a multitude of factors determined one's place, but U.S. officials often understood race in more dichotomous terms based exclusively on ancestry. This premise of racism confounded any clear place for Puerto Ricans in the hierarchy. As Anglo-Saxon lineage increasingly became the measure of whiteness in the United States, Spaniards and other Latins came to be perceived as a distinctly darker shade of pale. The latest census for the island had reported that black persons and those of mixed race were outnumbered by white persons but constituted a sizeable minority of the Puerto Rican population.[31]

Island leaders and officials shared racist thinking but defined race differently. They also had distinctly different views on politics, autonomy, and patronage. Prominent Puerto Ricans and their local followers expected elected officials to reward votes with patronage, especially because it would exemplify and thereby help institutionalize the principle that Puerto Ricans chosen by Puerto Ricans should fill island offices. To proceed otherwise would betray one's base and perhaps undermine autonomy. Typically, the opposition party was quick to cast such clientelism as corrupt and unprincipled cronyism. When majority-party status was out of reach, it was a standard Spanish-era practice to trumpet one's principles and decline to seek or accept office. Accordingly, when U.S. officials placed Muñoz Rivera and his allies under military rule in 1899, he resigned in "protest against the act of the Palace." The attempt to cast U.S. policy as Spanish tyranny did not convince U.S. officials, but it presented domestic audiences with a dramatic display of Muñoz Rivera as David confronting an imperial Goliath.[32]

To U.S. military governors, who were steeped in idioms of clean government and reform, Puerto Rican politics appeared to be a morass of corruption, duplicity, and political incompetence. Gestures such as Muñoz Rivera's resignation seemed more overwrought than heroic. The longest-serving U.S. governor-general, George Davis, who took his post in mid-1899, was suspicious of the islanders' Spanish and African heritage. In his view, the United States was an Anglo-Saxon nation beset by unassimilable racial inferiors incapable of self-government. Like Southern Redeemers contemptuous of Reconstruction, and other proto-Progressive reformers, Davis expected broad political participation to undermine good government, especially because democratic power in the hands of the lower classes caused corruption. He was thus primed to embrace his predecessors' judgments that even the island politicians who criticized corruption practiced it enthusiastically when in power. Muñoz Rivera was the "ringleader of the professional politicians," Davis surmised, and mired in their "hotbed of corruption." When they were in the opposition, they were unwilling to accept that they had lost the election, Davis charged. Worse, they dwelled at the nadir of the racial hierarchy, "only a few steps removed from a primitive state of nature." They were no better than disfranchised "Negro illiterates," he declared; "no more fit to take part in self-government than are our reservation Indians, from whom the suffrage is withheld"; and "far inferior . . . to the Chinese, who for very good reasons are forbidden to land on our shores." To progress toward liberty, they needed tutelage.[33] Davis, a Union veteran of the Civil War and Reconstruction, did not acknowledge that the charges of patronage and a violent refusal to accept adverse election results better described the Southern whites of the Confederacy and the Redemption than they did Puerto Ricans.

Although Davis's governorship would last less than a year, he had the ear of policymakers influential in crafting federal legislation. His disparagement thus threatened to redound to the enduring detriment of Puerto Ricans. Of course, Federales countered that Puerto Ricans were predominantly white, deserving of self-government, and superior to the "nearly all semi-barbarous" New Mexicans and to residents of Hawai'i and the Philippines.[34] But federal lawmakers were inclined to follow the lead and opinion of U.S. officials, not Puerto Rican politicians.

Having committed his administration to colonial rule in the Philippines, McKinley was convinced that constitutional challenges rather than armed conflict were now the more dangerous threat to his imperial vision. McKinley was keenly aware of the complexities and different constitutional priorities that shaped how Republicans and Democrats thought about empire vis-à-vis the Reconstruction Constitution. To steer debate in his favor, in August 1899 he chose Elihu Root as his new secretary of war. Root was a Wall Street lawyer without any military experience, but this suited the administration's new priorities: After ratification of the Treaty of Paris, the War Department's main task was administrative, not military. McKinley was "not looking for any one who knows anything about war," Root recalled.[35] Instead, a canny lawyer who accrued experience with the island would be invaluable to expansionists who wanted to shape legislation for empire.

Root was an incisive choice. He was among the most talented and successful jurists in the country. An active and influential Republican, he promoted expert administration as the balm for the disease of Tammany Hall Democrats and corrupt electoral politics generally. In 1898 he became president of the prestigious Union League Club of New York. His acceptance speech celebrated the club's support of African American soldiers during the Civil War and declared, without apparent irony, that the modern "purpose and spirit" of the club's support for the Union was rooted in "Anglo-Saxon pluck." At a dinner soon afterward, club members overwhelmingly supported expansion.[36]

And Root did not disappoint. Moving quickly in late 1899 and early 1900 with an eye to establishing a precedent applicable to the Philippines, he urged that Puerto Rico receive few rights and no citizenship. Federally appointed administrators rather than democratically elected officials should govern Puerto Rico, which he recommended not be made a traditional territory or future state.

Secretary Root wrenched the War Department into conformity with his views. Prior to Root's arrival, the War Department judges of the U.S. Provisional Court for

Puerto Rico had opened a two-year path to naturalization by accepting declarations of intention to become U.S. citizens. But that path required "residence in the United States," a criterion that Root deemed not to be satisfied by living on the island. Then, based on Root's objections, Governor Davis revised his public plans to prepare Puerto Ricans for "American Citizenship" and "statehood." Root also ordered Davis to stop requiring non-*criollo* voters simultaneously to renounce foreign allegiances and declare their intention to become U.S. citizens. Santiago Iglesias took the oath while it remained available and claimed that he had thereby become an American citizen. But Root saw the oath less as a path to U.S. citizenship and more as a trap that could leave a foreigner "a man without a country."[37]

Root aligned himself with reformers who equated restricted electorates with clean and effective government. Though the Republican Party still formally opposed Southern states' disfranchisement of formerly enslaved people and their descendants, Root and his subordinates stressed islanders' racial "inferiority" as they limited their suffrage and proposed to deny them home rule. Root openly called Reconstruction a failed experiment, for similar reasons. Governor George Davis now equated Puerto Ricans with New Mexicans, who lacked "capacity for State government" a half century after the acquisition of the territory.[38]

Root and Davis proposed to create what was essentially an imperial household with Puerto Rican dependents. One governor-general described them as "children" requiring "kindergarten instruction" in politics. Root recommended a "course of tuition under a strong and guiding hand." When Root's Senate ally, Republican lawyer Chauncey Depew of New York, stressed islanders' dependence, he chose women rather than children as his metaphor. Rejecting claims that the island was "a bride ... worthy ... of the ... American," he cited high rates of illiteracy and racial intermixture in Puerto Rico in insisting that she was a Jezebel instead. Davis recommended that the United States follow the British approach in Barbados, Trinidad, and Jamaica, where imperial government involved little democracy.[39]

Happily, Root wrote, Congress faced "no legal limitations." He and his law officer for the Division of Customs and Insular Affairs, Charles Magoon, invoked diverse judicial precedents that had been applied to disfavored, racialized U.S. communities. In a memorandum to Congress, Magoon claimed that "jurisdiction" and "sovereignty" over Puerto Rico did not extend "the territorial boundaries of the ... United States." In support of this view, Magoon and Root mustered decisions by judges and other officials that overlapped with but transcended the authorities identified by Lowell, the Harvard government professor, in his roughly contemporaneous exegesis. The War Department officials' citations featured consular courts, ships on the high seas, occupied lands, the guano islands, the District of Columbia, former and current territories, Mormons, slaves, the Chinese, other immigrants, free people of color before the Civil War, and American Indians. To evade the *Dred Scott* rules that the Constitution extended broad rights to the territories and demanded that they one day become states, Magoon and Root declared those aspects of the decision "overthrown" by the Civil War and subsequent decisions.[40]

Reconstruction could have provided them an additional "striking indication" of extensive federal power, but Root sidestepped that politically explosive precedent. Instead, he pointed in a very different direction. Except for the Thirteenth Amendment, the Constitution would not apply, he determined. The "great powers, rights, privileges, and immunities" of citizenship made it too precious to be extended to Puerto Ricans; the federal government could demand allegiance without promising naturalization. "Many persons ... from whom allegiance in some form is due ... are not citizens of the United States. Many soldiers ... , temporary sojourners, Indians, Chinese, convicted criminals, and, in another and limited sense, minors and women belong to this class." So too, Magoon concluded, did Puerto Ricans.[41]

Here, Root and Magoon proposed a revolution in Fourteenth Amendment citizenship doctrine. The founding-era rule that the Fourteenth Amendment formalized was that birth within lands over which U.S. sovereignty extended automatically conferred citizenship. Instead, Magoon now wrote, birth within the United States empire was not necessarily "birth within the territory ... of the United States."[42] Lawmakers could withhold what had come to be termed jus soli citizenship from newly acquired lands. The ostensibly ancient "right of the soil" was no longer unqualified.

The test of this bold strategy began on 3 January 1900, when Senator Joseph Foraker introduced legislation to establish a civil government for Puerto Rico, following the secretary of war's recommendations. Foraker included a presidentially appointed governor and upper legislative chamber, an elected lower legislative chamber, and a nonvoting delegate to the U.S. House of Representatives. The bill would not create a territory. But Foraker departed from Magoon and Root's proposed denial of citizenship. Instead, he sought to extend a form of citizenship to Puerto Ricans stripped of any significant "privileges" or "immunities." Foraker and the Senate Committee on Pacific Islands and Porto Rico insisted that the United States "have no subjects, and should not make aliens of our own." He felt comfortable in saying this, however, only because he believed that citizenship would bring islanders no "rights that the American people do not want them to have." It would entitle them to the governmental protection that women received, but not to political participation. Finally, Foraker's bill supported free trade for Puerto Rico, a policy that Root and McKinley promoted as just, albeit not legally required. As Root explained in his annual report, the loss of Spanish markets left Puerto Rico stranded in a competitive world. The alternatives, he wrote, were free trade or letting "the people starve."[43]

Foraker's bill created a quandary for antiexpansionist Democrats. Politically, empire was a potentially valuable issue for the fall election campaign. Democrats could lay groundwork for lines of attack by critiquing Foraker's bill now – but doing so would permit Republicans to alter the bill to blunt criticism. The alternative was to keep mum, which could permit Republicans to control the narrative at a pivotal juncture. At the level of policy, Democrats faced similar trade-offs. Like the president, secretary of war, and Republican lawmakers, they weighed their options in the shadow of courts. They acknowledged judicial supremacy and anticipated judicial review, but they treated law and the courts as pliable. If they attacked Republicans for denying islanders constitutional protections, then Republicans might cede ground and provide Puerto Ricans greater rights. That, in turn, could provoke the Supreme Court to find that Puerto Rico was a traditional territory.[44]

Because many saw Puerto Rico as a harbinger for the Philippines, such a holding would raise stark alternatives. On the one hand, it might produce the full integration of Filipinos that anti-imperialist Democrats dreaded. On the other hand, it might demonstrate the dreaded cost of retaining the Philippines, and so create a political consensus in favor of independence for the Philippines, which Democrats desired. Democrats instead chose to criticize Republicans for integrating Puerto Ricans too fully into the U.S. polity.

Republicans were receptive to the Democrats' critique. As one Republican senator explained, his party's "best constitutional lawyers in the Senate admit that ... it would not be safe" to "legislate for the Philippines as territory not a part of the United States" before hearing from the Supreme Court. Otherwise, the Court might decide to extend Filipinos citizenship and other constitutional protections. When Democrats worried that the Court might construe statutory free trade and citizenship as a signal that Congress recognized Puerto Rico as part of the United States, Republicans removed both provisions in favor of a temporary tariff set at 15 percent of prevailing rates. A tariff was attractive as a test issue for Republicans because it elided what Root called the divisive question of islanders' "moral right to ... the underlying principles of justice and freedom ... in our Constitution." Better yet, it could reach the Court before more sympathetic individual plaintiffs did so with claims to other rights. Speed mattered. The *New York Tribune* had just attempted to bring a test suit on citizenship by hiring a Puerto Rican employee despite the federal statutory prohibition on "alien" contract labor. The secretary of the treasury mooted that challenge by admitting the employee as an "isolated case." But planned lawsuits signaled that the reprieve would be brief. Foraker also replaced the island's delegate to the House in his bill with a Puerto Rican resident commissioner who would register with the U.S. secretary of state as foreign dignitaries did.[45]

But even Foraker's revised bill did not satisfy anti-imperialist Democrats. It reduced the likelihood of eventual statehood for Puerto Rico and the Philippines, but only through what Democrats saw as a dangerous expansion of federal power. In their view, the original sin was the determination to retain the Philippines, which necessitated the sacrifice of Puerto Rico to reduce the Pacific threat. Democratic senator and Confederate veteran from Tennessee William Bate described "Negrito" Filipinos as "physically weaklings of low stature, with black skin, closely curling hair, flat noses, thick lips, and large, clumsy feet." Such people, he asserted, "would prove a serpent in our bosom." Democratic representative William Jones of Virginia also favored release of the Philippines. This would free the United States to give Puerto Ricans "a Territorial form of government, such as is enjoyed by every other American territory." Presumably aware that the most recent census categorized 62 percent of Puerto Ricans as "white," 32 percent as "mulattoes," and just 6 percent as "of pure negro blood," Jones declared that most Puerto Ricans were "Caucasian" and proposed treating them as citizens. Jones said that the current Republican policy rivaled the worst abuses of centralized power known in U.S. history. He charged that it was the infamous *Dred Scott* decision all over again, since imperial rule over the new island (or in officials' parlance, insular) populations rested on the same theory that Justice Taney had applied to free African Americans. They were "conquered subjects" with "no rights which" the United States was "bound to respect." Jones also charged that the Republican policy was worse than Reconstruction. The Foraker Act would bring undemocratic Republican dominance and corruption; "no such dangerous and absolute power ... was ever before lodged in an irresponsible carpetbag government."[46]

In the weeks before passage of the Foraker Act, Federico Degetau had announced that the pressing question in the debate was whether the United States would have "two classes of citizens, two conditions of rights," with those occupying the higher category ruling those below.[47] Congress's answer was not reassuring. But with island elections under the act set for November, Degetau was optimistic. He insisted that history and law were on the Puerto Ricans' side and that the arcs of both would bend more quickly if he and his Partido Republicano were at the helm.

Santiago Iglesias and Luis Muñoz Rivera recognized the challenges. Campaigns meant competition for the labor vote. But Iglesias was reluctant to align his reconstituted labor movement too closely with either party, given the potential for co-optation and intralabor division. For their part, Muñoz Rivera and fellow Federales faced hostile U.S. officials, lacked strong mainland allies, and displayed elitism and commitments to whiteness that made it easy for opponents to depict them as racist and antilabor.

Foraker's bill became law in April of 1900. Despite the disappointments of the act, Degetau rallied his party around the conviction that the Constitution would soon bring islanders citizenship, rights, and self-government. The United States was a different sort of empire because it guaranteed equality, liberty, and republican government to all its people, he declared. Despite post–Civil War worries about Southern society, the United States had "not dared to deprive slaveholders or freedmen of the privileges and immunities of the Constitution" enshrined in the Fourteenth Amendment. Now, Degetau added, American Indians, heterogeneous European Americans, Chinese Americans, and others all enjoyed those rights. Degetau's claims meshed with his aspirations and with certain strands of U.S. jurisprudence, yet they little reflected how the contemporary United States actually treated immigrants, native peoples, and racial minorities. U.S. misconduct in the Philippines also belied U.S. commitment to law. Though the worst atrocities lay ahead in the Philippines, U.S. forces were already bloodily, brutally, and illegally suppressing the Filipino pro-independence forces with whom they had earlier been united in opposing Spanish rule. To make his case, Degetau used General Miles's promises to claim that Puerto Ricans would be included in the broad array of communities whom the Constitution would protect. Otherwise, he insisted, the United States would have to say, "Goodbye Washington, Goodbye Founding Fathers."[48]

Fluent in English, expert in U.S. law and policy, a student of U.S. history, and a devotee of a paternalistic brand of liberalism, Degetau proved an attractive candidate for resident commissioner. Republicanos soon nominated him. He campaigned on the pledge that "basic principles of the Constitution of the United States" guaranteed Puerto Ricans "the right to the fullness of the American citizenship" and eventually a place among the "autonomous states of the Union." If elected, he said, he would "brandish" Puerto Ricans' claims to citizenship, be it before federal courts or elsewhere in Washington.[49]

Degetau and his Republicanos wooed labor support in the campaign by offering an alliance that would bring workers payments from the party, a smattering of official posts, a prominent role in island politics and the accompanying prestige, and the ability to break the law for political ends with a substantial measure of official impunity. By aligning with Republicanos, workers would also strike a symbolic blow against racial hierarchy. They could abandon the *peninsular* Iglesias (a "foreigner") for a party headed by the island's leading man of color, José Celso Barbosa. Influential labor anarchists balked at this offer, but many other workers were tempted – and with Republicanos' help, they wrested away control of Iglesias's own Federación Regional.[50]

Iglesias was devastated, but not defeated. He characterized the Republicano offer to labor as a golden apple of discord, destined to sow division among workers. Iglesias and his allies regrouped as the Federación de Trabajadores Libres, or Federación Libre. Aware that the Federación Regional and the Republicanos had claimed the issue of race as their own, Iglesias's Federación Libre committed itself to strikes and greater openness to women members. Iglesias saw federal rule and an alliance with mainland labor activists as his best options under the circumstances. The Federación Libre began to build an alliance with the mainland Socialist Labor Party, which opposed the exploitation of workers on the mainland and in the colonies. The relationship quickly ripened into formal agreement under a declaredly Marxist socialist charter. When the Socialist Party fractured later that year, the Federación Libre aligned with Socialist Labor Party dissidents who favored closer ties to the powerful and more conservative American Federation of Labor. The dissidents soon also joined the new Socialist Party of America. In early 1900 the multilingual, multiethnic Socialist Party and its male and female members hosted Iglesias on a trip to New York City. There he gained access to labor activists and mainland press outlets. The question for Iglesias was whether these newfound friends and the exposure they brought would protect him and his followers during times of industrial strife on the island.[51]

The test came when Iglesias launched a San Juan–based general strike in August 1900. Republicanos unleashed a wave of repression calculated to prevent Iglesias from siphoning off supporters. The strike lasted several weeks. Hundreds of workers in San Juan left their jobs, while hundreds more refused to work in the sugar fields and in urban industries elsewhere on the island. Iglesias's friends in the Socialist Party and the labor movement in New York lobbied Washington, sent money to strikers, and provided favorable newspaper coverage. Nonetheless, Republicano officials arrested twenty-six strikers, including Iglesias, whom they charged with criminal conspiracy. Iglesias and other Federación Libre members were attacked by the violent *turbas*, a mostly working-class San Juan group associated with Republicanos and the Federación Regional. Governor Charles Allen and other island officials neither stopped the violence nor arrested the perpetrators. When the strikes finally ended in September, workers declared a moral victory. Employers had not met their demands, but the organized laborers had demonstrated their ability to launch and maintain a substantial work stoppage. Events such as these convinced the Federación Libre that connections with stateside organizations were crucial bulwarks against what they called politicians' plans to "have working people as slaves."[52] But more was needed to make real progress.

By late 1900, Muñoz Rivera's Federales faced plummeting electoral prospects. Republicanos had made significant gains among voters of color. Party leader Barbosa, the most prominent person of color in Puerto Rico, promoted the Partido Republicano as the party of island men of color and heir to the ideals of Abraham Lincoln. The alliance with the Federación Regional labor organization also swelled Republicano rolls. Federales' indifference to the plight of islanders of African ancestry contributed to this trend, especially because they ignored Puerto Rico's sharp socioeconomic divisions along racial lines. Federales explained that because Puerto Rico extended islanders of color the same rights and liberties as whites, they had no reason to complain. According to the Partido Federal, the foremost danger for the island's former slaves and their descendants was U.S. "absorption." Federalism in the United States masked racism, the party said, permitting such "great injustices" as the lynching and disfranchisement of African Americans. Sensing an opportunity, Republicanos charged that Federales were the true threat because they were the ones who treated islanders of color as "slaves."[53]

The Federales badly needed support, but they were not white enough for potential allies on the mainland and too white for potential allies on the island – or at least too invested in whiteness. To counter the Republicanos' alignment with mainland Republicans, Federales proposed an alliance with mainland Democrats. Presidential candidate William Jennings Bryan had encouraged this, with an anti-imperial jab, when he accepted the Democratic nomination: the "forcible annexation of territory to be governed by arbitrary power differs as much from the acquisition of territory to be built up into states as a monarchy differs from a democracy." The election of Bryan, Federales hoped, would bring a return to "true

American traditions" that included "an autonom[ous] form of government."
Predictably, white-supremacist Democrats did not rush to accept the Puerto Rican
political party as a full partner. Working-class *turbas* associated with the
Republicanos also attacked Federales, apparently with the sanction of island
officials. In two separate incidents in September, they gathered outside of Muñoz
Rivera's home, fired shots, and destroyed his printing press. This public violence by
working-class men of color against a man of Muñoz Rivera's standing and heritage
challenged traditional honor-based norms of deference and racial hierarchy.
The violence escalated into near-daily attacks as the election neared. Federales
charged that U.S. tolerance of the assaults revealed a pro-Republicano bias, which
was also evident in the pro-Republicano gerrymander of island voting districts. Two
days before the polls opened, Federales withdrew in protest and fear.[54]

On 6 November 1900, Puerto Rican Republicanos swept the House of Delegates
and elected Degetau resident commissioner. Mainland Republicans retained control
of the presidency and Congress. Within days, Degetau was in Washington,
determined to win citizenship for all islanders. His political career and islanders'
futures now depended on federal officials. Muñoz Rivera and Iglesias also went to
the mainland, both fleeing political violence, and resettled in New York. Muñoz
Rivera began laying groundwork for a return to power. Iglesias was less sure he
would go back. For the time being, he found work and lodging with socialist friends,
joined a local union, wrote for the mainland labor press, and studied English.[55]

Degetau and Muñoz Rivera had made stark, divergent choices about the best
course of action – the former favored law, Republicans, and collaboration; the latter
favored politics, Democrats, and confrontation. Yet in their separate ways, both
men, as well as Iglesias, sought the same thing: to realize the elusive promise of their
new metropole, from within.

McKinley's decisive victory over Bryan was a political vindication for
empire. Next came the legal challenges that Congress had set in motion when
legislating for Puerto Rico. By late 1900 the Supreme Court was set to review
several suits presenting racially charged questions about the relationship of
Constitution and empire that went to the heart of federal power and
individual rights. Plaintiffs' lawyer Frederic Coudert would later recall that
the cases provoked a "bitterness" akin to that sparked by the "Fugitive Slave
Law and the Missouri Compromise."[56] The Court faced a landscape already
marked by War Department administrators and Congress. Together, they had
proposed an imperial alternative to the Reconstruction Constitution: ceded
lands and their people could be treated as domestic for some purposes and as
foreign for others. For his part, Degetau was honing arguments that new
circumstances called for tried-and-true doctrine, particularly the
Reconstruction Constitution. With U.S. imperial turn in the balance and
Degetau in the wings, the Court took center stage.

3

"We Are Naturally Americans": Federico Degetau and Santiago Iglesias Pursue Citizenship

When Federico Degetau declared himself and other Puerto Ricans "naturally Americans," mainland newspaper reporters swooned. Their articles declared the first elected representative to reach the capital from the island to be among "the finest looking men" in Washington. He was a towering and "highly diplomatic" figure of "brilliant attainments," "splendid physique[,] and engaging presence." In portraits seen round the nation, Degetau symbolically swept aside portents of annexation as racial apocalypse. He was a handsome and well-heeled white gentleman in the brooding Romantic mold (Fig. 3.1). He expressed confidence that Puerto Ricans deserved citizenship; full constitutional rights; government "of, for, and by the people"; and "organized territory [status] for Porto Rico," which would pave the way for statehood. He wanted to be a traditional territorial delegate in lieu of a resident commissioner. And he announced plans to use the courts and Congress to secure these gains.[1]

Santiago Iglesias proclaimed his own demands for citizenship from a considerably weaker platform. After Degetau's allies rained violence down on him and drove him from San Juan, he found work in Manhattan, joined a cabinetmaker's union, and took up residence in Brooklyn. Like Degetau, he pinned hopes for himself and his island on the United States. He said that Puerto Rican workers needed "the American flag, which protects us in our citizenship rights," which "we now have," and the backing of U.S. labor organizations, which he saw as imminent.[2] Iglesias grasped the power of citizenship and had come up against its rhetorical limits when it was not amplified by a strong and supportive U.S. labor organization. Iglesias now set his sights on the country's largest one, the American Federation of Labor (AFL).

Both men's strategies were bold and ambitious. Degetau was relentless. He promoted and tried to embody Puerto Rican civilization wherever possible – before the press, at academic gatherings, in courts, and in Congress. As judges and lawmakers struggled with the relationship of the Constitution to empire, he also courted bureaucrats. He understood them to be both legal

FIGURE 3.1 Photograph of Federico Degetau y Gonzalez, *Harper's Weekly*, 22 Dec. 1900.

expositors in their own right and authorities who could influence other government institutions.

Degetau's confidence stemmed from his faith that law dominated politics in the United States, at least in matters of constitutional moment. Specifically, he expected officials acting in adjudicative capacities to hew to law regardless of political costs. He prodded agencies not bent on shaping constitutional meaning to decide constitutional questions, trusting that their decisions could steer judges, lawmakers, and executive officials in their own legal deliberations. Federal agencies were often the first on the ground, and sometimes they were the only governmental bodies to adjudicate thorny questions about Puerto Ricans' status and rights. Their assent would be valuable for Degetau; conversely, decisions against Degetau's claims could calcify into conventional legal wisdom. Administrators who dodged final reckonings created models for constitutional avoidance, which could also solidify into law.[3]

Faith in law also explains Degetau's priority on citizenship. Among other things, he understood citizenship to be a gateway to other legal benefits: rights, territorial status, and eventual statehood.[4]

Santiago Iglesias conjectured the opposite. He expected politics to drive legal outcomes and wanted to use legal outcomes to make political hay. He joined Degetau in seeking citizenship for Puerto Ricans. But he also treated the status more as a calling card with which to gain entrée to federal officials than as a switch whose flip would bring labor activists and other islanders robust, fully enforced rights.

Iglesias was similarly instrumental in his approach to race. He occupied a relatively privileged place in island racial hierarchies, yet aspired to lead an organized Puerto Rican labor movement notable for its multiracial composition and impulses toward racial egalitarianism. During early U.S. rule, Iglesias's aspirations had been crushed and his labor movement hobbled. To resurrect his career and the labor organization he founded, he was willing to compromise – even when it meant accepting some potential allies who were entangled with white supremacy.[5]

Degetau's first official acts in Washington included attending Supreme Court arguments in the earliest *Insular Cases*. In these cases the Supreme Court faced the seemingly stark choice of betraying the Reconstruction Constitution or dooming the nation's self-consciously imperial aspirations. Where the new oceanic empire was concerned, the justices were conflicted. All hailed from a legal elite accustomed to adhering to the structural constraints of the Reconstruction Constitution. This professional community valued fidelity to law and sophisticated legal reasoning.[6] But the appointment process also brought to the bench public figures invested in the success of the nation on the world stage. They understood their capacity to influence, empower, and impede administrative and political officials, potentially in ways that would interfere with important government objectives.

In some respects, then, the options that those on the Court faced mirrored the question dividing Degetau and Iglesias: Was law to drive politics or politics to drive law? The Reconstruction Constitution seemed to offer little space to reconcile competing juridical impulses – at least insofar as it bundled citizenship, constitutional rights, and statehood. But if it was possible to untangle them and parcel each out in stages, subsets, and degrees, then compromises might emerge.

For the justices, a slow, ambiguous, and distributed process of constitutional change had powerful appeal. It gave them control over the timing and consequences of their decisions. To the extent that the justices chose to experiment with new constitutional forms, the approach also permitted them to supplement their otherwise sparse toolkit. The president, War Department, and Congress had already sent preemptive signals to the Court that equipped it with political, administrative, and practical knowledge. The justices were now in a position to reciprocate. Dicta, minority opinions, narrow holdings, ambiguous reasoning, underdefined terms, the bracketing of questions, and openness to novel approaches could all signal the Court's preliminary plans. Nonjudicial officials could then critique, test, hone, and tacitly approve the innovations before the Court set them in constitutional stone.[7] On the other hand, in late 1900 the advocates who gathered in Washington to argue the *Insular Cases* were not resigned to an incremental or gnomic result. They wanted clear wins. The nation, too, was captivated by the possibility that the Court might satisfy advocates with clear, bold pronouncements.

The first two Insular Cases, *De Lima v. Bidwell* (1901) and *Downes v. Bidwell* (1901), concerned the imposition of tariffs on imports from Puerto Rico.[8] In the first, D. A. de Lima and Company challenged the application of the long-standing tariff on "articles imported from foreign countries" to goods shipped from Puerto Rico to New York. The case arose before the 1900 Foraker Act imposed a tariff specifically on United States–Puerto Rican trade. The second case featured Samuel Downes, who challenged the much lower Foraker Act tariff on similar shipments. If Puerto Rico was a foreign country, notwithstanding its cession by Spain, then D. A. de Lima and Company would win. If Puerto Rico was part of the United States, then the Foraker tariff would violate the constitutional rule that "all duties ... be uniform throughout the United States" and Downes would win. These questions implicated citizenship, said Frederic Coudert, the elite New York corporate lawyer who represented private litigants in both cases. He told the Court: "If the inhabitants of these islands are citizens of the United States, it would be admitted that the islands themselves were part of the United States." The *Insular Cases* as a whole presented the Court an opportunity to treat Puerto Rico and the Philippines differently.[9]

Degetau hoped for holdings that Puerto Rico was part of the United States rather than foreign, that Puerto Ricans were citizens, and even, perhaps, that Puerto Ricans were superior to Filipinos. Degetau and Coudert occupied similar ethnic and professional stations and sought the same outcomes in the cases, yet they aligned with opposing political parties. At a time when "Latin" countries were those that spoke Romance languages and when anti-Latin prejudice was widespread in the United States, both men boasted of their Latin heritage as they pursued recognition as top lawyers and political figures. Coudert and Degetau shared expertise in international and constitutional law, familiarity with elite transatlantic Latin circles, and bonds to their French ancestral homeland. Both believed that Latin peoples, such as French immigrants and Puerto Ricans, should be fully integrated into the United States. Degetau's Republican friends included policy makers who deprecated Puerto Ricans as racial subordinates. Coudert's primary academic mentor was the prominent Columbia law professor John W. Burgess, who promoted a "theory of the Teutonic government of the world."[10]

Coudert joined fellow Democrats and his mentor Burgess in opposing strict enforcement of the Reconstruction Amendments. Coudert conceded that the Fourteenth Amendment expanded the distribution of citizenship but claimed that citizenship offered few rights, a position also common among Democrats. Coudert advocated that those born in any sovereign U.S. territory receive jus soli citizenship, that is, citizenship by dint of what the Fourteenth Amendment termed birth "in ... the United States, and subject to the jurisdiction thereof." Anti-imperialist Democrats had made the same argument during congressional debates, but they had sought to prevent annexation by raising the specter of citizenship for Filipinos. Coudert's argument came dangerously close to awakening that Democratic bogeyman. Degetau had a richer vision of citizenship, which he associated with rights and white men. With Republicans dominating three branches of government, he expected enforcement of the Reconstruction Constitution in Puerto Rico.[11]

U.S. Attorney General John Griggs and Solicitor General John Richards rejected the restraints that the Reconstruction Constitution had long been thought to impose on empire. They urged the justices to hold that the government enjoyed wide discretion in how it governed Puerto Rico and Puerto Ricans. Able to build on the legal arguments of Secretary of War Elihu Root and his law officer Charles Magoon, Griggs and Richards fortified their position with analogies to disfavored U.S. people and places. Annexation had neither brought Puerto Ricans citizenship nor made Puerto Rico a part of the United States. Analogously, the Constitution accorded federal lawmakers great discretion in governing Mormons in Utah Territory, Confederate states occupied by Union troops, "appurtenant" guano islands, and U.S. consular courts in Japan. For federal power over citizenship, they cited *Dred Scott*, African slavery, residents of annexed territories whom Congress only belatedly naturalized, the "quasi-foreign" character of American Indians, and the probationary status of immigrants who had not been naturalized.[12]

Griggs lumped Puerto Ricans together with Filipinos as emphatically nonwhite. He spun an apocalyptic fable of sacrosanct citizenship polluted by unworthy and ignorant racial inferiors: "Suppose a cession of a small island with a half dozen inhabitants is desired as a fort." To require that the United States "accept them as citizens" would be "to put shackles on the national limbs." It was a remarkable metaphor: citizenship, traditionally associated with emancipation and individual liberation, was reinterpreted as a chain of national bondage. Citizenship mattered so much, Griggs declared, that political branches should forgo empire rather than permit the courts to intrude on the naturalization power. The worry was not Puerto Rican statehood. All sides agreed that a decision to admit a territory into the United States belonged with the political branches. Nor was the issue citizenship for Puerto Ricans, per se. The census categorized most Puerto Ricans as white. In the next six years the United States would absorb more immigrants from southern European polities such as Italy and the French and Spanish empires than there were residents of Puerto Rico. Congress also naturalized Hawaiians, whom the census described as majority "colored."[13] In Griggs's view the true threat was this: eight million racially degraded Filipinos.

Griggs cast Puerto Ricans as guinea pigs of empire. He urged the justices to proceed cautiously, lest this first experiment in expansion unleash hordes of undesirables. He proposed that Puerto Ricans be neither citizens nor aliens, but instead "noncitizen subject[s]." Here, Griggs articulated just the kind of second-class status that had outraged *criollo* Puerto Ricans under Spanish rule. His comment also bore striking similarities to the discriminatory measures inflicted on African Americans, American Indians, Chinese, and other racial minority groups. Yet Griggs saw no incompatibility between a liberty-loving democracy and a populace held in subjection: "To be called an American subject is no disgrace. The term does not imply anything as to the nature or form of the government of which one is a subject. It imports only that a person is within the protection and allegiance – either permanent or temporary – of a particular sovereignty."[14]

Both Coudert and Degetau rejected the analogy to African Americans and American Indians. The unique positions of those two groups, Coudert contended, actually strengthened Puerto Ricans' claim to citizenship. Noncitizen American Indians illustrated that the Fourteenth Amendment jus soli doctrine demanded allegiance at birth: most newborn American Indians owed primary allegiance to tribal communities and so were not citizens. But Puerto Ricans owed primary allegiance to the United States. Native Americans who were not born owing allegiance to an Indian nation were considered U.S. citizens. Why not treat Puerto Ricans the same way? When Democratic senator Donelson Caffery of Louisiana worried that such theories would sweep in Filipinos, Coudert's analysis provided a ready answer. No racial egalitarian, Coudert suggested that the Court treat "uncivilized" Filipinos as American Indians for constitutional purposes.[15]

As for African Americans, Coudert acknowledged that the *Dred Scott* decision had treated free African Americans as noncitizen subjects before the Civil War. But he urged the justices to reject the infamous precedent as aberrational, applicable only to those of African heritage, whom Taney's virulent racism had deemed "something different and apart from the rest of humanity," and only before slavery collapsed. Post-emancipation, Puerto Ricans did not and could not "occupy that *debased* position." Moreover, he stressed, Taney's "views have been repudiated by the American people in the Civil War, by three amendments to the Constitution of the United States, by this court, and by forty years of advancing civilization."[16]

Coudert argued simultaneously that the Court would risk infamy by denying Puerto Ricans citizenship, and that the status itself was unimportant. As a legal matter, it was a mere synonym for nationality, not a gateway to full constitutional rights or eventual statehood. In fact, "women, children and all persons in the Territories," as well as those who did not meet state literacy requirements for voting, were citizens while lacking political rights. By declining to distinguish Puerto Ricans from Filipinos, he suggested that citizenship would even be appropriate for the nontribal majority of that purportedly degraded people.[17]

Degetau differed with Coudert not only over the meaning of citizenship but also over how the Reconstruction Constitution's constraints on empire might be tested. Because no precedent had removed the constraints, Degetau expected the justices to enforce them, whatever the consequences. He believed that law and the Constitution should drive and shape politics. In contrast, Coudert and his adversaries expected the justices to chart their constitutional course pragmatically and instrumentally in order to minimize a decision's potentially destructive wake. Coudert reassured the Court that adherence to the Reconstruction Constitution would not cripple empire: "We have heretofore governed territories peopled by all kinds of races ... and given them the benefit of the Constitution, and we have had the best governed colonies ... in the world." Griggs and Richards sought the opposite result by similarly consequentialist means: they predicted a political nightmare if they lost.[18]

Although he was too late to add a test case of his own to the nine *Insular Cases* the Court had under consideration, Degetau did place himself, his people, and their status before the justices through a shrewd alternative. In early 1901 he applied for admission to practice before the U.S. Supreme Court, well aware that the Supreme Court bar was open only to U.S. citizens. When the Court admitted him, Degetau interpreted the victory broadly, claiming, "My admission ... fixed my personal Status and that of my constituents as American citizens." Articles in sympathetic island newspapers echoed the triumph: "The Great National Constitution Covers Puerto Rico," read the headline in one, which said Puerto Rico now had the same status as "other territories like Arizona." Mainland newspapers and lawyers also agreed with Degetau's spin. Charles Needham, the dean of Columbian Law School (today the George Washington University School of Law) announced, "Now I believe that the Constitution is in Puerto Rico."[19]

In May 1901 the Supreme Court issued its decisions in *De Lima v. Bidwell* and *Downes v. Bidwell*. The decisions were far less conclusive than Needham had predicted and Degetau had hoped. In a result that both Democrats and Republicans declared a victory, the justices ruled for the merchant in one case and the government in the other. *De Lima* invalidated application of the general U.S. tariff for imports "from foreign countries" to Puerto Rican goods shipped to the United States. Justice Henry Brown wrote for the Court that Puerto Rico "was not a foreign country within the meaning of the tariff laws." But then *Downes* upheld the Foraker Act tariff that expressly targeted mainland-island commerce. The four justices who had voted with Brown in *De Lima* dissented, and the *De Lima* dissenters found themselves in the *Downes* majority. Writing only for himself in *Downes*, Brown reasoned that Puerto Rico was "not a part of the United States within the revenue clauses of the Constitution" and thus was outside the constitutional mandate for uniform tariffs "throughout the United States."[20] According to Brown, the crucial factor in this decision was Congress, which had not treated Puerto Rico as a foreign country before 1900, even though it could have done so.

Degetau concluded that the decisions "produced a perplexity." They skirted the constitutional issues. Puerto Rico was within the nation for one statutory purpose but not for another constitutional one. In *Downes*, which contemporary observers considered the most important decision, no single opinion garnered five votes. Justice White's concurrence had the support of four justices, all of whom dissented in *De Lima*. Because four different justices dissented in *Downes*, eight of the nine members of the court disagreed with one of the results. Only Justice Brown voted with both majorities, which were both so slim that his vote was necessary to each.

It clarified matters little that the Court soon declared *Downes* and *De Lima* applicable to the Philippines.[21]

More confusing still, no majority opinion reconciled the results in the decisions with the *Dred Scott* rule that "all the provisions of the Constitution extended of their own force to the territories." That was surprising, because Democrats had vigorously claimed during the treaty-ratification debates that the *Dred Scott* decision stood in the way of Republicans' plans. One possible explanation for the omission was that the Foraker Act violated none of the Constitution's provisions; if so, the *Dred Scott* declaration that new territory is only "acquired to become a State" could well remain valid. That would be a significant challenge to Republicans' long-term plans. Another possible explanation was that *Dred Scott* had ceased to be binding precedent and thus merited little discussion one way or another. That would spell trouble for Republicans in a different way: *Dred Scott* was the best precedent for the proposition that Americans, even those never affiliated with tribes, could be denied citizenship.[22]

Justices in the *Downes* majority sought to reconcile Constitution and empire with pragmatic adaptation rather than adherence to precedent. The most notable opinion was Justice Edward Douglass White's concurrence, which had the support of every justice in the *Downes* majority besides Brown, and which proposed a new doctrine for Puerto Rico. He declared that, unlike prior territories, Puerto Rico had not been incorporated into the Union by statute or treaty. Thus, it would not necessarily become a state. Citizenship figured prominently in this analysis. White noted the frequency with which the federal political branches had expressly extended citizenship to the inhabitants of previously acquired territories. He stressed the silence of the Foraker Act on the question and concluded that the Constitution applied differently in Puerto Rico than in traditional territories. Yet neither his concurrence in *Downes* nor the substantive dissent in *De Lima*, which he joined, provided many details beyond the announcement that Puerto Rico was "foreign to the United States in a domestic sense" while also U.S. land under international law. He followed Attorney General Griggs, envisioning what might happen if "citizens of the United States discover an unknown island, peopled with an uncivilized race, yet rich in soil" and asking, "Can it be denied that [the power to acquire new territory] could not be practically exercised if the result would be to endow the inhabitants with citizenship of the United States...?" White concluded that the marriage of annexation to naturalization would leave the United States "helpless" in the age of empire.[23] To remain competitive as an emerging world power, the United States had to act like other empires and acquire, subject, and exclude.

The justices in the *Downes* majority also doubted the fitness of some races, especially Filipinos. Justice White's primary goal was to sanction empire and guard the mainland from purportedly savage Filipinos.

The justice later told Coudert that "he was much preoccupied by the danger of racial and social questions" concerning the Philippines and had been "quite desirous ... that Congress should have a very free hand." As the fifth vote for the judgments in both *Downes* and *De Lima*, Justice Brown shared White's concerns. He stressed "differences of race, habits, laws, and customs of the people," adding that a "false step at this time might be fatal to the development of what Chief Justice Marshall called the American empire."[24]

Yet neither opinion explicitly held that Puerto Ricans were *not* citizens. The four dissenting justices in *Downes* declared themselves prepared to hold that Puerto Ricans were citizens. So the decisions gave both sides of the debate over the island at least a thin reed of victory. Degetau maintained that the *Insular Cases* were consistent with his campaign to win citizenship and traditional territorial status. Stressing the justices' "practical unanimity that Porto Rico is 'a territory of the United States,'" he concluded that Puerto Rico was no more a "possession" or a "colony" than Arizona. Degetau's bravado notwithstanding, however, most observers understood that *Downes* had marked Puerto Rico as in some way subordinate and anomalous. Charles Magoon, the law officer for the Bureau of Insular Affairs within the War Department, saw the decisions as vindication of his aggressive administrative constitutionalism. He crowed that his views concerning the compatibility of Constitution and empire had won over the secretary of war, high-ranking officials in other departments, the political branches, the electorate, and even the Supreme Court.[25] And in fact Magoon had found support with administrators and elected officials and to some extent with the public and justices. But the Court had not adopted Magoon's views wholesale.

Presented with the opportunity to reject or validate the emerging colonial governance of noncitizen U.S. subjects and of U.S. lands that would never become states, the Court did neither. White compromised between constitutional fidelity and the exigencies of empire and imperial governance. He created the novel and ambiguous category of "unincorporated U.S. territory" – a chimera that was neither foreign nor domestic. Since a majority of the justices had yet to elevate this innovation into binding doctrine, the decisions left open many constitutional questions about empire.[26] Consequently, administrators, lawmakers, and even those outside the federal government found themselves called upon to provide answers and fill interpretive voids.

With the Supreme Court not yet prepared to settle the status of Puerto Ricans, Degetau sought to convince lawmakers and administrators to recognize him and his people as citizens. But he faced daunting obstacles. To his surprise, racial bias among mainlanders against Puerto Ricans was deep, widespread, and persistent. He told colleagues that it was "much more negative than the worst ideas we had heard or imagined." Degetau made the "great work of correcting this mistaken impression" a "foremost duty."[27] The lawmakers and bureaucrats he sought to convince were also likely to share the Court's worries about obstacles to empire. However, because Degetau's first faith was in law, not courts, the resident commissioner remained confident. He presumed that nonjudicial officials would adhere to the Reconstruction Constitution if pressed.

Degetau told his allies that mainlanders should judge and evaluate Puerto Ricans on the basis of leading islanders such as himself. Instead, they based their judgments on typical islanders and concluded that Puerto Ricans were a dependent, racially inferior people, much like Filipinos. Editorial cartoonists caricatured them as akin to African or American Indian "savages," recent immigrants from Europe, children, and women. Travel writers described their purportedly inferior "culture and state of civilization" (Fig. 3.2)[28]

To shift mainland opinion, Degetau took every opportunity to present himself and other leading Puerto Ricans as exemplars. Soon he was making near-daily visits to the Capitol, attending meetings with executive and judicial officials, securing the publication of his views in newspapers, and attending academic gatherings. He also responded forcefully to public affronts to Puerto Ricans' honor and to attacks on Puerto Ricans as a race.[29]

Degetau aimed to persuade his many mainland audiences that Puerto Rican elites were committed to liberty and experienced in self-government. Drawing on Spanish-era battles, Degetau developed a stylized history. First, he claimed, the Roman ancestors of Puerto Ricans had formulated principles that the founding fathers of the United States had used to draft the Constitution. Spain had joined the transatlantic struggle for liberty with its "noble and glorious" 1812 Constitution, in which Puerto Ricans had played a key role. Puerto Rico later sent representatives and senators to the Spanish Cortes under all but universal male suffrage. Puerto Ricans held the same status as Spaniards, and Puerto Rico constituted "a province of Spain equal to the other provinces" and endowed with more autonomy than U.S. states. In addition, in 1873 the efforts of island liberals ended slavery in Puerto Rico.[30]

Degetau extolled *criollo* Puerto Ricans' virtuous, virile pursuit of liberty, to blunt the charge that only Cuba had displayed the masculine wherewithal to rise up against oppression. He pointed out that Puerto Ricans, far from passive, had extracted substantial concessions from Spain without resort to arms. Their "ardent love of liberty" explained their enthusiasm for the U.S. invasion, he argued: U.S. forces would have faced stiff resistance had *criollos* not expected the United States to expand the liberal autonomy they had extracted from Spain in 1897.[31]

FIGURE 3.2A Detail from W. A. Rogers, "Uncle Sam's New Class in the Art of Self-Government," *Harper's Weekly*, 27 Aug. 1898, cover. From left to right, the figures represent a Cuban expatriate, a guerilla, Uncle Sam, Hawaii, and Porto Rico.

Degetau likened Puerto Ricans such as himself to Northern Republicans. Southerners, he noted, had fought a bloody war to preserve slavery. By contrast, Puerto Ricans, inspired by Lincoln's claim that "the Declaration of Independence ... gave liberty ... to the world for all future time," had won abolition peacefully. Similarly, the true tragedy of *Uncle Tom's Cabin*, he wrote, was the experience of "the whites [who] were more enslaved by our mounstrous [*sic*] crime than our legal victims."[32] This claim removed the voices and travails of those once held in bondage from Degetau's depiction of the island, and refocused attention on more acceptably white residents.[33]

Degetau also distanced Puerto Ricans from American Indians and indigenous Pacific Islanders. Mainlanders were wrong, he insisted, to equate Puerto Ricans with "some race of semi-savage 'Indians'" or the indigenous population of Guam, existing on "the boundaries of a savage condition."[34]

As he countered mainlanders' contemptuous slurs, Degetau also had to contend with islanders' demands for the progress toward status and rights he had promised them. To that end, Degetau forcefully availed himself of the latitude that the *Insular Cases* had created for extrajudicial institutions, focusing his efforts on Congress and executive-branch administrators. Even if

FIGURE 3.2B Detail from Victor Gillam, "The White Man's Burden (Apologies to Kipling)," *Judge*, 1899. Courtesy of Billy Ireland Cartoon Library and Museum. From left to right, the figures are identified as Filipino, Porto Rico, Cuba, Samoa (hidden), and Hawaii.

executive agencies did not provide Degetau with the answers he sought, the disputes he placed before them could potentially be transformed into federal-court test cases. He needed to act; otherwise, unwelcome and humiliating practices could harden into routine and, from there, conventional wisdom.

As Degetau's friend Ramón Lopez wryly observed, the United States could not be trusted to solve the problem alone: "That country is so big, and this one so small, that it is smart to always be pushing something, just so they'll remember us."[35]

Though Degetau befriended and cultivated key lawmakers, Congress was not receptive to his agenda. Legislators delayed because they saw Puerto Rico as a harbinger for the Philippines, as Degetau's modest campaign to have his own position reclassified from delegate to commissioner illustrates. That change would have permitted Degetau to speak but still not vote in the House of Representatives. Its real importance would have been the removal of a demeaning distinction in nomenclature between the elected representative from Puerto Rico and those from traditional U.S. territories. The chair of the House Committee on Insular Affairs, Henry Cooper, explained the obstacle to the proposal: many congressmen believed that "Puerto Rico can't be considered in itself" because the "Philippines also has to be taken into account." Degetau disagreed vehemently and dismissed "the Philippines and Hawaiians" as peoples with whom "we have almost nothing in common." Degetau reminded Cooper's committee that U.S. military authorities had promised Puerto Ricans (but not Filipinos) citizenship, and required Puerto Rican officeholders (but not Filipino ones) to take an oath to uphold the Constitution, give allegiance to the United States, and renounce fidelity to foreign nations.[36] Degetau only partially succeeded in securing gains for Puerto Rico by distinguishing it from the Philippines. The House Committee recommended the reclassification of Degetau's position and Foraker included it as part of a Senate bill on other Puerto Rican matters, but ultimately the provision was struck.[37]

Pivoting to the executive branch, Degetau pursued reforms that would benefit Puerto Ricans and erase distinctions between them and mainlanders. Access to federal civil service jobs fulfilled both criteria. The near-total exclusion of Puerto Ricans from the federal civil service was bad politics for Degetau and his fellow Republicanos. By giving hiring preferences to those born on the mainland over the island-born, the United States was essentially recreating the Spanish system of patronage that *criollo* liberals had long opposed. The lack of official opportunities mattered all the more because politics in Puerto Rican (as in the United States) still depended heavily on patronage and a kind of spoils system. Republicanos were quick to criticize the mainlanders who held "their" jobs. One group wrote Degetau to object to what it saw as governmental largesse flowing to second-rate hacks, the "clique of continental adventurers [in] official posts who are a discredit to the American government." Such complaints were long-standing and common among territorial residents (as among critics of Reconstruction). Degetau brought the matter to the president and secured a separate discussion with a civil service commissioner. Afterward he was pleased to report that, through his efforts, Puerto Ricans would receive a proportional share of jobs in the federal classified service. Several months later, the Civil Service Commission confirmed the island's quota in a statement to Congress.[38]

However, Degetau found his best wedge for Puerto Rican citizenship in the dispute over his own passport. Federal law prescribed that "no passport shall be granted ... for any other persons than citizens of the United States." Yet Degetau applied for and received a passport that omitted identifying its bearer as "a citizen of the United States." He protested to the State Department. His challenge soon attracted the attention of the Coudert firm, which had argued *De Lima v. Bidwell* and *Downes v. Bidwell*. The State Department let the complaint fester – yet another sign of the U.S. government's unwillingness to confront the full implications of empire. Coudert's firm proposed "to make a test case of it," but federal courts would compel federal executive officials to perform only public duties that they "are bound to perform without further question," Degetau's lawyer explained. Where their inaction rested on "an interpretation of the law," as in Degetau's case, the courts would not intervene.[39] Consequently, the challenge stalled.

Next, Degetau turned to his Washington network. Theodore Roosevelt had written Degetau that Puerto Ricans were "my fellow Americans," shortly before ascending to the presidency in 1901 after the assassination of William McKinley. In November Degetau secured a meeting with President Roosevelt to discuss citizenship for Puerto Ricans. He also scheduled meetings on the topic with Secretary of State John Hay and Justice Henry Brown. Degetau told Brown that "Puerto Ricans are and desire to be American, [and] although they believe that they have not been done justice, they still have faith." Roosevelt asked Degetau to elaborate his views in a letter.[40]

In his letter, Degetau solicited recognition of Puerto Ricans as citizens with careful arguments that did not apply to Filipinos. Recent legislation specific to Puerto Rico treated "*all inhabitants*" of the island as a single group. If some of the inhabitants were citizens, all were, he reasoned. To show that some were, he noted that the Treaty of Paris recognized some Puerto Ricans "as having accepted the nationality of the territory in which they resided." The *Insular Cases* held that Puerto Rico was "a territory of the United States." This closed the case, according to Degetau, on the unstated presumption that such nationals were necessarily citizens. Degetau raised a separate argument based on legislation that had grouped mainlanders and Puerto Ricans who resided on the island as "the people of Porto Rico." He asserted that such a "political body" could not comprise both U.S. citizens and citizens "of distinct nationality." Finally, Degetau reminded Roosevelt that Puerto Ricans had cooperated with U.S. rule during Spanish sovereignty after General Guy Henry promised them "protection as citizens of the American Union." The "only constitutional and just interpretation" was that Puerto Ricans had "American citizenship," he concluded.[41]

Rather than respond to Degetau's letter, U.S. officials evaded it. The secretary of state extended Puerto Ricans abroad "the same protection of person and property as is accorded to the native-born citizens of the United States." Then he and Roosevelt won legislation to authorize passports for U.S. insular residents, regardless of their citizenship.[42] They effectively undermined Degetau's call for citizenship by extending Puerto Ricans the rights of citizenship without the label – at least in the context of international travel (Fig. 3.3).

From Degetau's perspective, the concession was woefully inadequate, both politically and personally. In 1901 Degetau had used his passport to reunite with Ana Moreno Valerno, whom newspapers termed "his beautiful first love in old Madrid." She was the daughter of a count, sister-in-law of a Spanish Supreme Court magistrate, and niece of a former Spanish cabinet member. In early 1902 the pair established a household in Washington. Under U.S. and Spanish laws of marriage and citizenship, the union obliterated Moreno's lifelong identity as a Spaniard by cloaking her with Degetau's status. Degetau sought to test that status in U.S. eyes abroad. He asked a married Puerto Rican couple in France how they were classified by Albion Tourgée, the U.S. consul there. The islanders could not have hoped for an official more devoted to the Reconstruction Constitution. Tourgée had fought in the Union Army, pressed the egalitarian ideals of Reconstruction as a politician and judge, organized tens of thousands of U.S. citizens behind African Americans' rights, and brilliantly but unsuccessfully litigated *Plessy v. Ferguson* (1896). But sympathy was not enough. Tourgée was the representative of an administration bent on dismantling remnants of the Reconstruction Constitution. He followed policy and recorded the Puerto Rican couple as "allegiants of the United States" under its "protection."[43] Despite enjoying ostensibly equal protections abroad, Degetau discovered that his marriage as a Puerto Rican had transformed his wife from an aristocratic Spaniard into something less than a U.S. citizen.

Shifting course once again in his indefatigable campaign for citizenship, Degetau tried to elicit a favorable official pronouncement by bringing a claim similar to those in the *Insular Cases* of 1901: he challenged an import duty. He shipped from France paintings by a Puerto Rican artist and asked for the exemption from customs duties for "works of art, the production of *American artists*." The attorney general conceded that Puerto Rican artists were American artists. For Degetau, who equated nationality with citizenship, this was a victory. But, as with *De Lima*, the victory was not that clear-cut. As the attorney general cautioned, the status of American Indian artists illustrated that "it is clearly not inconceivable for a man to be an American artist ... and yet not a citizen of the United States."[44]

In another set of disputes, Degetau managed to neutralize bad decisions without securing good ones. In 1900, Hawaiian sugar planters faced

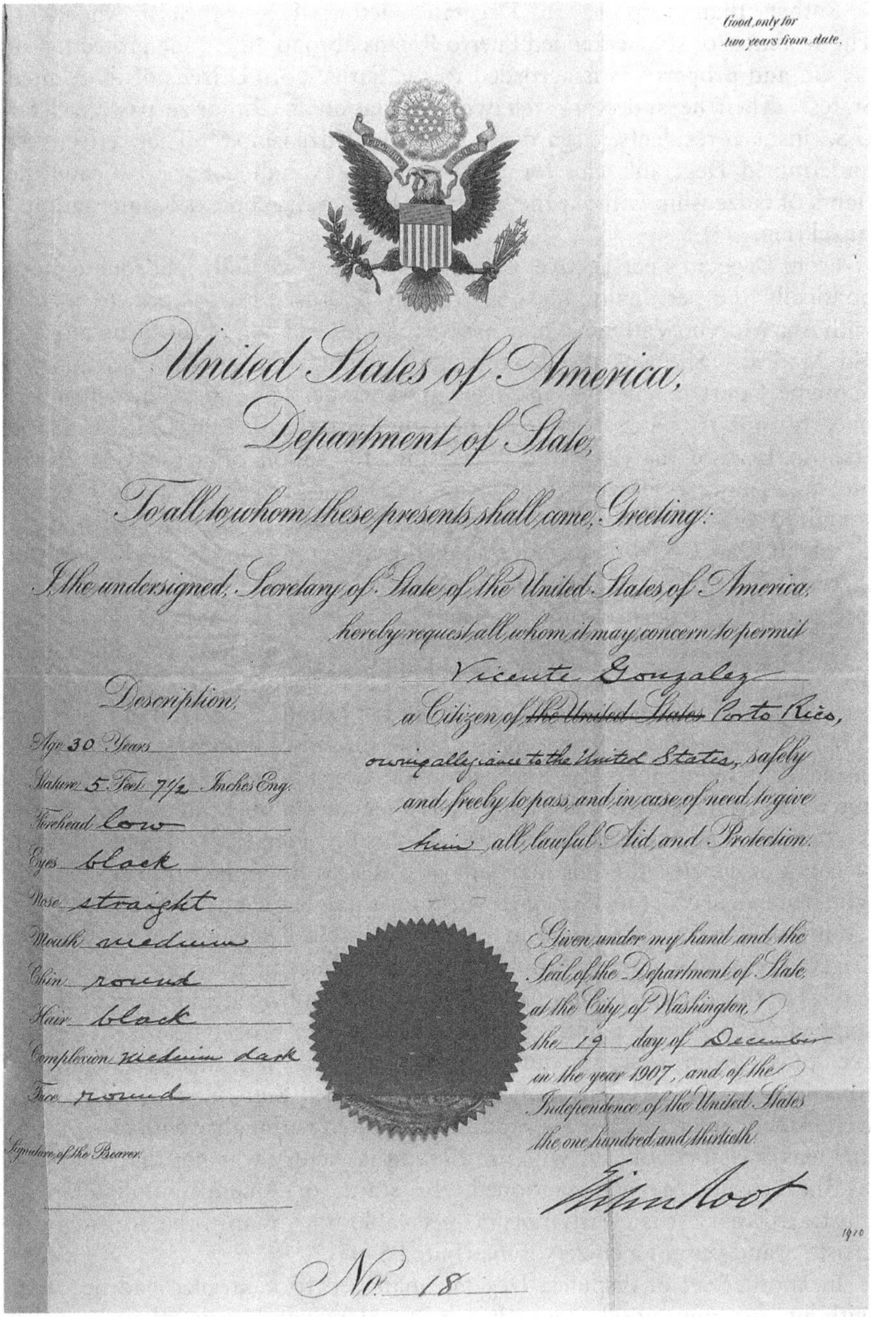

Good only for two years from date.

United States of America,

Department of State,

To all to whom these presents shall come, Greeting:

I the undersigned, Secretary of State of the United States of America, hereby request all whom it may concern to permit

Vicente Gonzalez

a Citizen of ~~the United States~~ Porto Rico,

owing allegiance to the United States, safely and freely to pass, and in case of need to give him all lawful Aid and Protection.

Description.

Age 30 Years

Stature 5 Feet 7 1/2 Inches Eng.

Forehead low

Eyes black

Nose straight

Mouth medium

Chin round

Hair black

Complexion medium dark

Face round

Signature of the Bearer.

Given under my hand and the Seal of the Department of State, at the City of Washington, the 19 day of December in the year 1907, and of the Independence of the United States the one hundred and thirtieth.

Elihu Root

1910

No. 18

FIGURE 3.3 Passport of Vicente Gonzalez, 19 Dec. 1907. Courtesy of Ancestry.com. The printed form identifying the bearer as a "citizen of the United States" was altered by hand to indicate that Gonzalez was a "citizen of Porto Rico, owing allegiance to the United States."

a tightening labor supply because of the Chinese Exclusion Act, a federal ban on immigration of persons under labor contracts, the migration of existing workers to the mainland, a score of small strikes, and a temporary Japanese bar on emigration. Planters responded by recruiting more than 5,000 impoverished Puerto Rican laborers. When the administration imposed no immigration delays on these migrants as they passed through New Orleans, Degetau pointed to the situation of "Mr. Alfonso Gómez y Stanley, a professor who . . . was [temporarily] detained at Ellis Island, N.Y., when it was known that he was a Porto Rican, and that he had no money." Degetau suggested that his new acquaintance Assistant Secretary of State David Hill could clarify when "Porto Ricans are to be considered as aliens, according to the immigration law, and when they are to be allowed to land as citizens of the United States." Hill's response was encouraging: "The error of holding [Gómez], even temporarily, evidently arose from the lack of knowledge of some officer as to the status of Porto Ricans." Degetau sought further clarification "concerning the Administration's opinion of the status of Porto Ricans," but with no pending claim hinging on the answer, the State Department remained frustratingly silent.[45] Though Degetau did not win citizenship for Puerto Ricans, he secured the admission that Gomez should not have been detained. Officials would thenceforth be hard pressed to cite Gomez's initial exclusion as authority. If officials had gotten away with such discriminatory treatment of islanders, then mainlanders could easily conclude that Puerto Ricans deserved no better.

Degetau's battle against discrimination was particularly effective in cases involving elites such as Gomez. Degetau aimed to represent Puerto Rico in the fullest sense of the word. He wanted to fulfill his constituents' aspirations and win his people citizenship by appearing before U.S. officials as an advocate or an aggrieved party, and he also wanted to exemplify Puerto Rican civilization.[46] Degetau's electoral, racial, and legal aims aligned most neatly in disputes over his own rights. In those cases, he could present himself to mainlanders and constituents as a competent and accomplished representative of Puerto Rico. This approach, however, placed Degetau's performance of patrician gentility above the experience of his constituents. Insofar as it alienated him from their experiences, it impeded his advocacy on their behalf. In this respect, the pursuit of one meaning of representation – exemplifying the "best" of Puerto Ricans – undercut its other meaning – advocating for Puerto Ricans. It also encouraged him to accept and even promote depictions of many islanders as akin to racially stigmatized U.S. communities.

Puerto Ricans who migrated to Hawai'i, for example, found themselves on the wrong side of Degetau's biases and representations. Those en route to Hawaiian sugar plantations, where field-workers eked out a harsh existence, were being arrested, held captive by officials at gunpoint, driven to mutiny by lack of food, and persistently barred by police from protesting their treatment. The anti-Chinese *San Francisco Examiner* reported that the Puerto Ricans passing through the area had "a sort of Chinese twang" and were "dark and look like negroes." In Hawai'i, planters whipped their workers, pitted ethnic groups against each other, and conspired to depress wages. More than a thousand Puerto Ricans left the plantations to seek better jobs. Police arrested them by the hundreds, primarily on charges of theft, prostitution, and vagrancy. One Puerto Rican newspaper reported that "our poor countrymen hid in the woods where they were persecuted by gunfire and set after with a pack of hunting dogs."[47]

Degetau demanded an investigation, though only of reported treatment that violated what he understood to be the migrants' rights as citizens. Like other affluent Puerto Ricans, Degetau considered labor relations to be private matters either beyond state purview or to be disposed of in local civil courts. Courts were increasingly making arrests, prosecutions, convictions, and governmental action the sine qua non of Reconstruction Constitution violations, and these became Degetau's preoccupations as well.[48]

When Hawaiian officials and planters denied that Puerto Rican migrants had been mistreated, Degetau was not inclined to press further. He did not want the workers to become the standard-bearers for his people's racial character. Instead he identified with the white territorial officials he envisioned as his peers. Hawaiian officials reinforced Degetau's credulity by flattering him and claiming his cause as their own. According to Degetau, one proposed a Supreme Court test case "to have the emigrants' citizenship rights recognized so that they could vote in Hawaii"; then came the flourish: "he hoped that I would argue the case . . ., understanding that this would guarantee success." Degetau naively concluded that "it doesn't seem likely that[,] were the complaints true, the planters would manifest such interest in investing Puerto Ricans with constitutional guarantees and in providing them the vote." No test case, broad rights, or franchise materialized in the wake of the investigation.[49]

Puerto Rican men in Hawai'i were disappointed. They charged that Degetau had fallen short as their representative. Signatories on one letter declared that Puerto Rico "feels sorry for its sons and daughters just as a . . . mother would for the son she adores," in effect asking Degetau to support the dependents whom the signatories could not. The authors appealed to Degetau's identification with Puerto Rico's emancipationist history by charging planters with racism and recreating "the times of the slaves and masters." The letter maintained that the leadership of Puerto Rico, lodged in the hands of its best men, had failed its constituents.[50]

Compounding Degetau's tepid advocacy, his strategy of presenting himself as an exemplar of Puerto Rican civilization did not succeed. It did not prevent mainlanders from judging Puerto Rico on its many mixed-race and desperately poor residents. To the contrary, Degetau's race-conscious strategy repeatedly backfired, as illustrated most starkly in his support for enrolling Puerto Rican children in the Carlisle Indian Industrial School in Pennsylvania and the Tuskegee Institute in Alabama. Richard Pratt founded the Carlisle School as an English-language vocational school for American Indians, describing his approach as "acculturation under duress." Of each of his young charges, he declared that he aimed "to kill the Indian in him, and save the man," thereby integrating Indian students into mainstream white U.S. culture. The Tuskegee Institute, established by Lewis Adams and Booker T. Washington, was originally intended to train African American schoolteachers.[51]

Degetau praised both schools and saw them as valuable and applicable to Puerto Ricans in need of uplift. He toured Carlisle as a representative of Puerto Rico, joined U.S. senators as an invited guest at the school's commencement, and worked to secure federal legislation to promote enrollment of Puerto Ricans there. At Tuskegee, he met with island students enrolled there, then exchanged letters and gifts with the famed Washington, the school's principal.[52]

Newspapers, colonial officials, Washington, and Pratt all underscored the appropriateness of the African American and American Indian schools for Puerto Ricans. Drawing on decades of experience in post-emancipation education that included time at the Freedmen's Bureau and involvement with the Carlisle School, Puerto Rico's first superintendents of public schools, John Eaton and Martin Brumbaugh, endorsed the enrollment of Puerto Ricans in Tuskegee and Carlisle. Booker T. Washington saw an opportunity to promote his school and also to elevate African Americans above new island peoples in the social hierarchy. As he told the press, "one-half of the population" in newly occupied Antillean lands were "mulattoes or Negroes," who would succeed in fulfilling obligations of U.S. citizenship only with "thorough intellectual, religious, and industrial training" of the kind Tuskegee was ideally positioned to provide. He later described one Puerto Rican student who was "quite savage" when he arrived, saying, "One of our boys," a "young American," gave him "a good thrashing" and he afterward "changed his methods." In a sense, the Puerto Rican student was beaten into citizenship. For Pratt, Puerto Ricans were a potential source of funds for Carlisle, if only he could convince federal officials to treat them as Americans Indians and provide them with scholarships. He asked a doubtless horrified Degetau to urge on the "Indian committee" the idea that "there is some Indian blood among your Porto Ricans and [that] on that ground there is a claim for them." Puerto Rican students and parents were quick to grasp the racist implications of the situation for them and their island. As one alumna of Carlisle complained, it was "an unforgivable injustice … choosing the only college they had for educating and civilizing the savage Redskin Indians for also educating and 'civilizing' the wretched Puerto Ricans."[53]

By mid-1902 it was clear that Degetau's tactics had produced mixed results. Some of his strategies had brought islanders valuable rights, but U.S. officials had not given Degetau what he most sought: equality with white citizens on the mainland. They resolutely declined to clarify Puerto Ricans' citizenship and territorial status. Administrators had not stepped into the breach as Degetau had hoped.

To add insult to injury, Degetau's efforts to sway public and official opinion did little to alter popular stereotypes that Puerto Ricans were backward and of mixed race. Despite the predominance of Catholicism in both the Philippines and Puerto Rico, the anti-imperialist Roman Catholic bishop John Spalding of Peoria announced in 1902 that in "the tropics the race is and, probably always will be, indolent, ignorant, weak and sensual." Degetau responded with largely futile indignation. William S. Bryan's popular book *Our Islands and Their People* was published in 1899 and then reissued in 1905 in an oversize edition. The collection of photographs and essays emphasized Puerto Rico's poverty and its residents' African ancestry, making the island's people into a commodified spectacle of the exotic. One photo from the collection features a naked, dark-skinned boy on a public road (Fig. 3.4).

FIGURE 3.4 Detail from "Road and Blockhouse between Aibonito and Coamo," in William S. Bryan, ed., *Our Islands and Their People* (New York, 1899), 408. The original caption read, in part, "The little boy in front is in full Porto Rican costume for young gentlemen."

The caption in the book describes the child as "in full Porto Rican costume for young gentlemen of his age."[54] Poor and naked dark-skinned children did not represent what Degetau viewed as the essence of Puerto Rico: *he* did. Accordingly, Degetau felt that the plight of the worst-off islanders should receive relatively little attention.

The labor leader Santiago Iglesias disagreed. He embraced Puerto Rico's poor population – albeit awkwardly at times, when its many brown members were concerned.

By late 1900, Santiago Iglesias was once again organizing Puerto Rican workers. The island labor leader sought citizenship for Puerto Ricans but distrusted Degetau, his allies, and the racially inflected paternalism that underlay their citizenship claims. Iglesias had had extensive experience advocating for workers in ways that got him into trouble with government officials. Citizenship could protect him from in such cases. Iglesias sought citizenship to impede oppression at the hands of elected Puerto Ricans, not to hasten home rule for political elites. He saw U.S. law and citizenship less as a panacea than as tools in a difficult and essentially political and economic struggle for liberation from local oppression. Thus, when it was rhetorically useful to do so, he was willing to argue what he knew not to be true, that the Supreme Court's *Insular Cases* decision had declared the Constitution fully in force in Puerto Rico. Where Degetau had aligned with Republicans, Iglesias sought the support of a very different but increasingly powerful mainland organization.

In late 1900, Iglesias's ally of choice was the American Federation of Labor. Formed in the 1880s as an umbrella organization for craft unions, the AFL was the preeminent labor organization in the United States. It was in the midst of unprecedented growth, fueled by high rates of immigration into the United States and continued growth in U.S. manufacturing output. In just the past year, the AFL reported adding more than 300,000 members. The AFL was also working to bring independent unions into its fold. Soon it would represent more than 80 percent of all unionized U.S. workers. Compared with labor movements in other affluent countries, the AFL was conservative. It sought gains within the existing wage-labor system, rather than its overthrow, and was committed to a "pure and simple" strategy of seeking economic gains without entangling itself in political or electoral struggles. It was also racist, vilifying U.S. residents of Asian descent and tolerating member unions' discrimination against African American workers.[55]

Still, Iglesias had few alternatives. Given the forces arrayed against labor activists in the United States, ranging from injunctions to state and federal troops sympathetic to management, few national organizations remained that both aspired to represent all industries and were in a position to offer Iglesias substantial protection. On 6 December 1900, Iglesias wrote to the AFL, claiming that there were "15,000 skilled workmen" in Puerto Rico, and not mentioning that many were men of color and unorganized workers.[56]

Iglesias's timing was propitious. In 1898 and 1899 AFL president Samuel Gompers had opposed imperialism as a threat to mainland labor, asking: "If the Philippines are annexed, what is to prevent ... hordes of Chinese and the semi-savage races" of "the negritos and Malays from coming to our country" and "engulfing our people and our civilization?" "Forcible annexation" of Puerto Rico would put "our political rights ... in jeopardy," Gompers claimed. But when annexation occurred anyway, he made the best of it. Gompers had demonstrated a similar pragmatism with immigrants from southeastern Europe: if their arrival could not be prevented, it was best to unionize them. It surely helped that Iglesias was a *peninsular* and that the census deemed Puerto Rico to be majority white. Gompers also knew firsthand how "skilled" immigrants from Puerto Rico and Cuba had formed durable enclaves among New York's tobacco workers during the last decades of the nineteenth century. Gompers's organizing efforts at their workbenches during those years had been his springboard into union leadership, and this must certainly have lifted Iglesias's hopes for a fruitful collaboration.[57]

Gompers moved quickly to integrate Iglesias into the American Federation of Labor. When they met in 1901, Gompers conveyed the AFL's commitment to collective bargaining and boycotts and its opposition to legislative intrusions, such as minimum-wage laws. Rather than seeking to overthrow capitalism, Gompers sought to portray organized labor as its mirror, a group of individual workers voluntarily associating to participate effectively in the marketplace.[58] His vision was far less radical than the anarchism, socialism, and communism with which Iglesias had previously shown sympathy. But its realization would be a huge advance in Puerto Rico, where collective bargaining was repressed by officials. And given the local political elites' antipathy toward him, Iglesias lost little by abandoning legislative strategies in favor of the union.

The AFL appointed Iglesias as its sole paid organizer in Puerto Rico and made his Federación de Trabajadores Libre an AFL affiliate. The AFL's support now brought Iglesias into the highest circles of Puerto Rican and U.S. government. At an AFL-arranged meeting with President McKinley, Iglesias presented a Federación Libre petition with 6,000 signatures, describing Puerto Ricans as being on the brink of starvation. McKinley promised to investigate. Following McKinley's assassination, Gompers introduced Iglesias to Theodore Roosevelt. When Gompers wrote the newly appointed governor of Puerto Rico, William Hunt, to ask that Iglesias be protected from harassment, President Roosevelt tasked Hunt with ensuring that Iglesias was not molested.[59]

As Iglesias's fortunes revived, so too did his feud with Degetau's Partido Republicano and its labor ally, the Federación Regional de los Trabajadores de Puerto Rico. Those organizations called Iglesias a foreigner and a leader without a movement. They were divided on whether his primary sin was anticapitalism or racism. Degetau typified a more elite, Republicano line of attack on Iglesias when he told Senator Foraker that Iglesias was a socialist Spaniard without labor bona fides. By contrast, when Federación Regional members charged that Iglesias was a Spaniard with no true *patria*, they added that the AFL would never "unite with the Puerto Ricans, many of whom they despise because they are black." To counter the latter charge, Iglesias echoed the

AFL's claim that African Americans were scabs who undermined unions, but said that, unlike on the mainland, "where most colored workers are the unwitting enemies of their unionized American coworkers," most Puerto Rican "colored workers" "are responding to the call to organize." Here, Iglesias echoed Degetau in seeking privileges and forms of belonging open to mainland whites by downplaying islanders' "blackness," the physical and cultural presence of former slaves and their descendants. Critics pounced. They charged that Iglesias's "position smacked of racism," especially because the AFL contained "unions that do not admit black workers."[60] As Iglesias boarded a steamship bound for Puerto Rico in November 1901, he faced stiff opposition.

When Iglesias arrived in San Juan a week later, officials there inadvertently boosted his popularity by arresting him on a charge of conspiracy to raise the price of labor during the August 1900 strikes. Unable to raise bail, Iglesias sent a protest to Governor Hunt and cables to the Associated Press and Gompers. Gompers immediately met with Roosevelt, whom Gompers reported to be "astonished" and full of "regret." Roosevelt ordered an investigation, and sympathetic accounts appeared in the mainland press. Predicting that prosecution could help the cause, Gompers bailed out Iglesias and counseled him to stand trial and "plead justification."[61]

Iglesias's defense at trial was that "Puerto Rico was covered by the American Constitution" and that "the Constitution follows the flag." In the streets, he demanded protection from extralegal violence. He accused the Federación Regional of shooting at Federación Libre offices, and the police of harassing Federación Libre members rather than arresting the gunmen. He had survived two murder attempts and eight armed attacks while the police did nothing. This unchecked violence became a test of U.S. commitment to upholding the Constitution. Puerto Rican workers must be allowed "freedom of association, press, and speech." Iglesias told a crowd of 1,500 labor demonstrators that island workers deserved full citizenship, accompanied by constitutional rights.[62]

Iglesias's standing got a second boost when Republicano judges convicted him and sentenced him to more than three years in prison. Republicano leader José Celso Barbosa privately told Degetau that, while "it is often said that all individual rights of the U.S. Constitution apply in Puerto Rico, ... practically that does not happen," as "just occurred with Iglesias." Here, Barbosa overestimated the constitutional protections on which mainland laborers could depend. Conspiracy convictions had fallen into disfavor there as an antilabor tactic only because more sweeping antilabor injunctions had replaced them. Whatever the case, Iglesias and Gompers condemned the conviction as a throwback to Spanish-era tyranny. The *New York Times* reported that Gompers was "prepared to carry the case to the United States Supreme Court on constitutional grounds." Iglesias predicted that "Governor

Hunt is American and will recommend the annulment of the laws because they conflict with methods eminently American."[63]

The cause garnered favorable press coverage. The *New York Evening Post* declared: "If we have annexed a lot of barbarous medieval statutes," they "must be stamped out like yellow fever or any other tropical plague." Iglesias worked with his one-time nemesis, Partido Federal head Luis Muñoz Rivera. The men shared a common enemy in the Republicanos, and Iglesias had contributed articles to the stateside paper that Muñoz Rivera had founded. Now Federales' papers in Puerto Rico and the mainland savaged Republicano judges and anti–Federación Libre violence, and advocated freedom of expression.[64]

Soon President Roosevelt and U.S. officials in Puerto Rico were convinced to revisit Iglesias's case. On 2 January 1902, Governor Hunt declared that "the right to organize to secure better wages by peaceable measures is perfectly lawful" and that contrary laws were "unworthy of an American government." At Roosevelt's urging, the U.S. attorney general told his island counterpart that Iglesias's conviction was at odds with the Constitution. In a letter to the appellate prosecutor, the Puerto Rico attorney general cited the "right to assemble" to condemn Iglesias's conviction as an "abridgement of personal liberty." The prosecutor conceded at oral argument that Iglesias's appeal was well taken. Six days later, the Puerto Rican Supreme Court reversed the conviction.[65] Iglesias was free, and triumphant.

The Federación Regional blunted Iglesias's gains with violence and charges that he was a racist Spaniard – but it was a hard case for them to make. The Federación Regional itself sometimes unleashed violence on people of color, and its Republicano partners pursued racial elitism. By contrast, Iglesias fought for workers. Degetau never fully took up the plight of Puerto Ricans in Hawai'i, while Iglesias and his colleagues credited the migrants' complaints. One Federación Libre leader even compared the labor migrants to the chattel slaves that Spain had once imported from Africa. In late 1902 Iglesias joined other Puerto Rican delegates in cosponsoring a resolution at the annual AFL convention that called for federal repatriation of Puerto Rican migrants in Hawai'i and prosecution of their abusers. Federación Regional depictions of Iglesias as a racist seemed even less convincing when he married an island woman of color, Justa Bocanegra. Nonetheless, *turbas* (mobs) associated with the Federación and Partido Republicano attacked Iglesias's wife in the streets of San Juan several weeks later. The police declined to arrest the perpetrators.[66]

The events of 1901 and 1902 strengthened Iglesias and his organization, while weakening Republicanos and the Federación Regional. During Iglesias's trial and appeal, Republicanos and Federación Regional members found themselves opposing a champion of workers' liberties. In the process, Iglesias accrued prestige and became a top labor leader. His legal victory inspired workers to assert themselves. Around three thousand Federación Libre members and sympathizers celebrated with a parade and mass meeting. By raising the issue of freedom of expression, the court's decision made inroads on a key right for labor activists. Although the AFL had resolutely opposed the U.S. imperial turn, the Federación Libre asked it to demand citizenship for Puerto Ricans. At its 1902 convention the AFL added a qualifier that disclaimed any support for imperial expansion but agreed to the demand.[67] Now Iglesias, the AFL, and Degetau were all working for the same goal.

As citizenship continued to elude Republicanos, it became clear that Degetau had been overly optimistic about prospects for full and immediate inclusion in the United States.[68] The *New York Times* captured his quandary in an editorial cartoon in 1903 that portrayed Uncle Sam as the overwhelmed white guardian of Cuba, Puerto Rico, and the Philippines (Fig. 3.5). In the cartoon, the three island infants of color are identical in dress, skin tone, and physique. Puerto Rico, the most docile of the three, occupies the perch closest to Uncle Sam's heart. Their elder brother, "American negro," sits on the floor, seeking the uncle's care. Similarities among the children suggest that the islanders resemble and also lag behind African Americans. And Uncle Sam's harried slouch does not bode well for any of them. The prospects for the kind of belonging that Degetau and his colleagues sought were bleak.

Iglesias's strategy fared better. Where Degetau kept faith with law, Iglesias treated law as a potential weapon in a fight that was, essentially, political and economic. He sought leverage over federal officials, not common cause with them. When he made his compromise with racism, it was to cement his bond with the AFL, not the Republican Party. A contemporaneous cartoon depicting the relationship between the American Federation of Labor and the same communities would have featured a hopeful and enthused Sam Gompers, not a beleaguered Uncle Sam. The Philippines would have joined African Americans on the floor – both largely excluded from the AFL. Cuba and Puerto Rico would have been lighter skinned, reflecting Gompers's sympathetic interest in both. But Puerto Rico alone would be drawn close to Gompers's heart, for Gompers had decided in late 1902 to visit the island.[69]

Republicanos were divided over whether law or politics was the more promising strategy. The party committed itself to membership in the U.S. Republican Party. Degetau publicly disagreed, contending that noncitizens could not honorably accept membership in mainland political parties. Instead, he planned to pursue what even sympathizers considered a quixotic strategy of engagement with federal entities over legal status. As he wrote, his "word of honor" compelled him to seek "the honor" of the Republicano nomination and "the honor of being reelected to continue the work I have undertaken in favor of [both] our American citizenship [and] the admission of Puerto Rico into the Union as an organized Territory[,] to become in the not-distant future a state." Republicanos complied, nominating him for another term as resident commissioner in 1902. But when the polls closed, the Federales had won a large minority of seats in

FIGURE 3.5 "Uncle Sam's Burden," *New York Times*, 5 July 1903, A9. The cartoon's original caption was "American Negro: 'Lift me up, too; I was here first!'" The figure on the floor is labeled "negro." From left to right, Uncle Sam holds the Philippines, Porto Rico, and Cuba.

Puerto Rico's House of Delegates. Degetau had survived, but by a much reduced margin of victory.[70]

Degetau's position now resembled Domingo Collazo's, another Ponceño who had relocated stateside. After years promoting an Antillean revolution against Spain, Collazo had joined the U.S. invasion of Puerto Rico in 1898. Collazo had put his faith in both the Republican administration, whose party also controlled Congress, and the United States, with its storied commitment to democracy, citizenship, and rights, and Degetau did the same. Republicans had disappointed both men. Neither executive-branch officials nor lawmakers had hewed to the Reconstruction Constitution and recognized Puerto Ricans as citizens with full constitutional rights, much less as residents of a future state.

Late 1902 found Puerto Rico still lacking self-government. Collazo was back in New York rather than in an official post on the island. Degetau was entering his second term, having failed to fulfill his campaign promises and to preserve his electoral standing on the island. Clearly, the men needed to adjust their approach.

4

"American Aliens": Isabel Gonzalez, Domingo Collazo, Federico Degetau, and the Supreme Court, 1902–1905

Little about Isabel Gonzalez suggested that she would present the Supreme Court with momentous decisions about empire, race, and citizenship. Not yet twenty-one years old in 1902 and facing financial hardship, she migrated from San Juan to New York, where she was to meet her uncle Domingo Collazo.

Because Puerto Ricans' right to enter the U.S. mainland was still uncertain, immigration inspectors challenged Gonzalez's fitness as an immigrant. They concluded that she was an undesirable alien, implied that Collazo was an inadequate head of household, and denied Gonzales entry. She and Collazo appealed that decision in federal court. They keenly felt the dishonor of being judged undesirable, but asserted in their court case only that Puerto Ricans were citizens, not aliens. That activism and restraint launched what the *New York Times* termed a "test case" on "the status of the citizens of Porto Rico."[1]

It was just the kind of case that Federico Degetau had been searching for. He made it the centerpiece of his second term as commissioner. Despite his inconclusive earlier attempts to clarify Puerto Ricans' status, Degetau still maintained that they were U.S. citizens. Once recognized as such, he insisted, they would have confirmation both that they held broad rights and that their island was on the road to statehood. Gonzalez was represented by Frederic Coudert, the lead attorney from the 1901 *Insular Cases*. In taking her case, Coudert hoped to convince the Court to integrate those narrow, vague, and fractured decisions into a more robust approach to the status of Puerto Rico and Puerto Ricans, albeit one that offered Puerto Ricans few new rights. At the root of this effort was the hope that law, rather than politics, would prevail and determine a more inclusive structure of empire.

The year 1902 started badly for Isabel Gonzalez. Her husband died of tuberculosis several months after she became pregnant for the second time. With an infant already in arms and her brother struggling to support their mother through factory work in New York City, she had few viable options in San Juan. One was to expand her household income through remarriage.

As she and her family would later craft the story, she pursued this path with a *criollo* named Adolfo Viñals, who had just ended two years of service with the U.S. Army's volunteer Puerto Rican regiment. But before they married, he too migrated stateside to work in a New York City factory.

Gonzalez now faced problems many of her countrywomen shared: poverty, family resources stretched thin by lack of local opportunity, personal honor teetering on a partner's good intentions, sex discrimination, and uncertain citizenship status. The ingredients essential for the test case Degetau and Coudert sought were already in place.[2] Gonzalez faced the constant possibility of setbacks and rebuffs, but she belonged to a family with a sophisticated and well-connected patriarch. And she was also a proud woman, and steadfast when provoked.

Gonzalez left San Juan for New York in mid-1902. She hoped to secure educational opportunities there for her younger sister, and she may also have expected to marry Viñals. Factory work would be a potential way to support herself in the meantime. Steaming away from San Juan, Gonzalez had reason to hope that she would be among the many Puerto Ricans whom Degetau would say had "frequently disembarked unmolested in New York." Her aunt had made a similar journey the year before, migrating to New York and then marrying Domingo Collazo. But on reaching port in New York, Isabel Gonzalez discovered that the rules governing migration to the mainland had changed while she was en route. Previously, although U.S. officials had carefully avoided granting citizenship to Puerto Ricans, they had not treated them as aliens for immigration purposes. That reluctance had sprung in part from concerns that anti-imperialists might use constitutional objections to such a policy to scuttle legislation for Puerto Rico, Hawai'i, and the Philippines.[3]

But enactment of the Philippine Organic Act in July 1902 removed that barrier. The act treated the Philippines much like Puerto Rico. Filipinos were to elect a lower legislative chamber but not their upper chamber or executive; they became "citizens of the Philippine Islands"; and their goods were subject to a tariff on arrival in the United States. In contrast to the tariff on goods from Puerto Rico, however, the one on goods from the Philippines rivaled the tariff on foreign goods and could not be quickly repealed. Although Puerto Rico circulated U.S. currency, the Filipino government could now coin its own money. The act for Puerto Rico was silent on the applicability of most provisions of the Bill of Rights, but the act for the Philippines simultaneously withheld the right to a jury trial on grand jury indictment and statutorily extended many other provisions of the Bill of Rights.[4]

Within weeks of the Philippine Organic Act, the Treasury Department reinstated the immigration policy it had put on hold in 1900. Thenceforth, Puerto Ricans would be "subject to the same examinations as are enforced against people from countries over which the United States claims no right of sovereignty." Following the new rules, port officials transferred Gonzalez to Ellis Island.[5]

There Gonzalez confronted a powerful arm of the U.S. administrative state. Exercising both prosecutorial and judicial functions and insulated from most formal judicial review, immigration inspectors on Ellis Island examined as many as 5,000 immigrants a day. Hundreds of inspectors made immigration determinations quickly and summarily. Inspectors sent difficult cases to the Board of Special Inquiry. There, an immigrant's hearing could end in minutes, without aid of legal representation or the chance to see and rebut evidence. And when Gonzalez arrived at Ellis Island she came up against a new commissioner who aspired to more efficient and stringent administration. President Theodore Roosevelt had appointed William Williams commissioner of immigration at Ellis Island several months earlier.[6]

Williams, a well-regarded Wall Street lawyer, doubled the exclusion rate at Ellis Island within his first year. His approach was infused with popular beliefs about morality and proper relations within families. It was also racially discriminatory. Williams described "radical sociological, industrial, racial and intellectual distinctions" between northwestern and southeastern Europeans and warned against policies that would "fill up this country rapidly with immigrants upon whom responsibility for the proper bringing up of their offspring sits lightly." Aggressively enforcing the statutory bar on aliens "likely to become a public charge," he directed inspectors to suspect anyone who arrived with less than ten dollars. They often labeled unmarried mothers and their children as likely public charges. Ellis Island policy dictated that women who were pregnant and not married had to be held for additional investigation. Single women were to be released only if a family member came to claim them. Like many social-welfare policy makers at the time, Williams and his subordinates assumed that women and children were dependents of men, despite the fact that many women were family breadwinners. Such policies had more to do with middle-class respectability than with the economic realities that most working-class women and their children faced.[7]

Pregnant and unmarried, Gonzalez presented to inspectors at Ellis Island as an abandoned woman. She lacked evident membership in an economically self-sufficient man's home and displayed inadequate sexual propriety. She had attempted to evade inspectors' scrutiny by carrying eleven dollars in cash, leaving her two-year-old daughter, Dolores, in the care of her mother in San Juan, and telegraphing ahead to her family in New York to pick her up. But her pregnancy was obvious, and she was held over for a hearing to determine whether she was "going to persons *able, willing and legally bound* to support" her. At the hearing, Gonzalez and her uncle, Domingo Collazo, argued that she was an upstanding, dependent woman in an honorable man's household. She explained her child and pregnancy through her status as a widow. Collazo transformed a missing fiancé into a husband who was not present owing to his work demands. Hedging his bets, Collazo also declared himself "willing to take

[Gonzalez] and provide for her." Wary inspectors sent Collazo home, urging him to produce the husband, saying, "His wife is here and he should come for her."[8]

Two days later, with Viñals still absent, Hermina Collazo appeared on Gonzalez's behalf. In the exchange that followed, inspectors again presumed a sex-based division of labor. Hermina Collazo explained that both she and her husband worked, but inspectors only inquired about her husband's pay. They questioned her about coming to testify without her husband and sought assurances that "in case this woman is released, you will stand by her and see that she does not get into trouble." The stenographer did not record her name, and the inspectors still insisted that they must see Gonzalez's husband.[9]

Isabel Gonzalez's brother Luis tried a new tack. He cast Isabel Gonzalez as a victim of *rapto*, a Spanish offense akin to breach of promise or seduction. Under Spanish law, a man committed *rapto* by using a promise of marriage to convince a woman who was a virgin to have sex with him. If the woman or her parents brought a successful *rapto* case, the man faced a choice: he could marry the woman and thereby restore her honor, or serve a prison sentence for his crime and pay a fine to compensate the woman for her lost honor. Luis assured the inspectors that his family had taken the necessary steps to restore his sister's honor by the first route. Though Isabel's lover had as yet declined to marry her, Luis vowed: "I have been to the church and have made arrangements and as soon as I have my sister with me, we are going there and are going to have them married. I have also gone to the authorities and told them[,] and everything is waiting for the release of my sister. . . . My aunt . . . has made arrangements and is sure of making a reconciliation . . . and will have them married." Luis apparently believed that this assurance would satisfy inspectors' concerns about Isabel Gonzalez's family's capacity to care for her, but instead the inspectors were indignant. "An arrangement then has been made by which a marriage is to take place without the husband's consent?" they asked. Luis affirmed that this was the case. The inspectors then followed Williams's policy and excluded Gonzalez as an undesirable "alien."[10]

With Isabel Gonzalez in detention on Ellis Island, the case shifted from the agency to the courts. Now, the relationship between Constitution and empire took center stage. In Williams's words, Gonzalez's challenge raised "the very difficult question of constitutional law[:] whether or not a Porto Rican was a citizen of the United States." On 18 August 1902, Collazo swore out a habeas corpus petition for Gonzalez. At about the same time, a friend put her in touch with a lawyer who filed Collazo's petition with the federal Circuit Court for the Southern District of New York. The court promptly paroled Gonzalez pending its decision. Williams hired a private lawyer who performed "exceedingly well." On October 7, Judge E. Henry Lacombe announced his decision. Because Gonzalez "was by birth an alien," she so remained, having not "in some appropriate way . . . since been naturalized." Williams was thrilled. The decision validated his action and the legal analysis undergirding it, advanced his racial agenda, and confirmed his authority over peoples from recently annexed lands. Within a week, the secretary of the treasury announced that Filipinos as well as Puerto Ricans would thenceforth "be examined as aliens."[11]

Lacombe's decision, though a loss for Gonzalez, gave her a chance to press the Supreme Court to decide whether those born in Puerto Rico, Guam, and the Philippines were aliens, nationals, subjects, or citizens. Collazo now reached out to Coudert, who had been looking for just such a dispute. Coudert took the case and prepared Gonzalez's appeal to the Supreme Court. The question was no longer whether Gonzalez and her family were "desirable." Instead, the suit would determine whether she was a foreigner. As Coudert saw it, it could also "settle the status of all the native islanders," including Filipinos, "who were in existence at the time the Spanish possessions were annexed by the United States."[12]

Degetau corresponded with Gonzalez's lawyers in early 1903. He then made the risky political decision to join the Gonzalez–Collazo–Coudert collaboration and appear in the case as a friend of the court. If the litigation produced no gains, it would arm the Federales against him. After all, Degetau had already failed to clarify the citizenship status of Puerto Ricans before political, administrative, public, and media audiences, and in two earlier attempted Supreme Court actions. Another failure would isolate him from fellow Republicanos as well. The speaker of the House of Delegates had already derided Degetau's strategy. Congressional support for presidential expansionism showed "that legislative action is not as free from executive influence as one would guess from reading books," he told Degetau. In other words, courts were unlikely to alter Puerto Ricans' status, absent strong legislative guidance. Degetau disagreed. Confident in the "profound respect" of the mainland public for its "judicial institutions," he insisted that a Supreme Court decision could change the situation. He even planned to capitalize on the anticipated favorable ruling by publishing immediately afterward an article in favor of statehood, in the New York *Independent*.[13]

In the meantime, Degetau continued to document instances in which an arm of the U.S. state had treated Puerto Ricans as citizens. At his request, the secretary of Puerto Rico's supreme court certified that U.S. military authorities had administered an oath to Degetau that required citizen-like obligations of national defense and the renunciation of all foreign allegiances common to naturalizations. Degetau also obtained a report of the House Committee on Insular Affairs that recommended Puerto Rico be represented by a congressional delegate of its own. He tracked a case in which the Treasury Department found a Puerto Rican traveler liable for custom duties applicable to U.S. residents, on the logic that Puerto Rico was "part of the United States, at least territorially. The question whether the parties are citizens of the United States is immaterial."[14]

Isabel Gonzalez and her family had their own motivations to pursue the appeal. Luis sought reunification of his family. On 5 February 1903 he wrote to Degetau from Staten Island, seeking help to return to San Juan, as his mother was unwell. Three months later Luis found another solution. He brought his mother, his younger sisters, and Isabel's daughter to New York. All too aware that unmarried mothers and their children could be excluded, the mother listed herself as married on the ship's manifest and claimed Isabel's daughter as her own. On May 18, Ellis Island officials cleared the ostensible nuclear family members for entry and released them into the care of Luis and his mother's sister, Hermina Collazo.[15]

Isabel Gonzalez strove to secure her own position and improve the status of other Puerto Ricans. Although her voice is absent from the administrative and trial records, other records reveal her decision to transform a dispute over the redemption of her individual honor and her access to opportunity in New York into a test case to win citizenship for all Puerto Ricans. While Gonzalez was out on bond, the *New York Times* later reported, "the young man, who she came here to find, turned up." The two wed, and she became "a citizen of this country through marriage," thus acquiring a right to remain on the mainland. Rather than end her appeal on those grounds, however, Gonzalez hid her marriage and her return to family life. As the named litigant and Coudert's client, she was uniquely positioned to influence his litigation goals, and seemingly did so on a key issue. In mid-1903 Coudert published an article advocating that Puerto Ricans be declared neither aliens nor citizens but nationals instead. Taking Britain and France as models, he wrote that "national" and alien were complements, mutually exclusive yet "together ... universally inclusive." Citizenship was narrower: all "citizens must be nationals, but all nationals may not be citizens." This intermediate status resembled the Court's rulings that Puerto Rico was domestic for one purpose yet not part of the United States for another. It also accommodated the justices' declared reluctance to recognize Puerto Ricans as citizens, which Coudert took to be insurmountable. Yet Collazo and Gonzalez rejected the approach, which would make Puerto Ricans full members of no country, "neither flesh nor herring." When Coudert filed his brief several months later, he subordinated the pursuit of the noncitizen nationality to a claim for full citizenship, as Collazo and Gonzalez preferred.[16]

The official record describes Gonzalez largely as immigration inspectors had: dependent, silent, and an object of state policy. Historians have only begun to correct this depiction of Gonzalez as a passive victim of governmental machinations.[17] In reality, Collazo enthusiastically supported Gonzalez's determination. For him, her case offered a chance to engage questions of Puerto Ricans' status in new ways. Moving beyond the world of revolutionary Antillean artisans with whom he had formed political clubs and published newspapers in the 1890s, Collazo began to build ties to island political leaders and acquire a voice in matters of island-mainland relations.

As he expanded his public role, he pursued a path similar to those already traversed by other Puerto Ricans who had assisted the U.S. invasion. Unlike the former opponents of Spanish rule who had secured official positions in post-annexation Puerto Rico, Collazo built relationships on the mainland and on the island. Thus, as Gonzalez's appeal was pending, he sought favor with Luis Muñoz Rivera, the leader of the Puerto Rican opposition party, by positively reviewing his new book of poetry, *Tropicales*. Collazo then sent Degetau a copy of the review. He described it as part "of a series that I propose to publish and that will take a political character." Degetau reciprocated by sending Collazo his own book, *Cuentos para el viaje*, which Collazo also praised. Soon they had friends in common.[18]

Collazo used the case to cast himself as an expert on U.S. law and politics, and he became a regular contributor for the island newspaper *La Correspondencia*. In one late-1903 piece, he argued that existing doctrine that permitted U.S. "possession of 'dependencies'" was inconsistent with the "institutions" and "democratic ... spirit" of the United States. Though he had previously told Degetau that the Court would "say that we are not Americans," he now "cherish[ed] hope." The alternative would be degradation. A denial of citizenship would bring Puerto Ricans down to the status of Filipinos, "denied ... constitutionally protected individual rights."[19] As Collazo saw things, Puerto Ricans lived in institutional limbo, suspended between colony and metropole, alien and national, and citizen and subject.

Whatever the Reconstruction Constitution had once required, the attributes and distribution of citizenship were now unsettled.

The briefs that the Supreme Court received in late 1903 in the *Gonzales v. Williams* appeal laid out competing visions of what the status of Puerto Ricans should be. The lawyers in the case knew that citizenship, Constitution, and empire all involved race. The question was not whether Puerto Ricans were similar to and different from other racialized communities subject to U.S. power, but how.[20]

Solicitor General Henry Hoyt classified Puerto Ricans as functionally equivalent to noncitizen nationals, a people internal to the United States who lacked key political rights. He had made the case against citizenship in his 1901 *Insular Cases* arguments. Now he characterized immigration laws as intended to exclude racial undesirables, and read "alien" to encompass Puerto Ricans. Hoyt thus asked the Court for a narrow decision based on racial difference, which he thought would be consistent with the attorney general's repeated recognition of Puerto Ricans as Americans. As he told the justices,

[My] proposition by no means is "Once a foreigner, always a foreigner ... in the new possessions." The proposition simply is, "Once a foreigner, ... still a foreigner as to certain civil rights, local and peculiar to the home territory and status" ... [;] although now Americans internationally, they retain their former alienage in large degree, and are excluded under the immigration laws.

Reviewing bars to entry by Chinese immigrants, prostitutes, those deemed idiots or insane, paupers, certain diseased persons, and anarchists, Hoyt highlighted Congress's desire to protect the mainland from "dangerous or burdensome" elements. He grouped Puerto Rico and the Philippines together, describing all the islands as remote in space, culture, and "civilization" and suffering problems of climate, "overcrowding," "primitive hygiene," "low ... standards of living and moral conduct," and the "extreme and willing indigency" that characterized the tropics. The Supreme Court, he concluded, ought to respect congressional intent to protect the mainland from these "evils."[21]

Coudert sought U.S. citizenship and nationality for Puerto Ricans, albeit in a highly discounted form. His brief analogized the United States to France and England, and Puerto Ricans to Europe's colonial subjects, African Americans, American Indians, women, and children. Coudert contended that the transfer of sovereignty over Puerto Rico and of Puerto Ricans' allegiance from Spain to the United States had also effected a transfer of subjection or nationality. If accepted, these points were sufficient to win Gonzalez entry, for existing immigration laws excluded only aliens. But Coudert went further. He repeated the claim that he had presented to the Court in 1901. Consistent with Gonzalez and Collazo's view that Puerto Ricans were citizens as well as nonaliens, he declared that finding Puerto Ricans to be neither aliens nor citizens would be tantamount to reviving *Dred Scott*. Significantly, he did not cast Puerto Ricans as white men who deserved full membership in the national polity. Women and people of color possessed a citizenship similar to the status that other empires bestowed on their subordinated peoples, so a similar recognition of Puerto Ricans as citizens would not impede U.S. imperial designs, he argued.

The question that the *Gonzales* case raised, Coudert contended, was how to adapt the post–Civil War jurisprudence of citizenship to a new problem: "imperialism, i.e., the domination over men of one order or kind of civilization, by men of a different and higher civilization." To distinguish between continental expansion and imperialism, Coudert retold the myth of a vacant West and Southwest. At acquisition, the territories there had contained only American Indians, who did "not long survive contact with civilization," and an "insignificant ... number" of people "largely of Caucasian race and civilization" whom the nation had absorbed. Puerto Rico, by contrast, had a large, stable population. Unlike the "frontier," where migration had "soon made the new lands thoroughly American[,] ... the problem of to-day cannot be solved either by extermination ... nor by assimilation."[22]

What to do with a people whom the nation would not assimilate, exterminate, or exclude? Coudert rejected the placement of Puerto Ricans in the "seemingly paradoxical legal category of 'American Aliens,'" which would turn the residents of domestic territories into outsiders. He built on his *Downes v. Bidwell* argument, that the international law of cessions had transformed Puerto Ricans into citizens. Because Puerto Rico was part of the United States under international law, he now added, ruling against Gonzalez "would declare the law of the United States, as expounded by its highest tribunal, to be that there exists under the jurisdiction of the United States a large class of persons who are strangers and aliens here and in every other nation of the globe."[23]

Coudert also appealed to the justices' paternalistic sentiments by playing on concepts of honor and gender. Having forcibly taken her, would the United States leave Puerto Rico, as symbolized by the unwed "Miss Gonzalez ... an undefined waif, on the sea of political uncertainty?" Or would the United States symbolically marry her, acknowledging that "she belongs to the United States, and may look to it for protection?" This was not only an evocative allegory but also suggestive of a tangible solution: Puerto Ricans could be citizens on the model of other dependents, including women. Doctrines limiting the claims of African Americans, American Indians, and women, among others, could serve as a model for the legal status of residents of the newly acquired territories. Grant citizenship but reduce its power, especially with regard to rights. Coudert saw "no room for quibble as to who are aliens," because congressional "reservation as to political status and civil rights" of Puerto Ricans was consistent with citizenship.[24]

Turning more concretely to case law, Coudert elaborated that citizenship, while widespread, brought few substantive rights. He chose decisions in which the Court had affirmed that men and women born within U.S. jurisdictions were citizens whatever their sex, race, or ethnicity. In the same decisions, the Court had eviscerated aspects of the Fourteenth Amendment that implied that U.S. citizenship carried a substantial array of rights. The *Slaughter-House Cases* (1873) virtually nullified the Privileges and Immunities Clause. *Minor v. Happersett* (1875), a decision about women's suffrage, eliminated voting as a potential federal citizenship right. The Court struck down a federal antidiscrimination law and forbade Congress to regulate private action under the Fourteenth Amendment in the *Civil Rights Cases* (1883). *Wong Wing v. United States* (1896) confirmed that the Constitution guaranteed some individual rights for all people but offered few protections specifically to citizens. Instead, they had to look to their states for the balance of their rights. Coudert could expect the justices to be receptive. In *Plessy v. Ferguson* (1896) and *Giles v. Harris* (1903) the Court had already blocked the invocation of the Fourteenth Amendment as a tool against transparent "caste" distinctions and deliberate African American disfranchisement. When women and people of color complained that their states denied them such rights, the Court increasingly declared itself impotent.[25]

Happily, Coudert contended, the Court's citizenship jurisprudence resembled and improved on that of other empires, notably France. The French approach to status helped Coudert delineate what he took to be the central confusion in the case: a failure to distinguish tiers of citizenship and subjection. In France, "the holder of political rights" was the "active" citizen, the status to which the word "citizen" referred in normal U.S. discourse. By contrast, U.S. law recognized as citizens nearly all U.S. nationals regardless of their political rights, including women, children, and African Americans. France also recognized the French nationality of its subordinate peoples, be they minors, married women, "Cochin" Chinese, "Taïti[ans]," or Algerians. But it divided these second-class nationals into two groups. Some, "such as minors, women and incompetents" were "passive citizens," a status identical with "subjection at common law" and carrying "full civil but no political rights." Others, "uncivilized or semicivilized tribes or people who become wholly subject to [French] jurisdiction," were called "subjects." They also received no political rights, and in lieu of traditional French civil rights, they held the traditional private-law rights of their locale. U.S. citizenship offered even less benefit. The Supreme Court had held that most rights deemed civil, except access to federal courts, came through state law and state citizenship and could generally be vindicated only at the state level. Granting Puerto Ricans a form of rights-poor citizenship would follow a model even more flexible than those of other great powers.[26]

According to Coudert, legal history also endorsed the recognition of Puerto Ricans as citizens along these sparse terms. *Dred Scott v. Sandford* (1857), which represented the opposite approach, had been essentially undone and superseded, Coudert argued, by the Civil War and the Fourteenth Amendment. So had the similarly reasoned *Elk v. Wilkins* (1884), which was reversed by the congressional Dawes Act (1887). Fortunately, four decades of Supreme Court decisions that had drained content from the Fourteenth Amendment meant that justices could facilitate imperialism without repeating the mistakes of *Dred Scott*. To render Puerto Ricans eligible for subjection, the Court merely had to declare them to be citizens.[27]

In his friend-of-the-Court brief, Federico Degetau took a dramatically different approach. As a former Spanish citizen, he associated his island with all the markers of male honor, including economic self-sufficiency, martial experience, and exercise of political and civil rights. He did not seek passive citizenship akin to that enjoyed by women and people of color. In fact, his brief barely mentioned female or working-class islanders such as Gonzalez.[28] Instead, he claimed for Puerto Ricans such as himself a robust citizenship associated with white men, civilization, economic and legal opportunities, political participation, and military and tax obligations. Drawing on his experiences with U.S. officials before and during his first term, he asserted that Puerto Ricans already occupied all these roles.

Key to Degetau's argument was his depiction of Puerto Rico as connected to the broader history of U.S. expansion. In a clever but specious analysis, he reasoned that when the Treaty of Paris vested Congress with discretion to determine the citizenship status of "native inhabitants" of Spain's former possessions, it referred to "the uncivilized tribes of the Philippine Islands" and not "Spanish citizens born in Porto Rico." Degetau portrayed the liberties Puerto Ricans had enjoyed under Spanish rule as indicative of their capacity for liberal politics, holding that it was a baseline below which no new government should fall. Under Spain, Puerto Ricans had such rights as representation in the national legislature, national citizenship accompanied by constitutional protections, "the same honors and prerogatives as the native-born in Castille," and broad autonomy.[29] But his attempt to conflate the status of *criollos* and *peninsulares* was more aspirational than real. It demanded that he ignore the long – and long-resented – history of Spanish favoritism toward the *peninsulares*.

Furthermore, Degetau located Puerto Ricans atop imperial-racial hierarchies within the United States. He claimed that Puerto Ricans differed from such disparaged groups as Filipino "*tribes*," "*Mongolians*," and the "*uncivilized native tribes* [of] *Alaska*." Though Puerto Ricans shared with American Indians struggles to define simultaneously the status of their people and their land, Degetau saw an unbridgeable divide in how the U.S. approached the two groups. American Indians could become U.S. citizens by renouncing tribal allegiances, which Puerto Ricans could not do because they had no foreign or tribal allegiance to renounce. Without explicitly mentioning Puerto Rico's former slaves and their descendants, Degetau implied that the island's political class shared with mainland Republicans a commitment to emancipation.[30] Puerto Ricans also resembled the French and the Mexicans who had been incorporated into U.S. citizenship in the nineteenth century after the Louisiana Purchase and the Treaty of Guadalupe Hidalgo.

Degetau used familial metaphors to assert the rights of Puerto Ricans, even when doing so came at the expense of other colonized peoples. He noted that President McKinley, using language that could have described a marriage contract, had Cubans grant their "honest submission" in order to receive from the United States "support and protection." In language suggestive of the relationship of parent and child, McKinley had Filipinos swear to "recognize and accept the supreme authority of the United States." By contrast, prospective Puerto Rican officeholders (including Degetau himself) had renounced their allegiance to Spain and agreed to "'support and defend the Constitution of the United States against all enemies home or foreign,'" thereby effecting "a plain renunciation of all foreign allegiance and an explicit acceptance of the duties of citizenship."[31] The oath invoked male realms of political rights and participation by speaking of defending the nation, holding political office, and upholding the Constitution. Taken together, Degetau's comparisons implied that Cuba had agreed to receive protection from the United States like a wife and the Philippines had accepted the authority of the United States like a child, but Puerto Rico had sworn allegiance to and taken up the defense of the United States like a man.

Degetau reminded the Court that the Foraker Act had envisioned Puerto Ricans as the beneficiaries of most U.S. laws. If they were not citizens, they would instead be disadvantaged by federal requirements of citizenship for ship captains, bank directors, and prosecuting litigants in the Court of Claims. He also emphasized that islanders paid U.S. taxes, swore allegiance to the Constitution, and were close to having a congressional delegate.[32]

Degetau's depictions of the best of the mainlanders and islanders as equals reinforced his core constitutional claim. By making Puerto Ricans into citizens of the U.S. territory of Puerto Rico, the U.S. political branches had activated the Fourteenth Amendment's Citizenship Clause at two separate levels. First, because the 1901 *Insular Cases* deemed the political branches to have made Puerto Rico U.S. territory, Puerto Ricans were "born . . . in the United States" and thus were U.S. citizens. Second, Degetau reprised his claim that the Foraker Act had both naturalized Puerto Ricans as U.S. citizens and made them citizens of Puerto Rico. Together, U.S. and Puerto Rican citizenship formed the "double allegiance" and "double citizenship" envisioned by the Fourteenth Amendment's recognition of most U.S. peoples as "citizens of the United States and of the state wherein they reside." Otherwise, Puerto Rican citizenship would be an alternative to U.S. citizenship, which would violate other laws. For example, mainlanders who relocated to Puerto Rico would, on becoming Puerto Rican citizens, be "deprived by Congress of their United States citizenship" in contravention of the Fourteenth Amendment bar on "'any law which shall abridge the privileges and immunities of citizens of the United States.'" Similarly, U.S. law would purport to define the status of aliens (Puerto Ricans) vis-à-vis another sovereign (Puerto Rico) in contravention of international law.[33]

Degetau's arguments asked the Court to consider him, an accomplished civil servant, rather than Gonzalez, an unmarried working-class mother, as the model for Puerto Rican citizens. "I myself, a native citizen of Porto Rico, could not be entitled to represent, in a political capacity, the hundreds of citizens of the United States, born or naturalized in the mainland, who have given me their suffrages, if I were an alien" rather than a citizen. Closing on a personal note, he reprised an earlier gambit: "If I were an alien, I could not have attained the highest honor in my professional career, that of taking, as a member of the bar of this Honorable Court, the oath to maintain the Constitution of the United States, this oath being incompatible with allegiance to any other power."[34]

At oral argument, on 4 December 1903, the Supreme Court appeared to agree with Coudert and Degetau, at least in part. According to one observer, Chief Justice Melville Fuller dismissed the contention that Degetau's admission to the Court's bar was "by courtesy" rather than "by right." As a result, the solicitor general all but conceded that Puerto Ricans could not be aliens.[35] Degetau's argument was largely successful. The justices were willing to consider that someone such as Degetau could be a U.S. citizen, or at least a semblance of one. Yet obviously, more than Degetau's individual status was at stake. As all parties in the case appeared to agree, Puerto Ricans and perhaps Filipinos held a common status under U.S. law. If Degetau was a citizen, then Gonzalez and perhaps very many Filipinos were citizens too. Once again, the specter of the Philippines and the racist underpinnings it invoked haunted and materially inflected the deliberations.

As Coudert rose to address the Court, it remained uncertain whether the justices believed that islanders were citizens. He sought to cast the alternative as a monarchical "subjection" best known to U.S. law through its association with *Dred Scott*.[36] But Justice William Day objected. The most recent appointee to the Court, Day had dealt with questions of law and empire as chairman of the Treaty of Paris negotiating commission. He had stood behind the assertion to Spanish negotiators that the United States could be trusted to treat Puerto Ricans honorably, notwithstanding the treaty provision giving Congress full discretion over their status. He now opposed attaching the monarchical term "subject" to U.S. insular peoples. Instead, he proposed the medieval term "liegemen," which applied to vassals who owed loyalty to a superior. Apparently he wanted to reject Coudert's proposal that the Court recognize a relatively modest version of citizenship and thereby avoid creating either subjects or new rights for Puerto Ricans. Although Day was reluctant to acknowledge explicitly that the Court had drained much meaning from citizenship, he had no qualms about how the United States treated women, people of color, or colonized peoples. Functionally, Coudert reiterated, it did not matter whether Puerto Ricans were "liegemen, nationals or subjects, all of which terms are absolutely identical as far as the law is concerned." The Court had to choose: reintroduce "subjects" into U.S. law, which Coudert disfavored, or extend Puerto Ricans citizenship.[37]

On 4 January 1904, Chief Justice Fuller announced the unanimous decision. First, the Court rejected Hoyt's assertion that Puerto Ricans were "aliens." "We ... cannot concede ... that the word 'alien,' as used in the [immigration] act of 1891, embraces the citizens of Porto Rico." Reviewing the Treaty of Paris and Foraker Act, Fuller explained that the United States had made "the nationality of the island ... American" and integrated Puerto Rico into the nation. In Puerto Rico, the United States had created a civil government with heads named by the president, implemented congressional oversight, established a U.S. district court, nationalized Puerto Rican vessels, and extended most federal laws to the island. While finding that the Treasury guideline under which Gonzalez had been held was invalid as applied to Puerto Ricans, the Court did not address whether Congress could resurrect similar rules by statute. For now, Puerto Ricans had "freedom of locomotion" everywhere subject to U.S. jurisdiction.[38] They could freely migrate from the island to the mainland.

As to whether Puerto Ricans were citizens, nationals, subjects, or liegemen, Fuller wrote: "We are not required to discuss ... the contention of Gonzales's counsel that the cession of Porto Rico accomplished the naturalization of its people; or that of Commissioner Degetau, in his excellent argument."[39] Having struck down the Treasury Department position that Puerto Ricans were aliens, the justices joined the numerous administrators who found it more profitable to evade clarification of the citizenship status of Puerto Ricans than to deny islanders this or that right.[40]

As Coudert would write several years later, the government's "determined opposition" to citizenship for Puerto Ricans had all but assured the Court would go no further. Its strategic silence rested on the possibility of a status somewhere between citizen and alien – what the *Nation* magazine termed "'nationals' of the United States" akin to "natives in the French colonies, or our own Indians." The justices avoided openly contradicting the widely held belief that U.S. citizenship and nationality were coextensive, while leaving lawmakers and administrators room to maneuver in governing new territorial acquisitions. As in *Downes v. Bidwell*, vagueness proved valuable to the Court as it sought to adjust constitutional democracy to empire. While Collazo complained that the Court "decided" in its opinion "that it had not decided anything," many read its indecision as an invitation to resolve the matter politically and administratively.[41] The decision created a vacuum to be filled by bureaucratic and legislative decisions and discretion. For the time being, it seemed that politics would drive law, and not the other way around.

Administrators and lawmakers could find much to celebrate in the government's loss, but the litigants and advocates who secured the favorable judgment had won at best a partial victory. The decision solidified Coudert's reputation as a leading lawyer of U.S. empire, but the clarification of Puerto Ricans' and Filipinos' status that he had sought still eluded him. And the decision was bittersweet for Gonzalez and Collazo. Although it facilitated the reunification of their extended family, it damaged their honor, which rested on being either a dependent in an adequate household or its head. Immigration inspectors had declared that neither Gonzalez nor Collazo occupied such a station, a conclusion that the Court's decision did not revise. Worse, the justices had declined to declare that Puerto Ricans were citizens by right. Indeed, the decision potentially put citizenship further out of reach. Some officials read federal naturalization statutes as applicable only to aliens. Under such a reading, the declaration that Puerto Ricans were not aliens left them with no path to citizenship.[42] For Degetau, who had campaigned on promises of winning citizenship for Puerto Ricans and, through that step, constitutional rights and the recognition of Puerto Rico as a territory on the road to statehood, the basic dilemma continued. In fact, clarification of the islanders' citizenship status now seemed further out of reach than ever.

Aware that the narrative told in *Gonzales v. Williams* (1904) had denied that Gonzalez was an appropriately dependent woman and that Collazo was a sufficiently independent man, the two moved on interconnected tracks to undo and rework the dishonor that U.S. officials had imposed on them. Both tried to adjust the public record to portray themselves as honorable. Their initial efforts to do so were more than a year in the making. On 1 September 1902, twelve days after her parole from Ellis Island, Gonzalez had given birth to her second daughter, Eva. The birth certificate listed Eva's mother as Isabel Viñals, formerly Isabel Gonzalez and now married to Eva's official (though most likely not biological) father, Adolfo Viñals. It declared that the new family made its home at Collazo's address. Whatever the truth of Domingo Collazo's and Luis Gonzalez's initial testimony to Ellis Island officials, Isabel Gonzalez and her family had within several weeks ensured that the official birth record corroborated their claims. Later, when the *New York Times* reported the day after the Court's ruling that Gonzalez was a woman who "had come here in search of a man who had promised to marry her and had failed to keep his promise," one of Gonzalez's lawyers ensured that the paper also announced her marriage. The article thus adapted a familiar Puerto Rican *rapto* narrative, of honor threatened and restored.

Collazo also turned to the press to restore his reputation. He secured repeated coverage of himself as a "well-to-do" uncle who gave immigration inspectors "guaranteed assurances" that Isabel Gonzalez would receive "support as a member of [his] family."[43] Subsequent years bore out Collazo's claims to be an honorable man who supported dependent female relations. He acted as a mentor to his niece's new husband, provided him a place of business, and opened his house to Gonzalez's relations. Within a few years, Collazo's household was supporting four female dependents.[44]

For Gonzalez, maintaining the stable and economically successful family that her honor demanded remained a public performance and a private struggle. In the years immediately after her case, Gonzalez did remain honorably dependent. She set up a household with Viñals in Staten Island, began raising her daughters Eva and Dora there, and she named the son she and Viñals had Adolfo Junior, after his father. To shore up her reputation, she permitted the *New York Daily Tribune* to publish a letter in her name that reminded readers of her detention "at Ellis Island as an 'alien likely to become a public charge,'" then boasted that the "forecast of my 'jailers' has not as yet been fulfilled." But the defiance masked vulnerability. In addition to young Adolfo, she and Viñals had a daughter who died in infancy. When Viñals's mother relocated to New York, it was the Collazos, rather than her son and Gonzalez, who were able to take her in. Eventually Viñals abandoned his marriage and his son and returned to Puerto Rico, leaving Gonzalez in the dishonorable station of an unmarried mother. By 1910 Dora was in an orphanage and Eva had joined the Collazo household. According to family lore, both changes were the result of economic desperation. Redemption came piecemeal, and incompletely. First,

Gonzalez met Juan Torres, a *criollo* clerk who had recently arrived in New York from Spain after a stint as a manager and salesman for the Singer (Sewing) Machine Company in the Dominican Republic. Like Gonzalez, Torres was separated from a spouse who lived in Puerto Rico and was the custodial parent of their child. In 1912 or so Gonzalez removed Dora from the orphanage and had a son with Torres, named Juan Eduardo. When Gonzalez married again in 1915, she and Torres each claimed the respectable (and nonbigamous) status "widowed." By this time the Collazos appear to have informally adopted Eva. Beginning in 1915, census records describe Eva as the Collazos' daughter rather than their niece. It now became possible for Isabel Gonzalez to present herself as the matriarch of a properly constituted family. When Luis Sanchez Morales, a prominent Republicano, remembered the case in print decades later, he praised Gonzalez's willingness to be a judicial "guinea pig" and described her long marriage and the many children and grandchildren to whom she devoted herself.[45]

Descendants recall that Gonzalez occupied such a role throughout the remainder of her life. Yet this too took effort, as reflected in her descendants' protectiveness about her history and their recollections of the shock one child received late in life on learning that the man who had raised him was not his biological father. Gonzalez's compromises and tribulations during her first decade as a nonalien in New York had far-reaching consequences.

In the immediate aftermath of her case, Gonzalez attempted to use the language of honor to shore up her family by continuing to appeal to Degetau as if he were her patron. She knew that Degetau had offered to help her brother pursue his studies. Signing a letter with her maiden name, she now asked Degetau to become the symbolic head of her needy household: "One reason I came to the United States was for the education of a little sister who I today have by my side and who I would like to place in one of these colleges of poor students in which many of our countrymen are placed" (Fig. 4.1). Gonzalez displayed a complicated, even paradoxical mix of independence and dependence. Her dependence on Degetau implicitly rested on an absence of husbands and fathers. And in seeking his male protection, she sought for her sister an education that would promote the sister's economic independence.[46]

Some months later, Isabel Gonzalez and Domingo Collazo wrote together, this time to secure a public voice for Gonzalez. In letters to the *New York Times* written in Gonzalez's name, they criticized the Supreme Court ruling in her favor for its willful blindness to a betrayal. Although the general at the head of the U.S. invasion of Puerto Rico had "proclaimed to the wide winds his 'liberating' speech," they wrote, his words were "nothing but bitter mockery and waste paper." Instead of recognition as "full-fledged American citizens," Puerto Ricans received "the actual incongruous status – 'neither Americans nor foreigners,' as it was vouchsafed by the United States Supreme Court apropos of my detention at Ellis Island for the crime of being an 'alien.'" In making this claim, Gonzalez and Collazo built on analogies that had been drawn on the mainland between annexation and

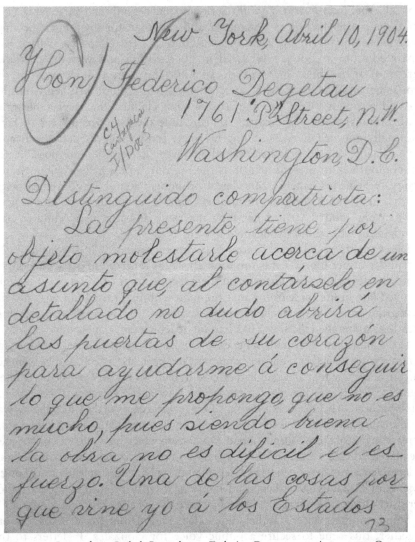

FIGURE 4.1 Letter from Isabel Gonzalez to Federico Degetau, 10 Apr. 1904, Centro de Investigaciones Históricas, Colección Ángel M. Mergal 5/I/5. Page one (above) and page four (below).

elopement (Fig. 4.2). But the romance between the United States and Puerto Rico had ended in a breach of promise much like the *rapto* that Gonzalez's brother had described to immigration officials in 1902. Having deceived Puerto Ricans and deprived them of one honorable status, Spanish citizenship, the United States was obliged to extend Puerto Ricans a new honorable status, U.S. citizenship. But instead, the island's predicament

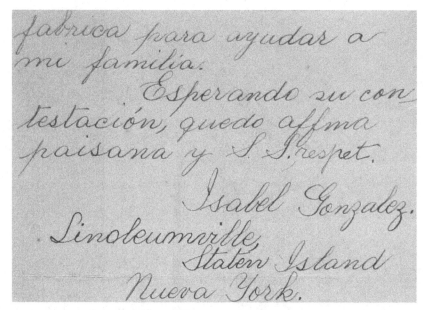

FIGURE 4.1 (cont.)

became the basis of investigations into Gonzalez's honor. In using this romantic metaphor to protest U.S. policies in Puerto Rico, Gonzalez and Collazo sought restoration of the "liberties and franchises" that constituted the active, male citizenship advocated by Degetau in her case. Their implicit claim was that, harmed like a woman, Puerto Rico ought to be recompensed like a man.[47]

Collazo also used the *Gonzales* case to comment publicly in his own name on Puerto Ricans' status. In letters to the editor of the *New York Times*, he declared that the decision left islanders in the position of amnesiacs "who have forgotten who they are." "If they ceased to be Spanish citizens and have not been Americans citizens [sic], what in the name of heaven have they been?" he asked. A new test case was not the answer, for "unless ... something extraordinary and unforseen [sic] happens to enable the highest tribunal to settle the question," the Supreme Court would leave Puerto Ricans' citizenship status "in suspense."[48]

Republicanos such as the speaker of the House of Delegates, Manuel Rossy, agreed that any continuation of Degetau's judicial strategy would be misguided. Rossy had expected Degetau to fail even before the justices issued their decision in the *Gonzales* case. "If the Supreme Court could make U.S. citizens of the inhabitants of a country based just on ... annexation," Rossy reasoned, with implicit reference to the Philippines, the United States "would have to concede citizenship to whatever upstart or enemy that it happened to annex." Consistent

FIGURE 4.2 Detail from R.C. Bowman, "She Can't Resist Him," *Minneapolis Tribune* (third quarter 1898), as reproduced in *Cartoons of the War of 1898 with Spain from the Leading Foreign and American Papers* (Chicago, 1898), 158. Courtesy of Internet Archive. The cartoon's original caption read, "It looks more like an elopement than an abduction." Clockwise from top left, the figures are Sagasta in the House of Spain, Porto Rico, and Gen. Miles.

with the view that Puerto Ricans should sit atop the racial ladder rather than seek to dismantle it, he claimed that this policy would mean that the United States "would not form a true nation, because germs destructive of its sovereignty would arise within it." Instead, he claimed, citizenship could be created only through federal legislation. Rossy remained optimistic that Republicanos could secure citizenship and perhaps eventual statehood through the party's alliance with U.S. Republicans. He and other Republicanos formalized plans to select and send delegates to the 1904 Republican National Convention.[49] This strategy emerged from a long tradition in island politics of striking a balance between principles and expediency, which sometimes meant forging partnerships with metropolitan parties.

Degetau was not convinced by this strategy. If Republicans planned "to keep us indefinitely as a dependency," he announced, he would not join them. Continuing to place his bets on securing a clarification of Puerto Ricans' status, Degetau stayed in Washington to play his remaining cards. Presumably because *Gonzales* had not come out as he had anticipated, he told the *Independent* that he would have to delay his article advocating statehood for Puerto Rico. Degetau nonetheless embraced the decision as "a stepping stone to a more decided recognition of the rights of Puerto Ricans in the United States." Republican support for eventual Puerto Rican statehood could depend on whether "the Supreme Court declares us American citizens," he believed. In an attempt to drum up a new test case, Degetau wrote the Board of Election Commissioners in Chicago about the voting rights of Puerto Ricans there. Board attorney William Wheelock replied that he had recently refused to register Puerto Ricans because he considered them noncitizens. *Gonzales*, he said, "carefully avoid[ed]" the "question of citizenship." Degetau could not challenge the decision in court because the board had no record of the identities of the aspiring voters. Degetau won floor privileges, though still no vote, in the House of Representatives, but because the Senate refused to act, he remained a resident commissioner rather than a delegate. He found a "peculiar indefiniteness" in this status: "in the language of the law, only a 'resident commissioner'" yet "with functions similar to those of a Delegate." Using his new powers, he introduced a bill to declare islanders to be citizens, but it promptly died in committee.[50]

When Degetau finally returned to San Juan in late June 1904, his political isolation was palpable. Republicanos moved ahead with their incorporation into the Republican Party despite his objections. As he predicted, the Republican Party was unwilling to back citizenship and territorial government for Puerto Rico; when Republicanos proposed such a plank for the party platform, the Republican National Convention rejected it. Degetau dismissed the two votes extended to Puerto Rico at the convention as a decision to "put Puerto Rico ... *on the colonial basis.*" Hawai'i and the Philippines also received two votes; other U.S. territories – even "Indian Territory" – got six.

Worse yet, U.S. Republicans actually embraced a "continuation of the present state of economic and political affairs" when they bragged of having "'organized the government of Porto Rico'" so that "'its people now enjoy peace, freedom, order, and prosperity.'"[51]

Battle lines within the Partido Republicano sharpened. Mateo Fajardo emerged as Degetau's main opponent for nomination as resident commissioner. A onetime member of the Puerto Rican Section of the Cuban Revolutionary Party in New York, Fajardo had joined the U.S. invasion of Puerto Rico alongside Collazo as part of the Puerto Rican Commission, but unlike Collazo he had stayed on the island. He became a Republicano and in 1902 was elected mayor of Mayagüez. When Fajardo apologized for U.S. Republican policies, claiming that "'before governing ourselves we should prove that we know how to do it,'" Degetau announced that the choice for Republicanos was between himself, a man who was "fighting for our citizenship," and Fajardo's cynical embrace of U.S. Republican colonialism. Nonetheless, Republicanos nominated Fajardo.[52]

The Federales sensed an opportunity. Like Fajardo, they favored politics over courts, but they rejected Fajardo's plan to influence Congress from within the U.S. Republican Party. Instead, they advocated a more confrontational approach, partly in an attempt to appeal to those Republicanos who were unhappy with their lack of power in their party and opposed to collaboration with U.S. Republicans. Resentment among island-born politicians over Spain's unwillingness to make government posts on the island available to Puerto Ricans remained fresh. That U.S. rule had not brought more and better government posts to islanders was particularly aggravating. To recruit these restless Republicanos, the Federales reconstituted themselves as an umbrella party, the Partido Unionista. Their platform was inclusive, seeking self-government, be it as a state of the Union, a U.S. territory, or an independent nation. Soon the Unionistas' ranks swelled.[53]

On November 8, the political landscape in Puerto Rico diverged yet further from Degetau's ideal. Fajardo lost. Voters chose Unionista Tulio Larrinaga as resident commissioner and placed the House of Delegates in Unionista hands. They would dominate Puerto Rican politics for the next two decades. At the imperial center, by contrast, Republican president Theodore Roosevelt won reelection and the Republican Party remained in control of Congress.[54]

Even as a lame duck, Degetau continued his pursuit of citizenship for Puerto Ricans. It was the topic of his final speech on the floor of the House of Representatives. He also launched a new test case on behalf a Puerto Rican job candidate, Juan Rodríguez, whom the Board of Labor Employment at the Navy Yard in Washington, DC, had declined to consider. Navy Yard rules stated that "no applicant will be registered unless . . . he is a citizen of the United States," so the application appeared to raise the question that the *Gonzales* Court had reserved. President Roosevelt had tried to avoid such problems by declaring that "birth or naturalization in Porto Rico" would also suffice. But as government lawyers would soon declare, Roosevelt's rule could be read as inapplicable to the job that Rodríguez sought. After the assistant secretary of state concluded that "as Mr. Rodríguez is not a citizen of the United States he is not eligible for registration," the board denied Rodriguez's application. Degetau returned to the courts to demand that the Washington Navy Yard board consider Rodríguez on his merits. On December 12, the Supreme Court of the District of Columbia denied the petition, and Degetau and Rodríguez appealed.[55]

Degetau implicitly acknowledged the appeal of Coudert's earlier arguments when he filed his brief on Rodriguez's behalf before the court of appeals in mid-February 1905. Having presumed in *Gonzales* that Puerto Ricans were either aliens or citizens, Degetau now expressly rejected the suggestion that Puerto Ricans be recognized as noncitizen nationals. But having learned that federal judges might rule otherwise, he also aimed to make citizenship more attractive to them by taking up Coudert's proposal that the Court recognize islanders as holding a basically inconsequential form of citizenship. He wrote that Congress had made most federal statutes, including many that referred to citizens and "not . . . 'nationals,'" applicable in Puerto Rico. Congress treated Puerto Ricans as citizens. Because the Supreme Court had "declared that Porto Rico is a territory of the United States," he asserted, Puerto Ricans were citizens under a federal statute declaring "'all persons born in the United States [with irrelevant exceptions] to be citizens of the United States.'" Despite his earlier portrayals of Puerto Ricans as independent male citizens, Degetau now deployed Coudert's depiction of citizenship as widely distributed and relatively modest in its implications. Degetau told the court that, unlike France or Spain, "our constitution is not based on the principle of the sovereignty *of the nation.*" It is "'we the people'" who "'ordain and establish'" it, he stated. But universal citizenship did not mean universal rights, Degetau assured the court. Citing the "'minors and married women'" who were citizens, he acknowledged "that political privileges are not essential to citizenship." The Court of Appeals for the District of Columbia lifted a page from *Gonzales* and ruled for Rodríguez. Rather than address Degetau's arguments, it held that President Roosevelt's instruction, that those demonstrating Puerto Rican citizenship "will not be required to show further evidence of citizenship," applied in this case as well.[56]

Five years of work had produced little progress on Degetau's promises to secure Puerto Ricans citizenship, full constitutional protections, traditional territorial status, and a path to statehood. Rather, the United States had consolidated a colonial regime in Puerto Rico on his watch. Statehood seemed less likely in 1905 than it had in 1899. When Degetau's wife made plans to visit her aristocratic family in Spain, she applied for a passport as a "resident of an insular possession" by marriage rather than as a U.S. citizen. In subsequent years, Degetau largely retired from politics. Still, he counted among his greatest accomplishments "the high distinction of appearing before the U.S. Supreme Court" to seek for Puerto Ricans the "definition of our *status* as American citizens."[57]

And yet Degetau's claims did win islanders concrete gains, including nonalien status, passports, a voice in Congress, free migration throughout U.S. lands, and access to federal civil service and Navy Yard jobs.

Isabel Gonzalez and Domingo Collazo also achieved mixed results. When federal officials impugned their honor, the niece and uncle advanced a powerful counternarrative. Still, the official story shapes perceptions of the family even today. The extended family had greater success overcoming federal obstacles to their reunification. As to status, Gonzalez and Collazo won a partial victory. It remained a point of pride that they had clarified that Puerto Ricans were not aliens, but a sore point that Puerto Ricans had yet to be recognized as citizens. Commentary on Puerto Rican affairs bearing Gonzalez's name occasionally emerged in subsequent years, and Collazo continued to be a leading voice within the Puerto Rican diaspora. His focus shifted from courts back to politics, which increasingly meant election work on the mainland and ties to the Partido Unionista.

Yet something important had been lost. From 1902 to 1904, Gonzalez, Collazo, and Degetau had put their faith in law and adjudication. They had approached judges and administrators with concrete legal disputes, asking them to settle legal claims that other federal officials would not. They had counted on bureaucracies and especially courts to follow legal principles. Afterward, Gonzalez disparaged the justices and Collazo abandoned his test cases for electoral politics. Yet Degetau kept the faith. With Degetau's retirement in 1905, Puerto Ricans lost their most fervent advocate for pursuing legal strategies to win U.S. citizenship. Maybe the political turn that Degetau's successors took would prove more successful.

5

Reconstructing Puerto Rico, 1904–1909

By 1905 the United States had established the empire that dared not speak its name. In Puerto Rico, the Philippines, and a string of possessions with smaller populations, it had installed a patchwork of undemocratic governance schemes, with no central office to coordinate them.[1] This makeshift empire was governed by inconsistency and ad hoc compromise. Republican officials circumvented the restraints of the Reconstruction Constitution yet never entirely renounced them. They advocated uplift, rights, and procedural regularity yet also facilitated the exploitation of colonial workers in deference to capital. Democrats favored undemocratic governance of populations of color yet opposed federal power. They advocated release of the Philippines, whose residents they judged to be racially degraded, yet considered retaining Puerto Rico if its population proved itself "white enough" for self-government. The Supreme Court neither required citizenship, full rights, and eventual statehood for these new acquisitions, nor rejected the Reconstruction Constitution outright. Justices signaled that the Reconstruction Constitution neither forbade empire nor attached any daunting consequences to it. The result was an empire structured and stitched together expediently by competing interests and often inconsistent impulses.

Puerto Rican leaders saw that this empire at odds with itself was unstable and charted their next moves accordingly. Santiago Iglesias and Domingo Collazo both chose to join with powerful mainland allies – Iglesias would strengthen and deepen his partnership with the American Federation of Labor; Collazo would enlist mainland Democrats to his anticolonial cause by appealing to their loathing of federal interference with state-level governance. The Bureau of Insular Affairs, which had overseen U.S. military governance of Puerto Rico in 1899 and 1900, saw the confusion in the makeshift U.S. empire and sought to rationalize it by resuming responsibility for Puerto Rico. Its ambitious and energetic chief, Colonel Clarence Edwards, would spearhead this effort and ally with Republican administrations that advocated a colonial department that would oversee all of the U.S. empire.[2]

But as Federico Degetau had learned, the United States' particular form of colonialism was resilient. In fact its ambiguity, ambivalence, and inconsistency were its essential features, not problems in need of definitive resolution, and in some respects were the sources of its strength and resilience.

On 17 February 1904, American Federation of Labor president Samuel Gompers looked toward the San Juan dock from the deck of the SS *Coamo* and "easily discerned" his colleague and warm friend Santiago Iglesias waiting for him there. In a coup for which Iglesias had empire partly to thank, the overextended AFL president was going to spend five weeks unionizing island agricultural workers.[3]

Gompers had opposed empire as inconsistent with his focus on white men in the trades, which he had used to quadruple AFL membership. But empire had arrived all the same. Annexation of Hawai'i, Puerto Rico, Guam, American Samoa, and the Philippines were faits accomplis. *Downes v. Bidwell* (1901) and the Philippines Organic Act (1902) signaled that empire could continue indefinitely. *Gonzales v. Williams* (1904) expressly authorized Puerto Rican (and perhaps Filipino) labor migration regardless of citizenship. U.S. oversight and governance overseas also continued to expand, now without sovereignty. In 1903 the United States supported Panamanian independence from Colombia and then secured sole control of a special canal-construction zone there. President Roosevelt soon announced a new corollary to the Monroe Doctrine: to prevent European interference, the United States would resolve its neighbors' debt defaults and internal disorders. These moves were related. As Elihu Root explained, "dominant influence" over the "route to the Panama Canal" was "the true justification and necessity for the Monroe Doctrine." When the Dominican Republic's foreign debt soared, the United States seized that nation's fiscal reins by taking over its customs houses. Following major protests in Cuba against blatant voting fraud, the United States reoccupied the country for three years.[4]

Unable to prevent such foreign adventures, Gompers and the AFL sought to mitigate them by emulating them. By organizing colonial workers in Puerto Rico, the AFL could insulate mainland members from competition. It could slow islanders' out-migration and increase stateside migrants' willingness to join unions. Puerto Rico was also the vanguard of what would grow into a Monroe Doctrine for labor. Although adamant about its own autonomy with respect to foreign labor movements, the AFL was expanding abroad. In late 1905 Gompers touted AFL "international unions" in Canada, Hawai'i, Cuba, Mexico, the Philippines, British Columbia, and, of course, Puerto Rico. Iglesias figured prominently in Gompers's ambitions to expand further into Latin America. He spearheaded the drive to produce Spanish-language AFL materials and provided Gompers with trusted counsel. Through Iglesias's organizing campaign, the AFL might be able to organize the Spanish-speaking masses for the first time.[5]

Working with Iglesias in Puerto Rico could also strengthen the AFL's defense against new, more radical labor currents. Mass strikes were rocking Europe and Latin America in these years. Anarcho-syndicalists played key roles in some; others were associated with the 1905 Russian Revolution. In the United States, the Industrial Workers of the World (IWW) eschewed AFL-style trade unionism in favor of "one big union" of all wage laborers. It also condemned color lines and opposed capitalism. These commitments could be attractive to radical island labor leaders, Puerto Rico's sugarcane workers, the island's racially diverse workforce more broadly, stateside agricultural laborers, and other unorganized workers on the mainland. Backing Iglesias could consolidate the AFL's dominant position in Puerto Rico, mitigate the IWW threat, display the union's concern for farm laborers, and demonstrate its ability to garner members outside of the trades.[6]

But even with AFL support, labor organizing in Puerto Rico presented major challenges. For the first two decades of the twentieth century, unemployment never dipped below 17 percent. Beset by recurring, almost structural, economic desperation, unemployed laborers had strong incentives to cross picket lines. Government favoritism toward capital bred repression. With the explosion of U.S. investment in Puerto Rico, agribusiness had insinuated itself into the island's corridors of power. The first civil governor, Charles Allen, had made securing mainland investments in sugar production a priority, and the most recent secretary of Puerto Rico, Charles Hartzell, was now counsel for the Porto Rico Sugar Company. The island's political elite wanted its share of the soaring wealth and thus sympathized with capital. In addition, internal conflicts continued to plague labor. As Iglesias and his urban, artisan-based union sought to organize sugar industry workers, who had long been associated with slavery and blackness, the Republicano-aligned Federación Regional de Trabajadores charged that he ignored and exacerbated the particular plight of workers of color.[7]

These were all formidable challenges, but the fields were ripe for unionization. Iglesias's Federación Libre was as ready for the work as it had ever been. Sugar was now king in Puerto Rico, and tobacco was also booming. U.S. tariff walls ensured preferable access to mainland markets for both island products. U.S. corporations expanded their holdings in these sectors, consolidating both industries and bringing the construction of some of the world's largest sugar mills. Sugar corporations became landlords, shopkeepers, and creditors to their employees. Such centralized control had the unintended consequence of creating favorable conditions for collective action: concentrated employers, standardized pay and conditions, and close communication among workers. Iglesias's Federación Libre had itself experienced rapid growth, secured Unionista allies, and gained a modicum of legitimacy under U.S.-influenced law.[8]

When he arrived in San Juan, Gompers promoted Iglesias's organizing efforts. Meeting with the governor, he deployed his familiar mainland strategy. He countered capital's influence by appealing to government's desire for impartial governance and higher standards of living. A conference with Unionista party head Luis Muñoz Rivera strengthened the anti-Republicano collaboration between Muñoz Rivera and Iglesias. Gompers also tackled the rift between Iglesias and the Federación Regional, though his efforts were undercut by the Federación Regional's opposition to racism, its enmity toward Iglesias, and Gompers's history of indifference toward mainland workers of color. Federación Regional leaders refused to merge into an organization headed by Iglesias, but Gompers refused to remove or demote him. When Federación Regional members interrogated Gompers about African American workers in the AFL, he declared: "The American Federation of Labor is the living aggressive organization and factor in American affairs to stand for the equal right [*sic*] of the Negro workingmen." In reality, the AFL condoned some member unions' exclusion of African Americans. Worse yet, Gompers blamed the victims, saying that one consequence of the legacy of stateside "slavery" was "the unpreparedness of the colored people" for "trade unionism."[9]

Together, Gompers and Iglesias exposed low wages in Puerto Rico, encouraged labor demand, and maneuvered to reduce the island's labor supply. Though he was no stranger to deprivation, Gompers was shocked by islanders' poverty: "I saw more misery and hunger ... in Porto Rico than I have ever seen in all my life, and I hope I may be spared from seeing the like again." Hunger stalked the countryside like the mythical bloodsucking chupacabra, a constant threat that could materialize almost instantly. To increase labor demand, Gompers and Iglesias sought to revive coffee exports, albeit in a market decimated by global oversupply and lack of U.S. tariff protection. Gompers praised Puerto Rican coffee; Iglesias pursued tariff protection and a union label of approval. The two men also lobbied to have Puerto Ricans work on the massive canal construction project in the U.S.-run Panama Canal Zone. Mindful of the risks revealed in the earlier migration to Hawai'i, they seized the opportunity in this case to bend the supply–demand curve in island workers' favor. Doing so had the further benefit to the AFL of redirecting potential Puerto Rican labor migration away from the mainland and toward the Canal.[10]

Gompers spent the bulk of his visit traveling around the island and organizing workers. Throughout, Iglesias stood at his side – translating, hosting, advising, representing, and reaping benefits from their close association. By the end of 1904 the men reported that 60,000 fieldworkers and forty-three unions had joined the island's labor movement.[11]

With AFL support, labor leaders in House of Delegates seats, and tens of thousands of workers behind him, Iglesias envisioned a comprehensive labor campaign that would include striking against employers and lobbying the federal government. Iglesias's congressional priorities were self-government and citizenship. Home rule would multiply the benefits of labor's electoral gains. According to Iglesias, U.S. rule and especially Gompers's visit had increased workers' rights to protest and associate. Citizenship would complete the process by providing islanders with the "same rights and privileges possessed by the people of all other states and territories." The campaign achieved a major success when, in 1904, Gompers demanded citizenship for Puerto Ricans, notwithstanding the possibility left open just months before in *Gonzales v. Williams* that Congress could subject noncitizen nationals to new immigration controls. Gompers did not recommend citizenship for Filipinos, for several reasons. He had a commitment to Iglesias, personal experiences and relationships with many Puerto Ricans, optimism about Iglesias's campaign, lingering hopes for the deannexation of the Philippines, and ambitions to organize other Latin American workers. Challenging expansionist Republicans' demeaning familial metaphors, Gompers declared: "It is an outrage ... to treat Porto Rico as a stepchild in the family of Uncle Sam."[12]

Although this endorsement strengthened Iglesias's hand with Congress in Washington, it had no immediate consequences. The Republican majority was divided on the extension of citizenship to Puerto Ricans. The Roosevelt administration and its congressional allies supported citizenship, but only because they thought it an easy and inexpensive way to placate islanders and thereby shore up colonial rule. In a letter soon to be shared with Congress, the secretary and future governor of Puerto Rico, Regis Post, praised citizenship as a "perfectly empty gift." Every thoughtful Puerto Rican "bitterly resents not being American citizens," he wrote, and because islanders already enjoyed what he saw as its key benefits, citizenship was safe to extend. In contrast, were the same Puerto Ricans to be new immigrants from abroad, they would be a "menace to our nation" and unfit for naturalization. Roosevelt agreed. He supported naturalizing Puerto Ricans even as he announced that they had the "largest measure of self-government that can with safety be given at the present." He envisioned a path to uplift through tutelage, not self-help. Many lawmakers concurred in the concession to an island that occupied a strategic location in relation to the future Panama Canal and could showcase U.S. methods of rule in Latin America. In the first half of 1906, Senate and House committees recommended granting Puerto Ricans citizenship, without recommending additional home rule. Lawmakers reasoned that citizenship for Puerto Ricans no longer threatened to create a "precedent" potentially "prejudicial to ... legislation for the Philippines." Nor were many rights or obligations embedded in that status. Perhaps travel documents or federal courts would become more accessible, but Puerto Ricans already swore to support the Constitution and were subject to U.S. laws.[13] This was a reversal of Justice Edward Douglass White's logic in the 1901 *Downes v. Bidwell* concurrence. There, White had reasoned that citizenship, which he knew carried few judicially enforceable rights, was nonetheless too consequential to extend to racially inferior peoples. Citizenship thus revealed itself to be all things – or nothing – to all people, too valuable to grant and yet too inconsequential to withhold.

Lawmakers had Puerto Rican proponents of citizenship in the constitutional and racial crosshairs. If citizenship was inconsequential, then seeking it was irrational – and hence evidence of racial inferiority. Presuming a baseline of U.S. rationality and practicality, colonial officials labeled the desire for citizenship emotional, and the people who "keenly felt" its denial "sentimental." But officials conceded that citizenship was not empty when they described the "practical" injury that each Puerto Rican suffered as a "man without a country" when abroad. Puerto Ricans were already treated as citizens when traveling, so "man without a country" was instead a code phrase. It referred to the psychological harm described in Edward Everett Hale's still popular 1863 story of the same name, in which the protagonist is sentenced to live out his life aboard U.S. naval vessels, never again to see or hear about his home country, the United States. He becomes "nervous, tired," and "heart-wounded," suffering in exile as a loyal American denied his national belonging.[14]

Puerto Ricans were correct that citizenship mattered, but this only made it harder to achieve. U.S. officials' presumptions about Puerto Ricans' degraded racial condition underlay islanders' legal and political subordination. Such officials were unlikely to extend Puerto Ricans consequential citizenship unless they could be convinced to change their evaluations of Puerto Ricans as a people. A representative of Unionista and Republicano mayors tried to convince them when he declared to Congress that Puerto Ricans "have shown all the qualifications" for the "high honor." Similarly, congressional proponents of citizenship cited the "high intelligence and culture" of Puerto Ricans in judging them as "worthy of the recognition" as citizens as U.S.-citizen Hawaiians. However, Republican speaker and so-called czar of the House, Joseph Cannon, worked from a similar premise to a different end. He declared Puerto Ricans unprepared for self-government and killed the citizenship bill.[15]

Congress did remove Puerto Ricans' humiliating ineligibility to naturalize. But even that modest concession reinforced Puerto Ricans' subordination. Before 1906, when Congress exempted nationals from the renunciation rule of the statute, some courts judged Puerto Ricans unable to naturalize because they had no foreign allegiance to renounce. At an AFL convention Iglesias described one court's absurd workaround: the Puerto Rican applicant had to renounce allegiance to the Republic of Puerto Rico, thereby renouncing the very U.S. polity he sought to join. The act also limited the power to naturalize to state and territorial courts of general jurisdiction. Puerto Rico had a U.S. district court of general jurisdiction that had long naturalized aliens. Because the U.S. attorney general had declared Puerto Rico to be organized territory, the court's judge asked the federal Bureau of Immigration and Naturalization to send naturalization forms. Instead, the bureau declared that no court in Puerto Rico could naturalize anyone: island residents had to relocate to the mainland to become citizens.[16] Few did. The attempt to open citizenship to Puerto Ricans had thus exacerbated their island's exclusion.

With citizenship and self-government elusive, Iglesias gambled that sugar workers had in 1905 pointed the way to renewed change by winning higher wages through work stoppages. After all, the core of Iglesias's strategy was to organize workers and undertake labor activism to improve working conditions. Launching successful strikes could increase Iglesias's lobbying power in Washington, turn workers into an electoral constituency, and stake out expressive claims. Such success had appeared out of reach without workers' first gaining citizenship, expressive freedoms, or electoral power. But in 1906 immediate and successful strikes seemed possible, so perhaps the cart *could* come before the horse. Through strikes, islanders could stake claims to citizenship, rights, and political participation.[17]

Gompers prepared Iglesias to lead a model strike. He put the moral and financial authority of the AFL behind what he envisioned as a new front in his union's constitutional struggle to invigorate laborers' freedom of expression. The goal was winning rights that would enable workers to upset economic relations, stop production, and organize fellow employees. Clashes were inevitable. Colonial officials resembled many of their stateside counterparts in praising gains in standards of living but rejecting the tactics that unions used to achieve them. Their conceptions of expressive liberty ended at license to utter "subversive," "incendiary" words impeding "those that have wished to work" and at trespasses on planters' interests. Gompers told workers to resist and "exercise every lawful right to secure the rights to which they are undoubtedly entitled." They should hew to this vision of law and to nonviolence unwaveringly. Otherwise, he warned, a "wholesale attack" on strikers could follow. Labor leaders could contest repression by recording and protesting violations. The strategy he outlined paralleled that of organized mainland laborers, who used law, evidence, and publicity to advocate for and achieve stubbornly elusive rights. There were many vocal radicals in the Federación Libre, but Iglesias hoped that the union's more conservative reputation would help temper the confrontation.[18]

Gompers anticipated appeals to higher authorities after constitutional differences were resolved against workers on the ground. When an officer of the Insular Police asked a mass-meeting speaker, "Who have you asked permission to celebrate this meeting?" the speaker cited "the permission I had been given by the U.S. Constitution." The officer disbanded the meeting, and the speaker provided Iglesias with a sworn statement about the event. Iglesias also publicized complaints about the police arresting strikers en masse and preventing strike supporters from speaking with potential strikebreakers.[19]

Gompers was optimistic that workers would secure immediate gains, but he did not deem it crucial. He counseled one impatient island labor leader, "All the ills which have grown up in Porto Rico in four hundred years cannot be rectified in a day." The reality was that the workers were weak and vulnerable; planters and sympathetic officials, powerful and insulated. Employers had access to strikebreakers and mercenary muscle. The governor controlled the Insular

Police and oversaw lower island officials. The island's political class wielded official power to charge and convict. And the formal alliance between labor groups and the Partido Unionista seemed to have little influence, given the racist and antilabor sentiments of key Unionista leaders, one of whom analogized workers to an "inferior race of the Siberian orangutans," with "fetid bodily smells." Employers and the police forcibly dispersed, beat, shot at, injured, arrested, prosecuted, fined, imprisoned, and even killed striking workers and their allies. Iglesias brought complaints to the governor and to Gompers, and Gompers passed them on to the press and President Roosevelt. The charges were dramatic; the police and hired thugs had come out in force. Ignoring violence against strikers by employers and police officers, prosecutors brought flimsy charges against the strikers themselves, as well as their leaders and propagandists. Some were acquitted but others were subjected to mass trials, sometimes culminating in fines and prison terms, without receiving basic procedural rights such as counsel, the opportunity to question witnesses, and a neutral forum. When Roosevelt ordered an investigation, Puerto Rico's governor Beekman Winthrop denied everything and blamed strikers for all the violence. By this time Gompers and Roosevelt were on opposite sides of election campaigns involving antilabor Republicans in the House of Representatives. Iglesias now reported receiving "no guarantees" of expressive freedoms from Roosevelt or elsewhere, and the strike collapsed. Organizing gains on the island evaporated. Instead, with defeat, "persecution, injustices, misery, treacheries," violence, vulnerability, and "fear and ignorance" stalked the cane fields.[20]

Iglesias and Gompers stayed the course. At Gompers's request, Iglesias refuted Winthrop's denial with detailed accounts, sworn workers' declarations, telegrams, workers' acquittals, lawyers' statements, mass petitions, and evidence of nonprosecution of antistrike crimes. Gompers ratified the refutation and forwarded it to Roosevelt. Charging that "the most sacred public rights conceded to Puerto Rico by the American Constitution are day by day violated," Iglesias's labor newspaper asked labor to find "higher powers and superior courts" within the federal government to lend assistance. Although neither vindication nor renewed strikes seemed imminent, their pursuit of freedom of expression had other benefits, such as fusing Iglesias's and Gompers's constitutional projects. Winning citizenship would strengthen Puerto Rican workers' claims to expressive freedom, which in turn would increase the value of citizenship. The men's cooperation was evident when the AFL carried the case of a prolabor island newspaper editor convicted of libel to the Supreme Court on "free press" grounds. Iglesias gained the practical, short-term power to hold public meetings, as colonial officials rejected the occasional Spanish minister's or island mayor's attempts to silence island labor.[21]

A decline in race-based divisions among labor organizations was a silver lining of the defeat. Shared oppression bred cooperation between the two *federaciones*, Regional and Libre. When urban strikes involving some workers from each of the *federaciones* broke out, necessity forced the unions to work together. When neither Republicanos nor Unionistas lent labor substantial island-level support, Gompers facilitated inter-*federación* cooperation by assisting strikers. Soon the organizations merged, Iglesias broke with the Unionistas, and island organized labor largely departed from electoral politics.[22]

To rebuild organized labor, from 1907 to 1909 Iglesias made the risky and controversial choice to eschew industrial strife and electoral politics and put his faith in benevolent colonial rule. Labor activism had "absolutely failed," Iglesias and his colleagues declared. "Capitalists and politicians arm-in-arm with the trusts" were free to debase "90% of the population" and make the island "a factory worked by slaves." Instead, Iglesias and the Federación Libre counted on the capacity of imperial law and administration to hold local elites at bay. Iglesias still demanded citizenship and its "rights and privileges." But he did not accept the bilingual *Porto Rico Review*'s judgment that a "citizen" was "not a charge to be cared for." He sought bureaus of labor and sanitation for Puerto Rico and governance of the island akin to that of a protectorate or the "English colony, New Zealand."[23]

While Iglesias organized on the island, Domingo Collazo repositioned himself as a journalist-politician seeking constitutional rights, self-government, and citizenship for Puerto Ricans. From his base in New York, the avowed antiracist sought to step onto the national political stage without succumbing to the racism that characterized the players he found there.

He failed. Collazo reaffirmed his principles where he could and contorted himself to avoid directly betraying his ideals in other cases – and, all the same, he ended up compromising himself, sometimes by openly deploying racist rhetoric. Part of the problem was that he chose parties as allies based on their views about citizenship and self-government, and not their lack of racism. His copartisans were Unionistas and white-supremacist Democrats. The former all but endorsed racial hierarchy. The latter were suspicious of Puerto Ricans' claims to whiteness.

Collazo's choice of these allies was born of a desperate process of elimination. Although Collazo had joined the U.S. invasion and also facilitated his niece's Supreme Court test case, Puerto Ricans still lacked anything resembling the participatory governance that Cuban revolutionary leader José Martí had deemed the essence of political legitimacy. Not only did statehood remain beyond reach, but also unavailable were alternatives such as autonomy, Canadian-style home rule, territorial government as in Oklahoma or even Hawai'i, and Cuban-style self-government. Puerto Rico was instead, Collazo said, "nameless and humiliated before the world." In a comment that anticipated his accommodation with U.S. racism, he complained that a "Jamaican negro" could naturalize, but not a Puerto Rican.[24]

Turning to politics, Collazo had few good options. He had ties to top Republicanos, but their party was in decline and accommodated colonialism; Unionistas were the fiery majority party. On the mainland, he rejected Republicans, those "bloodhounds of imperialism" who implemented "autocratic laws." Republican lawmakers had not naturalized Puerto Ricans; Republican lawyers had fought his niece's suit; Republican Supreme Court appointees had declined to recognize Puerto Ricans as citizens. Democrats won Collazo's support by leaning toward the anti-imperialist position articulated by William Jennings Bryan, whom prominent Antillean *independistas* had once supported.[25]

Next, Collazo went about the task of writing and organizing his way into Democratic and Unionista politics and a place among U.S. and Latin American journalists. In 1904 he organized Puerto Ricans with U.S. citizenship into a Puerto Rico American League to support "full American citizenship" for all islanders. In his writing, he had a knack for trenchant political commentary as well as sensational reports on such topics as German nudists and children who emitted electricity. Building on his relationship with the Partido Unionista, he secured a regular column in the island's most popular newspaper, the pro-Unionista *La Democracia*. Latin American newspapers soon provided him a larger platform. In 1908 Collazo served as one of Puerto Rico's delegates to the Democratic national convention, after which he joined the committee to notify Bryan of his nomination as the party's standard-bearer. He then served as secretary of a pro-Bryan Puerto Rican political club whose founders also included a one-time revolutionary colleague.[26]

Collazo's transition to nonjudicial venues and activities was propitious. In a string of cases between 1903 and 1905 that concerned subordinated and racially defined communities, the Supreme Court issued decisions that elevated evasion and deference to nonjudicial officials above rights and participation. Collazo's niece's suit was one. As he recalled, the Court provided no "explication of the island's status." Nobody, "least of all the Court," knew when it would. Other groups fared worse. The constitutional right to a jury trial was inoperative in the Philippines, by far the most populous territory, although it did apply in sparsely inhabited Alaska. The formal reason for the difference in Alaska was that the Alaska cession treaty naturalized nonnative residents and thus (presumably irrevocably) extended constitutional rights to that largely white population. But no such irrevocable rights were articulated in other cases, with nonwhite groups. *Lone Wolf v. Hitchcock* (1903), for example, allowed Congress to revoke treaty guarantees to American Indians at will. According to the Court, from American Indians' federally imposed "weakness and helplessness ... there arises the duty of protection, and with it the power." Dependence and obligation produced and were produced by subordination. In contrast, however, in *Giles v. Harris* (1903) the Court declared itself powerless to intervene when "the great mass of the white population" in a state "intends to keep the blacks from voting." In supporting the apparent nullification of the Fifteenth Amendment, many Northern and Republican newspapers braided metaphors of infancy and savagery with white supremacists' false indictments of Reconstruction. *Harper's Weekly* argued that empire presented a "problem identical with ... the Reconstruction period," which, "thanks to ... the Insular Cases, we have solved ... far more wisely." Whatever the case, these decisions reveal a doctrinal and judicial capriciousness in the interpretation of citizenship and rights, the primary coherence of which resided in the underpinning logic of race and racism.[27]

Within this new doctrinal landscape, Roosevelt and his party's promise of citizenship was what Collazo called a "gold brick," an apparently valuable item that was really worthless. Citizenship would not constrain U.S. rule in Puerto Rico because the increasingly influential *Insular Cases* had rights resting on the status of places rather than of people. Even citizens from the mainland lost rights when they landed in Puerto Rico. Republicanos erred in asserting that, as a matter of law, naturalization alone would transform the island's "colonial servitude" into what "is enjoyed in the Territories" acquired before the Civil War. The truth was that Roosevelt "consider[ed] Porto Ricans an inferior race" and had no plans to extend self-government to the island. The president's proffered citizenship was a "sonorous word without meaning."[28]

Puerto Rico's subordination should stand as a "'horrendous warning scarecrow'" to Latin America, Collazo asserted. The island was but one part of Republican administrations' ambition to establish "continental hegemony" throughout "Hispano-America." The policy, known as "dollar diplomacy," combined exploitative private U.S. investments, corrupt dealings, and deployment of economic, diplomatic, and military power. In Collazo's words, Central America was already falling "under a Republican protectorate." Financial ties would soon subject Haiti to U.S. rule. Cuba was "gravely injured by its pseudo caretakers in Washington." Santo Domingo sacrificed its international existence to a U.S. receivership. The Panama Canal Zone showcased the United States' "magnificent power," and further dollar diplomacy was inevitable.[29]

The Democrats' hazy promise that self-government was just over the horizon enticed an otherwise disillusioned Collazo. Presuming that Democrats would elevate anti-imperialism above anti–Puerto Rican racism, he declared that the redemption of Puerto Rico was imminent. Judicial unwillingness to enforce the constraints on empire in the Reconstruction Constitution created a political flexibility that Collazo now celebrated. Democrats opposed Republicans' "policy of colonial exploitation." The Democratic platform demanded traditional territorial status for Puerto Rico. Even though Republicans cynically claimed that the Constitution would then require financially ruinous taxes uniform with those in the states, the Republicans' own "exotic" governance "outside the U.S. Constitution" suggested that constitutional bounds were not so rigid.[30]

What Collazo did not emphasize and sometimes seemed at pains to avoid acknowledging was that Democrats were unreliable allies. First, they had not won a presidential election since 1892. Second, they had never administered the island empire. If and when they did, Puerto Rico might not be the priority island. As Collazo and his niece Isabel Gonzalez observed, Puerto Rican residents lacked the federal voting rights to attract the attention of mainlanders "deeply absorbed in their own problems." And if Democrats did turn to Puerto Rico, their doubts about Puerto Ricans' capacity for self-government could overwhelm their weak anti-imperialism, which was rooted less in an ethic of fairness than in the protection of their states from federal overreach and the protection of the nation from Filipinos (although judicial acquiescence in colonialism had already largely defused the latter concern).[31]

With Democrats out of power, Collazo was betting on their future successes and sympathies, but every passing year made the specter of Reconstruction animating Democrats' anti-imperialism more distant. Even so, from 1902 to 1908 Collazo's gamble made some sense. Democrats were still sufficiently worried about losing power in the South to pursue African American disfranchisement. Canonization of white-supremacist accounts of Reconstruction was well under way, though far from complete.[32]

Like Collazo, Unionistas eschewed law for politics and Republicans for Democrats. In lieu of total resistance to imperialism, Luis Muñoz Rivera and his colleagues sought to exploit the Democratic Party's vociferous opposition to Reconstruction and its celebration of the ensuing Redemption. Their strategy was to cast themselves as victims of federal aggrandizement in need of rescue. They told island voters and leaders in Puerto Rico and on the mainland that a new Reconstruction was under way in Puerto Rico. When Republicanos had been in power, Muñoz Rivera's New York–based, bilingual Spanish-English *Puerto Rico Herald* newspaper, which circulated by mail throughout the Americas, had announced: "We study history and see ... the scandals of the South repeated" in the "similarity between the *carpet-baggers* of the South and the *carpet-baggers* of Puerto Rico." Soon, "a thundering torrent of justice" from Washington would allow Muñoz Rivera and his colleagues to "redeem" Puerto Rico, just as the "South peacefully overcame its wretched exploiters." Unionistas here aligned their own constitutional concerns with those of Democrats by focusing on ostensibly tyrannical, violent, and racially inflected denials of home rule. They refashioned themselves into a legitimate, temporarily displaced and oppressed political class of whites, ready and able to govern a local population of color. Amid official reports of voter fraud in Republicanos' favor in 1902, these Reconstruction metaphors cast Republicanos as scalawag collaborators and Republican appointees on the island as carpetbaggers. Their common government was black Republican misrule.[33]

This was a risky analogy and electoral strategy in racially diverse Puerto Rico. Republicano opponents had returned near-universal manhood suffrage to Puerto Rico and called themselves the "party of the men of color" and Lincoln. In contrast, many Unionistas were open racial chauvinists. *La Democracia* tarred opponents as slaves who owed their "liberties and rights" to the "sacrifices of a generation of patriots" aligned with Muñoz Rivera. The Republicano indictment that the self-proclaimed "son of Spain" Muñoz Rivera was for *los blancos* (the whites) was credible, even though Muñoz Rivera could claim to be repurposing his pragmatic Spanish-era tactic of aligning with an otherwise-objectionable party to secure autonomy.[34]

Unionistas did not rebut mainlanders' doubts about Puerto Ricans' racial provenance by denying racial hierarchy. Instead, they asserted their elevated status within the hierarchy. They drew inspiration from Mormons, Cubans, and Boers, all of whom demanded autonomy and respect despite racially inflected Anglo or U.S. disparagement. In 1904 the Unionistas particularly focused on Japan and its victories in the Russo-Japanese War. *La Democracia* narrated that an island people once "contemptuously called ... monkeys" and denied recognition among "civilized nations" had now overawed a European opponent. Readers would have been familiar with the notion that Puerto Ricans had traded decadent Spanish neglect for modern, ascendant, and coercive U.S. power and now sought self-government. *La Democracia* described Japan as merely one step ahead: "Two centuries of lethargy" there preceded concessions to Western powers that had only recently ended with "restoration of the Mikado Power." The men of letters who were overrepresented among the political elite of militarily weak Puerto Rico could also take comfort in Japan's insistence that it be measured by its contributions to knowledge, not as a "fighting people only." Importantly, *La Democracia* cast Japanese achievements as representing ascendance within civilizational hierarchies, not challenges to them.[35]

Collazo struggled to infuse Unionistas' analogies with antiracism, but the attempt proved nearly incoherent. Collazo's frequent references to carpetbaggers recalled island *criollos'* Spanish-era resentments toward *peninsulares'* outsize role in Puerto Rican governance. Less convincing was his argument that Bryan, the Democrats, and the South did not disdain Puerto Ricans and revered Abraham Lincoln as the "true redeemer."[36]

Collazo had more success melding anti-imperialism and antiracism with the example of Japan. Focusing on the Japanese diaspora within the United States, he criticized the racism displayed by both sides. In early 1907 Japan complained about San Francisco's segregation of Japanese schoolchildren. Aware that "only the blacks and the Chinese sit in separate schools," the Japanese demanded classroom seats alongside the "Italians, Germans, and Jews." One compromise under consideration would have ended Japanese segregation in San Francisco schools while also reducing future Japanese immigration by subjecting it to severe restrictions modeled on those on Chinese travelers. Experienced with coercive and dishonoring immigration bars, Collazo wrote that he doubted the Japanese would want to "jump *from the frying pan*" of segregation "*into the fire*" of "meanness at U.S. ports." He predicted that the Japanese would invade the Philippines before accepting segregation in the United States. After Collazo penned the piece, the nations instead reached a "gentleman's agreement" that simultaneously ended anti-Japanese segregation in San Francisco schools and halted most issuances by Japan of passports to its United States–bound labor migrants. Collazo condemned Japanese racism as well. In lauding Japanese workers, he reported, Japanese newspapers in Hawai'i "spit" on Puerto Ricans as an inferior "'hybrid race.'" Declaring humanity "equal everywhere," Collazo exempted the racists themselves: "Perhaps the Californians are not wrong to oppose a flood of such yellow monkeys" as the Japanese.[37]

The racial slur was telling. Collazo was a Unionista, a one-time artisan, a fixture within the New York labor community, and a supporter of island workers at a moment of tension between Unionistas and the Federación Libre. Anti-Asian sentiment was one issue that could bridge the divide. Unionistas were not radical racial egalitarians. Gompers had coauthored a racist tract subtitled *American Manhood against Asiatic Coolieism*, and Collazo aligned with both sides by supporting two causes that rested on claims to U.S. membership: tariff protection for island-grown coffee, and citizenship for Puerto Ricans. The first meant joining the Federación Libre and Partido Unionista in bucking the Democratic Party's commitment to low tariffs, though perhaps only insofar as Republicans could maintain tariff protection for other domestic industries. Addressing congressmen and readers in New York and Puerto Rico, Collazo predicted that coffee protection would create and confirm membership and reciprocal allegiance. Were Puerto Ricans truly part of the United States, he reasoned, their coffee would be as American as Louisiana sugar and thus entitled to similar insulation from the vicissitudes of free trade. With the island's coffee industry on the verge of ruin, a protectionist tariff would rescue Puerto Ricans, elicit their gratitude, and thereby deepen their allegiance. Collazo added that stronger reciprocal duties of protection and allegiance long associated with citizenship were also reasons to employ Puerto Ricans in Panama Canal construction, as Gompers and Iglesias advocated. Envisioning such work as a step toward naturalization, he foresaw the government thereby securing a "hard-working, loyal and peaceful citizen."[38]

Antipathy toward Republicans, however, provided Collazo with an opportunity to synthesize his political alliances, artisan identity, and antiracism. One key reason was the AFL's turn toward electoral politics. As employers' antilabor lawyers and injunctions threatened to cripple unions, the AFL sought legislation to combat the court rulings. The union unsuccessfully opposed Republican speaker of the House Cannon's 1906 reelection.[39]

The anti-Republican alliance provided Collazo with an outlet for speaking against racism, albeit one secured only through willful blindness to Democrats' white supremacy. According to Collazo and an ally, Cannon treated Puerto Ricans as "negroes," too "ignorant" for citizenship or self-government. So did other Republican lawmakers. Collazo levied similar critiques against Republican presidents. Making no mention of Democrats' racism, he predicted waves of anti-Republican protest votes after Roosevelt's unfounded decision to discharge three companies of African American soldiers for a shooting death in Brownsville, Texas. Collazo was closer to Cuban revolutionary José Martí than to any Democrat when he criticized Taft for acceding to the "imbecile preoccupations" of two white officials who objected to traveling alongside a colleague of color. He also agreed with Unionista resident commissioner Tulio Larrinaga that officials' "persistent desire" to judge those denied self-government as inferior was a way to hide "some injustice, some moral wrong that it is necessary to cover, to justify."[40] Of course, the observation applied doubly to Democrats' treatment of African Americans.

The problem with waiting for Democratic redemption was that the 1904, 1906, and 1908 elections left Republicans in control of the federal government. As Collazo observed, Puerto Ricans had become "Sisyphus, forever rolling the boulder of our destiny" upward, only to see it "tumble and tumble again heavily into the abyss." With little to show for a decade of relative patience and no federal vote, Unionistas had "no other means of . . . protection than their own rights." Their primary weapon was control of the House of Delegates, which could prevent any budget from passing. In early 1909 delegates passed bills to tilt governance and patronage toward islanders. When the presidentially appointed Executive Council rejected the proposals, the House stonewalled the budget. Unionistas anticipated a punitive Republican response but hoped to rally U.S. opinion, secure a congressional hearing, sway some lawmakers, and avoid electoral backlash. If they were successful, greater self-government and more congenial colonial administrators might follow later.[41]

The crisis benefited Collazo. He acted as translator and secretary to Unionistas who secured meetings concerning the protest with President Taft, Secretary of the Interior Richard Ballinger, lawmakers, a Supreme Court litigator, a congressional committee, and reporters. Collazo cited the position in seeking entrée to the Senate's manager of Puerto Rican legislation, Republican Chauncey Depew of New York. Collazo's *La Democracia* column reported his pro-Unionista efforts, mainland expertise, and impressive access to the corridors of power. He also updated readers on presidential, congressional, and media responses to the protest for home rule.[42]

President Taft made the protest a reason to withhold self-government, and characterized Puerto Ricans as a race unfit for democracy. "Porto Rico has been the favored daughter of the United States," receiving "education" in governing itself. The metaphor cast Puerto Rico as the female child of the United States, invoking a double dependence that could only be half cured by time. Taft proposed that prior Puerto Rican budgets stay in place until subsequent ones replaced them, as was done in Hawai'i and the Philippines.[43]

The debate over Taft's proposal gave Collazo and other Unionistas an opportunity to build and consolidate support, especially among Democrats. As always, the tactic pitted Democrats' racism against their declining fear of federal power. Unionistas succeeded with Representative John Martin of Colorado, who ratified their account of the budget standoff and advocated a *"genuine home-ruling"* Puerto Rico rather than a "'carpetbag government' ... over whose selection the people governed have no voice." But, Martin observed, many mainlanders' "sense of vast superiority" over Puerto Ricans undermined support for island self-government. As during earlier legislative debates, racial disparagement of Puerto Ricans was bipartisan.[44]

Collazo and his Unionista allies remained hopeful about their longer-term prospects, but for the moment Taft's condemnation had brought Unionistas bad press. Congress enacted Taft's proposal to retain the prior year's budget until a new budget was passed that permitted the island's government to function even without the House of Delegates' consent. Collazo saw little hope that Taft would support Puerto Rican self-government. He echoed the New York *Sun*'s view that Taft was nostalgic for his days among the *"carpet baggers"* in the Philippines because "'it is not the same to be president of a republic as boss and lord of colonies.'" Still, Unionista leaders said that they'd won new congressional allies.[45] Collazo continued to predict that Democratic control of the national government would bring a "redemption" like that the party claimed to have secured in the South in reaction to Reconstruction, but the test was years away.

While Iglesias and Collazo were pursuing strategies centered outside the executive branch, Bureau of Insular Affairs chief Clarence Edwards sought to elevate himself and his office within it. He aspired to transform his bureaucracy within the War Department into a separate colonial department whose head would sit alongside the Secretary of War in the president's cabinet. Regaining oversight of United States–Puerto Rico relations was a crucial step toward centralizing all the U.S. empire under his control.

Edwards's plans were grand ones for an organization that began its existence in 1898 as the Division of Customs and Insular Affairs. When Congress created a civil government for Puerto Rico, the division lacked a long-standing career chief with the political muscle and institutional incentive to defend and expand its jurisdiction. Secretary of War Elihu Root remedied this with Edwards's appointment. Root felt that Edwards had positioned the agency to take on all of the duties that other countries assigned to their "colonial office." The mid-1902 Philippines Organic Act rewarded the transformation by elevating the division to a bureau. At a stroke, Edwards was put in charge of overseeing the bulk of lands and people within the formal U.S. oceanic empire and a substantial part, although not the majority, of its trade.[46]

Edwards had impressive connections, a West Point degree, ambition, and nearly two decades of advancement within the military. His army experience included training soldiers, managing information, and pacifying putative racial inferiors. By expanding his family's already impressive political ties and reaping their benefits, he had risen quickly within the army. Like many soldiers of his generation, he had served in the West as the army fought wars to subdue once-autonomous native nations. In the early 1890s he was praised as a military instructor at St. John's College (now Fordham University) before securing a desirable posting to the Military Information Division. He finished the decade as part of the anti-insurgency campaign in the Philippines, where he came under fire more than a hundred times and was repeatedly cited for gallantry.[47]

Edwards drew from these experiences as he built on Elihu Root's legal foundation. Under Edwards, the Bureau of Insular Affairs compiled masses of data on the colonies that it administered, made that information available to interested parties, and publicized the accomplishment. Soon, the bureau was a clearinghouse for colonial information. Newspapers reported on the many bureau clerks who organized, retrieved, and circulated the data, praising them as "experts in the matter of finance, the laws, the language, the method of record and all legislation either by or for such dependencies." The clerks produced fastidiously indexed files that eventually occupied 2,500 cubic feet of storage space. Edwards's ally Republican representative Herbert Parsons of New York advised that anyone seeking "assured facts in regard to any matter in the Philippines can ascertain them from this bureau." The value of the service became especially apparent when lawmakers, administrators, and others sought information on other colonies. The Washington *Evening Star* reported: "Not a day passes that many persons do not call at the insular bureau to inquire something about Porto Rican affairs, although it has ... nothing to do with that island." But there was nowhere else to turn. The *Washington Post* joked that the alternative was to approach "all the departments, bureaus, commissions, and institutions," whereby the information seeker would be "bound to learn much, even if it is not directly applicable to his question."[48]

The Bureau of Insular Affairs positioned itself as a repository of best colonial and dollar-diplomacy practices. It assumed that all U.S. colonies were unfit for self-government. President Roosevelt agreed, announcing that colonial people did not respect majority rule or minority rights. Under the circumstances, and still committed to retaining the new possessions and their populations, he favored federal tutelage. Influential reformers who gathered as "friends of the Indian and other dependent peoples" similarly saw a need for Puerto Rican uplift by the United States, and Edwards agreed with them. Edwards's law officer, Paul Charlton, pointed out that a colonial office could prevent conflicting precedents or theories of administration, as well as the duplication of activities. One governor of Puerto Rico declared that bureau oversight would "insure a uniform policy of administration, the value of which can not be overestimated."[49]

The bureau held itself out as a much-needed liaison and intermediary between colonial officials and the mainland, including Congress. Charlton and Parsons claimed that the bureau provided the Philippines invaluable services by lobbying for "legislation desired and needed" and by acting as the mainland agent for "their financial operations, the purchase of supplies, the securing of employees, etc.," while other possessions "suffered" as "orphans without any sympathetic bureau to assist them." When the officials in those lands saw the bureau's "successful and beneficent results," the men claimed, they tried to utilize the bureau and put themselves under its direction. In Hawaiian affairs, the absence of the bureau meant there was no check on other federal departments' "rapacity" in excluding local authorities from valuable waterfront real estate. Lacking access to the bureau or a federal vote, Alaska languished. Though Guam was annexed for its harbor, the press reported that the island struggled to secure appropriations to make the harbor safe. Indeed, reporters noted that its mere mention during cabinet meetings "brings out laughter." Another article lamented that each cablegram from Puerto Rico had "no one to whom it can go short of the president." Parsons explained that no bureau helped Puerto Rico sell bonds, seek aid or advice, or secure executive or administrative action or congressional legislation on the mainland. "What is everybody's business is nobody's business," he said.[50]

Finally, under Edwards the bureau established itself as the preeminent legal authority on empire. It recruited first-rate lawyers, claimed the entire law of empire as its bailiwick, emphasized legal complexities that made its legal expertise valuable, and seized opportunities to provide outside counsel. Its first law officer was Charles Magoon. His published legal analyses found support in the 1901 *Insular Cases*, ran to three editions in 1902–1903, and won him promotion to general counsel and then governor of the Panama Canal Zone. His replacement, Paul Charlton, was rewarded for his sterling performance with an appointment to a district court judgeship. The pair tackled a broad set of legal problems that arose from expansion. Where modern scholars vary, and count from three to twenty-one cases under the umbrella of the *Insular Cases* between 1901 and 1906, a War Department memorandum identified forty-four. In the bureau's hands, breadth created nuance. According to Charlton, the positions of the noncontiguous territories "are so anomalous and irreconcilable with each other that no general rule for the application of the Constitution or laws" to them existed. Their peoples occupied equally uncertain positions. Puerto Ricans and Filipinos were nonaliens of either "non-descript citizenship" or noncitizenship. Stranger yet, they could not naturalize prior to 1906. According to Charlton, the naturalization statute applied only to aliens, which Puerto Ricans and

Filipinos were not. It required renouncing foreign allegiance, which colonials' U.S. allegiance foreclosed. It also demanded five years' residence in the United States, which did not encompass Puerto Rico or the Philippines. The difficulty of the legal landscape brought a substantial volume of work, and "legal questions affecting insular matters" flowed to the bureau from Washington and the colonies. Eminent administrative law scholar Ernst Freund, for example, requested an explication of the bureaucracy of empire, and the Interstate Commerce Commission asked for interpretation of the word *territory* in its statute. The bureau drafted, edited, and evaluated congressional bills, including those opening oaths of naturalization to Puerto Ricans.[51] In effect, bureau lawyers functioned as a federal law office for empire before Congress ratified that role.

The bureau implemented these services in the Philippines and advertised them within and beyond official Washington. Its primary constituency was not the private sector but political actors seeking a better-administered empire. Executive-branch officials were thrilled; opponents of empire were not. As U.S. authority outside the states grew, potential battlegrounds included both the post–Civil War acquisitions of Alaska, Hawai'i, Puerto Rico, Guam, and American Samoa, and Caribbean nations such as Panama, Cuba, and the Dominican Republic, where the United States was now intruding on sovereign prerogatives.[52]

Republican executives sought to transform the Bureau of Insular Affairs into a colonial office like those at the helm of European empires, but Democrats frustrated all such attempts from 1903 to early 1909. One supporter reasoned: "Uncle Sam now has many and vast colonial interests, and must provide the machinery and means to develop and govern them, or they will be hindrance rather than a help." Representative Parsons urged abandoning what he depicted as the discredited French model of cross-departmental distribution of colonial responsibility, advocating instead the centralized British colonial office model, which Parsons claimed hastened self-government. Congressional anti-imperialists heard fighting words, interpreting such recommendations as a declaration that "the colonial system of the United States has been established permanently." As Collazo put it, it was a declaration of an intent to institutionalize the "universal Empire of the United States." Some still hoped that statehood, traditional territorial status, or independence would soon reach the outlying possessions; if the inept running of the empire hastened its collapse, all the better. The danger was competent centralization that expanded and entrenched colonialism. Proponents of centralization used the euphemism "insular" for "colonial," knowing the latter term "might arouse some prejudice."[53]

In an attempt to overcome congressional paralysis, the bureau dramatically expanded its reach by participating in the U.S. turn from formal expansion to informal modes of control. The executive branch withheld U.S. sovereignty when it governed new lands after 1900, thereby minimizing congressional input. It used the resulting discretion to install bureau officials abroad, and by 1907 current and former bureau officials governed much of Cuba, the Canal Zone, and the Dominican Republic. Law Officer Charles Magoon became governor of the Panama Canal Zone, then of reoccupied Cuba. Edwards became chief of the Office of Administration, Isthmian Canal Affairs. Edwards's right-hand man, Frank McIntyre, joined Secretary of War Taft in Havana to arrange United States–Cuba relations. According to the *New York Tribune*, the bureau was "confided all Cuban affairs." Bureau officials experienced in Cuban customs work then oversaw the U.S.-run customs house in the Dominican Republic. The secretary of war chose McIntyre to inspect Dominican operations. Bureau officials seized these opportunities to showcase their offerings. According to George Colton, the first U.S. head of Dominican customs, bureau officials were expert intermediaries between Washington and its charges. They "rescued" the Panama Canal Zone "from chaos," he declared, and were supervised within the bureau by "one of the greatest civil lawyers of America." Colton's successor won praise for reports "full of valuable information." The asserted expertise of the bureau's legal team extended to the Panama Canal Zone and Cuba.[54]

By 1909, the Bureau of Insular Affairs had established itself as the single agency to which administration of the entire empire could be ceded – provided that the United States was willing to acknowledge that it held colonies and would continue to do so for the foreseeable future. The bureau faced no competing bureaucratic aspirant to primacy in colonial affairs. The Department of the Interior showed little appetite for its presidentially imposed role as recipient of territorial executive officers' reports to Washington. When asked about it, department officials "laughed and said that the order didn't seem to amount to very much, that they had nothing to do with Porto Rico." But without congressional signoff, the bureau's aspiration to become the department for all the U.S. empire remained just that. Only the Philippines fell within the bureau's formal jurisdiction; other lands annexed since the Civil War did not. The majority of territorial trade, territorial land, and territorial residents whom U.S. records judged to be white lay beyond bureau authority. Census takers recorded vastly more Puerto Ricans than Filipinos as white.[55]

The Puerto Rico budget crisis was a test of Edwards's alliance with Republicans. Early signs boded well. President Taft asked Congress to place Puerto Rico within the bureau's jurisdiction. The bill's Senate sponsor, the Republican Chauncey Depew of New York, with whom Collazo had sought a meeting, reported that Taft considered the measure "very essential." The bill's House sponsor, Republican Marlin Olmsted of Pennsylvania, expected "considerable opposition." Perhaps, like Collazo, Democrats saw little daylight between the "frank hostility" of Northern military rule and the "'egotistical, cowardly, hypocritical,'" "'corruption'" of the carpetbaggers now in charge. To Olmsted's surprise, Democrats focused their attacks on the diminution of popular control over the budget rather than dividing their fire to reach the bureau's new authority too. When even that limited challenge failed in mid-1909, the Bureau of Insular Affairs became the official guardian of Puerto Rico.[56]

Puerto Rico was a new showcase for Edwards and his bureau. He envisioned expanding the bureau's role as a provider of information not otherwise available by gathering Puerto Rico data and opening it to all comers. He strengthened the bureau's reputation for colonial best practices, in league with the island's new governor, George Colton. Colton had joined the Philippines invasion, organized Philippine and Dominican customs matters, and written and worked with the Bureau of Insular Affairs to secure congressional passage of the Philippines tariff law. Soon Colton publicly declared victory for his and the bureau's methods by announcing that Puerto Rico's once-nettlesome House of Delegates now embraced "cooperation and harmony." Edwards also acted as an intermediary for officials across the island–mainland divide. He provided mainlanders occupying high governmental posts in Puerto Rico with news of Washington, assistance with mainland transactions, and help in interactions with stateside officials. Edwards accompanied a presidentially commissioned investigation of Puerto Rico, then drafted a report and proposed legislation that reached the president and lawmakers. He testified before Congress, supplied it with information, lobbied members, and guided presidential support for legislation on Puerto Rico. Olmsted, the chairman of the Committee on Insular Affairs, solicited and compiled Edwards's legislative suggestions, introduced them as a Puerto Rican reform bill, and prepared to shepherd it through his committee and the House. Olmsted's Senate counterpart stood ready to attempt the same.[57]

At this stage, the bureau mustered its legal expertise behind a test case in favor of citizenship. The approach minimized the threats that citizenship otherwise posed to the bureau's reputation as a font of good government, its role as a mediator, and its legal authority. One measure of the bureau's competence at colonial government was public opinion, which in Puerto Rico overwhelmingly favored citizenship. The Republican Party concurred. Were the Republican-controlled Congress not to naturalize Puerto Ricans soon, they would feel disappointed and betrayed. But congressional debate on citizenship for Puerto Ricans could strain the bureau's ability to mediate relations between the United States and Puerto Rico. Attorney General of Puerto Rico Henry Hoyt predicted that Southern lawmakers would "seize the occasion to comment upon the large population of negroes in Porto Rico, the brutality of the negro, his undesirability as a citizen, including inflammatory discussion of rape." Governor Colton foresaw "agitation and ill feeling" if lawmakers overtly grafted mainland white-supremacist tropes onto Puerto Rico. Many officials, on the other hand, worried that the Supreme Court would respond to collective congressional naturalization of Puerto Ricans by extending them full constitutional protections, which would reduce the bureau's discretion on the island.[58]

By contrast, if an adjudicator recognized Puerto Ricans as citizens, no racist congressional debate would occur and no congressional act could be cited by the courts as a precedent for further liberalization of U.S. rule. Law Officer Charlton told Edwards that citizenship would not bring Puerto Ricans new individual rights. A test case would also burnish the bureau's legal reputation by putting it out ahead of the implications of a new Supreme Court decision. The decision, in *Kopel v. Bingham* (1909), involved the transfer of a criminal defendant from New York to Puerto Rico, pursuant to a federal law applicable only to territories "organized" by Congress with territorial legislatures and governors. Holding that the transfer was statutorily authorized, the Court declared that Puerto Rico was a "completely organized territory." This declaration had implications for citizenship. A separate federal statute gave "organized territories" full constitutional rights, and as Hoyt explained, that was "all that the word citizenship means." Thus, if "organized territory" had the same meaning in both contexts, then Puerto Ricans were citizens. Leading island lawyers, former president Roosevelt, former secretary of war Root, and *Insular Cases* lawyer Frederic Coudert stated or were reported to state that the Court might well declare Puerto Ricans to be citizens if the government pressed. Hoyt's reasoning was not airtight, however. If citizenship was more than rights, then Hoyt's equivalence failed. To explain the Court's acceptance of Puerto Rican tariff nonuniformity, Hoyt was left reading the *Insular Cases* as confined to customs matters.[59]

Edwards, Hoyt, Colton, and Secretary of War Jacob Dickinson wanted the clarification of Puerto Ricans' status that had eluded Degetau when he was resident commissioner. Like Degetau, these men initially expected federal agencies to provide a quick legal answer. In late 1909 they combed incoming passport applications for Puerto Ricans self-identifying as citizens. They planned to send such an application to Secretary of State Philander Knox, who set the rules for passports, who would then refer it to Attorney General George Wickersham for an opinion. Hoyt, however, was not confident that Wickersham would get the final word. He saw "enough doubt," he explained, "as to what the Supreme Court would say upon that subject to justify the abandonment of the idea of seeking an administrative determination," which the men did. But a judicial determination was also beyond reach. As Degetau had learned, passport issuance was discretionary; hence, unreachable by suit. The men were unable to extract a citizenship decision from the Supreme Court. As the House of Representatives Committee on Insular Affairs afterward reported, the Court had intimated it "will not seek a ford until it comes to the stream."[60] Edwards and the others had sought the same clarification as Degetau and had reprised his failure instead.

At this point, Edwards's failure to build a coalition transcending party, class, or orientation toward empire stopped his ambitions short. By mid-1910, depending on the Taft administration was a losing proposition. As Progressive insurgents within the party, such as Senator Robert La Follette of Wisconsin, faced off against an old guard typified by House speaker Cannon's iron rule, Taft was unwilling or unable to bridge the gaping divide. Instead Taft alienated the insurgents, to the bureau's detriment. The first loss was Alaska. Taft declared its small, scattered population inadequate for self-government. His "heavy pressure" brought to the Senate a bureau-authored bill that would place Alaska under the jurisdiction of the Bureau of Insular Affairs. Insurgents blocked its passage. Reflecting the Republican Party's distance from Reconstruction, Republican senator William Borah of Idaho blamed Alaska's ills on "carpetbaggers who have been sent in there."

A loss with regard to Puerto Rico followed. Taft and his allies pressed for a bureau-authored bill reformulating the island's organic law. It included provisions granting the bureau authority to appoint an executive secretary for the island, approve Puerto Rico's civil service rules, sign off on colonial officials' leave requests, and set rules for deposits of island funds. Democrats rebelled. A decade before, Representative William A. Jones of Virginia had disparaged Republican imperial rule as worse than Reconstruction. Having proudly contributed to Virginia's state-constitutional disfranchisement of African Americans in the interim, he was now the leading Democrat on the House Committee of Insular Affairs. As such, he linked new bureau authority to "government more autocratic than autonomic, more military than civil." The bill's backers chose to abandon the challenged provisions rather than mount a defense that would have required substantial Republican unity.

Anti-imperialist lawmakers came within a half dozen flipped votes of winning an amendment to strip the bureau of the authority over Puerto Rico it already had. When Democrats then exploited Republican divisions to seize the House in the 1910 election, the bureau's prospects faded. Republicans would not retake Washington for a decade. Legislation would never again expand the U.S. territory over which the bureau exercised authority. Thenceforth, the bureau would govern its existing portfolio and assist with the executive branch's overseas adventures.[61] In Puerto Rico, however, the limitation made little difference. Even without augmented authority, the Bureau of Insular Affairs' existing oversight of the island made it predominant.

By 1910 it was clear that internal conflict was a durable feature of empire in the United States. This conflict resulted in a structure from which Iglesias, Collazo, and Edwards could and did extract marginal, piecemeal gains. Iglesias strengthened his connections to Gompers and won a modicum of expressive freedom. Collazo raised his profile among Unionistas and Democrats and cultivated an anti-imperial alliance between them. Edwards's Bureau of Insular Affairs brought Puerto Rico within its jurisdiction while staffing or overseeing much of the United States' informal empire.

But even with powerful mainland allies, none of the three men managed to elevate his favored position on empire to dominance. Better working conditions, island autonomy, and a colonial department all remained beyond reach. The formidable forces of deference to capital, colonial governance, and fear of federal power survived their efforts.

Citizenship contained similar multitudes. The prospect of congressional naturalization of Puerto Ricans presented Edwards, Collazo, and Iglesias with potential trade-offs. If Congress withheld citizenship, the Bureau of Insular Affairs would face Puerto Ricans' resentment. If Congress extended it, the Supreme Court might equate such naturalization with territorial incorporation and thus reduce the bureau's discretion.

For Unionistas, citizenship aligned with their goal of home rule. The Senate had agreed with this premise in 1900; worried that the Court would cite citizenship as a reason to liberalize U.S rule in Puerto Rico, senators had withheld the status. But as the Supreme Court's apparent comfort with empire grew, lawmakers and jurists grew more confident that collective naturalization could be disentangled from democracy. Iglesias envisioned island workers wielding a rights-rich form of citizenship. But as Democrats settled into control of the House, it was the all-but-rightsless citizenship that Democrats had pioneered for African Americans in the South that Republicans proposed to extend to Puerto Ricans.

6

The Jones Act and the Long Path to Collective Naturalization

After bruising defeats, Santiago Iglesias, Domingo Collazo, and colonial officials all prioritized citizenship as they plotted their ways forward – but not the same kind of citizenship. The aspiration enjoyed broad support among Republicans, Democrats, and Unionistas. Yet citizenship was not inevitable in 1910; nor was its meaning transparent or uncontested.

Iglesias envisioned a kind of dependent citizenship. He saw Puerto Rico becoming a permanent U.S. possession in which benevolent federal administrators would protect workers from local elites and educate them into self-sufficiency.[1] Collazo and many of his allies in the island's Unionista majority party desired robust citizenship of the type associated with the Reconstruction Constitution. Convinced that Puerto Rico would fail as an independent nation, Collazo looked to Democrats to become the majority party in the United States and then extend to Puerto Ricans citizenship, full constitutional rights, and self-government. But Democrats themselves favored a more ambiguous citizenship for Puerto Ricans that could thread the needle between their opposition to empire as federal overreach and their advocacy of racist governance and African American dispossession. Top colonial officials and key Republican lawmakers favored "empty" citizenship. Naturalization would placate Puerto Ricans and signal permanent U.S. rule over Puerto Rico without bringing Puerto Ricans new rights, greater self-government, or eventual statehood.

Amid growing support for legislation to extend citizenship to Puerto Ricans, Iglesias placed his faith in U.S. officials' protection. With the island economy and polity dominated by U.S. corporations and local elites, Iglesias was unable to sustain labor activism with the support of AFL president Samuel Gompers alone. He needed a powerful institutional ally within the U.S. government. In late 1909 he welcomed the inauguration of George Colton as governor of Puerto Rico and the initiation of oversight by the Bureau of Insular Affairs, of which Clarence Edwards was chief. Iglesias looked to progressive U.S. administrators to govern the island's worker-citizens as good parents nurtured maturing children. Workers should be protected as "American citizens," he declared, with "full constitutional rights." His descriptions of those rights, however, were as gauzy and vague as mainlanders' odes to citizenship.

Primarily, Iglesias envisioned federal power protecting workers from Unionistas' "persecutions" and U.S. corporations' attempts to make the island a "great factory for ... exploiting cheap labor." He envisioned an island bureaucracy dedicated to helping workers. Iglesias began by building on the backlash in Washington against Unionistas for provoking a budget crisis. Iglesias and his allies cast Unionistas as elitist proto-tyrants. As heads of the Spanish-era autonomous cabinet, Muñoz Rivera and his followers had jailed journalists, disrupted labor meetings, treated workers as "submissive slaves," and opposed broad suffrage as bad for "whites." Today, they charged, Unionistas rejected "American administration," "American methods," and American labor reforms.[2]

When Iglesias objected to immigrants of dubious racial stock enjoying clearer paths to naturalization than Puerto Ricans, he tacitly endorsed the same notions of racial inferiority that others just as easily applied to Puerto Ricans. In seeking "uplift" that would place island workers on the path of white organized labor in the United States, he chose a term that many progressive reformers celebrated as a salve to supposed racial inferiority. Indeed, mainland proponents of Puerto Rican independence were predisposed to hear Iglesias's arguments in just that way. U.S. dollar diplomacy was often justified by the presumed racial inferiority of affected peoples. Had Iglesias instead chosen to lionize the entirety of the masses while deprecating the elites, he could have pointed to the examples of Reconstruction and Jim Crow. However, knowing those analogies would have infuriated Democrats, he avoided both of them.[3]

Racism made Colton and Edwards receptive to Iglesias. They condemned Luis Muñoz Rivera's "intolerant bossism" and shared Iglesias's belief that "American principles and influence" were island labor's only defense. Racial condescension animated their views. Colton recounted his stints in New Mexico, the Philippines, the Dominican Republic, and now Puerto Rico as time spent among races "as different from ours as possible among human beings." Casting the problem in animalistic terms, he described Puerto Ricans as "ignorant" people who "followed their leaders blindly, with little more than an instinct" and thereby threatened to make the island into a "veritable Haiti."[4]

U.S. government officials, including Colton, Edwards, Secretary of War Jacob Dickinson, and President William Howard Taft, advocated legislation that would extend Puerto Ricans citizenship while strengthening colonial governance. They envisioned greater gubernatorial authority, limited democratization of the upper legislative chamber, infrequent elections and legislative sessions, a literacy or property requirement that would disfranchise most voters, and a larger administrative apparatus that included a department focused on labor. Offering easy access to such citizenship would reinforce colonial power and confirm Colton's claim that "Porto Rico is American territory and will always remain so." Streamlined individual naturalization, rather than collective citizenship, would prevent federal courts from construing the legislation as promising either statehood or the extension of full constitutional rights. And by requiring naturalization for voting, the bill would both expand and conceal disfranchisement.[5]

By early 1910, Iglesias and colonial officials had joined forces. Despite its disfranchisement provision, Iglesias supported an administration bill that would foreclose independence, weaken Unionistas, and create an administrative department dedicated to workers' welfare. Iglesias also "worked long and faithfully" for a successor bill to naturalize Puerto Ricans collectively. With Taft's star on the wane, Iglesias's lobbying prowess and his access to Gompers and the AFL's Democratic connections strengthened the Bureau of Insular Affairs' hand in Congress. According to Gompers, Iglesias could "easily persuade anyone with his intelligence, earnestness, and force of character." Though the AFL generally lobbied only on matters directly affecting trade unionism, Iglesias won its support for the administration-backed citizenship bills. High AFL officials approached dozens of lawmakers, secured supportive statements from most senators, then published and distributed a pro-naturalization pamphlet. The support was valuable for the Republican-aligned bureau because Gompers had credibility as a former anti-imperialist who was friendly with Democrats.[6]

In Puerto Rico, Colton and Iglesias implemented a variation on the progressive ideal of industrial democracy, in which unions and management would cooperate to regulate the conditions of labor. Labor's local electoral defeats notwithstanding, Colton praised Iglesias's Federación Libre as "representing ... the largest class of people on the Island." Like many Progressives fearful that economic inequalities would drive industrial strife and class conflict, he described a "righteous obligation of the most fortunate" to "contribute to the welfare of the whole people." Colton won enactment of bills that strengthened protective legislation for women and children, the island's labor bureaucracy, eight-hour work rules, and workplace safety, and also occasionally selected labor leaders for island posts. While Unionistas depicted such acts as intrusions on "Puerto Ricans' indestructible right to rule their own destinies," Iglesias and Gompers commended Colton. Iglesias saw industrial peace as the path to "civil rights and political guarantees" for workers. When tobacco strikers won partial gains, he urged them back to work. A government crackdown on anarchist labor activists strengthened his hand.[7]

Iglesias believed workers in Puerto Rico were too weak to strike, but activists on his left flank asserted that it was he who lacked manly independence. The booming tobacco trade continued to house labor militants and anarchists who sustained more than their share of strikes. These leaders had experience organizing new workers, including many women whose early twentieth-century entry into the trade coincided with the Federación Libre's support of women's suffrage in 1908. Such successful activism supported anarchists' critique that workers should – and could – stand up for themselves, if only Iglesias would let them, rather than merely "aspiring to suck the Washington dairy from [President] Taft's teat."[8]

After 1909, Iglesias's bet on dependence and citizenship won modest gains. By keeping union members "friendly to the American Government," he earned the goodwill of colonial administrators and congressmen and insulated himself from the prevalent charge of "black socialism," a coded reference to anarchism as well as race. Capitalizing on industrial peace, he doubled union membership on the island to 10,000. Working alongside insular officials and winning their praise strengthened his hand with workers, though it brought no guarantee of officials' support during future battles against U.S corporations. Iglesias pursued dependent citizenship, and rallied scores of island unions behind pro-citizenship petitions, positioning himself for the "attendant glory" if citizenship materialized.[9]

In the middle of 1909, it seemed that Collazo's Democrat-Unionista alliance could bear fruit. Collazo relished the Republicans' internecine warfare and diminishing political prospects. As senators abandoned Taft's colonial policy, Collazo observed the tension between the president and his predecessor, Theodore Roosevelt. In 1910, Democrats retook the House. With the futures of Puerto Rico and the Philippines increasingly disaggregated, Collazo envisioned that Puerto Rico could transcend its colonial status and avoid the informal subordination that dollar diplomacy had imposed on nearby countries. The new Democratic chair of the House Committee on Insular Affairs, William A. Jones of Virginia, gave Collazo reason for optimism. Jones believed that the Constitution already held sway in Puerto Rico; thus, "no legislation is necessary to confer American citizenship" there. However, because this view had "never received judicial or other governmental sanction," Jones also favored naturalizing islanders "en masse."[10]

To hasten Democrats' redemption of Puerto Rico and the rights, citizenship, and home rule that could accompany it, Collazo wrangled Democratic voters, promoted naturalization and self-government, and attacked colonial officials. Borrowing a page from his 1890s playbook, Collazo organized the Puerto Rican diaspora in New York into the Alianza Puertorriqueña (Puerto Rican Alliance). He again stepped forward as secretary, but this time among a rarified group of officers that included businessmen, political operatives, journalists, a prominent musician, and a medical doctor. Collazo had sought to overthrow metropolitan and colonial political parties in the mid-1890s, but now the Alianza aimed to unite them. It would "canvass the country" for Democrats and counted Unionista party head Luis Muñoz Rivera as a member. Displaying his knack for public relations, Collazo gave interviews and secured press coverage that portrayed him as leading a club with hundreds of members, representing thousands of Puerto Ricans. Before mainland media, Congress, and reform gatherings, the Alianza advocated citizenship, self-government, and an elected Puerto Rican senate. As the 1912 election neared, Collazo helped form the citywide Latin-American Democratic Association in New York, in which he again filled the post of secretary. He fostered a connection between Muñoz Rivera and former Democratic presidential candidate William Jennings Bryan, and won himself a meeting with Woodrow Wilson, the Democratic presidential hopeful. As a delegate to the Democratic National Convention and a member of the committee to notify the nominee, Collazo accepted Muñoz Rivera's exhortation to attack Republican governance and seek "home rule" from Democrats.[11]

At the Alianza, Collazo tapped into Democrats' comparisons of colonial governance to carpetbagger rule in the South. When island leaders protested alleged abuses by Republican officials, Collazo led the Alianza to demand investigation of reports of Governor Colton's "repeated ... drunken carousels." But Collazo had miscalculated the rhetorical half-life of postbellum politics and underestimated the political strength of Colton's superiors in Washington. Edwards castigated Collazo's "defaming campaign" against Colton, a teetotaler, who had already been thoroughly investigated and "completely vindicated." As the bureau's law officer responsible for providing legal counsel, Felix Frankfurter ordered an investigation of Collazo by William Flynn, the former head of the U.S. Secret Service.[12] As documents critical of Collazo accumulated, the bureau ensured that they were retained for future use; its extensive and cross-indexed records included a file specifically dedicated to Collazo. But whatever harm Collazo's activism was doing to his long-term prospects for an official role in Puerto Rican affairs, he had more pressing problems.

The closely related rise of U.S. dollar diplomacy and growing Unionista support for independence together threatened Collazo's aspirations. Unionistas had long benefited from calling independence the "last refuge of our honor," an outcome inferior to statehood but better than colonial subjection. Muñoz Rivera understood independence to be an "abstract ideal." Nevertheless, support for independence cloaked Unionistas in anticolonial patriotism. It was also a demand that U.S. officials could not dismiss with racial insults, given U.S. support for Panamanian, Cuban, and Dominican independence. As statehood grew increasingly remote, Unionistas placed greater emphasis on independence, eventually making it their foremost long-term goal.[13]

The shift in policy soon attracted an unexpected bedfellow: Senator Elihu Root. He now preferred the "clearly defined policy" of dollar diplomacy, which would maximize the control Republican expansionists coveted and minimize the obligations that Democratic anti-imperialists feared. It would also keep foreign powers out, leave U.S. sovereignty and governance at home, and permit the United States to protect "peace and order" abroad. The policy already applied to Cuba, Santo Domingo, and Central America, Root said, and it was what "we ought to do with Porto Rico."[14] Unionistas' romantic yearnings for unattainable independence suddenly had the potential to bolster Root's proposal. Many Unionistas, including Collazo, were appalled by the prospect of Puerto Rico becoming subject to the type of domination that the United States was extending throughout the Caribbean.

Collazo launched a sophisticated media campaign to discredit Root's proposal. In *La Democracia* he recalled the warning issued by the apostle of Cuban independence, José Martí, that economic dependence on a stronger country bred political dependence. Cuba had suffered that fate; heavily dependent on sugar exports to the United States, it had never escaped U.S. oversight. Republicans now maintained this "new colonial system" of dollar diplomacy throughout the hemisphere, Collazo wrote. Dominican, Panamanian, and Nicaraguan sovereignty were vastly diminished. Colombia, Honduras, Costa Rica, and El Salvador faced similar threats. Puerto Rico could hardly hope for better, given its long U.S. occupation, reliance on U.S. markets, and proximity to the mainland.[15]

Both parties, Democrats and Republicans, supported citizenship for Puerto Ricans. Root did not. Naturalization would only breed resentment, he predicted, as islanders would expect a role in "governing ... the rest of the country" that they would never be granted. Root had planned to outline his opposition to citizenship in a major Senate speech, until Collazo cleverly preempted him. A private conversation with Root about his plans for the island had been published, and Collazo showed the article to periodicals throughout New York. National coverage followed. Collazo and his Unionista and Alianza allies then shaped the mainland narrative to portray the Puerto Ricans as an often-deceived people who were bitterly disappointed that Root had disregarded his party's earlier promise of citizenship. *Harper's Weekly* reprised Isabel Gonzalez's family metaphors, with Puerto Rico darkened: "Uncle Sam's attitude" toward "stranded and helpless" Puerto Rico "is most unbecoming. He won't marry the dusky maiden, he won't divorce her, he won't even promise a permanent engagement, or to be a big brother to her."[16]

The campaign was a success. *La Democracia* praised Collazo as a "forceful writer and tireless fighter," and Unionistas again stopped short of opposing U.S. citizenship. Neither the Democratic nor the Republican Party changed its platform in favor of Root's vision. For now, Collazo's expectation survived – an expectation of citizenship and rapid granting of "autonomous government as ample and liberal as that of Canada," under U.S. sovereignty.[17] But as Collazo had begun to discover after he impugned Governor Colton, his aspirations for autonomy ran contrary to a powerful bureaucracy in Washington: the Bureau of Insular Affairs.

Clarence Edwards sought to entrench the authority of his Bureau of Insular Affairs over Puerto Rico just as Democrats' power increased markedly from 1909 to 1911. Internal division weakened Republicans, and Democrats won enough races in 1910 to capture the House of Representatives and narrow Republicans' Senate majority. Edwards favored retaining Puerto Rico as a formal colony, even as the United States increasingly engaged the rest of the Caribbean and Latin America through dollar diplomacy. He proposed that the bureau improve colonial governance of Puerto Rico. Building on the bureau's experience as an intermediary in dealings among Republicans in Puerto Rico, the upper reaches of the War Department, Congress, and the White House, Edwards aimed to incorporate elected Puerto Ricans, congressional Democrats, and U.S. and Puerto Rican labor leaders into a consensus around his proposals. In addition to disfranchisement and a new island department focused on labor, his priorities included an elected senate and an absolute gubernatorial veto. To Governor Colton, this division of lawmaking power would produce good laws subject to sufficient check. Edwards also favored collective naturalization. With the futures of Puerto Rico and the Philippines no longer conjoined, bureau law officer Felix Frankfurter judged that reform a cheap, convenient way to end Puerto Ricans' anomalous status and "remove the most disturbingly insistent source of discontent" on the island.[18] It was also the only reform proposed by the bureau that enjoyed broad support in both Washington and San Juan – and even then, it was for disparate reasons. The authority and ability of the bureau's legal experts to maintain and navigate ambiguities in the meanings of citizenship were crucial to any compromise.

Colton and the Bureau of Insular Affairs began their consensus-building work with island leaders. Iglesias's Federación Libre strongly favored collective naturalization, as did most Unionistas. Neither organization supported a scheme of individual naturalization that would then require citizenship to vote. Given the poverty, limited transportation, scant administrative resources, and spotty communication on the island, many Puerto Ricans would not apply, and that scenario could seriously threaten the Unionistas' majority. It would certainly threaten Iglesias's plans to make citizenship a cornerstone of labor activism. Worse, U.S. racial prohibitions might bar some Puerto Ricans, including the island's many artisans of color, from naturalizing individually. And such prohibitions would have the incidental effect of highlighting Puerto Ricans' blackness and racial mixture. As Collazo and his niece Isabel Gonzalez had discovered, requirements that a person demonstrate eligibility for citizenship were fraught with peril, especially for women. Indeed, the Taft administration's first draft of a naturalization bill would have made unmarried adult women ineligible.[19]

Colton and the bureau were able to forge a compromise because neither the Partido Unionista nor the Federación Libre was firmly opposed to disfranchisement. Thus, they were willing to support collective naturalization coupled with disfranchisement on lines other than citizenship. A similar compromise solved governance. Unionistas were so enthusiastic about securing an elected senate that they were willing to put aside their goal of complete home rule and suspend their enmity toward organized labor long enough to accept a new labor department with a presidentially appointed head. Republicanos, for their part, were in no position to dissent from a proposal that fulfilled their priorities of collective naturalization and an elected senate. The island's political and labor leaders united behind a draft bill.[20]

Ambiguities in the meaning of citizenship permitted the Taft administration to back the compromise bill with minimal changes. According to one astute observer, "a great body of public opinion" continued to reflect the belief that the "grant of citizenship would carry with it the implied promise of ultimate statehood." Both Republicano proponents and mainland opponents of citizenship often held that view. But Taft did not reject the naturalization provision on that ground. Instead, he mitigated it by declaring naturalization "entirely disassociated from any thought of statehood." Secretary of War Stimson opined that because "no substantial, approved public opinion in the United States" even "contemplates statehood," Puerto Ricans should aspire instead to become an "overseas self-governing territory." The only substantial change proposed by Taft and his congressional allies was to the proposed senate for Puerto Rico; some seats would be elective immediately, but the rest would phase in over the following thirty-six years.[21]

Stimson, Colton, and Edwards sought congressional Democrats' support for the bill by appealing to the bipartisan commitment to white supremacy – but they had to tread carefully. Unionista leaders insisted that Puerto Ricans ranked high on the racial ladder. As one leader told Congress, post-annexation New Mexico, Louisiana, and Florida "could not have equaled the present civilization of Porto Rico." Some Democratic members of Congress agreed, citing numerous Puerto Rican virtues, from their "high order of intelligence" to loyalty, probity, and civic virtue. Other Democrats ridiculed islanders as inferior. The bureau reported that when Muñoz Rivera used his limited English to "read with some difficulty" a statement of "emphatic opposition" to a proposed law, Democratic representative Harvey Helm of Kentucky humiliated him by eliciting his affirmation to the leading question: "Do I understand that you unreservedly and unequivocally favor the bill?"[22]

Stimson, Colton, and Edwards proved their mettle as imperial liaisons. Aware that in 1899 Democrats had leapt at the chance to show Republicans that the racial theories underlying Reconstruction were incompatible with empire, Colton made that claim his own. He wrote Edwards that federal officials must not repeat Reconstruction's mistake of ignoring racial hierarchy. In Puerto Rico, he said, unqualified voters and "unprincipled leaders" had sidelined "intelligent people" and created the "same condition" that "existed in our Southern States during the days of 'reconstruction.'" Because Colton's analysis was likely to offend the "accredited" Unionista "representatives" of Puerto Rico, to whom Democrats were inclined to defer, Edwards and Stimson proceeded discreetly. They invited a bipartisan embrace of white supremacy by forwarding Colton's observation to Tennessee Democrat Finis Garrett and encouraging him to share it with others on the House Committee on Insular Affairs. Edwards and Stimson got the desired result. When Democrats took control of the House, they introduced legislation that closely resembled the administration's own measure.[23]

Toward the end of the Sixty-First and Sixty-Second Congresses (1909–1911 and 1911–1913), the Bureau of Insular Affairs and its allies struggled to remove final obstacles to the bills they favored. Doing so was important, because Unionistas' willingness to compromise rested on Muñoz Rivera's control over the more radical members of his party. The longer that compromise failed to produce legislation, the more tenuous Muñoz Rivera's position became and the less credible Colton's promises appeared. Yet the U.S. Senate displayed little urgency. Its emphasis on consensus created several opportunities for individual lawmakers to delay legislation, which is what happened during both sessions. Isolated senatorial opposition scuttled passage of the administration's bill in the Sixty-First Congress. It also prevented passage of a collective naturalization bill in the next, despite lobbying by Stimson and the bureau, as well as Gompers, to persuade the holdout, then-Democratic senator James Clarke of Arkansas.[24]

When lawmakers reconvened in 1913, it would be Democrats who would decide Puerto Rico's fate. They would face the same choices as the previous administration: grant the island formal independence and control it through dollar diplomacy, redeem Puerto Rico by granting it home rule, or enact Colton's grand compromise.[25] Each approach had its challenges. Independence had support among some Unionista leaders but few mainland ones. A partly overlapping set of Unionistas expected Democrats to fulfill promises to extend rights, citizenship, and self-government to Puerto Ricans. But many Democrats inclined toward Colton's proposal to pair naturalization with continued colonial rule – although Unionistas might not accept so little from Democrats, from whom they had expected so much. Finally, a new administration meant new bureaucrats on the island, which meant forging a new relationship with Iglesias. His continued acquiescence to disfranchisement was contingent on his having a good relationship with bureaucrats, but that remained to be seen.

The Democratic Party's assumption of control of both the executive and the legislative branches in March of 1913 did not bode well for the Bureau of Insular Affairs. Despite Edwards's attempts to broaden its appeal, the bureau had long been aligned with Republicans. The previous year, Edwards had declared that "any departure from the McKinley-Roosevelt-Taft policy in dealing with the islands would set them back years." Powerful Democrats had recently called for deannexation of the Philippines and the transfer of Puerto Rico to the Department of Interior. Then, several months before the 1912 election, the Taft administration had promoted Edwards and replaced him as bureau chief with his long-time assistant, Frank McIntyre. After the election, McIntyre challenged Democrats to think bigger. Redeeming Puerto Rico would sacrifice white supremacy to federalism. Now that rebel yells and "Dixie" had echoed through Washington's streets on Woodrow Wilson's inauguration day, better that Democrats continue federal rule and thereby advance white supremacy.[26] With the bureau's legal-colonial expertise at their disposal, Democrats saw that they could pursue such a policy without reneging on pledges to naturalize Puerto Ricans and expand self-government, and without triggering unwelcome constitutional consequences such as statehood.

McIntyre aligned himself and his bureau with the people, politics, and priorities of a Democratic Party increasingly untroubled by empire. According to Collazo, McIntyre "proclaimed himself 'a Democrat.'" Natural allies included members of Congress who were supportive of the bureau's work; Democratic Party members with experience in colonial governance of the Philippines; and two Wilson appointees, Secretary of War Lindley Garrison and Governor of Puerto Rico Arthur Yager. To distance themselves from the bureau's partisan reputation, McIntyre and his staff emphasized that empire was no longer a divisive national issue. The mainland public supported U.S. rule in Puerto Rico. Democrats had won control of the House without mentioning the Philippines in their platforms. Past Republican presidents and colonial officials agreed with many Democrats that Puerto Ricans should be U.S. citizens.[27]

McIntyre and his colleagues courted congressional Democrats by adjusting their defenses of colonialism and drawing sharper contrasts between empire and Reconstruction. Where Democrats condemned Reconstruction for turning the racial order upside down, the bureau claimed to do the opposite. Its political tutelage of peoples unprepared for self-government put racial orders right side up, it said, blaming lack of democracy and governmental dysfunction on the failings of subjects, not rulers. In such locales, only federal officials were in a position to implement policies on the model that white supremacy demanded. Echoing a justification for dollar diplomacy, McIntyre told one Democratic senator that progress for most Puerto Ricans required the "introduction of ideas which do not exist in the Latin-American countries." Bureau officials also worked to stave off charges of carpetbagging. Confident that an absolute gubernatorial veto was sufficient to maintain U.S. control, McIntyre advocated replacing the mainlander-dominated appointed upper legislative chamber with an elected senate. For other posts, he favored a "minimum of Americans" and a maximum of Puerto Ricans. These positions would make McIntyre indispensable to stateside officials and Puerto Rican political aspirants. He uniquely combined knowledge of Puerto Rican politics and influence within Washington's corridors of power.[28]

McIntyre assumed that both national parties had stopped treating the conflict over empire as a proxy war over Reconstruction. He was correct. By 1914 white supremacy had triumphed, politically, legally, and culturally. African Americans were now disfranchised throughout the former Confederacy, and the Republican Party platform no longer mentioned black men's voting rights. Jim Crow was ubiquitous across the South, and segregation existed beyond it as well. Federal courts did not enforce the Reconstruction Amendments to protect African Americans' rights. For only the second time since the Civil War, Democrats controlled the federal government. White-supremacist attacks on Reconstruction had also gained national acceptance and found expression in major artistic and academic works. Thomas Dixon's book *The Clansman* (1905) depicted "the awful suffering of the white man during the dreadful reconstruction period." William Dunning's *Reconstruction, Political and Economic, 1865–1877* (1907) described Reconstruction as "an era of corruption presided over by unscrupulous 'carpetbaggers' from the North, unprincipled Southern white 'scalawags,' and ignorant freedmen." Cinema further popularized these views, most notably in D. W. Griffith's *The Birth of a Nation* (1915).[29] The acceptance of white supremacy by both parties and the white U.S. public made McIntyre's task easier.

McIntyre's gambit succeeded. He convinced Democrats that "political divisions should not go beyond the national maritime line." In early 1914, the party abandoned its efforts to transfer Puerto Rico to the Department of Interior and espoused the key features of Colton's grand compromise that McIntyre advocated: a largely or entirely elected island senate; an absolute or near-absolute gubernatorial veto; a rule that any new voters meet some required mix of literacy, property ownership, or taxpaying; and creation of an island Department of Labor. These provisions enjoyed broad bipartisan support.[30]

The constitutional and political challenges associated with the legislation now centered on citizenship. The legitimacy of the federal government's extending its rule overseas was no longer in question. The remaining challenge was legislating without producing unwanted legal consequences. Democrat William A. Jones of Virginia, a member of his party's narrow congressional majority and the chair of the House Committee on Insular Affairs, worried that if Puerto Ricans won statehood, they would sometimes hold "the balance of power in the Congress." Citizenship might set that eventuality into motion. The difficulty was that colonial officials and lawmakers also saw compelling reasons to extend citizenship. Himself a Confederate veteran and Redeemer Democrat, Jones had savaged Republican imperial governance in 1900 as worse than Reconstruction. He reiterated his stance that Puerto Ricans were citizens and that the Constitution applied to Puerto Rico. Democratic colleagues on his committee agreed that the United States should not "permanently keep" and rule people as "subjects and not citizens." Demands for citizenship had united Puerto Rican political and labor leaders under Colton and seemed popular with islanders. It might also "greatly improve" U.S. relations "to the whole of Latin America." Citizenship would signal permanent U.S. retention, thus neutralizing Puerto Ricans' demand for independence as a negotiating tactic. It would also end the "embarrassment" of Puerto Ricans' uncertain eligibility for jobs reserved for citizens.[31]

Frankfurter, who had retained his post after the change in administration, pointed toward a solution in a memorandum that assured Congress of its control over the legal consequences of granting citizenship to Puerto Ricans. His memo surveyed fourteen years of the Supreme Court justices' inaction, ambiguities, and occasional clear holdings. He also reviewed the legal and political precedents that had emerged from U.S. governance of Cuba, Hawai'i, the Panama Canal Zone, and the Dominican Republic. He argued that constitutional rights, citizenship, U.S. sovereignty, and self-government in dependent locales were entirely within congressional control. "If Congress chooses to grant citizenship" but withhold statehood or full constitutional rights, "the Supreme Court will respect such exercise."[32]

Federal lawmakers were convinced. In a pair of leading bills on the future of Puerto Rico and the Philippines, Jones took up Degetau's decade-old suggestion of placing the Philippines and Puerto Rico on separate paths. But contrary to Degetau's recommendation, his proposed legislation did not change the colonial status of either. Nor did it treat the decreased consequences of citizenship as an opportunity to reaffirm that all Americans were citizens. Instead, one bill abstractly promised independence to the Philippines but provided no timetable, set no process in motion, and declined to naturalize Filipinos in the interim. The other slated Puerto Ricans for collective naturalization – hence, permanent retention. Both bills withheld self-government and full constitutional rights. They provided bills of rights that excluded jury and tariff uniformity provisions. The governors and top judicial officers were to be presidential appointees. Each created an elected senate to be checked by a combination of absolute gubernatorial, presidential, and congressional vetoes and by a rule that old budgets would continue in force if new ones were not enacted. New voters would have to meet a mix of alternative literacy, taxpaying, and property-owning requirements. Elections and legislative sessions would be less frequent.[33]

When Democrats took control of the federal government in 1913, Luis Muñoz Rivera declared that Unionistas' "joy knew no bounds." Democrats had demanded that places "be governed according to the will of the inhabitants." With Puerto Rico no longer a test case for the Philippines, it could be judged on its own merits. Leading Unionistas' early interactions with Democratic leaders convinced them that they would obtain access to the administration, a statutory grant of "home rule to Porto Rico," and appointments of Puerto Ricans rather than mainland carpetbaggers to island posts. But Collazo was skeptical. Given recent political events, the one-time herald of Democratic redemption now "complained . . . of the indifference of both parties to the affairs of the island."[34]

Democrats were quick to confirm Collazo's fears and disabuse Unionistas of their illusions. In October Muñoz Rivera complained that repeated appointments of mainlanders to island posts "in no way lived up to the home rule" promises. Collazo had hoped that he, at least, would secure a position of some sort. He had extensive service in Democratic politics and endorsements from the secretary of state, a Democratic senator, Muñoz Rivera, and the Democratic National Committeeman for Puerto Rico. But when bureau officials placed these endorsements alongside the earlier critical reports in Collazo's personnel file, his candidacy went nowhere.[35]

Democratic inaction stifled Unionistas' hopes as well. In the new congressional session Democrats showed no inclination to enact reform legislation for Puerto Rico. Wilson's message to Congress offered no definite Puerto Rico policy. Samuel Gompers declared imminent reform "extremely doubtful." Where Congress did act was on its commitment to lower sugar tariffs. Though Bureau of Insular Affairs officials, Puerto Rican political and labor leaders, island sugar producers, and Collazo all warned Democrats that eliminating tariffs on foreign sugar would decimate the island's economy, Democratic lawmakers nonetheless slated sugar protection for elimination. Only rising sugar prices and Democrats' policy reversal following the outbreak of World War I in 1914 prevented economic ruin for Puerto Rico.[36]

Pessimistic about the prospects for Unionista-Democrat cooperation, Collazo dedicated himself to what he termed "the greater Latin American family." He discontinued his column in *La Democracia* and published fewer English-language letters about Puerto Rico. Instead, he contributed to the new Spanish-language New York newspaper *La Prensa* and continued to write for a Venezuelan newspaper. Within New York's Puerto Rican community he became a popular speaker known for giving highly informative talks. He also led the Democrats' Latin America Bureau and became secretary of the New York All-Americas Chamber of Commerce.[37]

As Unionistas' frustration with the status quo mounted, a majority of party members inclined toward the views of such radical Unionistas as speaker of the House of Delegates José de Diego. He opposed U.S. citizenship and demanded instead what amounted to second-class sovereignty, such as that Elihu Root had described and representative Jones's bill for the Philippines promised. Although Collazo judged this position "suicidal to the island's interest in the Congress," the Unionistas altered their platform during the United States' Sixty-Third Congress (1913–1915) to prioritize independence. Muñoz Rivera and his loyal copartisan Cayetano Coll y Cuchi explained to the House Committee on Insular Affairs in 1914 that U.S. citizenship would foreclose independence without suggesting the "most remote intention on the part of the United States to ever grant statehood." Collective naturalization would make islanders "citizens of an inferior class" and Puerto Rico "perpetually a colony, a dependency." Jones's bill promising the Philippines eventual independence soon became law, but Jones offered Puerto Rico no similar option. He had long demanded citizenship rather than independence for Puerto Ricans. Given mainland opinion in favor of retaining Puerto Rico, Jones declared Unionistas' hopes vain. Muñoz Rivera pressed Congress to offer some ultimate status: "If you tender statehood now," he said, we would "accept" that. But congressional leaders instead declared that "Porto Ricans don't know what they want" and set the issue aside. Democrats apparently retained sufficient sensitivity to federal tyranny to prefer inaction. Perceiving the Hobson's choice, Unionistas deemphasized independence and narrowed their ambitions to incremental advances.[38]

Many Democrats now joined Jones in giving precedence to racism over Puerto Rico's self-government. Senator James Vardaman of Mississippi, a notorious white-supremacist, described the misfortune of bringing "into the body politic" a people who would "not in a thousand years ... understand the genius of our government," adding that there was "enough of that element ... already to menace the nation with mongrelization." He cast federal administration of Puerto Rico as an unpleasant reality for a distant and different people: "The Porto Ricans are going to be held against their will," he acknowledged, and "I am from the South, where for years we had a carpetbag government, and I know from experience how intensely disagreeable that is." Yet Vardaman did not suggest that Jones's proposed legislation violated a sacred constitutional principle. Nor did he assert that ostensible Reconstruction-era misrule was being visited on the island. With Reconstruction vanquished, Vardaman preferred to swallow the bitter pill of federal rule than to risk racial infection of the body politic. He supported the balance struck in Jones's bill: modest expansion of self-government paired with "empty" citizenship calculated to facilitate indefinite U.S. administration.[39]

Speaking before Congress, Muñoz Rivera and his Unionista colleague Coll y Cuchi lamented Democrats' "meager and conservative" proposal. They argued that U.S. colonial rule in Puerto Rico replayed the post–Civil War phenomenon of carpetbagger officials who self-interestedly reported that the "rebels of the South were unprepared for self-government." But Democrats opposed treating Puerto Ricans as white. Instead, they offered Puerto Ricans a citizenship that Muñoz Rivera and Coll y Cuchi dismissed as farcical. Jones's proposed legislation would provide citizenship without granting home rule or a vote in federal elections. The island leaders' sense of betrayal was palpable: "For 16 years we have endured this system of government" and did not lose hope because the Democratic Party was "encouraging us by its declarations." Puerto Ricans "have been a colony for 400 years, and we do not want to be a colony," they explained. Honor compelled rejecting the "second class" status on offer. The citizenship that U.S. officials deemed too symbolically important to extend Puerto Ricans from 1899 to 1901 had come to be seen by 1916 and 1917 as so hollow it was an insult.[40]

By this time, however, Jones's proposal had gained supporters in many quarters. It was decided that collective naturalization would be accompanied by a one-year opt-out provision. A new, wholly elected legislature would be checked by a conditional gubernatorial veto and absolute presidential and congressional vetoes. As before, old budgets would continue in force if not replaced. Elections and legislative sessions would be held half as frequently. Workers would benefit from a new Puerto Rican Department of Agriculture and Labor, but suffer under a voting requirement of literacy or taxpaying for new voters, and eventually for all voters. The heads of the island's executive and judicial branches would remain presidential appointees. President Wilson, Governor Yager, and Democratic sponsors in Congress backed this proposal, and Republican colonial officials had championed similar measures. Republicanos had long sought citizenship and liberalization of the island's government. Though Unionistas had sought more, they doubted they could achieve it and so mostly offered reluctant support. As Collazo declared upon reentering the fray, any failure to secure citizenship at this stage would primarily benefit colonial "bureaucrats."[41] The bill closely resembled the compromise that Colton had forged and that Iglesias had backed in 1910. But Iglesias's understanding of the value of citizenship and the expendability of the franchise had shifted considerably in the interim.

Woodrow Wilson's election came as Iglesias confronted the limits of his strategy of governmental protection through dependent citizenship. The strategy had not mitigated the imbalance between islanders' endemic poverty and corporations' profits. With electoral power still out of reach, strikes were the obvious alternative. The approach was similar to that in 1906: by asserting and defending a right to strike, workers would build self-confidence, forge social networks, accrue experience for future strikes, gain doctrinal ground, improve their working conditions, and mitigate immediate setbacks by grounding them in a longer-term project of legal and social change.[42] But predictions that success would breed success were not always fulfilled. In 1906, sugar strikes had collapsed amid widespread repression, causing the labor movement to retrench. This time, Iglesias could expect to draw on officials' goodwill, Gompers's close relationship with Wilson, and workers' experience asserting and defending a right to strike. Nonetheless, the prospect was daunting.

The stark and persistent juxtaposition of islanders' dire straits and employers' commercial advantages, stinginess, and corruption demonstrated workers' need for higher wages. Island conditions shocked mainlanders. McIntyre claimed that the masses of Puerto Ricans dependent on agricultural work were worse off than "the most miserable negro" in the post–Civil War South. Gompers labeled the poverty and associated "misery" and "degradation" in Puerto Rico "appalling." Cheap, overcrowded housing menaced health and "every sense of decency." Medical care was often nonexistent. Real wages were stagnant. Workers' diets were "miserably inadequate." By contrast, employers in the island's leading export sectors, tobacco and sugar, were organized, well financed, politically influential, and cutthroat in their business dealings. The American Tobacco Company controlled more than three quarters of the island's tobacco production. Tariff protection ensured that the absentee capital that had consolidated the sugar industry retained access to U.S. markets on favorable terms. Employers laid siege to unions and depressed wages by relocating jobs from higher-wage island towns to lower-wage ones. Political influence insulated these corporations from protective labor legislation. It also won them authority during strikes to pay and house police officers, thereby seemingly transforming the officers into employers' agents. Although sugar employed more than a third of all agricultural workers, the labor force vastly outnumbered the available jobs. Producers reduced wages below subsistence levels. The large plantations sold food and supplies to workers at exorbitant prices and engaged in outright wage theft.[43]

Iglesias had reason to be optimistic that Gompers, the president, and colonial officials would offer strikers more support than they had in 1906. Gompers had grown more willing to support strikes, at a time when national industrial strife and union membership were rising together and when the rapidly growing Industrial Workers of the World was staging dramatic walkouts. President Wilson was a potential ally. Gompers had supported Wilson during the 1912 campaign and was now the president's trusted advisor. Wilson backed labor bills, assisted the labor movement, accepted its recommendations for government appointments, treated Gompers as the representative of all wage earners, and found places for labor leaders in federal agencies affecting workers' interests. Such agencies were on the rise and of growing relevance to Puerto Rico, as reflected in the formation that year of the Department of Labor, which understood Puerto Rico to be among its concerns.[44] For his part, Iglesias had spent recent years building good relationships with Taft-era colonial officials.

The tests came between 1914 and 1916, when workers laid down their tools by the tens of thousands. In 1914, employees of the American Tobacco Company's Porto Rico American Tobacco Company went on strike, eventually winning improvements in working conditions. Around the same time, World War I caused a rise in consumer prices and sugar prices, which were driven up to levels "never dreamed of" shortly after a round of wage cuts. Although not unionized, disgruntled cane workers lived, traveled, and labored together, and so had opportunities to articulate their resentments to one another and formulate responses. In January 1915 a group in Bayamón launched a strike that spread across the island. It involved more than 17,000 workers before it collapsed without achieving permanent islandwide gains. A year later, 10 percent of all employed islanders joined a second strike that swept through the fields before it also ended without permanent gains.[45]

Iglesias and his colleagues stepped forward to lead and support strikers, who clashed repeatedly with island officials. During the tobacco strike, police and judges subject to oversight by the new governor, Arthur Yager, joined with employers' hired strikebreakers to break up labor demonstrations and attack and prosecute strikers. Then, during the sugar strikes, Yager ordered the enforcement of "order and peace" "at all costs and by means of force." Violence, destruction, and repression resulted. Police and paid thugs killed numerous strikers. Two police officers received grievous injuries, and dozens of strikers suffered wounds. Around 4 percent of the island's population was arrested. After just one incident, more than 100 strikers were convicted.[46]

Iglesias's clash with Yager was partly personal, as he lacked the friendly relationship he had had with Yager's predecessor. Like other governors, Yager prioritized mainland investment. His elite education, powerful connections, and institutional leadership experience also inclined him to favor U.S. corporate interests. Because Yager and Wilson were old friends, Gompers had little success convincing President Wilson to rein him in.[47]

Iglesias evaluated the propriety of government actions, workers' rights, and labor tactics by whether they alleviated workers' plight. More radical than his patron Gompers, Iglesias remained a socialist his entire life. He took up the long-standing argument within AFL circles that governmental bars on workers' collective organizing reduced labor to chattel, in violation of the Thirteenth Amendment bar on slavery and involuntary servitude. Enslaved workers had a right to strike to "break ... their chains," he declared. Iglesias also argued for workers' rights to freedom of speech, publication, assembly, and association, all of which he aggressively asserted. He was more circumspect about delineating in that ensemble of rights other tactics, such as secondary strikes, intimidation, and demonstrations, to impede replacement workers' entry into workplaces. Yet it was the combination of expressive and other tactics that promised to help workers seize the reins of power. They brought workers into unions and acclimated them to self-assertion, fostered labor unity and ideological cohesion, asserted the dignity of labor, and indicted economic injustice.[48]

Yager rejected Iglesias's analysis wholesale. Capitalism was not bondage, he insisted, and workers' misery was not the government's responsibility. Prior Spanish misrule had created the island's bad economic conditions, and Puerto Rico's large "surplus population" thwarted easy solutions. It was not the government's place to encourage voluntary settlements of strikes in the public interest. Better labor contracts were the sole legitimate purpose of strikes. Industrial strife aimed just at organizing "would not accomplish any useful purpose" but would cause only economic losses and lethal violence. While Yager recognized free speech rights, he gave them a conventionally narrow, predominantly political domain. "Peaceful and orderly" meetings were permissible but large, noisy, threatening gatherings were not. Police were to protect dissenting workers' rights to cross picket lines, not unions' desire to convince and perhaps intimidate such workers.[49]

Iglesias instructed workers to press their rights aggressively, document all violations, and seek adjudication. He hoped to turn more distant agents of the state against those suppressing strikers and advance the AFL's project of "influencing legal thought." He repeated Gompers's directive: "Every constitutional, statutory and inherent right should be exercised in the effort to associate, assemble, and meet and express their thoughts and views." Inherent rights included rights to which workers should feel entitled even when legal authorities did not yet recognize them. Iglesias also sought a forum in which "justice for the workers in their fights will be recognized." Antilabor courts were bad candidates, yet judicial process was Iglesias's model. He envisioned opportunities to testify, a neutral body open to constitutional and other legal claims, power to secure testimonial and other proofs, a formal record, and a culminating decision. In the meantime, he benefited from Gompers's "excellent publicity bureau."[50]

Iglesias created an extensive, detailed record of this repression. Telegrams, notarized affidavits, letters, and reports poured in from strikers and their supporters. "More than 1,000 country workers ... filed complaints" in a single instance, he recounted. The complaints focused on denial of expressive freedoms and wanton violence. With superiors' support, police abused and "violently and illegally" disbanded workers' "peaceful" and "orderly" parades, public meetings, small gatherings, acts of symbolic expression, and speeches. A patron leaving a movie as police broke up a labor meeting swore seeing "a policeman beating a man with a stick.... The poor victim beg[ged] the policeman to stop beating him (the victim), saying these words, 'Don't hit me more,' and then the policeman shoot [sic] him, and the poor man said to said policeman, 'Please don't kill me that I am going out,' and then the policeman shoot [sic] again the second time, killing him."[51]

Having prepared his claims, Iglesias searched for a receptive forum. Iglesias first presented Yager with charges of official wrongdoing during the 1914 tobacco strike. Yager responded by conducting a pro forma investigation, then rejecting the accusations, which would have invited charges of his own malfeasance or failure to supervise his subordinates. Instead, he labeled Iglesias a "trouble maker." Iglesias had little to gain from courts, which were more likely to enjoin labor activities than protect them. The island's House of Delegates also remained hostile to labor. Federal elected officials voiced support for a wide-ranging congressional investigation, but other matters always took precedence. Long-cultivated alliances also failed Iglesias. Early in the Wilson administration, McIntyre had encouraged Iglesias and Yager to develop a working relationship, advocated Iglesias's appointment to a government post, and urged Yager to nudge employers toward conciliation. But when the two men clashed, McIntyre protected his bureau from charges of misadministration by siding with Yager and declaring Iglesias a "violent" lawbreaker unfit even for a "minor capacity in the government." Iglesias's constitutional claims were dismissed as echoes of Gompers's "usual extreme

statements regarding the suppression of free speech, right of assembly, etc."
The president retained his faith in Yager.[52]

Iglesias found a governmental ally in the congressional Commission on Industrial Relations. The commission was a Progressive-era institution created to address conflicts between labor and capital. Its chairman aimed to "put the *law* itself to work for the public service." After hearing from Iglesias and island officials, the commission's director of research and investigation authored an influential report that endorsed Iglesias's view. Reaching Congress on 23 August 1915, the report found that "rural police and local magistrates" had "violated the personal rights of the strikers" and shown "wanton brutality," and island laborers suffered severe deprivations. "Responsibility rests upon the American Nation" for such colonized peoples, the commission declared, who "morally and legally" are "wards of the Nation."[53]

Iglesias had secured important interim returns. Laborers gained confidence, and an overwhelming number survived the strike, built relationships with other participants, and learned strategies to deploy next time. By documenting and responding to workers' complaints and investigating and condemning colonial officials who were not otherwise punished, federal actors validated workers as witnesses and complainants who deserved to be heard. Workers' accounts were now part of the historical record. By calling for federal action against the existential threat that "industrial feudalism" posed to the republic, the report of the director of the high-profile Commission on Industrial Relations confirmed the importance and viability of the strikers' broader legal claims.[54] Iglesias foresaw workers fighting for what they still lacked: better wages and working conditions, expanded rights, and power within island politics.

In 1916, Iglesias announced at the American Federation of Labor's annual meeting that a federal statute "granting American citizenship to the Porto Ricans (collectively)" remained a priority. The aspirations he attached to the status were hardly recognizable, however. Gone was his advocacy of citizenship that would secure the protection of a benevolent administrative state. As workers struck, organized, and withstood and challenged official repression, they acted less as wards than as assertive political, legal, and economic agents. Iglesias now lauded citizenship as a helpful tool in struggles to expand workers' rights and political clout.[55] Wisely, however, Iglesias identified no concrete rights of citizenship. Were the status to appear too valuable or meaningful, lawmakers might balk at extending it. The approach also reflected Iglesias's dynamic vision of citizenship. Citizenship would help secure hearings at which he could assert a right to strike. When federal decision makers sided with labor, new rights would begin to take hold and sometimes be associated with citizenship. Citizenship for him did not come with specific rights at the outset. Rather, he believed rights would emerge out of an iterative and elaborative process once the foothold of citizenship was achieved. His view of the value of citizenship was instrumental, and flexible, to be forged as opportunity allowed.

One corollary of Iglesias's view was that Puerto Ricans must be collectively naturalized, as Jones's bill proposed. For workers to bring citizenship-based claims to U.S. institutions, Puerto Rico had to remain part of the United States. As pro-independence Unionistas like José de Diego understood when they opposed such measures, collective naturalization was a "chain which will tie us forever" to the United States. Aware that lawmakers' support for citizenship partly rested on the understanding that it would not commit Congress to a particular future status for Puerto Rico, Iglesias declared it "very premature" to settle the question of eventual Puerto Rican statehood. After all, New Mexico and Oklahoma had to wait "one or two generations" for a decision.[56]

The value of remaining under U.S. sovereignty had increased for Iglesias as the U.S. government had grown to include new bureaucracies favorable to labor. After Puerto Rico created an island bureau of labor, for instance, Iglesias and Gompers asked U.S. Secretary of Labor William Wilson to recommend a new bureau chief to Yager. Wilson was formerly the international secretary-treasurer of the United Mine Workers, and he proposed longtime labor organizer F. C. Roberts. Yager agreed, and Roberts soon became Iglesias's stalwart defender. He lionized labor leaders and their movements as engines of Americanization and progress in Puerto Rico. He blamed strikes and the accompanying disorder not on laborers but on employers' greed, intimidation, and intransigence. Now, Jones's pending bill proposed to elevate labor concerns from the bureau level to the department level by creating a Department of Agriculture and Labor. The department's head would join the island's upper legislative chamber, the Executive Council. McIntyre counseled Yager that any such new department's head should be a "representative of labor."[57]

Iglesias vociferously opposed disfranchisement. He had previously been willing to support bills with disfranchisement provisions if they also provided for collective naturalization, but now he promised a "knock-out blow" for any bill that would unite "American citizenship" with "disfranchisement," as did Yager, McIntyre, and Jones's. His change of heart sprang from two events: the failure of the recent strikes, and his recent decision to harness island workers' growing militancy by founding the Puerto Rican Socialist Party. As the party name suggests, Iglesias had a more positive view of governmental power than Gompers. He and his colleagues had yet to test their electoral strength in an island election, but they espoused "democratic ideals" in the hope that broad suffrage would protect labor. Citizenship should bring new rights, not eliminate those long enjoyed under both Spanish and U.S. rule. The solution was "the people" exercising "their own means of correcting the evils."[58]

Iglesias's new stance confronted Democrats with a potential conflict between their fears of an inverted racial hierarchy and federal overreach. The solution of

House Democrat James Davis of Texas was to leave it to Puerto Rico to disfranchise, as his state had done: "We are acting for ourselves down there in Texas" by disfranchising, he declared, adding in reference to Puerto Ricans, "These people are not acting for themselves. When they treat themselves that way I have no objection" to their disfranchisement. Other Democrats gave even higher priority to racial hierarchy. Advocates of disfranchisement sought Senator Vardaman's vote by telling him it would "benefit the whites against the colored people." On 23 May 1916, Yager won. The House of Representatives passed a Puerto Rico reform bill that would make literacy or taxpaying a requirement to vote in the island's general elections.[59]

Iglesias and Gompers now sought to defeat the bill in the Senate. In December, Iglesias elicited support from Democrat John Shafroth of Colorado, the chairman of the Senate Committee on Pacific Islands and Porto Rico. Iglesias then visited the Capitol to state his case personally to each senator, and had island and mainland unions send senators letters against disfranchisement. Soon Iglesias reported that friendly senators were waging "a splendid battle" against disfranchisement. His cause gained an important ally when Republican progressive Robert La Follette of Wisconsin exercised his senatorial prerogative to prevent a vote until the issue was resolved. Gompers wrote La Follette to praise his stand for "the fundamental liberties of the people" and reiterated Iglesias's view that it was better "the bill be killed rather than it pass with unjust disfranchisement."[60]

By early 1917, imminent war forced the hands of colonial officials seeking to preserve disfranchisement. The Wilson administration now judged Puerto Rico reform to be urgent. The president opposed with increasing ferocity the oppression of weaker nations by stronger ones, and a failure to liberalize U.S. rule in Puerto Rico would expose Wilson to accusations of hypocrisy. Wilson laid out his vision in his high-profile January 1917 "Peace without Victory" speech. "Governments derive all their just powers from the consent of the governed," he said. "No right anywhere exists to hand peoples about from sovereignty to sovereignty as if they were property." He recast the Monroe Doctrine as a guarantor of national self-determination. As the United States sought to rally nations to the Allied cause, the indefinite U.S. retention of nonconsenting, non-self-governing, noncitizen Puerto Ricans undercut his most powerful ideals.[61]

Reform was particularly important to U.S. relations with the Caribbean and the rest of Latin America. The United States was not trusted in the region. It had recently established military rule in Haiti and set up a military police state in Santo Domingo. The sale of the Danish West Indies (today, the U.S. Virgin Islands) to the United States almost fell through because of Danish fears that island residents would not receive U.S. citizenship. Newly appointed Secretary of War Newton Baker declared: "The whole moral dominance of the Government of the United States in the American Mediterranean is involved

in our treatment of the people of Porto Rico, and these unfortunate delays give
... illustration for argument as to our neglect of the real interests of peoples
associated with us."[62]

Puerto Ricans' "impatient desire for citizenship" must not be tested, Baker
warned. Federal officials were wary of German adventurism, and Puerto Rico
lay on a key access route to the recently opened Panama Canal. Successful
passage of reform would improve islanders' morale, encourage military
enlistment and patriotism, and discourage "internal disturbance," as well as
insurrections and "plots against the Panama Canal."[63]

With the congressional term winding down and U.S. entry into World War
I imminent, Congress faced "direct and insistent urging" from Wilson and
Newton to enact Puerto Rican reforms. Backers of the bill concluded that
Senate passage required appeasing La Follette by jettisoning disfranchisement.
On 2 March 1917, the revised version of Colton's grand compromise became
law. The new statute collectively naturalized Puerto Ricans, unless they chose to
opt out; islanders also gained a bill of rights. But the law lacked jury and tariff-
uniformity guarantees. Puerto Rico also gained an Executive Council–level
Department of Agriculture and Labor. The new elected senate would be
checked by a conditional gubernatorial veto and absolute presidential and
congressional vetoes. Elections would be held every four years rather than
every two, and legislative sessions would switch from annual to biennial. Old
budgets would continue to remain in place until new ones were enacted, and the
U.S. president would continue to appoint the island's top judicial and executive
officials. How Puerto Ricans and U.S. officials would shape the meaning and
impact of the law, and the citizenship it bequeathed, remained a question for the
years to come.[64]

From 1900 to 1904 U.S. Supreme Court justices had joined administrators and
lawmakers in taking a tentative, innovative, and pragmatic approach to the
relationship between the Constitution and the U.S. imperial project.
Lawmakers took no stand on the U.S. citizenship of Puerto Ricans or the
eventual statehood of Puerto Rico. Many administrators conceded piecemeal
rights to Puerto Ricans to avoid deciding constitutional questions concerning
their status. The Supreme Court was unwilling either to adopt or reject the view
that the United States could hold colonies populated by nonindigenous
noncitizen subjects. These political and administrative actors recognized that
citizenship need not confer on recipients any specific – or many – rights. Even so,
War Department officials and congressional leaders from both parties came to
pursue policies consistent with the maintenance of colonies and colonized
peoples.[65]

This bipartisan support for empire was possible because Reconstruction was
finally dead. The citizenship at the center of the Jones Act remained a contested
and unstable construct that could be deployed for competing ends. Democrats,
Republicans, and Bureau of Insular Affairs officials gambled that courts would

accept collective naturalization disassociated from new constitutional rights and eventual statehood. Colonial officials expected citizenship to entrench colonial governance. It would both placate Puerto Ricans bitter about lack of self-government and undermine proponents of independence. Relatedly, the Jones Act disproved Collazo's prediction that Democrats would provide Puerto Ricans citizenship, rights, and self-government all at a stroke. But citizenship had brought Collazo a role in Democratic electoral politics, and now he wanted to build on that. Iglesias planned to wield citizenship on behalf of labor, claiming rights and demanding hearings for worker citizens. That he had risked losing naturalization to retain suffrage suggested a judgment that citizenship-based claims would fare much better now that they would be supported by political mobilization.

Conclusion

A month after the naturalization bill was passed, Puerto Ricans, like all U.S. citizens, were at war. President Wilson signed the formal declaration 6 April 1917. Involvement in the conflict that had convulsed Europe since 1914 transformed the United States. The federal government grew, assumed new responsibilities, and gained unprecedented power. The economy boomed in response to wartime demand for goods and labor. The labor movement was strengthened as union representatives served alongside business leaders on federal boards to regulate wages, prices, and the allocation of labor power to essential industries. The nation conscripted more than two million male citizens, hardened its borders, and curtailed civil liberties amid calls for all citizens to display patriotism.[1]

As the war in Europe continued, the constitutional counterrevolution in favor of empire at home neared its climax. For three decades before the U.S. imperial turn, the Reconstruction Constitution had made citizenship, bundled together with rights and statehood, a national imperative. That constitutional understanding had now been largely displaced by the territorial nonincorporation doctrine, which deconstitutionalized citizenship, rights, and statehood where empire was concerned. It also unbundled them; naturalization brought Puerto Ricans little closer to full constitutional rights and eventual statehood than had annexation. As a result, geography and race were often more determinative of Puerto Ricans' fortunes than citizenship.

Productive legal ambiguity remained the norm. With the prioritization of geography and race, citizenship would prove to be an especially partial and contingent status in Puerto Rico. For three central actors in Puerto Rican affairs – the War Department, Iglesias, and Collazo – citizenship was an adaptable and helpful tool during and after World War I, for each in a particular way. Collazo and Iglesias sought it because they perceived it to be honorable, and because they knew others wanted it and would support their efforts to secure it. But citizenship was imperfect. The status did not bring either man the rights, membership, democracy, or protection that he had sought. Citizenship mattered, but it also deceived.

Since the War Department had first governed Puerto Rico, in the years 1898 to 1900, the island's constitutional structure had been utterly transformed. In annexed places, the territorial nonincorporation doctrine had supplanted the Reconstruction Constitution as the prime determinant of membership, rights, and ultimate statehood. Citizenship was no longer either the preeminent constitutional status nor the herald of full constitutional rights and statehood that Federico Degetau had surmised during his crash course on the Reconstruction Constitution. Territorial nonincorporation sustained colonial governance. Regardless of citizenship, it marked the island as permanently subordinate, and islanders as racially inferior.

This ambiguity of citizenship reverberated in matters of conscription and military appointments. Colonial officials struggled to get residents of Puerto Rico equal access to West Point, Annapolis, and the Merchant Marine. Members of the army's Porto Rico Regiment faced greater obstacles to advancement than those in the regular army. For complex reasons, susceptibility to conscription varied not with citizenship or nationality, but by colony of residence. The Selective Service Act (1917) authorized conscription of citizens, according to population-based quotas, from each state, territory, and the District of Columbia, but not from Puerto Rico or the Philippines. Seeing "great economic advantage" in military service at a time when the War Department thought to place the entire army "under the conscription provision of the law," Bureau of Insular Affairs chief Frank McIntyre implemented the draft in Puerto Rico. Yager warned him there could be a "campaign for renunciation" of citizenship to avoid conscription, but McIntyre kept such refusals under 300 by reading citizenship out of the Selective Service Act: Puerto Ricans were statutorily "entitled to the protection of the United States" and hence "required to render service" to it, regardless of citizenship status. The evolving policy caught Ubaldino Ramírez Quiñones – and others – in its crosscurrents. To avoid being drafted before he received the dentistry diploma necessary to become an officer in the Dental Reserves Corps, Ramírez Quiñones had declined citizenship. When his diploma arrived, military superiors declared his noncitizenship a disqualification for the Dental Reserve Corps – yet he was eligible for conscription. Worse yet, the Bureau of Insular Affairs judged his refusal of citizenship to be irreversible.[2]

War Department officials enforced the subordinate status of Puerto Rico after ratification of the Nineteenth Amendment (1920), which banned state and federal governments from denying the right to vote to citizens on the basis of sex. Genera Pagán was a member of the Federación Libre, which had supported women's suffrage for years. When Pagán tried to register to vote under the new amendment, Yager sent the question of her eligibility up the bureaucratic chain and got a negative response from the judge advocate general. The Puerto Rican Supreme Court later elaborated that the Nineteenth Amendment did not extend to Puerto Rico. Island suffragists found themselves suspended between feminism and anticolonialism, and discovered that citizenship was, as regarded their access to the vote, irrelevant. When the island government declined to act further on the matter, some suffragists provoked anticolonialists' fury by seeking congressional intervention. Puerto Rico belatedly ended the conflict in 1935 by finally granting women the vote.[3]

Puerto Ricans on the mainland and in Hawai'i learned the same kind of lesson as the Puerto Rico's suffragists: their place of origin trumped their citizenship. The Bureau of Insular Affairs tracked how Puerto Ricans who left the island were "Americans but strangers," as an island newspaper put it. For three years, starting in World War I, federal law required an identity card or a passport for intra–United States travel involving Puerto Rico, citizen or not. Until the territorial Supreme Court intervened, Hawaiian officials declared their Puerto Rican residents to be noncitizens ineligible to vote, congressional statutes notwithstanding. In New York, Puerto Ricans were sometimes rejected as witnesses for naturalizations on grounds of their noncitizenship. Factories, shipyards, and military bases misclassified Puerto Ricans as aliens and paid them less or laid them off first. One island newspaper reported Puerto Ricans' citizenship was "useless" at the Port of New York because officials there treated them with the "same harshness as the poor Italian immigrants." When Puerto Ricans on the mainland sought proof of citizenship, colonial officials struggled to provide it. The State Department limited passports to those traveling abroad. After distributing at least one ad hoc certificate of citizenship, the Bureau of Insular Affairs disclaimed authority to continue. A bureau broadside informing "the people of the mainland that the Porto Ricans are their 'fellow citizens'" left sufficient confusion that the Puerto Rican government eventually began issuing its own certifications of Puerto Rican migrants' citizenship.[4]

In many cases, racism underlay the confusion over whether naturalized Puerto Ricans were citizens. Sometimes military officials condoned or promulgated policies expressly elevating race above citizenship. When South Carolina's arch white-supremacist senator, Benjamin Tillman, objected to any "Porto Rican negroes" joining Puerto Rican troops who were slated for training in his state, some of the troops were instead trained in Puerto Rico in segregated army camps. Puerto Rican naval enlistees reported that "gringoes ... make fun of us, not knowing that we are citizens." They recalled a commanding officer who "forced a colored Porto Rican to box" a stronger man to show that "Americans are strong enough to whip any foreigner." The racial segregation and disparagement stung, in part because racial hierarchies were consequential in Puerto Rico too. These navy enlistees sought to ascend the racial hierarchy, not reject it. They objected to the "colored companies" in which they were placed, insisting that they were of "true Spanish descent" and adding, "[We] don't think a drop of negro blood runs in our veins."[5]

Clearly, citizenship was doing little to buoy Puerto Ricans' hopes of achieving equality with white mainlanders, full constitutional rights, or island self-government. This reality contrasted sharply with President Wilsons' rhetoric on self-determination as the guiding principle of U.S. war aims, politics, and international relations. Many people in dependent lands had understood those words as a repudiation of empire, especially because their author was the powerful president of a nation forged in an anticolonial revolution. Had Federico Degetau survived, he likely would have heard echoes of the Reconstruction Constitution. Wilson's words were intended to have a much narrower focus, however. As Wilson soon made clear, the right to immediate self-determination ended at the color line; only whiteness conferred full rights of self-determination. Puerto Rican political leaders condemned the glaring mismatch between Wilson's aspirations and their island's condition.[6]

In contrast, Wilson's intentions were good news for the Bureau of Insular Affairs. Even so, any opportunities for the bureau to extend its power were limited – primarily because U.S. governance of Caribbean locales beyond Puerto Rico and the Philippines was in retreat. The Dominican occupation ended in 1922, and U.S. Marines left Nicaragua soon after that. Threats of a U.S. occupation of Cuba or Mexico, or a Honduran receivership, had also passed. Nonbureau entities governed Haiti (the U.S. Marines and the State Department, from 1915 to 1934); the Panama Canal Zone; Hawai'i and Alaska (Department of the Interior); and Guam, American Samoa, and the Virgin Islands (U.S. Navy). Even in Puerto Rico, the bureau shared authority with the presidentially appointed governor. And when Republican Warren Harding succeeded Woodrow Wilson as president, he chose a corrupt, incompetent, and racist governor, E. Montgomery Reily. "Porto Ricans are children," Reily wrote to Harding, and he could not "associate" with the island's "half-blooded negro" commissioner of immigration. With the increasingly powerful Iglesias demanding the transfer of Puerto Rico to the Department of the Interior, and the Philippines slated for independence, it seemed more likely that the bureau would be extinguished than that it would be elevated into a colonial department along British lines.[7]

To resist Puerto Ricans' demands for improved governance, War Department officials touted citizenship. They rewrote the history of Puerto Ricans' collective naturalization, promoted the expressive significance of citizenship, and stopped dismissing the status as an "empty gift." They hoped to quell Puerto Ricans' discontent and deemphasize colonial aspects of Puerto Rico's governance. McIntyre opportunistically described Puerto Ricans' path to citizenship as an example of federal deference to islanders' interests and wishes. Congress withheld citizenship before 1905 to avoid triggering the Constitution's financially burdensome revenue clauses, he said.

After 1905, War Department officials, presidents, and congressmen had joined Puerto Ricans in support of citizenship. Legislation had been delayed only by its entanglement with other issues. Lawmakers' doubts about Puerto Ricans' fitness for citizenship did not deter it, nor did World War I hasten it.[8]

McIntyre's was a shrewd and self-serving rewriting of history. In reality, Congress withheld citizenship in 1900 to create a legislative test case for the Philippines. It added the provision potentially contravening constitutional revenue clauses to narrow that case.[9] The revenue clauses were no insurmountable obstacle: the expedient of passing Puerto Rican funds through the Treasury would have cured any problem. Citizenship bills repeatedly fell to senators' objections. Many lawmakers saw Puerto Ricans as racial inferiors. And World War I was indeed the raison d'être for collective naturalization, which was enacted despite opposition from the elected representative of Puerto Rico.[10]

McIntyre's revisionist account incorporated Secretary of War John Weeks's view, conveyed to (but not heeded by) Governor Reily in 1921: citizenship should not be described as an "empty gift," for its glorification as a valuable and undifferentiated status was the sine qua non of successful governance. "To the people of Porto Rico, as to all Americans," Weeks said, "the first appeal of our country is to the heart." Puerto Ricans had the same citizenship as those in all U.S. states and former territories. It carried "every right and privilege" and demanded the "same service and loyalty."[11] Now War Department officials defended U.S. rule by celebrating islanders' citizenship and the juridical dignity and equality that it ostensibly bestowed.

The War Department's tactic of celebrating citizenship relied on officials' confidence that Puerto Ricans could not use their citizenship to overthrow colonial rule. That confidence, in turn, reflected a revolution in the meaning of citizenship, away from protecting its holders' autonomy. The Supreme Court had asserted the prior view in *Hodges v. United States* (1906), which held that the Reconstruction amendments empowered Congress to prevent race discrimination only by governmental actors. As the Court explained, to hold otherwise would undermine liberty by rejecting the national judgment after the Civil War that "declined to constitute" African Americans as "wards of the nation …, but gave them citizenship" instead. Unincorporated territories were not the only place where third-class citizenship was developed. American Indians' relationship to U.S. citizenship followed a parallel trajectory away from substantive visions. Before annexing Puerto Rico, the United States had launched an Indian policy that aimed to end American Indians' dependence through coterminous naturalization and assimilation. By 1920 most American Indians were U.S. citizens – yet the status had neither ended their subjugation and inequality nor displaced federal guardianship as their defining status. Many lacked rights and remained subject to Indian Office administration. Arizona declared all

Indians, regardless of citizenship, to be "under guardianship," hence ineligible to vote.[12] Courts that once cited federal duties to honor treaty guarantees as the reason behind federal oversight now pointed to Indians' alleged inability to manage their own affairs. Guardianship survived citizenship unless Congress said otherwise, the Supreme Court reasoned in *United States v. Celestine* (1909) and *United States v. Nice* (1916). When the collective naturalization of American Indians that many had sought a generation or two before finally came in 1924, it produced little excitement. No Puerto Rico case recognized citizen-wards quite so explicitly as *Celestine* and *Nice*, but a judicial test was brewing.[13]

The relationship of naturalization to territorial incorporation reached the Supreme Court after the District Court for Porto Rico and the Puerto Rico Supreme Court each overturned convictions of defendants who had been denied jury rights. In the cases *In re Tapia* (1917) and *Muratti v. Foote* (1917), the respective courts declared that post-naturalization Puerto Rico was incorporated. In the subsequent brief to the Supreme Court, U.S. Attorney General Howard Kern advanced Felix Frankfurter's claim that the "great diversity" in forms of U.S. governance in occupied lands proved that Congress had discretion to fix a place's status without reference to the status of its people. He also analogized Puerto Ricans to American Indians, whose dependence survived their mass naturalization.[14]

To the War Department's satisfaction, the Supreme Court treated the Reconstruction Constitution as a paper tiger to be brushed aside by the unfolding of empire. In early 1918 the justices summarily reversed both decisions. The Court's terse citation to a handful of prior *Insular Cases* (1901–1914) offered little clarification of controlling doctrine. But, whatever Puerto Rico's actual status, McIntyre was satisfied that it had not changed. As Secretary of War Weeks later told Republican president Warren Harding, confusion was in fact central to U.S. policy. Every former president and secretary of war who expressed himself on the matter was "committed against" a "promise of statehood," he wrote. But presumably because such expressions could outrage Puerto Ricans, he advised that the best approach was to say nothing.[15]

Thus it was that doctrinal and political confusion concerning the status of Puerto Rico fortified colonial officials' authority over the island. No pre-1899 acquisition with a recorded population as large and dense as Puerto Rico's had ever been relegated to territorial status, much less indefinitely. Yet it remained unclear to an observer whether Puerto Ricans would ever "be given their statehood or their independence or whether their legal status [was] to be left dangling, like Mahomet's coffin, betwixt the heaven of their aspirations and the earth of their disillusionment."[16]

In the meantime, Iglesias told the American Federation of Labor that Puerto Rico and Puerto Ricans, respectively, were an unincorporated organized territory and U.S. citizens "not under the Constitution." These pairings were novel, awkward, counterintuitive, and ambiguous. But they were amenable to empire. In just over twenty years, the conventional legal wisdom that annexation brought citizenship together with full constitutional rights and eventual statehood had dissolved. Neither annexation nor citizenship now appeared likely to trigger rights or statehood. The Court was unlikely to alter Iglesias's complaint that "after twenty years of American domination, we have not been able to know what the Congress of the United States intends to do with us." That was precisely the legal and political goal, not the problem.[17]

Collazo had voiced a similar lament twelve years earlier in the midst of his pursuit of citizenship, rights, and autonomy for Puerto Ricans. Before 1898 he had advocated revolution. Afterward, he pressed constitutional claims on federal officials. Pragmatically willing to secure islanders benefits under either the Reconstruction Constitution or Democrats' constitutional commitment to home rule, he turned to military officials, Supreme Court justices, and elected Democrats. But none of them vindicated his constitutional vision.

By mid-1917 that constitutional vision lay in tatters, collective naturalization notwithstanding. Only the possibility of a governmental post on the island remained of Collazo's plan to leverage his citizenship and stateside residence and take a hand in island affairs. The wartime expansion of the federal government brought Collazo his last, best chance at a patronage appointment in Puerto Rico.

Collazo deployed his relationships with Democrats, Unionistas, Iglesias, and Gompers. Aspiring to become treasurer of Puerto Rico, he moved to San Juan, entered Unionista-dominated politics, and secured recommendations from mainland Democratic colleagues with whom he had worked during the presidential campaign. But the Bureau of Insular Affairs remained hostile, and Yager declined to appoint him. Then, seeking closer alignment with Iglesias and Gompers, Collazo published a letter in the San Juan *Times* echoing their attacks on Governor Yager. Around the same time, Yager defeated an attempt to place Collazo on the censorship board. Collazo moved back to the mainland. Once there, he provided evidence of islanders' poverty before the National War Labor Board (NWLB) to support Iglesias's and Gompers's complaints. He helped organize a meeting of Ibero-Americans in New York for a cause that Gompers and Iglesias shared: prevention of U.S. military intervention in Mexico. Gompers recommended Collazo to President Wilson as translator for the planned investigation of conditions in Puerto Rico. But the Bureau of Insular Affairs' memory was long. McIntyre gathered evidence against Collazo from the bureau's copious files. Before the issue came to a head, however, Republicans took control of the federal government, and momentum for the investigation fizzled.[18]

Collazo's failure to win Democratic patronage by 1920 reflected Democrats' unwillingness to end colonialism in Puerto Rico and set the island on the path of prior territories. Despite eight years of Democratic rule, the Bureau of Insular Affairs' authority and Puerto Ricans' wardship remained entrenched. Stateside political consensus in favor of colonialism ruled out major constitutional innovations. Collazo abandoned his theory that Congress could promise Puerto Rico statehood without causing the Supreme Court to enforce the Constitution's revenue clauses there. Traditional territorial status would cost the island $21 million annually, he declared in New York newspapers. Puerto Rico's best hope was an improved colonial status, with Puerto Rico becoming a self-governing community "after the English fashion in Canada or Australia."[19]

At this point Collazo largely abandoned Puerto Rico as a field of politics. He focused instead on becoming a political boss in New York City. Citizenship and the suffrage it often provided made the shift possible. To integrate thousands of registered New York voters of Puerto Rican descent into the Democratic machine, Collazo created political clubs and fostered alliances between existing organizations. To overcome divisions of class, race, and borough – as well as disagreements over Puerto Rican independence – he promoted a consensus around a moderate set of aspirations: patriotic anti-imperialism, island self-government, and citizenship rights. Bridging the color line was vital to the creation of an ethnic Puerto Rican voting bloc. But it was difficult. New York's color line was entrenched. Collazo's revolutionary colleague of color, Arturo Schomburg, who maintained close social ties with Puerto Ricans and mainland-born African Americans, chose to live in the black community in Brooklyn. Working-class activist Bernardo Vega recalled a white Puerto Rican family whose white neighbors drove them from their building because the family invited Puerto Ricans of color into their home. Emphasizing the common roots of the *colonia* (the community of Puerto Ricans resident in New York), Collazo celebrated the love of homeland that animated *independistas*, including many politically active *colonia* elites. Speaking to workers, he memorialized artisans of color and other veterans of the revolutionary anti-imperial struggle in which he had participated in the 1890s. Collazo described the poet, fellow typesetter, and eventual revolutionary soldier Francisco Gonzalo Marín as the "black Lord Byron."[20]

Collazo's strategy circumscribed his ability to speak out. At one point he became concerned that runaway debt, corruption, and overtaxation would so reduce business profits in Puerto Rico as to discourage new investments there. He wanted to persuade mainland decision makers that a class war could be the result. Normally, that would mean a letter to the editor of a large-circulation, English-language New York newspaper, but associating himself with such an analysis could alienate labor interests. Instead, Collazo wrote under his niece Isabel Gonzalez's name, and once again she became the instrument for others' ambitions. Because experience had taught Collazo the importance of ensuring beforehand that Gonzalez would vouch for him if asked, it is easy to imagine that she approved and perhaps helped craft "her" letter to the *New York Times*. The former partners in litigation and propaganda remained linked by family ties, including those between Gonzalez and her daughter Eva, whom Collazo treated as his child.[21]

Collazo also united the *colonia* through criticism of common enemies and attention to common complaints. When Governor Yager's successor, E. Montgomery Reily, proved disastrous, Collazo organized protests against him. In New York newspapers, Collazo advocated that Puerto Rico be governed by Puerto Ricans. A committee he led demanded that Democrats invite New Yorkers of Puerto Rican descent to participate in their own governance by nominating someone for a local office. As *colonia* leaders increasingly made citizenship a basis for claims to better treatment in New York, he celebrated those who fought for "citizenship rights." When election boards of registry failed to recognize the citizenship of applicants of Puerto Rican descent, Collazo complained. The strategy worked; Collazo became the *colonia*'s representative at Tammany Hall.[22]

By the time Collazo died – of a heart attack, on 23 September 1929 – he was deeply enmeshed in shifting Puerto Ricans' influence from the island to the mainland. Early on, many Puerto Ricans had turned to the island's resident commissioner for help, regardless of where in the United States they were. But as stateside Puerto Ricans gained political clout, they found it more effective to lobby their own congressional representatives. In fact, island residents eventually realized that congressmen who represented heavily Puerto Rican mainland districts were in a better position to advocate for the island.[23]

This dynamic was the result of the island's colonial condition. Thus, though Collazo experienced his turn toward New York as limiting his horizons, the *colonia* would soon outstrip the colony in political importance to the United States.

By contrast, Santiago Iglesias leveraged citizenship to carry Puerto Ricans' struggles to the national stage. War did not dim his enthusiasm for this approach. Instead, the island labor leader reformulated his concept of citizenship to meet new circumstances. Before the war, he had celebrated citizenship as an additional basis for claiming rights and gaining a federal hearing. As World War I shifted the federal government's stance toward unions from one of conflict to cooperation, Iglesias recast citizenship as providing entrée to new federal bureaucracies that regulated the labor supply. Such access brought opportunities to participate in the national strategies of the American Federation of Labor at a time when those strategies paid handsomely.

At the root of the opportunity was President Wilson's decision to commit the United States to world war. To build national capacity, Wilson partnered with willing nongovernmental organizations and punished dissenters. Thus, when the Industrial Workers of the World and the Socialist Party of America opposed the war, they faced official repression. Gompers's full-throated support of Wilson, on the other hand, bought the AFL a prominent seat at the table, especially because Wilson needed uninterrupted industrial production following the record number of strikes carried out during the six months following the United States' entry into World War I. Gompers had twice backed Wilson for president, including in the 1916 reelection campaign that Wilson won by a slim margin. Jettisoning his long-held pacifism, Gompers engineered the defeat of resolutions brought by powerful antiwar factions within the AFL, and instituted an AFL-wide policy against strikes. In turn, Wilson placed Gompers on the advisory commission of a national defense council and made him chair of the commission's labor committee. He became the first U.S. president to address the annual AFL convention. He placed five Gompers allies on the War Labor Conference Board to articulate the principles of wartime industrial relations. That board proposed the National War Labor Board to adjust industrial disputes. Wilson agreed. He chose as cochair Frank Walsh, the Gompers ally who had been chair of the Commission on Industrial Relations, which was friendly to Iglesias.[24]

The NWLB held special promise for Iglesias, if only it would hear him. It was a quasi-adjudicative institution that could potentially displace colonial officials as the key arbiters of labor strife in Puerto Rico. The board conducted hearings on complaints, usually made by workers. After taking evidence, it issued decisions that aimed to protect workers' and employers' rights while also advancing the public interest in such matters as equitable pay and living wages. The board had no enforcement authority, but the backing of the president during wartime gave it considerable persuasive power. Iglesias's challenge was to establish that the board was the proper authority to manage island labor strife.[25]

Where island labor was concerned, Yager considered his authority paramount. This was a recipe for conflict, given his conservative labor politics. He had already clashed with Walsh over the breadth of workers' expressive freedoms. He then split with the Department of Labor's Puerto Rico conciliator F. C. Roberts over how to measure labor strife, and on the propriety of conciliating a dispute before it expanded into an islandwide strike. Viewing the dispute as his to resolve, he engineered the reassignment of Roberts, outside Puerto Rico. When the American Federation of Labor sent its own investigators, Yager condemned their attempts to rouse workers to industrial activism and moved to deport them unless they tempered their rhetoric.[26]

Iglesias rejected Yager's claim to primacy over labor matters on the island. He demanded the benefit of the new national policies. Thus, when a contract fight loomed in the sugar industry in late 1917, Iglesias welcomed the special agent sent by the Department of Labor to conciliate. Though sugar growers refused to negotiate and Yager declined to step in, Iglesias sought federal intervention. Even after the harvest season opened in December, he was willing to delay the strike at Gompers's request. But when further outreach to federal officials also failed, sugar workers laid down their tools. By April 2 the strike included thousands or tens of thousands of workers. When the usual violence and repression followed, Iglesias and Gompers complained to the NWLB and President Wilson.[27]

The complaints stressed workers' citizenship, in an effort to strengthen workers' freedom of expression and complement it with other protections rooted in the public interest and in wartime obligations. In each case, the invocation of Puerto Ricans' citizenship reinforced the claim that Puerto Rico should benefit from policies applicable throughout the United States. Thus, Iglesias and Gompers argued that renewed violence and repression demonstrated that "Porto Rico workers are not protected in their rights as free citizens." As a result, though sugar prices had doubled and island living costs outstripped those on the mainland, sugar wages in Puerto Rico were barely half those in Cuba, Hawai'i, Honduras, and the Bahamas. Island workers were "practically starving." Because the victims were citizens, their poverty and suffering contravened the public interest of the United States. As the men put it: "It is hardly conceivable that such a thing still happens in a country enjoying American citizenship." The strike cut sugar production, but the fault for indirectly providing "aid and comfort to the enemy" lay with Yager and the growers, Iglesias charged. As one labor leader told President Wilson, citizen "workers have been loyal to you and the nation." In line with federal policy, they sought productive conciliation, which growers rejected and Yager refused to provide.[28]

A resolution was reached because the broader War Department did not share Yager's distaste for the federal labor bureaucracy. Although War Department officials defended Yager, they urged him to take more active steps to alleviate islanders' poverty and supported a federal investigation in Puerto Rico. Because the NWLB was also preparing to investigate, President Wilson combined the two inquiries.[29] Colonial Puerto Rico was set to become a new front in what Frank Walsh promoted as the federal war on domestic industrial autocracy.

During the same period, President Wilson wanted to use Iglesias and Gompers's nascent Pan-American Federation of Labor (PAFL) to rally organized labor throughout the Americas to get behind U.S. war aims. Iglesias distinguished himself in this effort. He had conceived the PAFL as a response to the specter of united pan-American capital. The institutional framework was to come from Gompers's existing work with Mexican labor leaders to prevent United States–Mexico military conflicts. As Gompers's foremost adviser and spokesperson on Latin American and especially Caribbean affairs, Iglesias drafted the case for the PAFL and served with Gompers on the implementation committee. But when the United States entered World War I, Wilson moved to co-opt the project. By the time Iglesias and other U.S. labor leaders finally reached Mexico in 1918, they were actively collaborating with administration officials. The labor men encouraged Mexico to join the war on the allies' side and reported back to the U.S. ambassador. The administration then discreetly funded the PAFL newspaper, and in November 1918 Secretary of Labor William Wilson addressed its first conference. With active fighting over in Europe, Gompers secured Mexican trade unionists' support for President Wilson's peace aims.[30]

The Pan-American Federation of Labor seemed a promising field for Iglesias. When a U.S. street railway union denied a charter to a Puerto Rican local, Iglesias had Gompers object that such discrimination undermined the PAFL. At Iglesias's urging, the PAFL demanded that Puerto Ricans receive greater citizenship rights and escape War Department "despotism." Within the PAFL, Iglesias gathered increasing influence, which culminated in his appointment as its paid Spanish-language secretary. He also became the official American Federation of Labor representative to the labor movements of Latin America. Those duties took him to the Dominican Republic, Cuba, the Virgin Islands, and Central America, and brought him into contact with matters in Venezuela and Peru as well.[31]

Iglesias rose so high within the PAFL because Puerto Rico was the only place in Latin America then under U.S. sovereignty, and because the PAFL was no federation of equals. Gompers treated the PAFL as a vehicle for his imperial designs, a strategy soon dubbed "labor's Monroe Doctrine." As with the policy it mimicked, Gompers's approach masked dominance and self-dealing with a language of cooperation and protection. Latin American unions were not necessarily anxious to become clients of the AFL, especially where radicalism, race, and immigration were concerned. Gompers and the AFL risked alienating Latin American labor movements by condemning socialism and denouncing communism as intolerable "aggression." Racism further tested Latin American delegates' goodwill. The AFL vociferously objected to meeting wartime labor demand in the United States with Mexican workers. Gompers defeated an effort to have the PAFL address anti-Mexican discrimination by AFL unions. Instead, Gompers sought a total halt to immigration, in part to safeguard the United States' "racial purity." Gompers's ally, Secretary of Labor Wilson, drafted legislation authorizing the deportation of aliens who joined radical groups. Given that most PAFL delegates hailed from Latin America in 1919, Iglesias's role as Gompers's junior Latin American partner made him a particularly valuable surrogate. Iglesias never fully internalized Gompers's conservatism. He led a Socialist Party, praised revolutionary Russia, and lent his name to fundraising efforts, thereby inviting charges of radicalism, and braved Gompers's occasional criticism. Nevertheless, he had a close working relationship with Gompers. Iglesias implicitly and then explicitly assented to the AFL's exclusionism – in part because stateside demand for migrant Puerto Rican workers might rise as a result.[32]

Iglesias's decision to join Gompers in open opposition to others' liberty of movement departed strikingly from his own experience. As a four-time migrant, he had depended on access to mobility. But his decision was in line with a hardening of nationality and national borders during and after World War I. For its part, the United States soon subjected aliens from outside the Americas to national quotas that favored northern and western Europe. It also expanded exclusion from Chinese immigrants to Japanese ones. The self-determination and international equality that Gompers and the Wilson administration had trumpeted in forming the Pan-American Federation of Labor and negotiating the European peace were part of this broader shift. In Gompers's and eventually Iglesias's hands, the right of labor to autonomy within national borders included the power to insulate itself from external threats. Citizenship, in other words, carried the right to exclude.[33]

When Iglesias defended immigration restrictions, he emphasized the disappointing results of labor migration from Puerto Rico, declaring such migration "detrimental" to the sending community, the émigrés, and workers in the receiving community. During World War I, 12,000 islanders worked in stateside army camps. Many grew ill and died, and survivors returned home with little to show for their work. Puerto Rican labor activist Joaquin Colón López declared these migrants the "worst compensated, most ignored, longest suffering, most abandoned" citizens in the country. As the Great Migration of African Americans from the rural South to the urban North gained steam in the 1920s, Southern planters sought to replace farmworkers who left with Puerto Rican labor. U.S. officials supported such efforts, even though they generally produced poor results. A large labor migration to Arizona launched in 1926 collapsed soon afterward amid migrants' dissatisfaction and protest. Nativism, ethnically tinged "red scares," violence against immigrants and racial and ethnic minorities, and white resentment of nonwhite strikebreakers erupted throughout the United States. Work open to migrant Puerto Ricans was often below prevailing wages, and taking such jobs could harm or anger local workers. Migrants' deaths, illnesses, absences, financial ruin, and loss of contact with home in turn wreaked havoc back in Puerto Rico. Iglesias was well positioned to see how emigration could also prevent reforms at home. Colonial officials' fantasies of annually sending 100,000 islanders elsewhere to work bred a fatalistic attitude toward Puerto Rico's endemic, extreme poverty.[34]

By the time Iglesias expressly assailed immigration at the PAFL's 1927 conference, he had also grown substantially more dependent on the island's prolabor voters. Labor's World War I gains were never consolidated and institutionalized. Instead, between 1918 and 1922 the Great War ended, a massive stroke disabled President Wilson, and Republicans rode an antilabor backlash to take control of the federal government. The planned investigation of labor conditions in Puerto Rico died in the planning stage, and economic recession enveloped the nation. The AFL had swelled to four million members but then shrank by a third. In Puerto Rico, workers in the increasingly consolidated sugar industry won gains, then lost them. Male unemployment on the island soared from 20 percent in 1920 to 30 percent in 1926. Strikes decreased. Malnutrition and hunger worsened. Yet workers persevered. Membership in the Federación Libre tripled from its pre-1916 level to nearly thirty thousand, then remained at that level throughout the 1920s. From 1920 through the 1930s, workers and their allies provided Iglesias's Socialist Party with a quarter of all island votes. Leveraging that support into alliances and power, Iglesias became resident commissioner from 1933 until his death in 1939.[35]

Iglesias's political ascent was the final step in his remarkable transformation. Iglesias had entered adulthood in 1890s Cuba as an anti-imperial revolutionary labor activist who was subject to arrest for seeking Cuban independence from Spain. More than three decades later, little beyond labor activism remained of his résumé. He had become a U.S. citizen, Puerto Rico's elected representative in Congress, and an ally of mainland labor leaders intent on refashioning pan-American labor relations in the image of an imperialistic U.S. foreign policy. The glue that had always bound Iglesias's shifting labor-activist personae was faith in citizenship. At his memorial, Iglesias's son-in-law and successor in office declared that Iglesias died having "won his battle" by living to see "the workingmen and the common people recognized as citizens." He did not add that Iglesias had reinvented the status of citizenship even as he reinvented himself. Iglesias had variously conceived of citizenship as facilitating migration, promising rights or supporting claims, averting self-government, preventing immigration, and preserving U.S. sovereignty. He pursued these intellectual contortions in part because he always saw citizenship as an effective, pragmatic foundation on which to build alliances and advance substantive projects.[36]

But his steadfast pursuit of citizenship for Puerto Ricans also reflected his broader faith in government as a potential agent of positive change. In seeking to advance his ideals, he repeatedly turned to imperial officials and those who had their ear. He identified as a socialist throughout his life and admired communist Russia, both of which were attitudes that exemplified his faith in the potential for state power to be used for the good of the working class. The best evidence of Iglesias's commitment to government-centered aspirations for betterment may well be his choice to embody it as his legacy. He and his wife, Justa, named their first five daughters Libertad, Fraternidad, Igualdad, Justicia, and América.[37] Iglesias's successful campaign for collective naturalization had brought them all citizenship in 1917.

Unequivocal endorsement of territorial nonincorporation finally came through a test case that Iglesias had helped to engineer. In April 1918

Iglesias's colleague, the veteran labor organizer José Balzac, criticized governor of Puerto Rico Arthur Yager in print as an "odious grave-digger of the people." A criminal libel prosecution followed, and Balzac sought to make the trial a referendum on Yager's labor policies. He demanded a jury and time to bring Iglesias to the court as a witness. The court denied both requests, then convicted him. Iglesias posted bond. Balzac appealed to the U.S. Supreme Court. He retained Jackson Ralston, who had represented such labor activists as Samuel Gompers in Supreme Court cases and other appeals involving libel and constitutional law. Now closely following the case, Gompers wrote Ralston that he hoped the decision would bring Puerto Rico the Constitution in full. But the 1918 *In re Tapia* decision permitting the denial of constitutional jury rights in Puerto Rico foreclosed that result, leaving Ralston few good arguments.[38]

Worse, Ralston faced an unsympathetic bench. Six of the sitting justices had been appointed by Republican presidents who came to the White House after Republicans abandoned any serious commitment to protecting African Americans' rights. One, Joseph McKenna, had joined Justice White's concurrence in *Downes v. Bidwell* (1901). He was among five Republicans appointed by McKinley, Roosevelt, or Taft, each of whom had advocated the imperial turn. The sixth Republican appointee was Taft himself, now chief justice. Woodrow Wilson appointed the three others after his Democratic Party had irreversibly overthrown Reconstruction. As a result, opposition to federal overreach no longer rivaled white supremacy as a guiding principle of Democrats' approach to empire. Unlike their predecessors, the new justices had no history of upholding strands of the Reconstruction Constitution at odds with territorial nonincorporation doctrine. By the time these justices had come to the Court, Justice White's territorial nonincorporation doctrine and the Court's seeming receptivity to noncitizen nationality had both become mainstream ways to explain and justify empire.[39]

In *Balzac v. Porto Rico* (1922), the justices rejected the Reconstruction Constitution rule that tied annexation and citizenship to full constitutional rights. Writing for a unanimous Court, Taft proclaimed the territorial nonincorporation doctrine. Though the Court had previously indicated that statutory naturalization triggered incorporation, Taft rejected that presumption. Because White's concurrence and its progeny had "fixed the attention" of legislators on the question of incorporation, the prospective rule would be that "incorporation is not to be assumed without express declaration" or its equivalent. Because Congress had not spoken, Puerto Rico remained unincorporated, and thus the Constitution did not require jury trials there.[40]

In a sign of things to come, Taft clarified neither what constitutional rights turned on the line between incorporated and unincorporated status, nor how such rights were to be identified. This remains the law a century later. Truly, ambiguity has been the handmaiden of empire.[41]

Balzac also contributed to the conventional legal wisdom that the Constitution empowered federal lawmakers to deannex lands, maintain perpetual territories, and admit new states. Taft portrayed statehood as but one status to which lands acquired by the United States could ascend. Later Supreme Court decisions reasoned – though never quite held – that deannexation and perpetual territorial status are valid alternatives. Because incorporation was the "step ... leading to statehood," the Court declared taking that step to be "not our province" but instead one to "be begun and taken by Congress." With the Philippine Independence Act (1934), Congress established a transition process that culminated in the Philippines' independence from the United States in 1946. Six years later Congress permitted Puerto Rico to establish itself as a relatively autonomous U.S. commonwealth. Even now the Court has shown no hesitation in recognizing the legitimacy of either arrangement. It treats Filipino independence as fact, and in 2016 described the commonwealth status of Puerto Rico as the result of Congress exercising its constitutional power over territories. The Court has never directly confronted the question of whether either arrangement is constitutional, but it has ready means to uphold both. Constitutional text and the Court's own precedents commit to the political branches decisions to admit new states and recognize foreign governments.[42] Practicalities and long acquiescence make contrary holdings all but unthinkable.

Collazo and Iglesias learned the lesson that politics can trump constitutional law, and even reshape it. Their aspirations consistently included the relationship that citizenship forged between individuals and officialdom. Abandoning revolution for reform, the one-time firebrands accrued personal power by participating in government at the federal, state, territorial, and local levels. Late in life, they made politics central to their public projects, a shift spurred by fights for citizenship, and by citizenship already secured.

Afterword

In the century since the collective naturalization of Puerto Ricans, it has become clear that citizenship is still important. Citizenship distinguished Puerto Ricans from Filipinos, most significantly by bringing Puerto Ricans the enduring freedom to migrate within the United States. Today, more U.S. citizens of Puerto Rican descent live off the island than on it. Puerto Ricans on the mainland comprise the nation's second-largest group of Latinos. They have become a formidable political constituency. Mainland life has also brought many Puerto Ricans into close-up encounters with the hard edges of U.S. racial hierarchies. Perhaps partly as a result of discrimination, mainland Puerto Ricans are less likely than those on the island to describe themselves as white.[1] As the Puerto Rican diaspora has grown, Iglesias's affirmation that citizenship would chain the island to the mainland in perpetuity has proven prophetic.

Not only has citizenship mattered, but it has had the capacity to be determinative. The 1957 Supreme Court decision in *Reid v. Covert* involved the wives of two active-duty soldiers stationed on U.S. military bases abroad. Each woman was charged with killing her husband on an overseas base, and they faced courts-martial rather than juries. Both were convicted, and both appealed to the Supreme Court on the grounds that they had a right to a jury. When the Court first heard the women's consolidated case, it cited earlier decisions declaring it "clearly settled" that the right to a jury trial did not extend beyond the incorporated United States. A year later, the Court reversed itself: four justices "reject[ed] the idea that when the United States acts against citizens abroad it can do so free of the Bill of Rights." A fifth vote came from John Marshall Harlan II, who now opposed the "sweeping proposition" that constitutional jury rights "have no application to the trial of American citizens outside the United States." As Justice Anthony Kennedy observed later, the focus on citizenship in *Covert* was typical: "In cases involving the extraterritorial application of the Constitution, we have taken care to state whether the person claiming its protection is a citizen."[2]

The Court's reversal probably would not have surprised Frederic Coudert. He described the *Insular Cases* as a choice for the Court between upholding its "reverence for the Constitution" and allowing "the United States properly to govern a people so alien." These two conflicting desires, he told *Columbia Law Review* readers, "were reconciled by [an] ingenious and original doctrine" whose "very vagueness ... was valuable." Those who held such views inhabited a world constituted by racial hierarchy and conceived in racist terms. Neither Coudert nor the U.S. officials studied in this book transcended that world, a failure that poisoned even their best intentions. Perhaps that failure was an implicit admission of the impossibility of harmonizing constitutional ideals with imperial realities.[3] We have learned that lesson in the perils of empire after 120 years and more of suffering for Puerto Ricans. It is not over yet.

Puerto Rico is still an unincorporated territory. Self-government and constitutional rights there are tenuous. The *Insular Cases* are still binding precedent. The Supreme Court has never clarified whether the Fourteenth Amendment demands citizenship for those born in Puerto Rico or merely permits Congress to act. Looking back at the Court's work, the eminent Puerto Rican jurist José Trías Monge took a more pessimistic view than Coudert. The justices, he charged, had abetted the longest-surviving democracy on earth in remaining responsible for the "oldest colony in the world."[4]

Today, harms to Puerto Ricans from racism, association with foreignness, and lack of federal voting rights are glaring. So is the rare and shocking spectacle of case law as racist as that recounted here remaining largely untouched by time. During the decade and a half of research and writing that culminated in this volume, Puerto Rico's plight went from bad to worse. Yet the longer story is more mixed, perhaps even encouraging. Relationships between the U.S. nation and its people and lands have not unswervingly bent toward subordination and exclusion. The premise of this book is that the promise of citizenship, eventual statehood, and full constitutional rights for all is a promise worth remembering. It is a reminder of what has been lost, of what might be pursued, and of how an imperial power might do justice to the oldest colony in the world.

Notes

ACKNOWLEDGMENTS

1. Sam Erman, "*Puerto Rico and the Promise of United States Citizenship*," PhD diss., University of Michigan, 2010, iii–viii; Sam Erman, "Meanings of Citizenship in the U.S. Empire: Puerto Rico, Isabel Gonzalez, and the Supreme Court, 1898–1905," *Journal of American Ethnic History* 27 (Summer 2008): 26–27; Sam Erman, "Citizens of Empire: Puerto Rico, Status, and Constitutional Change," *California Law Review* 102 (2014): 1181n.

INTRODUCTION

1. This understanding of "concepts" of citizenship derives from Rebecca J. Scott and Jean M. Hébrard, *Freedom Papers: An Atlantic Odyssey in the Age of Emancipation* (Cambridge, MA, 2014); Rebecca J. Scott, "Public Rights, Social Equality, and the Conceptual Roots of the Plessy Challenge," *Michigan Law Review* 106 (2008): 777–804.
2. Katie Anastas and James Gregory, "Timeline and Map of Woman Suffrage Legislation State by State 1838–1919," Mapping American Social Movements through the 20th Century, http://depts.washington.edu/moves/WomanSuffrage_map.shtml; Michael Perman, *Struggle for Mastery: Disfranchisement in the South, 1888–1908* (Chapel Hill, NC, 2000), 5–6, 9–22; Plessy v. Ferguson, 163 U.S. 537 (1896); Joy Ann Williamson, Lori Rhodes, and Michael Dunson, "A Selected History of Social Justice in Education," *Review of Research in Education* 31 (2007): 195–224.
3. On Reconstruction, equality, and the peculiar status of Washington, DC, see Kate Masur, *An Example for All the Land: Emancipation and the Struggle over Equality in Washington, D.C.* (Chapel Hill, NC, 2010). For ease of exposition and because I have uncovered little use by those I study of the District of Columbia as a precedent for empire, I do not discuss implicit citizenship in the national capital as an alternative to citizenship in a state or future state.
4. Classic examples include W. E. B. Du Bois, *Black Reconstruction in America: An Essay toward a History of the Part Which Black Folk Played in the Attempt to Reconstruct Democracy in America, 1860–1880* (Oxford, 1935); Eric Foner,

Reconstruction: America's Unfinished Revolution, 1863–1877 (New York, 1988); C. Vann Woodward, *Origins of the New South, 1877–1913*, rev. ed. (Baton Rouge, LA, 1999 [1951]). See also Richard White's synthesis of Reconstruction and the Gilded Age, *The Republic for Which It Stands: The United States during Reconstruction and the Gilded Age* (Oxford, 2017). Among many works on the Civil War and Reconstruction amendments as a constitutional moment or second founding, see Bruce Ackerman, *We the People: Transformations* (Cambridge, MA, 2000).

A century after the U.S. imperial turn, scholars have taken their own turn toward empire. For an early example, see Amy Kaplan, *The Anarchy of Empire in the Making of U.S. Culture* (Cambridge, MA, 2002). No such turn was required for scholars already working on territories acquired by the United States in 1898–1899. See, for example, Christina Duffy Burnett and Burke Marshall, eds., *Foreign in a Domestic Sense: Puerto Rico, American Expansion, and the Constitution* (Durham, NC, 2001); José Trías Monge, *Puerto Rico: The Trials of the Oldest Colony in the World* (New Haven, CT, 1997). Modern scholars also see longer-term origins to U.S. empire than did some contemporaries. See Jack Ericson Eblen, *The First and Second United States Empires: Governors and Territorial Governments, 1784–1912* (Pittsburgh, 1968); Sarah H. Cleveland, "Powers Inherent in Sovereignty: Indians, Aliens, Territories, and the Nineteenth Century Origins of Plenary Power over Foreign Affairs," *Texas Law Review* 81 (Nov. 2002): 1–284; David Reynolds, *America, Empire of Liberty: A New History* (London, 2009). On 1898–1899 as an imperial turn, see Bartholomew H. Sparrow, *The Insular Cases and the Emergence of American Empire* (Lawrence, KS, 2006), 3–9, 40; Juan R. Torruella, *Global Intrigues: The Era of the Spanish-American War and the Rise of the United States to World Power* (San Juan, PR, 2007); Walter Lafeber, "The 'Lion in the Path': The U.S. Emergence as a World Power," *Political Science Quarterly* 101 (1986): 705–718. For a recent canvass of scholarship attempting to define colonialism, empire, or imperialism, see Paul A. Kramer, "Power and Connection: Imperial Histories of the United States in the World," *American Historical Review* 116 (Dec. 2011): 1349 and n. 3. For a court-focused work on the imperial turn, see Efrén Rivera Ramos, *The Legal Construction of Identity: The Judicial and Social Legacy of American Colonialism in Puerto Rico* (Washington, DC, 2001).

5. On the term *territorial nonincorporation*, see Christina Duffy Burnett, "Untied States: American Expansion and Territorial Deannexation," *University of Chicago Law Review* 72 (Summer 2005): 799–800 and n. 8. For works defining and listing the *Insular Cases*, see, for example, Sparrow, *Insular Cases*; Christina Duffy Burnett, "A Note on the *Insular Cases*," in Burnett and Marshall, *Foreign in a Domestic Sense*, 389. On the post-1897 U.S. turn toward long-term nonsettler colonialism, see Charles R. Venator-Santiago, *Puerto Rico and the Origins of US Global Empire: The Disembodied Shade* (New York, 2015); Lanny Thompson, *Imperial Archipelago: Representation and Rule in the Insular Territories under U.S. Dominion after 1898* (Honolulu, 2010), 23–25.

6. By contrast, Krishanti Vignarajah portrays a rapid judicial settlement in favor of the new approach. See Vignarajah, "The Political Roots of Judicial Legitimacy: Explaining the Enduring Validity of the *Insular Cases*," *University of Chicago Law Review* 77 (2010): 790.

7. As Robert W. Gordon observes in his article "Introduction: J. Willard Hurst and the Common Law Tradition in American Legal Historiography," to declare oneself a

practitioner of legal history is to envision certain phenomena to be *"distinctively legal"* (*Law & Society Review* 10 [Fall 1975]: 10). Studying how relative outsiders to law engaged with unquestionably legal institutions, actors, and content provides one way to mitigate the artificially narrowed vision that can otherwise result. It does so without risking the conflation between law and power or authority that Naomi Mezey perceives in scholarship on legal consciousness and the everyday: see "Out of the Ordinary: Law, Power, Culture, and the Commonplace," *Law & Social Inquiry* 26 (2001): 153. See also Dave Cowans, "Legal Consciousness: Some Observations," *Modern Law Review* 67 (2004): 928–958.

8. Accounts that focus on politics include Xi Wang, *The Trial of Democracy: Black Suffrage and Northern Republicans, 1860–1910* (Athens, GA, 2012), 216–266; Woodward, *Origins of the New South*, 324–325. For examples from cultural history, see David W. Blight, *Race and Reunion: The Civil War in American Memory* (Cambridge, MA, 2001), 291, 345; Nina Silber, *The Romance of Reunion: Northerners and the South, 1865–1900* (Chapel Hill, NC, 1993), 178–185. As the first study to conjoin the twentieth-century constitutional histories of empire and Reconstruction, *Almost Citizens* takes an approach whose promise has been expounded in Burnett, "Untied States"; Juan R. Torruella, *The Supreme Court and Puerto Rico: The Doctrine of Separate and Unequal* (Río Piedras, PR, 1985); Sanford Levinson, "Why the Canon Should Be Expanded to Include the Insular Cases and the Saga of American Expansionism," *Constitutional Commentary* 17 (2000): 241–266; Rebecca J. Scott, *Degrees of Freedom: Louisiana and Cuba after Slavery* (Cambridge, MA, 2005).

9. On legal doctrines hostile to racial discrimination that survived *Plessy v. Ferguson* (1896), see Pamela Brandwein, *Rethinking the Judicial Settlement of Reconstruction* (Cambridge, 2011); Richard H. Pildes, "Democracy, Anti-Democracy, and the Canon," *Constitutional Commentary* 17 (Summer 2000): 295–319. On twentieth-century implementation of black disfranchisement and Jim Crow, see C. Vann Woodward, *The Strange Career of Jim Crow* (Oxford, 2001 [1955]); Perman, *Struggle for Mastery*. Glenda Elizabeth Gilmore's groundbreaking *Gender and Jim Crow: Women and the Politics of White Supremacy in North Carolina, 1896–1920* (Chapel Hill, NC, 1996) describes early twentieth-century activism by African American women. On white Southerners' post-1898 cultural productions, see, for example, W. Fitzhugh Brundage, *The Southern Past: A Clash of Race and Memory* (Cambridge, MA, 2005). On post-1898 Civil War remembrance, see, for example, Thomas J. Brown, "Civil War Remembrance as Reconstruction," in *Reconstructions: New Perspectives on the Postbellum United States*, ed. Thomas J. Brown (Oxford, 2006), 207, 218.

10. On the general trend toward a "longer" Reconstruction, see Thomas J. Brown, "Introduction," in Brown, *Reconstructions*, 7.

11. Within the booming literature on citizenship, any selection of works discussing or illustrating its promise is necessarily partial. Consider Laurent Dubois, *A Colony of Citizens: Revolution & Slave Emancipation in the French Caribbean, 1787–1804* (Chapel Hill, NC, 2004); Scott, *Degrees of Freedom*; Hilda Sabato, "On Political Citizenship in Nineteenth-Century Latin America," *American Historical Review* 106 (Oct. 2001): 1290–1315; Martha S. Jones, *Birthright Citizens: A History of*

Race and Rights in Antebellum America (Cambridge, 2018); Patrick Weil, *The Sovereign Citizen: Denaturalization and the Origins of the American Republic* (Philadelphia, 2013). On citizenship facilitating governmental authority, see Linda Kerber, *No Constitutional Right to Be Ladies: Women and the Obligations of Citizenship* (New York, 1998); Myriam Cottias, "Gender and Republican Citizenship in the French West Indies, 1848–1945," *Slavery and Abolition* 26 (Aug. 2005): 233–245; Kunal M. Parker, "State, Citizenship, and Territory: The Legal Construction of Immigrants in Antebellum Massachusetts," *Law and History Review* 19 (Autumn 2001): 583–643. Works on the contingent and constructed nature of citizenship include Peter Sahlins, *Unnaturally French: Foreign Citizens in the Old Regime and After* (Ithaca, NY, 2004); Frederick Cooper, Thomas C. Holt, and Rebecca J. Scott, "Introduction," in *Beyond Slavery: Explorations of Race, Labor, and Citizenship in Postemancipation Societies* (Chapel Hill, NC, 2000), 1–32; Emmanuelle Saada, *Empire's Children: Race, Filiation, and Citizenship in the French Colonies*, trans. Arthur Goldhammer (Chicago, 2012). On display and performance of citizenship, see Caryn Cossé Bell, *Revolution, Romanticism, and the Afro-Creole Protest Tradition in Louisiana 1718–1868* (Baton Rouge, LA, 1997). A classic work that predefines citizenship, and then measures people and polities against it is T. H. Marshall, *Citizenship and Social Class and Other Essays* (Cambridge, 1950), 1–75. On the dangers of presupposing what citizenship meant in undertaking historical scholarship, see William J. Novak, "The Legal Transformation of Citizenship in Nineteenth-Century America," in *The Democratic Experiment: New Directions in American Political History*, ed. Meg Jacobs, William J. Novak, and Julian E. Zelizer (Princeton, NJ, 2003), 85–119.

12. Unlike Degetau, Collazo, and Iglesias, most island men were impoverished, unorganized, nonvoting agricultural laborers. Puerto Rican women had even less access to electoral politics and formal leadership. See Yamila Azize, *La mujer en la lucha* (Río Piedras, PR, 1985); Astrid Cubano-Iguina, "Political Culture and Male Mass-Party Formation in Late-Nineteenth-Century Puerto Rico," *Hispanic American Historical Review* 78 (Nov. 1998): 631–662; Eileen J. Suárez Findlay, *Imposing Decency: The Politics of Sexuality and Race in Puerto Rico, 1870–1920* (Durham, NC, 2000).

13. On the value of studying midlevel actors, see Daniel P. Carpenter, *The Forging of Bureaucratic Autonomy: Reputations, Networks, and Policy Innovation in Executive Agencies, 1862–1928* (Princeton, NJ, 2001); Karen Barkey, *Empire of Difference: The Ottomans in Comparative Perspective* (Cambridge, 2008). Despite Stephen Skowronek's memorable phrase, the turn-of-the-twentieth-century federal government was not solely dominated by "courts and parties." Although Skowronek observed the uneven influence of administrative institutions in this period when he introduced the courts-and-parties formulation in *Building a New American State: The Expansion of National Administrative Capacities, 1877–1920* (Cambridge, 1982), the concept has had enduring influence as an impediment to perceiving the full scope of administrative influence in the U.S. state. See Richard R. John, "Rethinking the Early American State," *Polity* 40 (2008): 332. Jerry L. Mashaw, "Federal Administration and Administrative Law in the Gilded Age," *Yale Law Journal* 119 (2010): 1365, offers a corrective to American political development accounts of muscular administration emerging only in the 1930s.

14. 32 Cong. Rec. 436.

15. A growing body of work demonstrates the extent to which the late nineteenth-century United States was an empire engaged in settler colonialism. The harvest season has been particularly bountiful in the field of American Indian history. See, for example, Jeffrey Ostler, *The Plains Sioux and U.S. Colonialism from Lewis and Clark to Wounded Knee* (Cambridge, 2004); Andrew Denson, *Demanding the Cherokee Nation: Indian Autonomy and American Culture, 1830–1900* (Lincoln, NE, 2004); Margaret D. Jacobs, "Maternal Colonialism: White Women and Indigenous Child Removal in the American West and Australia, 1880–1940," *Western Historical Quarterly* 36 (Winter 2005): 453–476; Richard White, "The American West and American Empire," in *Manifest Destinies and Indigenous Peoples*, ed. David Maybury-Lewis, Theodore Macdonald, and Biorn Maybury-Lewis (Cambridge, MA, 2009), 203–224; Steven Sabol, *The Touch of Civilization: Comparing American and Russian Internal Colonization* (Boulder, CO, 2017); Philip P. Frickey, "Doctrine, Context, Institutional Relationships, and Commentary: The Malaise of Federal Indian Law through the Lens of *Lone Wolf*," *Tulsa Law Review* 38 (2002): 5–36; Symposium on Settler Colonialism and the American West, *Journal of the West* 56, no. 4 (Fall 2017). Other works address additional communities, including those evident in the titles of Gunlög Fur, "Indians and Immigrants—Entangled Histories," *Journal of American Ethnic History* 33 (Spring 2014): 55–76, and Laura E. Gómez, *Manifest Destinies: The Making of the Mexican American Race* (New York, 2007).

16. Law and judges were never entirely subservient to the causal power of politics. As Paul Frymer contends in "Law and American Political Development," *Law & Social Inquiry* 33 (Summer 2008): 779–803, American political development (APD) scholars have tended to underestimate the institutional nature of courts. Thomas M. Keck adds that regime theory scholars too often presume that governing coalitions dictate judicial results; see Keck, "Party Politics or Judicial Independence? The Regime Politics Literature Hits the Law Schools," *Law & Social Inquiry* 32 (Spring 2007): 517. On the prior scarcity of APD work concerning the judiciary, see Reuel Edward Schiller, "'Saint George and the Dragon': Courts and the Development of the Administrative State in Twentieth-Century America," *Journal of Policy History* 17 (Jan. 2005): 110–124. Keith E. Whittington calls for a better understanding in APD of how law influences judges, in "Once More unto the Breach: PostBehavioralist Approaches to Judicial Politics," *Law & Social Inquiry* 25 (Apr. 2000): 613. For a foundational account of the Court as a political institution, see Robert A. Dahl, "Decision-Making in a Democracy: The Supreme Court as a National Policy-Maker," *Journal of Public Law* 6 (1957): 279–295. See also Barry Friedman, *The Will of the People: How Public Opinion Has Influenced the Supreme Court and Shaped the Meaning of the Constitution* (New York, 2009). On judges facing situations in which competing political pressures leave them free to choose among a range of options, see, for example, Keck, "Party Politics," 517–518; Vignarajah, "Political Roots."

1898: "THE CONSTITUTIONAL LION IN THE PATH"

1. A. T. Mahan, *The Interest of America in Sea Power, Present and Future* (Boston, 1897), 137–172, 224–225, 234, 256, 302–314; *The World Almanac* (New York, 1891), 16, 232; *The World Almanac and Encyclopedia* (New York, 1898), 51, 335.
2. Mahan, *Interest in Sea Power*, 302–314.

3. Ibid., 257; *Slaughter-House Cases*, 83 U.S. 36, 71 (1873); Appellant's Brief, Gonzales v. Williams, No. 225, 192 U.S. 1 (30 Nov. 1902), 32.
4. Mahan, *Interest in Sea Power*, 257.
5. U.S. Const., am. XIV, secs. 1, 2; Civil Rights Cases, 109 U.S. 3, 20 (1883); Eric Foner, *Reconstruction: America's Unfinished Revolution, 1863–1877* (New York, 1988), especially xxv, 251–261, 602–603; Ira Berlin et al., *Slaves No More: Three Essays on Emancipation and the Civil War* (Cambridge, 1992); David W. Blight, *Race and Reunion: The Civil War in American Memory* (Cambridge, MA, 2001); Walter Dean Burnham, *Critical Elections and the Mainsprings of American Politics* (New York, 1970); Charles W. Calhoun, *Conceiving a New Republic: The Republican Party and the Southern Question, 1869–1900* (Lawrence, KS, 2006); Pamela Brandwein, *Rethinking the Judicial Settlement of Reconstruction* (Cambridge, 2011), 30; Rebecca J. Scott, *Degrees of Freedom: Louisiana and Cuba after Slavery* (Cambridge, MA, 2005), 8, 43–45, 265–267; Xi Wang, *The Trial of Democracy: Black Suffrage and Northern Republicans, 1860–1910* (Athens, GA, 2012).
6. Calhoun, *Conceiving a New Republic*, esp. 4, 207, 226–267; Wang, *Trial of Democracy*, 49, 79, 82, 92, 94, 96, 105, 113–114, 188, 216–300; Scott, *Degrees of Freedom*, 47–48, 53, 87; Foner, *Reconstruction*, 279, 342–343, 425–444; Wang, *Trial of Democracy*, 49, 79, 82, 92, 94, 96, 105, 113–114, 188, 227, 254, 267–300; Brandwein, *Rethinking the Judicial Settlement*, 9–10, 126, 143, 153; C. Vann Woodward, *Origins of the New South, 1877–1913: A History of the South*, rev. ed. (Baton Rouge, LA, 1999 [1951]), 289, 322; Mark Elliott, *Color Blind Justice: Albion Tourgée and the Quest for Racial Equality from the Civil War to* Plessy v. Ferguson (Oxford, 2008), 248; J. Morgan Kousser, *The Shaping of Southern Politics: Suffrage Restriction and the Establishment of the One-Party South, 1880–1910* (New Haven, CT, 1974), 31.
7. Blight, *Race and Reunion*, 4–5, 102, 110–112, 138–139, 216, 394–397; Foner, *Reconstruction*, xix, 582, 609–610; Woodward, *Origins of the New South*, 51–74, 431–434, 440–443; C. Vann Woodward, *The Strange Career of Jim Crow* (Oxford, 2001 [1955]), 56–61; William Archibald Dunning, *Essays on the Civil War and Reconstruction and Related Topics* (London, 1904 [1897]), vii–viii; William A. Dunning, *Reconstruction, Political and Economic, 1865–1867* (New York, 1962 [1907]), 205–210; Richard H. Pildes, "Democracy, Anti-Democracy, and the Canon," *Constitutional Comment* 17 (2000): 301; Kousser, *Shaping of Southern Politics*, 3, 11, 243–244; Joseph Gerteis, *Class and the Color Line: Interracial Class Coalition in the Knights of Labor and the Populist Movement* (Durham, NC, 2007), 23, 33–34, 127–128, 146–147; Matthew Hild, *Greenbackers, Knights of Labor, and Populists: Farmer-Labor Insurgency in the Late-Nineteenth-Century South* (Athens, GA, 2007), 1, 3–4, 150–151, 174–175, 201; Marilyn Lake and Henry Reynolds, *Drawing the Global Colour Line: White Men's Countries and the International Challenge of Racial Equality* (Cambridge, 2008), 49–74; Nina Silber, *The Romance of Reunion: Northerners and the South, 1865–1900* (Chapel Hill, NC, 1993), 185–195; Cecilia Elizabeth O'Leary, *To Die For: The Paradox of American Patriotism* (Princeton, NJ, 1999), 121–128.

   By this time, a significant body of academic and popular literature reinforced white-supremacist distortions of Reconstruction. British historian James Bryce's acclaimed *The American Commonwealth* (1888) and Columbia historian William Dunning's *Essays on the Civil War and Reconstruction* laid the groundwork for an academic consensus that condemned Reconstruction. A popular school of Southern historical fiction romanticized slavery and the Confederacy, memorializing the "Lost Cause" and justifying white supremacy. As Silber, *Romance of Reunion*, 163; Mark Elliott, "Race, Color Blindness, and the Democratic Public: Albion W. Tourgée's Radical Principles in *Plessy v. Ferguson*," *Journal of Southern History* 67 (May 2001): 309–312; and Barbara A. Gannon, *The Won Cause: Black and White Comradeship in the Grand Army of the Republic* (Chapel Hill, NC, 2011), relate, contrary voices had not yet abandoned the field.

8. Plessy v. Ferguson, 163 U.S. 537, 540 (1896); Scott, *Degrees of Freedom*, 88; Gerald J. Postema, "Introduction: The Sins of Segregation," *Law and Philosophy* 16 (1997): 241–242; Michael Perman, *Struggle for Mastery: Disfranchisement in the South 1888–1908* (Chapel Hill, NC, 2001), 83–90, 117–121; Williams v. Mississippi, 170 U.S. 213, 221–222 (1898); Woodward, *Origins of the New South*, 321–322.

9. Eric T. Love's groundbreaking *Race over Empire: Racism and U.S. Imperialism, 1865–1900* (Chapel Hill, NC, 2004) rejects the view that a misguided attempt at racial uplift, a "white man's burden" of sorts, weighed in favor of expansion. Instead, Love observes that race was always an argument against annexation during the period. Elsewhere, as in the Jim Crow South, and at other times, as during the slave trade or after 1898, the United States opted for racial subjugation over disengagement. I argue that it was only racism as constrained by the Reconstruction Constitution that motivated the three-decade halt to annexations. On other causes of the hiatus, see Erik Overgaard Pedersen, *The Attempted Sale of the Danish West Indies to the United States of America, 1865–1870* (Frankfurt, Germany, 1997), 75–76, 80, 112, 170–172; Love, *Race over Empire*, 20–23, 153; Robert L. Beisner, *From the Old Diplomacy to the New, 1865–1900*, 2nd ed. (Arlington Heights, IL, 1986), 14, 50, 106; Charles S. Campbell, *The Transformation of American Foreign Relations, 1865–1900* (New York, 1976 [1965]), chs. 3, 10; Charles Callan Tansill, *The Purchase of the Danish West Indies* (New York, 1968 [1932]), 146, 151; Isaac Dookhan, *A History of the Virgin Islands of the United States* (Kingston, Jamaica, 1994), 253–254; Alfred L. Castle, "Tentative Empire: Walter Q. Gresham, U.S. Foreign Policy, and Hawai'i, 1893–1895," *Hawaiian Journal of History* 29 (1995): 87–88; Cyrus Veeser, *A World Safe for Capitalism: Dollar Diplomacy and America's Rise to Global Power* (New York, 2002), 33; Louis A. Pérez Jr., *Cuba between Empires, 1878–1901* (Pittsburgh, 1983), 59–65; Tennant S. McWilliams, "James H. Blount, the South, and Hawaiian Annexation," *Pacific Historical Review* 57 (Feb. 1988): 25–46; Thomas J. Osborne, *"Empire Can Wait": American Opposition to Hawaiian Annexation, 1893–1898* (Kent, OH, 1981), 107. The causes historians identify include party politics, turnover in office, corruption charges, competing domestic and budgetary concerns, militarism fatigue, fear of military vulnerability and hard-to-incorporate alien peoples, adequate existing markets, anticolonialism and anti-imperialism, commitment to self-determination, reaction against Reconstruction, industrial and labor opposition, and lack of a need to preempt other empires' annexationist designs. The classic overview of American Indian history remains Francis Paul Prucha, *The Great Father: The United States Government and the American Indians* (Lincoln, NE, 1995 [1984]), 676.

10. Cong. Globe, 7 Apr. 1871, 524; Northwest Ordinance, sec. 13; Don E. Fehrenbacher, *The Dred Scott Case: Its Significance in American Law and Politics* (Oxford, 1978), 74–77, 142; Jack Ericson Eblen, *The First and Second United States*

Empires: Governors and Territorial Government, 1784–1912 (Pittsburgh, 1968), 1–51; Dred Scott v. Sandford, 60 U.S. 393 (1857); Christina Duffy Burnett, "Untied States: American Expansion and Territorial Deannexation," *University of Chicago Law Review* 72 (Summer 2005): 802–803. On U.S. authority over uninhabited guano islands as a precursor to empire, see Christina Duffy Burnett, "The Edges of Empire and the Limits of Sovereignty: American Guano Islands," *American Quarterly* 57 (Sept. 2005): 779–803.

11. *Dred Scott*, 60 U.S. 393 (1857); Slaughter-House Cases, 83 U.S. 36, esp. 72–73 (1873); ibid., 119 (Bradley, J., dissenting); Leo S. Rowe, *The United States and Porto Rico* (New York, 1904), 87–89; Sarah H. Cleveland, "Powers Inherent in Sovereignty: Indians, Aliens, Territories, and the Nineteenth Century Origins of Plenary Power over Foreign Affairs," *Texas Law Review* 81 (Nov. 2002): 197; Fehrenbacher, *Dred Scott Case*, chs. 6, 15; Austin Allen, *Origins of the Dred Scott Case: Jacksonian Jurisprudence and the Supreme Court, 1837–1857* (Athens, GA, 2006), 168, 179, 217–219; Brandwein, *Rethinking the Judicial Settlement*, 28–31, 57, 98–104.

Chief Justice Roger Taney's lead opinion in *Dred Scott* rested on several additional premises: states could not grant U.S. citizenship, Congress had not naturalized African Americans, and citizenship in a state and in the United States must generally coincide. In a blow to woman's suffrage, *Minor v. Happersett*, 88 U.S. 162 (1875), denied that citizenship enfranchised. For an example of antebellum jurists' competing accounts of who held citizenship and what it meant, see State v. Manuel, 20 N.C. 144 (1838); Rights of Free Virginia Negroes, 1 U.S. Op. Atty. Gen. 506 (1821).

12. *Compilation of Reports of the Committee on Foreign Relations, United States Senate, 1789–1901*, vol. 8 (Washington, DC, 1901), 218; Love, *Race over Empire*, 41; Pedersen, *Attempted Sale of the Danish West Indies*, vii, 162–167; Nicholas Guyatt, "America's Conservatory: Race, Reconstruction, and the Santo Domingo Debate," *Journal of American History* 133 (Mar. 2011): 981; Frank Moya Pons, *The Dominican Republic: A National History* (Princeton, NJ, 1998 [1995]); William Javier Nelson, *Almost a Territory: America's Attempt to Annex the Dominican Republic* (Newark, DE, 1990); Allison L. Sneider, *Suffragists in an Imperial Age: U.S. Expansion and the Woman Question, 1870–1929* (Oxford, 2008), 47. David Healy and Robert Beisner identified the hiatus in annexations as problematic in their respective monographs, *US Expansion: The Imperialist Urge in the 1890s* (Madison, WI, 1970), 4, and *From the Old Diplomacy to the New*, 13–14. The annexation of Alaska demonstrated that the contiguity of the territories to be acquired did not distinguish the two periods. As Matthew Karp elaborates in *This Vast Southern Empire: Slaveholders at the Helm of American Foreign Policy* (Cambridge, MA, 2016), antebellum U.S. expansion had a proslavery flavor that did not survive the Civil War.

13. "St. Domingo and the United States," *Spectator* [London], 29 Jan. 1870, in *Littell's Living Age*, 5 Mar. 1870, 635–636; Cong. Globe, 7 Apr. 1871, 526; ibid., 11 Jan. 1871, appx. 30; Love, *Race over Empire*, 59.

14. 31 Cong. Rec. 5936, 5938, 5790, 5792, 5777–5778, 5842, 5903, 5921, 5937, 5998; 26 Cong. Rec., appx. 481–482; Love, *Race over Empire*, 103–104, 129–130, 150; George S. Boutwell, "Hawaiian Annexation," address before Boot and Shoe Club of Boston, 22 Dec. 1897, *Advocate of Peace* 60 (Jan. 1898): 19; Stephen M. White, "The Proposed Annexation of Hawaii," *Forum* 23 (Aug. 1897): 731; James Bryce,

"The Policy of Annexation for America," *Forum* 24 (Dec. 1897): 385; Castle, "Tentative Empire," 83; Carl Schurz, "Manifest Destiny," *Harper's*, 1 June 1893, 737; A Disciple of Daniel Webster, "Why Should We Annex Hawaii," *New York Herald*, 23 Feb. 1893; Eric Love, "White Is the Color of Empire: The Annexation of Hawaii in 1898," in *Race, Nation, and Empire in American History*, ed. James T. Campbell, Matthew Pratt Guterl, and Robert G. Lee (Chapel Hill, NC, 2007), 84; Thomas M. Cooley, "Grave Obstacles to Hawaiian Annexation," *Forum* 15 (June 1893): 399; 26 Cong. Rec. 1821–1822; "Hawaii," *Nation*, 9 Feb. 1893, 96; E. L. Godkin, "How Are We to Govern Hawaii?" *Nation*, 2 Dec. 1897, 432–433. Although residents of Japanese and Chinese descent formed a substantial minority of the population on the islands, they were overwhelmingly foreign-born and thus potentially excludable from citizenship on annexation. See *Report of the General Superintendent of the Census, 1896* (Honolulu, 1897), 31, 34.

15. 31 Cong. Rec. 5998, 5788; Love, "White Is the Color of Empire," 95; John Foster to Benjamin Harrison, 14 Feb. 1893, in *Foreign Relations of the United States 1894: Affairs in Hawaii: Appendix II* (Washington, DC, 1895), 201; William McKinley, "The President's Message," *Evening Star Almanac and Hand-Book 1898* 4 (Jan. 1898): 436–437; "A Voice from Hawaii," *Seattle Post-Intelligencer*, 28 July 1897, 8; *Annexation of the Hawaiian Islands*, H.R. Rep. No. 1355, 55th Cong., 2d sess. (17 May 1898), pt. 1, 61. For express acknowledgments of consequences of annexation, see "Statement of Gen. Schofield," *New York Tribune*, 15 Mar. 1893, 2, cited in Lorrin A. Thurston, *A Hand-book on the Annexation of Hawaii* (St. Joseph, MI, [1897?]), 72; 31 Cong. Rec. appx. 612; "More American Talk," *Los Angeles Times*, 11 Oct. 1897, 5; "Republican Party Platform of 1896," *The American Presidency Project*, comp. Gerhard Peters and John T. Woolley, www.presidency.ucsb.edu/ws/?pid=29629 (2017); Osborne, "*Empire Can Wait*," 84, 104–105; Love, *Race over Empire*, xvii, 106, 146, 154.

Several dynamics contributed to the renewed pressure for expansion: expansion by other territorial empires, rising tariff walls, desires to access foreign markets, U.S. investment in naval capacity, a martial spirit haunting officialdom, and other empires' designs in the Americas. See Healy, *US Expansion*, 12, 26–27, 43–44; Beisner, *From the Old Diplomacy to the New*, 4–5, 10–12, 14, 19, 23–24, 78–79, 81, 87–89, 95, 98–131; Walter LaFeber's *The New Empire: An Interpretation of American Expansion 1860–1898*, 35th anniv. ed. (Ithaca, NY, 1998); Jedidiah J. Kroncke, *The Futility of Law and Development: China and the Dangers of Exporting American Law* (Oxford, 2016), 73; Mahan, *Interest in Sea Power*; Kristin L. Hoganson, *Fighting for Manhood: How Gender Politics Provoked the Spanish-American and Philippine-American Wars* (New Haven, CT, 1998), 3–4, 10, 24, 81; George Herbert Ryden, *The Foreign Policy of the United States in Relation to Samoa* (New Haven, CT, 1933), 519, 555; Veeser, *World Safe for Capitalism*, 4–5, 33. Tansill, *Purchase of the Danish West Indies*, 200; Love, *Race over Empire*, 153.

16. Sylvester K. Stevens, *American Expansion in Hawaii, 1842–1898* (Harrisburg, PA, 1945), 157–158, 126–127, 170; Veeser, *World Safe for Capitalism*, 30–42; *Compilation of Reports of Committee on Foreign Relations, United States Senate, 1789–1901: Diplomatic Relations with Foreign Nations – Affairs in Cuba*, vol. 7 (Washington, DC, 1901), 309–312; Isaac Dookhan, "Changing Patterns of Local Reaction to the United States Acquisition of the Virgin Islands, 1865–1917," *Caribbean Studies* 15 (Apr. 1975): 50; Gordon K. Lewis, "An Introductory Note

to the Study of the Virgin Islands," *Caribbean Studies* 8 (July 1968): 12; W. D. Boyce, "Advantages of Making the Canal Zone a Free City and Free Port," *Journal of Race Development* 5 (July 1914): 81; Schurz, "Manifest Destiny."

17. Nicholas Thomas, *Islanders: The Pacific in the Age of Empire* (New Haven, CT, 2010), 272–281; Ryden, *Foreign Policy in Relation to Samoa*, xii–xvii, 555, 574–575; Teemu Ruskola, "Canton Is Not Boston: The Invention of American Imperial Sovereignty," *American Quarterly* 57 (Sept. 2005): 860–861, 870–872, 876–877.

18. R. A. Humphreys, "Presidential Address: Anglo-American Rivalries and the Venezuela Crisis of 1895," *Transactions of the Royal Historical Society* 17 (1967): 150, 153; Jennie A. Sloan, "Anglo-American Relations and the Venezuelan Boundary Dispute," *Hispanic American Historical Review* 18 (Nov. 1938): 494; Veeser, *World Safe for Capitalism*, 30–32; Pérez, *Cuba between Empires*, 66–67, 171–186; Beisner, *From the Old Diplomacy to the New*, 12.

19. *Elk*, 112 U.S., at 122, 121 (1884) (Harlan, J., dissenting); Prucha, *Great Father*, 560–561, 676, 679; *Kagama*, 118 U.S. 375 (1886); Cleveland, "Powers Inherent," 58, 61–63; Heather Cox Richardson, *Wounded Knee: Party Politics and the Road to an American Massacre* (New York, 2010).

20. David Wallace Adams, *Education for Extinction: American Indians and the Boarding School Experience, 1875–1928* (Lawrence, KS, 1995), 22–24; Jacqueline Fear-Segal, *White Man's Club: Schools, Race, and the Struggle of Indian Acculturation* (Lincoln, NE, 2007), xi–xii; Frederick E. Hoxie, *A Final Promise: The Campaign to Assimilate the Indians, 1880–1920* (Lincoln, NE, 2001 [1984]), x, 42, 44, 50, 52, 70–71, 74–75, 79–80, 152–154; Prucha, *Great Father*, pt. 6; Cleveland, "Powers Inherent," 63; Frederick E. Hoxie, *This Indian Country: American Indian Political Activists and the Place They Made* (New York, 2012), 237–244.

21. Sarah Barringer Gordon, *The Mormon Question: Polygamy and Constitutional Conflict in Nineteenth-Century America* (Chapel Hill, NC, 2002), 1, 47, 77, 81, 85, 90, 98, 114–116, 120, 129, 219; Gerald L Neuman, "Constitutionalism and Individual Rights in the Territories," in *Foreign in a Domestic Sense: Puerto Rico, American Expansion, and the Constitution*, ed. Christina Duffy Burnett and Burke Marshall (Durham, NC, 2001), 184–187; John Nieto-Phillips, "Citizenship and Empire: Race, Language, and Self-Government in New Mexico and Puerto Rico, 1898–1917," *Journal for the Center for Puerto Rican Studies* (Fall 1999): 53–56.

Full constitutional rights did not stop the bureaucratically weak federal government from regulating organized and active workers via criminal prosecutions, antilabor injunctions, and violence. See Christopher L. Tomlins, *Law, Labor, and Ideology in the Early American Republic* (New York, 1993), 44–51, 61–63; Josiah Bartlett Lambert, *"If the Workers Took a Notion": The Right to Strike and American Political Development* (Ithaca, NY, 2005), 10, 13, 22, 44–51, 56, 58, 65; William E. Forbath, *Law and the Shaping of the American Labor Movement* (Cambridge, MA, 1991), 61–65, 77–78, 83, 108, 111, 125–126; David Ray Papke, *The Pullman Case: The Clash of Labor and Capital in Industrial America* (Lawrence, KS, 1999), xiii, 33–35, 38, 41, 49, 75–76, 98; Richard Schneirov, Shelton Stromquist, and Nick Salvatore, "Introduction," in *The Pullman Strike and the Crisis of the 1890s: Essays on Labor and Politics*, ed. Richard Schneirov, Shelton Stromquist, and Nick Salvatore (Urbana, IL, 1999), 1; Melvyn Dubofsky, "The Federal Judiciary, Free Labor, and Equal Rights," in ibid., 162–165; David Montgomery, "Epilogue," in ibid., 238. Gordon, *Mormon Question*, 5, 134, 219, 225, describes how federal antipolygamy laws imposed shared state norms on territories. In *Public Vows: A History of Marriage and the Nation* (Cambridge, MA, 2000), ch. 5, Nancy F. Cott observes the racial associations opponents drew between polygamy and racial degradation.

22. *Wong Kim Ark*, 169 U.S. 649, 683–684 (1898); In re Ross, 140 U.S. 453 (1891); Cleveland, "Powers Inherent," 206; *Chae Chan Ping*, 130 U.S. 581 (1889); *Fong Yue Ting*, 149 U.S. 698 (1893); Page Act of 1875, 18 Stat. 477; Chinese Exclusion Act of 1882, 22 Stat. 58; Chinese Exclusion Act of 1884, 23 Stat. 115; Scott Act 1888, 25 Stat. 504; Geary Act, 27 Stat. 25 (1892); Cleveland, "Powers Inherent," 129–134, 149; Andrew Gyory, *Closing the Gate: Race, Politics, and the Chinese Exclusion Act* (Chapel Hill, NC, 1998), 1; Lucy E. Salyer, "*Wong Kim Ark*: The Contest over Birthright Citizenship," in *Immigration Stories*, ed. David A. Martin and Peter H. Schuck (New York, 2005), 51–85. In *At America's Gates: Chinese Exclusion during the Exclusion Era, 1882–1943* (Chapel Hill, NC, 2003), 6, Erika Lee identifies Chinese exclusion with U.S. transformation into a self-defined racial "gatekeeping" nation.

23. Alberto Elena and Javier Ordóñez, "Science, Technology, and the Spanish Colonial Experience in the Nineteenth Century," *Osiris* 15 (2000): 74, 78–79; Leslie Bethell, ed., *The Cambridge History of Latin America*, vol. 2: *Colonial Latin America* (Cambridge, 1997), 34; Rondo Cameron, *A Concise Economic History of the World: From Paleolithic Times to the Present* (Oxford, 1989), 191; James W. Cortada, "A Case of International Rivalry in Latin America: Spain's Occupation of Santo Domingo, 1853–1865," *Revista de Historia de América* 82 (July–Dec. 1976): 53–82; Astrid Cubano Iguina, *El hilo en el laberinto: Claves de la lucha política en Puerto Rico (siglo XIX)* (Río Piedras, PR, 1990), 77; Anthony E. Kaye, "The Second Slavery: Modernity in the Nineteenth-Century South and the Atlantic World," *Journal of Southern History* 75 (Aug. 2009): 627–650.

On the roots of *criollo* and its subordinate connotations, see J. H. Elliott, *Empires of the Atlantic World: Britain and Spain in America 1492–1830* (New Haven, CT, 2006), 234–239. Extensive slave-based production of sugar for export in the Spanish Antilles was part of the "second slavery" that arose in the nineteenth century in response to a complex set of economic and international-relations dynamics. See Dale Tomich and Michael Zeuske, "Introduction, the Second Slavery: Mass Slavery, World-Economy, and Comparative Microhistories," *Review (Fernand Braudel Center)* 31 (2008): 91–100.

24. Pérez, *Cuba between Empires*, 89–96; Ada Ferrer, *Insurgent Cuba: Race, Nation, and Revolution, 1868–1898* (Chapel Hill, NC, 1999), chs. 1–3. On Spanish economic exploitation of Puerto Rico, see Maluquer de Motes, "El mercado colonial antillano en el siglo XIX," in *Agricultura, comercio colonial y crecimiento económico en la España contemporánea*, ed. Jordi Nadal and Gabriel Tortella (Barcelona, 1974), 322–357. On rural deprivation in Cuba, see Louis A. Pérez, "Toward Dependency and Revolution: The Political Economy of Cuba between Wars, 1878–1895," *Latin American Research Review* 18 (1983): 131.

25. Francisco A. Scarano, *Puerto Rico: Cinco siglos de historia* (New York, 1993), 430–431, 436–449, 451; José Trías Monge, *Puerto Rico: The Trials of the Oldest Colony in the World* (New Haven, CT, 1997), 10–11; María Dolores Domingo Acebrón, *Rafael María de Labra: Cuba, Puerto Rico, Las Filipinas, Europea y Marruecos, en*

la España del sexenio democrático y la restauración (1871–1918) (Madrid, 2006), 34; Jesse Hoffnung-Garskof, *Racial Migrations: New York City and the Revolutionary Politics of the Spanish Caribbean, 1850–1902* (Princeton, NJ, forthcoming), chs. 1–2; Fernando Bayrón Toro, *Elecciones y partidos políticos de Puerto Rico (1809–1976)* (Mayagüez, PR, 1977), 45–49, 51–67; Reece B. Bothwell Gonzalez, *Puerto Rico: Cien años de lucha política*, vol. 1. pt. 1 (Río Piedras, PR, 1979); David Ortiz Jr., *Paper Liberals: Press and Politics in Restoration Spain* (Westport, CT, 2000), 21–22; A. G. Quintero Rivera, "Background to the Emergence of Imperialist Capitalism in Puerto Rico," *Caribbean Studies* 13 (Oct. 1973): 50.

26. Hoffnung-Garskof, *Racial Migrations*, chs. 1–2; Jesse Hoffnung-Garskof, "To Abolish the Law of Castes: Merit, Manhood and the Problem of Colour in the Puerto Rican Liberal Movement, 1873–1892," *Social History* 36 (Aug. 2011): 312–314, 318; Cubano, *El hilo en el laberinto*, 80–83; Bayrón Toro, *Elecciones*, 51–67; Scarano, *Puerto Rico*, 430–431, 451–453; Astrid Cubano Iguina, "Political Culture and Male Mass-Party Formation in Late-Nineteenth-Century Puerto Rico," *Hispanic American History Review* 78 (1998): 641–643; Bothwell, *Puerto Rico* 1:1:5; Jay Kinsbruner, *Not of Pure Blood: The Free People of Color and Racial Prejudice in Nineteenth-Century Puerto Rico* (Durham, NC, 1996), 47–50, 129–133.

27. A. G. Quintero-Rivera, "Socialist and Cigarmaker: Artisans' Proletarianization in the Making of the Puerto Rican Working Class," *Latin American Perspectives* 10 (Summer 1983): 19, 23; Kirwin R. Shaffer, *Black Flag Boricuas: Anarchism, Antiauthoritarianism, and the Left in Puerto Rico, 1897–1921* (Urbana, IL, 2013), 24; Córdova, *Resident Commissioner*, 49; Gervasio L. García and A. G. Quintero Rivera, *Desafío y solidaridad: Breve historia del movimiento obrero puertorriqueño* (San Juan, PR, 1986), 18–20, 22–23, 27–28; Hoffnung-Garskof, *Racial Migrations*, ch. 2; Scarano, *Puerto Rico*, 478–480; Juan Ángel Silén, *Apuntes para la historia del movimiento obrero puertorriqueño* (San Juan, PR, 1978), 22; Galvin, *Organized Labor Movement*, 22, 23, 35.

28. Scarano, *Puerto Rico*, 445, 448; Hoffnung-Garskof, *Racial Migrations*, chs. 1–2.

29. Miles Galvin, *The Organized Labor Movement in Puerto Rico* (London, 1979), 30–33; James L. Dietz, *Economic History of Puerto Rico: Institutional Change and Capitalist Development* (Princeton, NJ, 1986), 98; Laird W. Bergard, *Coffee and the Growth of Agrarian Capitalism in Nineteenth-Century Puerto Rico* (Princeton, NJ, 1983), 193, 196–197; U.S. Census, *Number of Inhabitants: Puerto Rico* (Washington, DC, 1952), 6, www2.census.gov/prod2/decennial/documents/23761117v1ch12.pdf; Trías Monge, *Puerto Rico*, 15–17; Galvin, *Organized Labor Movement*, 33; Fernando Picó, *La guerra después de la guerra* (San Juan, PR, 1987), 14, 28–30, 33; Henry K. Carroll, *Report of Porto Rico* (Washington, DC, 1899), 48–52; Gonzalo F. Córdova, *Resident Commissioner, Santiago Iglesias and His Times* (Río Piedras, PR, 1993), 12–13; Luis A. Figueroa, *Sugar, Slavery, and Freedom in Nineteenth-Century Puerto Rico* (Chapel Hill, NC, 2005), 198, 206–207; Scarano, *Puerto Rico*, 471–477; Robert C. McGreevey, "Borderline Citizens: Puerto Ricans and the Politics of Migration, Race, and Empire, 1898–1948," PhD diss., Brandeis University, 2008, 47–48; A. G. Quintero Rivera, *Conflictos de clase y política en Puerto Rico* (Río Piedras, PR, 1977), 124–126.

30. Scarano, *Puerto Rico*, 454, 461, 516–519, 524; Pérez, *Cuba between Empires*, 11, 14–15, 97; Hoffnung-Garskof, *Racial Migrations*, chs. 1–4; Certificate, 18 June 1874, CIHCAM 6/VII/12; Astrid Cubano, "Reformas electorales y práctica política en Puerto Rico (1874–1900)," in *Legitimidad, representación y alternancia en España y América Latina: Las reformas electorales (1880–1930)*, coord. Carlos Malamud (Mexico City, 2000), 87–88, 94; Hoffnung-Garskof, "To Abolish the Law of Castes," 324; Ortiz, *Paper Liberals*, 34; Germán Delgado Paspera, *Puerto Rico: Sus luchas emancipadoras (1850–1898)* (Río Piedras, PR, 1984), 449–451.

31. Scarano, *Puerto Rico*, 460–461, 514–515, 517–521, 590; Trías Monge, *Puerto Rico*, 11; Ana Georgina Sagardia de Alvarado, "United States–Puerto Rican Relations: The Changing Citizenship Status of the Puerto Rican People under the United States Sovereignty (1898–1917)," PhD diss., University of California, Berkeley, 1983, 22–23; Hoffnung-Garskof, *Racial Migrations*, ch. 5.

32. Dietz, *Economic History*, 26–27, 29; Bergard, *Coffee*, 146n3, 149, 153–155, 157, 182–183, 192–193, 197, 211–212; Galvin, *Organized Labor Movement*, 30–33; Picó, *La guerra*, 27; Scarano, *Puerto Rico*, 462–466; Cubano, *El hilo*, 85, 115, 147–148; *Statistical Abstract of the United States, 1893, Sixteenth Number* (Washington, DC, 1894), 338.

33. Cubano, "Reformas electorales," 94–95; Hoffnung-Garskof, *Racial Migrations*, ch. 5; Ileana M. Rodríguez-Silva, *Silencing Race: Disentangling Blackness, Colonialism, and National Identities in Puerto Rico* (New York, 2012), 128.

34. Cubano, "Reformas electorales," 87–89, 94–95; Hoffnung-Garskof, *Racial Migrations*, ch. 5; Elliott, *Empires of the Atlantic World*, 234–239; Rodríguez-Silva, *Silencing Race*, 128; Scarano, *Puerto Rico*, 522–524.

35. U.S. War Department, *Report on the Census of Porto Rico, 1899* (Washington, DC, 1900), 34; Hoffnung-Garskof, "To Abolish the Law of Castes," 312–314, 334–336; Cubano, "Reformas electorales," 88–89; Rosa E. Carrasquillo, *Our Landless Patria: Marginal Citizenship and Race in Caguas, Puerto Rico, 1880–1910* (Lincoln, NE, 2006), 91–92; Hoffnung-Garskof, *Racial Migrations*, chs. 2, 5–6; Rodríguez-Silva, *Silencing Race*, 109, 111, 113–116, 128; Eileen J. Suárez Findlay, *Imposing Decency: The Politics of Sexuality and Race in Puerto Rico, 1870–1920* (Durham, NC, 1999), 9–10, 20, 24–25, 43–45, 47, 55–58, 74, 85–86, 91–100; McGreevey, "Borderline Citizens," 103; Santiago Iglesias Pantín, *Luchas emancipadoras (Crónicas de Puerto Rico)*, 2nd ed., vol. 1 (San Juan, PR, 1958), 62, 64; Córdova, *Resident Commissioner*, 25; Scarano, *Puerto Rico*, 479–480; García and Quintero Rivera, *Desafío y solidaridad*, 27; Ángel Silén, *Apuntes para la historia*, 22. Martí envisioned the violence as necessary for revolution. Autonomista elites displayed ritualized violence of the sort displayed in challenges to duels. Disturbingly, the familial metaphor had the potential to tap into notions that servants, and at one time even slaves, constituted parts of elite households.

36. Hoffnung-Garskof, *Racial Migrations*, chs. 1–5; Pérez, *Cuba between Empires*, 16–17, 42, 99–100, 109, 112–138; Gerald E. Poyo, *"With All, and for the Good of All": The Emergence of Popular Nationalism in the Cuban Communities of the United States, 1848–1898* (Durham, NC, 1989), xvi–xvii, 103–107; Scott, *Degrees of Freedom*; Ferrer, *Insurgent Cuba*, 112–138; Scarano, *Puerto Rico*, 529.

37. Gordon K. Lewis, *Puerto Rico: Freedom and Power in the Caribbean* (New York, 1963), 42–45; Scarano, *Puerto Rico*, 524–527, 530, 534–535, 540–542, 549; Córdova, *Resident Commissioner*, 26–27, 33–34, 36, 58; Christina Duffy Ponsa,

"When Statehood Was Autonomy," in *Reconsidering the Insular Cases: The Past and Future of the American Empire*, ed. Gerald L. Neuman and Tomiko Brown-Nagin (Cambridge, MA, 2015), 18, 24–26; Edward S. Wilson, *Political Development of Porto Rico* (Columbus, OH, 1905), 36–37; "The Puerto Rican Independence Movement and the Status Issue under Spanish Rule: Selected Sources, 1892–1897," *Centro* 10, nos. 1–2 (1998): 16–17; Trías Monge, *Puerto Rico*, 12–15; Sagardia, "United States–Puerto Rican Relations," 28–30; McGreevey, "Borderline Citizens," 35; Cubano, "Reformas electorales," 88–89; Iglesias, *Luchas*, 1:67.

38. Pérez, *Cuba between Empires*, 59–68, 140–143, 168–180, 185–186.
39. Sagardia, "United States–Puerto Rican Relations," 87–88; "Suspencion," *El Liberal*, 22 Apr. 1898; Federico Cedó Alzamora, *La Guerra del 98 y Mayagüez* (Mayagüez, PR, 2014), 31; José Trías Monge, *Historia constitucional de Puerto Rico*, vol. 1 (San Juan, PR, 1999 [1980]), 130. Muñoz Rivera's newspaper, *El Liberal*, made the case for convening the legislature on 6, 9, 11, 24, and 31 May; 11 June; and 4 and 5 July 1898.
40. 31 Cong. Rec. 6344; *Annexation of the Hawaiian Islands*, pt. 2, 1; Tom Coffman, *Nation Within: The History of the American Occupation of Hawai'i*, rev. ed. (Kihei, HI, 2009), 308; Newlands Resolution, J.R. No. 55, 30 Stat. 750 (1898). Mary Dudziak addresses the relative lack of restraint on federal power during wartime in *War Time: An Idea, Its History, Its Consequences* (Oxford, 2012). Thomas Osborne deemphasizes the war as a driver of the annexation, in *"Empire Can Wait,"* 121–126.
41. 31 Cong. Rec. 5987; Schurz, "Manifest Destiny"; Richard L. Forstall, ed., *Population of the States and Counties of the United States: 1790 to 1900* (Washington, DC, 1996), 3; U.S. War Department, *Census of Porto Rico*; U.S. War Department, *Report on the Census of Cuba, 1899* (Washington, DC, 1900), 72; *Report of the Philippine Commission to the President*, vol. 1 (Washington, DC, 1900), 11–16; Ferrer, *Insurgent Cuba*, 77–96; "Gen. Emilio Aguinaldo: The Big Man of the Philippines," *Los Angeles Times*, 11 May 1898, 4.
42. Ángel M. Mergal, *Federico Degetau: Un orientador de su pueblo* (New York, 1944), 27, 30–34, 39–41, 43–46, 49–50, 121, 131–132, 134–137, 141–148, 183–189; M. Degetau to Hermano, 10 Dec. 1862, CIHCAM 20/L2; Declaratoria de Da. Consuelo sobre bienes y deudas de D. Matías, 27 Sept. 1864, in A. M. Melgar, Documentación relacionada con la vida y la obra de D. Federico Degetau, 1941, 20, CIHCAM 20/L2; Hoffnung-Garskof, *Racial Migrations*, chs. 1–2, 5; Trías Monge, *Puerto Rico*, 10–13; Scarano, *Puerto Rico*, 445, 448; Certificate of Federico Degetau upon receiving his law license, 29 Oct. 1888, in Melgar, "Documentación"; Bonifacio Sánchez, "Notas acerca de la personalidad de Don Federico Degetau en sus distintos aspectos," CIHCAM 20/L2, 78; Certification of waiver of military service, 5 Mar. 1883, CIHCAM 6/VII/19; Córdova, *Resident Commissioner*, 25; Certification of membership in El Porvenir, 20 Jan. 1882, CIHCAM 6/VII/16; CIHCAM 11/L2; various documents, CIHCAM 10/III/7–8 and I/3; Draft, Federico to his aunt, n.d., CIHCAM 1/V/20; Ortiz, *Paper Liberals*, 4–6, 9; Arístides Díaz, "Federico Degetau y González," *El Autonomista*, 22 May 1897, CIHCAM 22/L1; [Federico Degetau?], "Las cosas de Puerto Rico," paper unknown, n.d., CIHCAM 22/L1; "El país es el juez," *El Globo*, 17 Oct. 1887, CIHCAM 22/L1; "La política en Puerto-Rico," *El Globo*, 19 Oct. 1887, CIHCAM 22/L1.

43. Lewis, *Puerto Rico*, 42–45; Hoffnung-Garskof, "To Abolish the Law of Castes," 324–326; Wilson, *Political Development*, 37–38; Ponsa, "When Statehood Was Autonomy," 17; Scarano, *Puerto Rico*, 526–527, 541; Córdova, *Resident Commissioner* 31, 53–54; Laurent Dubois, *Avengers of the New World: The Story of the Haitian Revolution* (Cambridge, MA, 2004); Gannon, *Won Cause*, 6–8, 146, 177; A. Fernando Juncos to Federico Degetau, 30 Jan. 1898, CIHCAM 2/II/12; Mergal, *Orientador*, 50.

44. Ramos y Velex to Degetau, 27 July 1898 ("por ofricar de Ysaac sacfriado por su padre Abraham"); Rafael M. Labra to F. Degetau, 7 Aug. 1898, CIHCAM 2/III/71 ("olvida"); Federico Degetau to Praxedes Sagasta, 15 Oct. 1898, CIHCAM 2/III/80 ("guerra civil"); draft, Federico Degetau to Mac Kinley [*sic*], 18 Oct. 1898, CIHCAM 2/III/81 ("estrecho vinculo"; "indestructible vinculo de origen"); Treaty of Paris, 30 Stat. 1754, 1761 (1899); Degetau to Brioso, Matienzo, and Muñoz, 14 Jan. 1896, CIHCAM 1/VII/16; draft, Federico Degetau to [Rossy?], 17 Jan. 1897, CIHCAM 1/VII/17; various documents, CIHCAM 2/I–II; F. Degetau y González, "Justicia y equidad," *El País*, 19 May 1897, CIHCAM 22/L1; Federico Degetau to Vicente Romero Giron, 21 Oct. 1898, CIHCAM 2/III/84; Mergal, *Orientador*, 50, 162–165; Certification of Permission to Embark for Puerto Rico, 23 Sept. 1898, CIHCAM 2/III/77; [Illegible] to Federico Degetau, 26 Oct. 1898, CIHCAM 2/III/86; John MacArthur to F. Degatau [*sic*], 31 May 1899, CIHCAM 2/IV/6; "A el 'Diario,'" *El País*, 15 Sept. 1900, CIHCAM 22/L1.

45. Iglesias, *Luchas*, 1:14–15 ("modestos obreros"), 15–19, 31–32, 36; Araceli Tinajero, *El Lector: A History of the Cigar Factory Reader*, trans. Judith E. Grasberg (Austin, TX, 2010), 36–44; Hoffnung-Garskof, *Racial Migrations*, ch. 3; Shaffer, *Black Flag Boricuas*, 23, 29–30; Córdova, *Resident Commissioner*, 47, 51; Juan Carreras, *Santiago Iglesias Pantín: Su vida, su obra, su pensamiento (datos biográficos)* (San Juan, PR, 1965), 9.

46. Iglesias, *Luchas*, 1:38–39 ("era franco y hablaba en la colonia sin reserva de ninguna clase"; "el hecho de haber nacido en España constituía en cierto modo una garantía para mí en aquel momento"), 31–32, 37, 43–44, 59, 62, 64–65, 88; McGreevey, "Borderline Citizens," 103; Shaffer, *Black Flag Boricuas*, 31; Galvin, *Organized Labor Movement*, 19, 29, 37; Santiago Iglesias, José Ferrer y Ferrer, and Eduardo Conde, *A los obreros de Arecibo* (Puerto Rico, 1898), CPMN, Movimiento obrero puertorriqueño: hojas sueltas (1898–1937); "La consigna," *Ensayo obrero*, 20 Mar. 1898, 1; "De ayer a hoy," *Ensayo obrero*, 10 Apr. 1898, 1; Mariano Negrón Portillo, *Las turbas republicanas, 1900–1904* (Río Piedras, PR, 1990), 24–27, 119; Córdova, *Resident Commissioner*, 59.

47. Hoffnung-Garskof, *Racial Migrations*, chs. 5, 1–4; Manifest, Brig *Morning Light*, 19 May 1889, 42, NY NARA M237/533/465; 1892 Census, E-D-04; Hoffnung-Garskof, "To Abolish the Law of Castes," 314, 325–326, 333–334, 342. Census takers recorded nearly every resident of a Brooklyn block where Collazo lived and worked in the 1890s as "white." *Lain's Brooklyn Business Directory 1891–1892* (1892), 202; 1880 Census, EDs 12, 21; 1900 Census, EDs 17–18, 30–31. The first instance I have found of Collazo himself being recorded as white is from 1904; see 1904 Census 34/19. The last is Standard Certificate of Death for Domingo Collazo, 26 Sept. 1929, Bureau of Records, Department of Health of the City of New York.

Though race in Puerto Rico existed on more of a continuum and took a less binary form than in the United States, it was also a highly consequential and ascriptive category there. See Kinsbruner, *Not of Pure Blood*, 1, 9, 32; Hoffnung-Garskof, *Racial Migrations*, ch. 1.

48. Carmelo Rosario Natal, *Puerto Rico y la crisis de la Guerra Hispanoamericana (1895–1898)* (Hato Rey, PR, 1975), 297–298 ("esclavitud disfrazada" "mentida autonomía" "emancipación absoluta"); "Un periódico y un libro," *Patria*, 1 July 1896, 3 ("órgano de la clase obrera"); "Abrumador Deferencia," *La Doctrina de Martí*, 25 July 1896, 1 ("obra de reparadora justicia"); Pedro Deschamps Chapeaux, *Rafael Serra y Montalvo: obrero incansable de nuestra independencia* (Havana, 1975), 121 ("mueran ... las diferencias y las clasificaciones etnográficas, en los labios de los que se estiman de patriotas cubanos"), 115–119, 121, 128–129; "Nuestra labor," *La Doctrina de Martí*, 25 July 1896, 1 ("germen de horrors"); *La Doctrina de Martí*, 10 Oct. 1896, 1 ("república con todos y para todos"), quoted in Deschamps, *Rafael Serra*, 117; Hoffnung-Garskof, *Racial Migrations*, chs. 4–6; Jesse Hoffnung-Garskof, "The Migrations of Arturo Schomburg: On Being *Antillano*, Negro, and Puerto Rican in New York, 1891–1938," *Journal of American Ethnic History* 21 (Fall 2001): 3–49; "Administración de 'Patria,'" *Patria*, 20 Aug. 1895, 1; Bernardo Vega, *Memorias de Bernardo Vega: Contribución a la historia de la comunidad puertorriqueña en Nueva York*, ed. César Andreu Iglesias (Río Piedras, PR, 1980), 72–73; Pérez, *Cuba between Empires*, 90; Poyo, *"With All,"* 116–118, 133; Scarano, *Puerto Rico*, 531, 533; "Puerto Rican Independence Movement," 16; José Martí, "Club Borinquen," *Patria* (New York), 10 Apr. 1894, reprinted in Carlos Ripoll, comp., *Escritos desconocidos de José Martí: Cuba, Puerto Rico, propaganda revolucionaria, juicios, crítica, Estados Unidos* (New York, 1971), 88–89; Biblioteca Histórica Cubana, *La revolución del 95 según la correspondencia de la delegación cubana en Nueva York*, vol. 3 (Havana, 1933), 382–383; "Socios del Club," Las Dos Antillas Political Clubs Minutes, 1892–1908, Folder MG 57, Las Dos Antillas (translation), Schomburg Center for Research in Black Culture, New York Public Library; "Patria Libre," *La Doctrina de Martí*, 2 Oct. 1896, 1; "El peligro," ibid., 30 Dec. 1897, 1; S. Figueroa, "Cuba, para los Cubanos," ibid., 2 Oct. 1896; "El honor de Grant," ibid., 30 Apr. 1897, 1; D. Collazo, "¡No más corderillos!" ibid., 6 Aug. 1896, 3; "Deber cumplido," ibid., 6 Aug. 1896, 4; Aline Helg, *Our Rightful Share: The Afro-Cuban Struggle for Equality, 1886–1912* (Chapel Hill, NC, 1995), 88.

49. [Roberto H. Todd], *Memoria de los trabajos realizados por la sección Puerto Rico del Partido Revolucionario Cubano, 1895 á 1898* (San Juan, PR, 1993 [1898]), 147–149 ("gobierno constitutivo"; "estado ó nación"), 21–30, 129–150, 232–233; Ibrahim Hidalgo de Paz, *Cuba: 1895–1898: Contradicciones y disoluciones* (Havana, 1999), 258–259; Cedó Alzamora, *La Guerra*, 33, 189; Córdova, *Resident Commissioner*, 61–62; Harold J. Lidin, *History of the Puerto Rican Independence Movement*, vol. 1 (Hato Rey, PR, 1981), 164–165; Héctor Andres Negroni, *Historia militar de Puerto Rico* ([Spain?], 1992), 367–368; Ángel Rivero, *Crónica de la Guerra Hispanoamericana en Puerto Rico* (Madrid, 1922), 429–437; *Annual Reports of the War Department for the Fiscal Year Ended June 30, 1898: Report of the Major-General Commanding the Army* (Washington, DC, 1898), 131; Kal Wagenheim, with Olga Jimenez de Wagenheim, *The Puerto Ricans: A*

Documentary History (New York, 1973), 91; "Plans a Surprise in Puerto Rico," *Chicago Daily Tribune*, 25 July 1898, 1.
50. María Cadilla de Martínez, *Rememorando el pasado heroico* (Arecibo, PR, 1946), 545n425.

THE CONSTITUTION AND THE NEW U.S. EXPANSION: DEBATING THE STATUS OF THE ISLANDS

1. For one example, see Robert Wooster, *Nelson A. Miles and the Twilight of the Frontier Army* (Lincoln, NE, 1993), 38–56.
2. Juan Ramos y Velex to Federico Degetau, 27 July 1898, CIHCAM 2/III/69 ("matadero"); Nelson A. Miles to the Inhabitants of Porto Rico, Headquarters of the Army, Ponce, Puerto Rico, 28 July 1898, in *Annual Reports of the War Department for the Fiscal Year Ended June 30, 1898: Report of the Secretary of War, Miscellaneous Reports* (Washington, DC, 1898), 41; Sidney Shalett, "War Suspended, Peace Assured," *New York Times*, 13 Aug. 1898, 1; "General Henry's Words of Wisdom," *San Francisco Call*, 19 Oct. 1898, 1; Oath of Allegiance of Jesus [M. Rossy y?] Calderón, 19 Oct. 1898, AG/OG/CG/179/justicia, ciudadanía, 19 octubre 1898–1899; Albert A. Nofi, *The Spanish-American War, 1898* (Boston, 1997), 252–256; Germán Delgado Pasapera, *Puerto Rico: Sus luchas emancipadoras (1850–1898)* (Río Piedras, PR, 1984), 591–592; Mariano Negrón Portillo, *Cuadrillas anexionistas y revueltas campesinas en Puerto Rico, 1898–1899* (Río Piedras, PR, 1987), 15–26; Ángel Rivero Méndez, *Crónica de la guerra hispanoamericana en Puerto Rico* (Madrid, 1922), 274–276, 280, 429–437; Fernando Pico, *Cada guaraguao: Galería de oficiales norteamericanos en Puerto Rico (1898–1899)* (Río Piedras, PR, 1998); Henry K. Carroll, *Report on the Industrial and Commercial Condition of Porto Rico* (Washington, DC, 1899), 55; Parole of Pedro Sam Clemente, 10 Aug. 1898, AG/OG/CG/179/Justicia, ciudadanía, 19 octubre 1898–1899, C.F. 135, D.P. 1898; "Citizenship of the Porto Ricans," *San Francisco Call*, 19 Oct. 1898, 1; Wooster, *Miles*, 38–56. During his Indian War days, General Miles promised to be "their friend" if a group of American Indians returned to their camp; Nelson Miles, *Serving the Republic: Memoirs of the Civil and Military Life of Nelson A. Miles* (New York, 1911), 243–244. In 1896 Miles relied on his experience battling Native peoples in the U.S. West to assert that American Indians were "a doomed race" of "unruly children" who should be "civilized" under the expert rule of army men who had "reconstructed States"; Nelson Miles, *Personal Recollections and Observations of General Nelson A. Miles Embracing a Brief View of the Civil War, or, From New England to the Golden Gate* (Chicago, 1896), 341–342, 351, 347. Henry also spent years fighting American Indians in the U.S. West. He and Miles had sought to have responsibility for Indian affairs transferred from the Department of the Interior to the War Department, which they contended was particularly well equipped to govern dependent wards of the United States. See Marcus R. Erlandson, "Guy V. Henry: A Study in Military Leadership," Master of Military Art thesis, U.S. Army Command and General Staff College, 1985, 63; Miles, *Personal Recollections*, 345–347.

3. For a short history of naturalization oaths, see U.S. Citizenship and Immigration Services, Naturalization Oath of Allegiance to the United States of America, www.uscis.gov/us-citizenship/naturalization-test/naturalization-oath-allegiance-united-states-america (updated 25 June 2014).

4. "Chinese Exclusion in Puerto Rico," *New York Times*, 21 Jan. 1899, p. 4; G. Meiklejohn to Guy Henry, 26 Jan. 1899, MD NARA 350/8/C80-2; Charles Magoon, Memorandum, in *Relations of Puerto Rico to the Constitution*, H.R. Doc. No. 594, 56th Cong., 1st sess. (1900), 2; Memorandum, [1 May 1900?], MD NARA 350/5A/184; G. Meiklejohn to Secretary of Treasury, 17 Jan. 1899, MD NARA 350/5A/184; G. Meiklejohn to Guy Henry, 17 Jan. 1899, MD NARA 350/5A/184; Guy Henry to Assistant Secretary of War, 9 Feb. 1899, MD NARA 350/5A/184-1; G. Meiklejohn to Secretary of Treasury, 23 Feb. 1899, MD NARA 350/5A/184; Insular Affairs War Department Record Card, Immigration to and from Porto Rico, General Record 1-3, MD NARA 350/4/84; Federico Degetau to Secretary of Treasury, 5 Oct. 1902, CIHCAM 3/VI/56; Robert C. McGreevey, "Empire and Migration: Coastwise Shipping, National Status, and the Colonial Legal Origins of Puerto Rican Migration to the United States," *Journal of the Gilded Age and Progressive Era* 11 (Oct. 2012): 553–573; Héctor I. Santos, "Cabotage Laws: A Colonial Anachronism," *Revista de derecho puertorriqueño* 36 (1997): 3; *Customs Tariff and Regulations for Ports in Porto Rico in Possession of the United States* (Washington, DC, 1898), MD NARA 350/8/C25-5; Secretary of Treasury to Secretary of War, 4 Mar. 1899, MD NARA 350/8/C170-2; Philippine Customs Service, *Chinese and Immigration Circulars (Annotated)*, vol. 1 (Manila, 190[8?]), 89; 30 Stat. 151 (1897); DeLima v. Bidwell, 182 U.S. 1, 180–181 (1901); Acting Secretary of War to Attorney General, 20 June 1899, 3, MD NARA 350/8/C182-70.

5. Hay to Day, 28 and 26 Oct. 1898, in *Papers Relating to the Treaty with Spain*, S. Doc. No. 148, 156th Cong., 2d sess. (1901), 37, 35; Eric T. Love, *Race over Empire: Racism and U.S. Imperialism, 1865–1900* (Chapel Hill, NC, 2004), 159–178.

6. Love, *Race over Empire*, 181.

7. *A Treaty of Peace between the United States and Spain: Message from the President of the United States, Transmitting a Treaty of Peace between the United States and Spain, Signed at the City of Paris, on December 10, 1898*, S. Doc. No. 62, pt. 2, 55th Cong., 3d Sess. (1899), 53, 6, 3, 22–62; Hay to Day, 29 Nov. 1898, in *Papers Relating to the Treaty with Spain*, 61; United States–Russia Treaty of 1867, 18 Stat. 671, 673 (1867); Newlands Resolution, 30 Stat. 750, 751 (1898); "Constitution of the Spanish Monarch – Madrid, June 30, 1876," in *British and Foreign State Papers: 1875–1876*, vol. 67 (London, 1883), 118. One approach to evading the Reconstruction Constitution that made its way into the final treaty text was to make no mention of U.S. receipt of sovereignty over the islands. But such silence was hard to equate with lack of formal sovereignty, because Day and McKinley insisted that Spain by treaty cede the Philippines to the United States. An apparent legacy of the earlier presumption that U.S. citizenship would accompany annexation found its way into Article XI of the final treaty, which guaranteed Spaniards the same judicial rights in Puerto Rico as "citizens of the country to which the courts belong." An indication that this understanding of the clause is correct is Secretary of War Elihu

Root's strained attempt to reach the opposite result by reading "citizens" as "populace" and "belong" as "operate under" to produce the claim: "By citizens is meant inhabitants owing allegiance to the authority maintaining law and order." Elihu Root to George Davis, 19 Feb. 1900, MD NARA 350/5A/1137-22.

8. *Papers Relating to the Treaty with Spain*, 8–9. For expansionist arguments that the Treaty of Paris trumped the Constitution, see [Elihu Root?], Memorandum, n.d., MD NARA 350/5A/1444-9.

9. Carl Schurz, "American Imperialism: An Address Opposing Annexation of the Philippines, January 4, 1899," in *American Imperialism in 1898*, ed. Theodore P. Greene (Boston, 1955), 77–84, as quoted in Paul A. Kramer, *The Blood of Government: Race, Empire, the United States, and the Philippines* (Chapel Hill, NC, 2006), 117; 32 Cong. Rec. 642, 959; Robert L. Beisner, *Twelve against Empire: The Anti-Imperialists, 1898–1900* (New York, 1968), 216, 219–220, 225; Servand D. Halili Jr., *Iconography of the New Empire: Race and Gender Images and the American Colonization of the Philippines* (Quezon City, the Philippines, 2006), 32–33. My discussion of Senate debates on the Treaty of Paris and surrounding events is indebted to Michael Cullinane, *Liberty and American Anti-Imperialism, 1898–1909* (New York, 2012), and Love, *Race over Empire*.

For a sample of the scholarship addressing interrelationships among race, legal policy, and empire, see Lanny Thompson, "The Imperial Republic: A Comparison of the Insular Territories under U.S. Dominion after 1898," *Pacific Historical Review* 71 (Nov. 2002): 535–574; Kramer, *Blood*; Mark S. Weiner, "Teutonic Constitutionalism: The Role of Ethno-Juridical Discourse in the Spanish-American War," in *Foreign in a Domestic Sense: Puerto Rico, American Expansion, and the Constitution*, ed. Christina Duffy Burnett and Burke Marshall (Durham, NC, 2001), 48.

10. Carman F. Randolph, *The Law and Policy of Annexation with Special Reference to the Philippines Together with Observations on the Status of Cuba* (New York, 1901), vii; Christina Duffy Burnett and Burke Marshall, "Introduction," in Burnett and Marshall, *Foreign in a Domestic Sense*, 6; Carman F. Randolph, "Constitutional Aspects of Annexation," *Harvard Law Review* 12 (Dec. 1898), 292–293, 297–301, 308–310; Simeon E. Baldwin, "The Constitutional Questions Incident to the Acquisition and Government by the United States of Island Territory," *Harvard Law Review* 12 (Jan. 1899), 400–407. That tribal Filipinos might be denied U.S. citizenship, Randolph wrote, did not solve the problem, for millions of other racially inferior Filipinos would still become U.S. citizens; Randolph, "Constitutional Aspects," 305, 309–310.

11. 32 Cong. Rec. 639, 433–439, 93–96, 565, 641, 837; Cullinane, *Liberty and Anti-Imperialism*, 58; Thompson v. State of Utah, 170 U.S. 343, 349 (1898); Late Corporation of Church of Jesus Christ of Latter-Day Saints v. United States, 136 U.S. 1, 44 (1890), summarized at 32 Cong. Rec. 96. Senate Democrats justified disparagement of Filipinos by describing their racial mixture, Asian and Pacific Islander heritage, and lack of experience with republican governance. Because the tropics were inhospitable to whites, the senators contended, the extermination of indigenous and other nonwhite inhabitants, followed by white settlement, was not a viable solution. Vest also cited *Dred Scott*'s anti-imperial strands, which demanded eventual statehood for U.S. territories. The claim that nationality was equivalent to citizenship depended on overlooking American Indians.

12. C. C. Langdell "The Status of Our New Territories," *Harvard Law Review* 12 (Jan. 1899): 365–392; James Bradley Thayer, "Our New Possessions," *Harvard Law Review* 12 (Feb. 1899): 464–485.

13. 32 Cong. Rec. 295, 833, 293, 287–288, 834, 836, 325–329; Cullinane, *Liberty and Anti-Imperialism*, 33–34; Mormon Church v. United States, 130 U.S. 1, 42, 44 (1890).

14. 32 Cong. Rec. 639, 837. Among many excellent works on the long life of Civil War animosities and traumas that could counterbalance Northern and Southern whites' reconciliatory impulses, see Caroline E. Janney, *Remembering the Civil War: Reunion and the Limits of Reconciliation* (Chapel Hill, NC, 2013); Barbara A. Gannon, *The Won Cause: Black and White Comradeship in the Grand Army of the Republic* (Chapel Hill, NC, 2011).

15. Samuel J. Thomas, "Holding the Tiger: Mugwump Cartoonists and Tammany Hall in Gilded Age New York," *New York History* 82 (Spring 2001): 155.

16. On U.S. attempts to assimilate American Indians in the late nineteenth century and growing white pessimism about the project at the turn of the twentieth century, see Jacqueline Fear-Segal, *White Man's Club: Schools, Race, and the Struggle of Indian Acculturation* (Lincoln, NE, 2007); Frederick E. Hoxie, *A Final Promise: The Campaign to Assimilate the Indians, 1880–1920* (Lincoln, NE, 1984).

17. 32 Cong. Rec. 567; Cullinane, *Liberty and Anti-Imperialism*, 38; Beisner, *Twelve against Empire*. Republican senator George Hoar of Massachusetts won little support from his Republican colleagues when he advanced legal arguments against empire that were rooted in Reconstruction.

18. 32 Cong. Rec. 571, 1845–1848, 327–329, 561, 438–439, 472, 529–530, 959–960; Love, *Race over Empire*, 187–188, 194–195; Cullinane, *Liberty and Anti-Imperialism*, 32, 37, 42–43; "How the Vote Was Taken," *New York Times*, 7 Feb. 1899, 1. Some senators valued the commercial, security, and humanitarian benefits of ratification. Others questioned such logic. For some senators, their local constituencies' opposition to annexation outweighed any national benefits to be gained. Senator Caffery, for example, from the large sugar-growing state of Louisiana, saw the sugar output of recent and potential U.S. acquisitions as a threat to his constituents. On European powers' "hypocritical techniques of annexation without sovereignty," see Martti Koskenniemi, *The Gentle Civilizer of Nations: The Rise and Fall of International Law 1870–1960* (Cambridge, 2001), 110–125, 151–152.

19. Abbott Lawrence Lowell, "The Status of Our New Possessions – A Third View," *Harvard Law Review* 13 (Nov. 1899): 176, 173–174, 166–69, 175; 11 Stat. 119–120, secs. 1, 6 (1856); *Revised Statutes of the United States, Passed at the First Session of the Forty-Third Congress, 1873–1874*, 2nd ed. (Washington, DC, 1878), 1080–1081, title 72, secs. 5570, 5576; Jones v. United States, 137 U.S. 202, 224, 203–204 (1890); Duncan v. Navassa Phosphate Co., 137 U.S. 647, 651 (1891); Fleming v. Page, 50 U.S. 603, 615 (1850); Christina Duffy Burnett, "The Edges of Empire and the Limits of Sovereignty: American Guano Islands," *American Quarterly* 57 (Sept. 2005): 779, 782; Liliana Obregón, "The Civilized and the Uncivilized," in *The Oxford Handbook of the History of International Law*, ed. Bardo Fassbender and Anne Peters (Oxford, 2012), 917–919, 922–925; In re Ross, 140 U.S. 453, 454, 464 (1891).

20. Naomi Mezey described the broader problem in understanding how legal consciousness and law constitute each other as that of determining "how the individual shells of experience and perception become the coral reef of culture." Review, "Out of the Ordinary: Law, Power, Culture, and the Commonplace," *Law & Social Inquiry* 26 (Winter 2001): 160. As if that question were not hard enough, the coral polyps in these waters are sentient, able to shape their shells, desirous of producing particular reefs, and prone to making adjustments in light of experience.

21. Santiago Iglesias Pantín, *Luchas emancipadoras: Crónicas de Puerto Rico*, 2nd ed., 2 vols. (San Juan, PR, 1958–1962), 1:90 ("habían jurado defender y morir por la bandera española en sus puestos"; "continuaron ... gozando de las mismas posiciones"; "jurando a la vez respetar y defender la bandera americana"); Memorandum, C.F. 74, D.P., 1898, 22 Oct. 1898, AG/DE/SPR/COS/Registro de Correspondencia, caja 1.

22. Iglesias, *Luchas*, 1:82–83 ("Ahora no tiene usted nada que temer; el pabellón Americano le ampara[;] ... puede considerarse un ciudadano libre"), 77–78, 87–88, 92–97, 130–131, 133–134; Kirwin R. Shaffer, *Black Flag Boricuas: Anarchism, Antiauthoritarianism, and the Left in Puerto Rico, 1897–1921* (Urbana, IL, 2013), 34; Iglesias, *Luchas*, 2:60; "Labor Leader Was Jailed," *San Juan News*, 2 Aug. 1900, 1, AG/OG/CG/233/disturbios, #11709, cuatro copias del periódico *San Juan News* 1900–1902; Igualdad Iglesias de Pagán, *El obrerismo en Puerto Rico: Época de Santiago Iglesias (1896–1905)* (San Juan, PR, 1973), 58; Carroll, *Report*, 316–318.

23. Iglesias, *Luchas*, 1:99 ("extranjero"), 96 ("somos anexionistas"), 88, 92–93, 95; "El juicio oral y publico," *El porvenir social*, 15 Apr. 1899, 1, CPMN, roll S-450 ("en contraposición con las leyes de la gran República Americana"); Carroll, *Report*, 316–318; Bolívar Pagán, "Memorial Addresses: Remarks by Commissioner Pagán of Puerto Rico," in *Memorial Services Held in the House of Representatives of the United States Together with Remarks Presented in Eulogy of Santiago Iglesias, Late a Resident Commissioner from Puerto Rico* (Washington, DC, 1940), 31; Iglesias, *Luchas*, 2:240; "De la Corte de Justicia," *El porvenir social*, 31 May 1899, 1, CPMN, roll S-450. Carlos Sanabria reviews prior analyses of the ideology of Iglesias and his colleagues in "Samuel Gompers and the American Federation of Labor in Puerto Rico," *Centro Journal* 17 (Spring 2005): 140–161. On articles in Iglesias's paper favoring socialism and anarchism, see Shaffer, *Black Flag Boricuas*, 38–53; Kirk Shaffer, "Tropical Libertarians: Anarchist Movement and Networks in the Caribbean, Southern United States, and Mexico, 1890s–1920s," in *Anarchism and Syndicalism in the Colonial and Postcolonial World, 1870–1940*, ed. Steven Hirsch and Lucien van der Walt (Boston, 2010), 296. As Gervasio Luis García insists in "I Am the Other: Puerto Rico in the Eyes of North Americans, 1898," *Journal of American History* 87 (June 2000): 55, accounts attributing all evils in Puerto Rico to U.S. rule overlook elite Puerto Ricans' participation in these dynamics.

24. General Orders, No. 160, Headquarters Department of Porto Rico, San Juan, 12 Oct. 1899, MD NARA 350/5A/1286-2; Iglesias, *Luchas*, 1:135, 159–160; "Al General Davis," *El porvenir social*, 18 July 1899, 2, CPMN, roll S-450; "To General Davis," *El porvenir social*, [Oct./Nov.?], 1899, 2, CPMN, roll S-450.

25. On labor and the Populists, see Matthew Hild, *Greenbackers, Knights of Labor, and Populists: Farmer-Labor Insurgency in the Late-Nineteenth-Century South* (Athens, GA, 2007). On links between federal inaction and the construction of a racial caste system in the U.S. South, see Desmond King and Robert C. Lieberman,

"Finding the American State: Transcending the 'Statelessness' Account," *Polity* 40 (July 2008): 376–377. On U.S. troop involvement in strikebreaking and similarities in depictions and understandings of the Civil War, the Indian Wars, the Philippine-American War, and industrial strife, see Priscilla Murolo, "Wars of Civilization: The US Army Contemplates Wounded Knee, the Pullman Strike, and the Philippine Insurrection," *International Labor and Working Class History* 80 (Fall 2011): 77–102; Louis Carroll Wade, "Hell Hath No Fury Like a General Scorned: Nelson A. Miles, the Pullman Strike, and the Beef Scandal of 1898," *Illinois Historical Journal* 79 (Autumn 1986): 162–184; David Ray Papke, *The Pullman Case: The Clash of Labor and Capital in Industrial America* (Lawrence, KS, 1999); Troy Rondinone, "'History Repeats Itself': The Civil War and the Meaning of Labor Conflict in the Late Nineteenth Century," *American Quarterly* 49 (June 2007): 397–419.

26. Leo S. Rowe, *The United States and Porto Rico* (New York, 1904), 248–249; Iglesias, *Luchas*, 1:129 ("las muchedumbres campesinas e industriales que estaban bajo el dominio y control de los caciques"), 119; Brief Filed by Leave of the Court by Federico Degetau, No. 225, Gonzales v. Williams, 192 U.S. 1 (Nov. 1903), 26; G. Henry to Adjutant General, 15 Feb. 1899, MD NARA 350/5A/168-3; *To the People/Al País* ([PR], [1899?]), CIHCAM 22/L1; *Programa del Partido Federal* ([1899?]), 10–11, 13, 15–16, CIHCAM 6/L3; *Petition to the President of the United States of the Agriculturalists of Puerto Rico* (Washington, DC, 1899), MD NARA 350/8/C182-8; "Spain Preferred to Our Neglect" and "Tomorrow's Celebration," *Diario de Puerto Rico*, 24 Feb. 1900, CIHCAM 12/L2; F. Degetau y Gonzales, *Al País* ([PR], [1900]), CIHCAM 12/L2; "La libertad individual en la constitutición de los EE. UU.," *El País*, 15 May 1900, CIHCAM 12/L2; "La libertad en la constitución de los EE. UU.," *El País*, 23 May 1900, CIHCAM 12/L2; Copy, Guy Henry to Adjutant General of the Army, 22 May 1899, Centro de Investigaciones Históricas, Colección de Caribeño de Justicia y Paz, caja 15, cartapacio 10, documento 6; Francisco de P. Acuna to Guy Henry, 17 Apr. 1899, MD NARA 350/5A/81-3; Geo. Davis to Adjutant General, 20 Sept. 1899, Centro de Investigaciones Históricas, Colección de Caribeño de Justicia y Paz, caja 15, cartapacio 14, documento [8]; *Industrial and Other Conditions of the Island of Puerto Rico, and the Form of Government Which Should Be Adopted for It*, S. Doc. 147, 56th Cong., 1st sess. (1900), 178, 201; "Serpentinas," *El Territorio*, date unknown [May 1899?], CIHCAM 12/L2; Spencer C. Tucker, ed., *The Encyclopedia of the Spanish-American and Philippine American Wars: A Political, Social, and Military History* (Santa Barbara, CA, 2009), 44; Miriam Jiménez Román, "Un hombre (negro) del pueblo: José Barbosa and the Puerto Rican 'Race' toward Whiteness," *Centro* 8 (Spring 1996): 8, 16; "Various Topics," *University of Michigan Chronicle* 9 (27 Oct. 1877): 18; César J. Ayala and Rafael Bernabe, *Puerto Rico in the American Century: A History since 1898* (Chapel Hill, NC, 2007), 54; General Order No. 15, in H.R. Doc. No. 60-1484 (1909); *Asamblea republicana: Celebrada en San Juan, Puerto Rico: Los días primera y dos de julio de 1899* ([San Juan, PR,] 1899), 3–5, CIHCAM 6/L2; Federico Degetau, "The Porto Ricans as Soldiers and as Legislators," *Philadelphia Record*, 23 May 1901, CIHCAM 12/L2.

Degetau's brief quoted Degetau's own certificate. "El banquete republicano," newspaper and page unknown [July 1899?], CIHCAM 12/L2, quoted Barbosa as declaring "that our sentiments have been for the north, the great homeland of the party of Lincoln." On subsequent nurturing of ties to mainland Republicans, see *Informe de los delegados del Partido Republicano de Puerto Rico ante la Convención Nacional Republicana celebrada en Chicago, en 21 de junio de 1904* ([San Juan?], PR, 1904), 4–12, CIHCAM 6/L8. For descriptions of Barbosa as a man *de color* (of color), see, for example, Iglesias, *Luchas*, 1:59. Barbosa himself used the phrase, describing his party as the "party of the men of color," as Eileen J. Suárez Findlay, *Imposing Decency: The Politics of Sexuality and Race in Puerto Rico, 1870–1920* (Durham, NC, 1999), 142–143, relates in findings that draw in part from the newspapers *La Defensa* and *El Águila*.

27. *Asamblea republicana*, 29 ("los pueblos monárquicos y centralizados"), 21–23; F. Degetau y Gonzalez, "El dilema," *El País*, 20 Mar. 1900, CIHCAM 18/L2 ("Puerto Rico será un Territorio Republicano hoy y mañana un Estado de la Unión, ó Puerto Rico será lo que entre los anglo-sajones se llama 'una Colonia de la Corona'"; "la ciudadanía americana se redujo al monopolio de 74 millones de oligarcas"); *To the People/Al País*; Draft, F. Degetau to G. Davis, 30 Mar. 1900, CIHCAM 2/IV/18; Major Egan and F. Degetau, Investigation of the Charges of Excessive Punishment Brought against Mr. Benjamin Delvalle, Acting Superintendent of the Boy's Charity School, 29 Mar. 1900, CIHCAM 10/II/35 et seq.; Certification of Eugenio de Jesús López [Gartamlide?], 8 Jan. 1900, CIHCAM 6/I/17; Charles Allen to Frederico Degetau, 25 Nov. 1900, CIHCAM 2/V/6; [Illegible] to Federico Degetau, 9 June 1900, CIHCAM 2/IV/21; Headquarters, Department of Porto Rico, General Order No. 37, [3?]1 Mar. 1899, CIHCAM 2/IV/5; José Barbosa et al. to Federico Degetau, Sept. 1900, CIHCAM 2/IV/29; Federico Degetau to Adolfo Marin, [Mar. or Apr. 1899?], CIHCAM 2/IV/13; articles collected in CIHCAM 18/L1, 26–53, 79–128; David W. Blight, *Race and Reunion: The Civil War in American Memory* (Cambridge, MA, 2001). At CIHCAM 12/L2, see "En el Ateneo: Conferencias interesantes," *La Correspondencia*, 15 Apr. 1900; "Protesta," *El País*, 7 July 1899; "Los examenes generales," *La Correspondencia*, 19 June 1900; F. Degetau to Manuel Rossy, 31 Aug. 1900, in "Un acuerdo," *El País*, 20 Sept. 1900; "Conferencia importante," newspaper unknown, 9 Sept. 1899; "Ateneo," *La Correspondencia*, 5 May 1900; title unknown, *La Correspondencia*, 6 May 1900; "Lo de beneficencia," *El País*, 1 Apr. 1900; "Lo del asilo de huérfanos," *La Correspondencia*, 3 Apr. 1900; "Lo de beneficencia," *El País*, 4 Apr. 1900; F. Degetau y Gonzales, "Antecedentes del debate," *El País*, 4 Mar. 1900, CIHCAM 18/L2; "La constitución Americana: Conferencia de Degetau," *El País*, 17 Apr. 1900; F. Degetau y González, "Educacion civica," Parts I–VI, newspaper unknown, [Aug. 1900?]; "La constitución de los Estados Unidos," *El País*, 23–24 Apr. and 2 May 1900; "Los dos incondicionalismos," *El País*, 20 July 1899.

28. Degetau, "La constitución Americana" ("latinos"; "la existencia del individuo como centro de relaciones jurídicas"); Degetau, "El dilema" ("avergonzada"; "de su propia honra y de su buen nombre"); F. Degetau y González, "La votación del Bill Payne," *El País*, 17 Mar. 1900, CIHCAM 18/L2; F. Degetau y González, "Por honor y por deber," *El País*, 22 Mar. 1900, CIHCAM 18/L2; F. Degetau y González, "La palabra del Choctaw," *El País*, 27 July 1899, CIHCAM 12/L2; F. Degetau y González, "Puerto-Rico ante el Congreso," *El País*, 16 Mar. 1900, CIHCAM 18/L2. On other Republicano leaders' failures to appreciate the depth of the racial bias that Puerto Ricans faced on the mainland, see Federico Degetau to Manuel Rossy, 4 Jan. 1901, CIHCAM 2/VI/2.

29. "Spain Preferred to Our Neglect"; *Programa del Partido Federal*, 10, 15–16; Astrid Cubano Iguina, "Political Culture and Male Mass-Party Formation in Late-Nineteenth-Century Puerto Rico," *Hispanic American Historical Review* 78 (Nov. 1998), 642–643; "Tomorrow's Celebration"; Jack Ericson Eblen, *The First and Second United States Empires: Governors and Territorial Governments, 1784–1912* (Pittsburgh, 1968); Kathryn A. Flynn, ed., *2012 Blue Book* (Santa Fe, NM, 2012), www.sos.state.nm.us/Public_Records_And_Publications/NMCentennialBlueBook. pdf; "N. O. Murphy Made Governor of Arizona," *San Francisco Chronicle*, 17 July 1898, 20; John Bartlett Meserve, "The Governors of Oklahoma Territory," *Chronicles of Oklahoma* 20 (Sept. 1943), 222–223, http://digital.library.okstate.edu/ Chronicles/v020/v020p218.html.

30. "Luis Munoz Rivera," *San Juan News*, 14 Feb. 1899, 1, MD NARA 350/5A/21/ 168-7; "Entre claro y oscuro," *El Liberal*, 10 Jan. 1899, 1 ("habló alto"); Gonzalo F. Córdova, *Resident Commissioner, Santiago Iglesias and His Times* (Río Piedras, PR, 1993), 31.

31. John Higham, *Strangers in the Land: Patterns of American Nativism, 1860–1925* (New Brunswick, NJ, 1955), 39–90; Mae M. Ngai, "The Architecture of Race in American Immigration Law: A Reexamination of the Immigration Act of 1924," *Journal of American History* 86 (Feb. 2001): 67–92; Carroll, *Report*, 183. Jiménez Román, "Un hombre," 11, argues that African appearance, more than African ancestry, drove many racial characterizations. Findlay, *Imposing Decency*, 6–17, 23–24, 27, 37–39, describes a dominant racial hierarchy structured around relative lightness and darkness, in which a person's place resulted from judgments about their morality, cultural activities, dress, speech patterns, previously enslaved relations, wealth, social standing, classifications in official records, and reputation. Luis A Figueroa, *Sugar, Slavery, and Freedom in Nineteenth-Century Puerto Rico* (Chapel Hill, NC, 2005), 204, points to rising official rates of whiteness in post-emancipation Puerto Rico. On U.S. views, see Ariela Gross, *What Blood Won't Tell: A History of Race on Trial in America* (Cambridge, MA, 2008), 10–11; Rebecca J. Scott, *Degrees of Freedom: Louisiana and Cuba after Slavery* (Cambridge, MA, 2005), 262. Neil Foley discusses struggles over racial characterizations of Mexican Americans in *The White Scourge: Mexicans, Blacks, and Poor Whites in Texas Cotton Culture* (Berkeley, CA, 1997).

32. "Luis Munoz Rivera"; Summary, Fidel Guillermety et al. to Francisco del Valle, C.F. 256, D.P. 1898, 29 Oct. 1898, AG/DE/SPR/COS/Registro de Correspondencia, caja 1; General Orders No. 17, Headquarters Department of Porto Rico, 10 Feb. 1899, MD NARA 350/5A/21/168-6; Memorandum for the Assistant Secretary, MD NARA 350/5A/21; Pedro A. Cabán, *Constructing a Colonial People: Puerto Rico and the United States, 1898–1932* (Boulder, CO, 1999), 167; General Orders No. 17, 10 Feb. 1899. On honor achievable through clientelism, which was common in Puerto Rico, see Emanuel Pfoh, "La formación del estado nacional en América Latina y la cuestión del clientelismo politico," *Revista de Historia de América*, no. 136 (Jan.-Dec. 2005): 129–148; Bertram Wyatt-Brown, "Andrew Jackson's Honor," *Journal of the Early Republic* 17 (Spring 1997): 1–36; Barbara Schröter, "Clientelismo politico: ¿Existe el fantasma y cómo se viste? / Political Clientelism: Does the Ghost Exist and What Is It Wearing?" *Revista Mexicana de Sociología* 72 (Jan.-Mar. 2010): 149. On being out of office as an opportunity to display honorable virtue, see Juby Bieber, "A 'visao do sertao': Party Identity and Political

Honor in Late-Imperial Minas Gerais, Brazil," *Hispanic American Historical Review* 81 (May 2001): 340–342.

33. Henry to Adjutant General, 15 Feb. 1899; Geo. W. Davis, "Report of the Military Governor of Porto Rico on Civil Affairs," in *Annual Reports of the War Department for the Fiscal Year Ended June 30, 1900*, vol. 1, pt. 13 (Washington, DC, 1902), 115–117; S. Doc. No. 56-147, at 58, 4; Ayala and Bernabe, *Puerto Rico in the American Century*, 31–32; C. Vann Woodward, *The Strange Career of Jim Crow*, commemorative ed. (Oxford, 2002 [1955]), 54–56; Glenda Elizabeth Gilmore, *Gender and Jim Crow: Women and the Politics of White Supremacy in North Carolina, 1896–1920* (Chapel Hill, NC, 1996), 123; Michael Perman, *Struggle for Mastery: Disfranchisement in the South, 1888–1908* (Chapel Hill, NC, 2000); Shelton Stromquist, *Reinventing "The People": The Progressive Movement, the Class Problem, and the Origins of Modern Liberalism* (Urbana, IL, 2006), 56–82; Woodrow Wilson, "The Study of Administration," *Political Science Quarterly* 2 (June 1887): 197–222; Henry to Adjutant General of the Army, 22 May 1899; Guy Henry to Adjutant General, 9 Dec. 1898, MD NARA 350/5A/81.

34. "Spain Preferred to Our Neglect"; Davis, "Report of the Military Governor," 13; "Tomorrow's Celebration"; *Puerto Rico: Hearings before Committee on Ways and Means*, 56th Cong., 1st sess. (1900), 51.

35. Philip C. Jessup, *Elihu Root*, vol. 1 (New York, 1938), 215, gives the source of the quotation as "Addresses on Government and Citizenship, pp. 503–504." See also ibid., 183–189, 221–222. Tariffs on mainland-island trade were already generating test cases and administrative inquiries. See Coudert Brothers to Elihu Root, 19 Oct. 1899, MD NARA 350/5A/1116; "Cuba a Foreign Land in Law," *New York Times*, 9 Nov. 1899, 7; Virginia Kays Veenswijk, *Coudert Brothers: A Legacy in Law: The History of America's First International Law Firm 1853–1993* (New York, 1994), 135; Bartholomew H. Sparrow, *The Insular Cases and the Emergence of American Empire* (Lawrence, KS, 2006), 55; "Outside of Tariff Laws," *Washington Post*, 15 Feb. 1900, 4.

36. *The Union League Club of New York* (New York, 1898), 87–88; "Elihu Root for President," *New York Times*, 30 Dec. 1897, 1; Jessup, *Elihu Root*, 1:183; Elihu Root, "The Political Use of Money: Address of September 3, 1894," and Elihu Root, "The Civil Service: Address of September 21, 1894," in *Addresses on Government and Citizenship by Elihu Root*, vol. 1, ed. Robert Bacon and James Brown Scott (Cambridge, MA, 1916), 141–144, 180, 190; 227–230; "Oratory at the Union League," *Chicago Tribune*, 23 Feb. 1899, 1.

37. Elihu Root to George Davis, 6 Feb. 1900, AG/OG/CG 179/expediente: justicia, ciudadanía, marzo 1900, 7171; Headquarters Department of Porto Rico, Circular No. 15, 17 June 1899, MD NARA 350/5A/81-12; Headquarters Department of Porto Rico, Circular (Corrected), 15 Aug. 1899, MD NARA 350/5A/21/168-16; [George Davis] to Secretary of War, 12 Feb. 1900, AG/OG/CJ/179/Justicia, ciudadanía, marzo 1900, 7171; Guide to Puerto Rican Records in the National Archives, New York City (Aug. 2013), 4, www.archives.gov/nyc/finding-aids/ puerto-rican-records-guide.pdf; Juramento de fidelidad á los Estados-Unidos de América of Vicente Soto, 22 July 1899, AG/OG/CG/179/justicia, ciudadanía, 19 octubre 1898–1899; George Davis to Elihu Root, 28 Sept. 1899, MD NARA 350/ 5A/21/168-19; George Davis to Elihu Root, 28 Sept. 1899, MD NARA 350/5A/21/

168-18; General Orders, No. 160, 3–4; Córdova, *Resident Commissioner*, 101; Pagán, "Memorial Addresses," 29, 32; Wrapper, AG/OG/CG caja 179, expediente: justicia – renuncia – ciudadanía, junio 1900, 10649; Juramento de fidelidad á los Estados Unidos de América of Manuel Santiago Pantin, 10 Apr. 1900, AG/DE/76–16/1, Legajo número 1: España, 1024. For evidence that the oath is Iglesias's, see Santiago Iglesias to Committee on P.I. and Porto Rico, 3 Jan. 1911, DC NARA, 46/Sen 62A-F17/Army Vetinary Bill to Citizenship Granting of to Porto Rico (containing Iglesias's signature); 1920 Census PR/San Juan/Santurce/27/20A; Iglesias de Pagán, *El obrerismo*, 112. In AG/OG/CG/179/justicia, ciudadanía, marzo 1900, 7171, see Root to Davis, 6 Feb. 1900; John Hay to Secretary of War, 27 Jan. 1900. See also Clarence Edwards to Geo. Davis, 7 Mar. 1900; Memorandum Card, 27 Feb. 1900, MD NARA 350/5A/311/1286-4; John Hay to Secretary of War, 10 Apr. 1900, MD NARA 350/5A/180G/1286-5. The issue of the competence of the court to naturalize turned at least in part on whether the Provisional Court was "a district or supreme court of the Territories." *Revised Statutes, 1873–1874*, 378, Title XXX, sec. 2165 (1874); "U.S. Provisional Court," *Boston Daily Globe*, 18 June 1899, 18.

38. George Davis, "Extract from Annual Report of the Commanding General, Department of Porto Rico, to the Adjutant General, Dated August 15, 1899," MD NARA 350/5A/168-20; Pérez, *Cuba between Empires*, 307–312; Henry to Adjutant General, 9 Dec. 1898; Nell Irvin Painter, *Standing at Armageddon: The United States 1877–1919* (New York, 1987), 9–10, 228–230; General Orders, No. 160, 3–4; C. Vincent comp., *The Platform Text-Book* (Omaha, NE, 1900), 140, 162; Henry to Adjutant General, 9 Dec. 1898; Elihu Root, *Address of the Honorable Elihu Root, Secretary of War, Delivered at a Meeting of the Union League Club, Held on the 6th Day of February, 1903, to Honor Its Fortieth Anniversary*, 7–10; Nina Silber, *The Romance of Reunion: Northerners and the South, 1865–1900* (Chapel Hill, NC, 1993), 137, 141, 156; Elihu Root, *The Military and Colonial Policy of the United States: Addresses and Reports* (Cambridge, MA, 1916), 164; Davis to Adjutant General, 20 Sept. 1899; S. Doc. No. 56-147, 49–65 (1900). On Root's policy in Cuba, which resembled that in Puerto Rico, see Pérez, *Cuba between Empires*, 311–312; Jessup, *Elihu Root*, 1:288; Scott, *Degrees of Freedom*, 187. For Root casting lawyers of southern and eastern European extraction as alien contagions to the bar, see Elihu Root, Address, 15 Jan. 1916, *New York State Bar Proceedings* (Albany, NY, 1916), 474–481.

39. Henry to Adjutant General, 15 Feb. 1899; Henry to Adjutant General, 9 Dec. 1898; *Five Years of the War Department: Following the War with Spain, 1899–1903, as Shown in the Annual Reports of the Secretary of War* (Washington, DC, 1904), 33–34; 33 Cong. Rec. 3619; S. Doc. No. 56-147, 81; Davis, "Extract." Like Root, Senator Depew was an elite business lawyer. He had become general counsel for the Vanderbilt railroad empire in 1876. On the Jezebel stereotype, see Deborah Gray White, *Ar'n't I a Woman? Female Slaves in the Plantation South* (New York, 1999 [1985]), 27–61. Marilyn Lake and Henry Reynolds, *Drawing the Global Colour Line: White Men's Countries and the International Challenge of Racial Equality* (Cambridge, 2008), describe how a broad swath of English-speaking polities drew on common ideas about race and looked to each other's white-supremacist policies as they implemented their own discriminatory practices.

40. *Five Years of the War Department,* 31–32, 40; Charles E. Magoon, *Report on the Legal Status of the Territory and Inhabitants of the Islands Acquired by the United States during the War with Spain, Considered with Reference to the Territorial Boundaries, the Constitution, and Laws of the United States,* S. Doc. 234, 56th Cong., 1st sess. (1900), 11–13, 23, 40, 1, 37–39, 51–55, 60; Jessup, *Elihu Root,* 1:226; Charles E. Magoon, *Reports on the Law of Civil Government in Territory Subject to Military Occupation by the Military Forces of the United States, Submitted to Hon. Elihu Root, Secretary of War, by Charles E. Magoon, Law Officer, Bureau of Insular Affairs, War Department, Published by Order of the Secretary of War,* 3rd ed. (Washington, DC, 1903), 20; [Root?], Memorandum, 34–60.

41. Rowe, *United States and Porto Rico,* 87; Magoon, *Report on the Legal Status,* 71, 22–26, 33–34, 38, 67–72. The omission of mention of Reconstruction was doubly notable given Davis's recent declaration that he had modeled governance of the island on "the military Government which existed in the Southern States during the period of reconstruction following the Civil War." Davis, "Extract." When Magoon had discussed Reconstruction in an earlier memo to Root, he had limited his discussion to the powers exercised by the United States in the formerly independent Texas. Turning to allegiance, Magoon cast it as a substantive status, obligating the United States, inter alia, to protect Puerto Ricans in their property and person.

42. Magoon, *Report on the Legal Status,* 71–72. On contemporary recognition of this history, see *Wong Kim Ark,* 169 U.S. 649 (1898); Frederick Van Dyne, *Citizenship of the United States* (Rochester, NY, 1904), 7–12. The rule also required birth within the allegiance or jurisdiction of the United States. Magoon did not suggest that Puerto Ricans failed to meet that requirement.

43. S. Rep. No. 249, 56th Cong., 1st sess. (1900), 12–13, 1; 33 Cong. Rec. 2473, as quoted in José A. Cabranes, "Citizenship and the American Empire: Notes on the Legislative History of the United States Citizenship of Puerto Ricans," *University of Pennsylvania Law Review* 127 (1978): 428; Elihu Root to William McKinley, 18 Aug. 1899, as quoted in Jessup, *Elihu Root,* 1:373; 33 Cong. Rec. 630; Richard W. Leopold, *Elihu Root and the Conservative Tradition* (Boston, 1954), 27–28; "Plan to Rule Puerto Rico," *New York Times,* 4 Jan. 1900, 11; Root, *Military and Colonial Policy,* 165–168; Magoon, *Report on the Legal Status,* 22–23, 66–67, 70–72; *Five Years of the War Department,* 22–23, 40; Jessup, *Elihu Root,* 1:375; Geo. Davis to Elihu Root, 14 Feb. 1900, MD NARA 350/8/C182-43. A longtime proponent of African American voting rights, and racial justice more broadly, Foraker was well aware of how inconsequential U.S. citizenship could become for disfavored groups. Perman, *Struggle,* 262–263.

44. Four justices so found as to Hawai'i in 1901. See *Downes v. Bidwell,* 182 U.S. 244, 305 (1901) (White, J., concurring in judgment); ibid., 344–345 (Gray, J., concurring in the judgment).

Nonjudicial officials' attempts to influence constitutional meaning during these months were forms of executive, administrative, and legislative constitutionalism. McKinley framed and prefigured the debate. Capable of rapid, decisive action, the War Department led the legal offensive. Congress also asserted itself, but as a multimember body that, to act, had to tamp down conflicts over principles and their implications. Its structure discouraged settling underlying controversies in favor of incremental, less-than-systematic policies. Examples of work on executive and legislative constitutionalism abound. On presidents shaping constitutional meaning, see Keith E. Whittington, *Political Foundations of Judicial Supremacy* (Princeton, NJ, 2007). Cornelia T. L. Pillard reviews theoretical defenses of executive constitutionalism in "The Unfulfilled Promise of the Constitution in Executive Hands," *Michigan Law Review* 103 (Feb. 2005): 676–758. The classic statement of presidential power as the power to persuade is Richard Neustadt, *Presidential Power: The Politics of Leadership* (New York, 1960). George C. Edwards, *The Strategic Presidency: Persuasion and Opportunity in Presidential Leadership* (Princeton, NJ, 2009), argues that presidents succeed by spotting and exploiting opportunities. For a description and defense of one form of legislative constitutionalism, see Robert C. Post and Reva B. Siegel, "Legislative Constitutionalism and Section Five Power: Policentric Interpretation of the Family and Medical Leave Act," *Yale Law Journal* 112 (2003): 1943–2059. On the tendency of compromises to leave underlying theoretical questions unanswered, see Cass R. Sunstein, "Incompletely Theorized Agreements," *Harvard Law Review* 108 (May 1995): 1733–1772. One source of diversity in Congress was seniority; freshmen members rubbed elbows with colleagues whose tenures could stretch back to the Civil War. See also Kenneth A. Shepsle, "Congress Is a 'They,' Not an 'It': Legislative Intent as Oxymoron," *International Review of Law and Economics* 12 (1992): 239–256. The Constitution imposed a second significant constraint on the lawmaking power. Gillian E. Metzger provides an incisive introduction in "Administrative Constitutionalism," *Texas Law Review* 91 (June 2013): 1897–1935. I share Sophia Z. Lee's focus on administrators' "interpretation and implementation of constitutional law" and on the "relationship between administrative and court" and other types of constitutionalism; see Sophia Z. Lee, "Race, Sex, and Rulemaking: Administrative Constitutionalism and the Workplace, 1960 to the Present," *Virginia Law Review* 96 (June 2010): 801. See also Jeremy K. Kessler, "The Administrative Origins of Modern Civil Liberties Law," *Columbia Law Review* 114 (June 2014): 1083–1166; Karen M. Tani, "Administrative Equal Protection: Federalism, the Fourteenth Amendment, and the Rights of the Poor," *Cornell Law Review* 100 (May 2015): 825–899. Daniel P. Carpenter, *The Forging of Bureaucratic Autonomy: Reputations, Networks, and Policy Innovation in Executive Agencies, 1862–1928* (Princeton, NJ, 2001), defines autonomy in such a way as to require convincing another to forgo an existing preference. The concept blurs into administrative constitutionalism when the bureaucrat is able to convince others to accept her legal analysis rather than undertake their own. Internal hierarchy and responsibility for colonial governance allowed the secretary of war to choose which disputes would become judicial cases and which policies could be put in place and then presented to courts as faits accomplis. These dynamics challenge conventional depictions of weak federal bureaucracies during the Gilded Age. On the importance of institutional structure to bureaucratic capacity, see Carpenter, *Forging of Bureaucratic Autonomy*; Jerry L. Mashaw, "Federal Administration and Administrative Law in the Gilded Age," *Yale Law Journal* 119 (2010): 1362–1472.

For critiques of scholarship that treats courts as relatively subservient to external forces, see Thomas M. Keck, "Party Politics or Judicial Independence? The Regime Politics Literature Hits the Law Schools," *Law & Social Inquiry* 32 (Spring 2007): 511–544; Matthew E. K. Hall, "Rethinking Regime Politics," *Law & Social Inquiry*

37 (Fall 2012): 878–907. On writing history that accounts for both the unpredictability of outcomes and the genuine constraints that historical actors faced, see Scott, *Degrees of Freedom*, 6–7, 264, 269.

45. "Free Trade Abandoned: Senators' Views Changed," *New York Tribune*, 28 Jan. 1900, 1; *Five Years of the War Department*, 32; Jorge Cruz, S. Doc. No. 281, 56th Cong., 1st sess. (1900), 2; Rowe, *United States and Porto Rico*, 129, 90, 130; 35 Cong. Rec. 2042; "Jorge Cruz, the Excluded Porto Rican," *Great Round World*, 19 Apr. 1900, 75–77; Alfred S. Johnson, ed., *The Cyclopedic Review of Current History*, vol. 10 (Boston, 1901), 352; "The Week," *Nation*, 12 Apr. 1900, 272; Jorge Cruz, S. Doc. No. 311, 56th Cong., 1st sess. (1900); S. Rep. No. 249, 56th Cong., 1st sess. (1900), 7–8, 17; "Tariff for Puerto Rico," *New York Daily Tribune*, 1 Feb. 1900, CIHCAM 18/L1, 29; Foraker Act, secs. 3–4, 39 31 Stat. 77, 77–78, 86 (1900); Cabranes, "Citizenship," 432–433; *Civil Government for Porto Rico: Hearings before the Committee on Pacific Islands and Porto Rico United States Senate, 63d Cong., 2d sess., on S. 4604 a Bill to Provide a Civil Government for Porto Rico, and for Other Purposes* (Washington, DC, 1914), 18–19; *Civil Government for Porto Rico: Hearings before the Committee on Insular Affairs, House of Representatives, 63d Cong., 2d sess., on H. R. 13818, a Bill to Provide a Civil Government for Porto Rico, and for Other Purposes* (Washington, DC, 1914), 32–33; 33 Cong. Rec. 2008, 2659, 3632, 3690; John W. Foster, *The Practice of Diplomacy* (Boston, 1906), 63; "Changes," *Louisville Courier-Journal*, 28 Mar. 1900, 2; J. B. Foraker, "Porto Rico: It Belongs to the United States, but Is Not the United States, nor a Part of the United States," in *A Testimonial to the Public Services of Hon. Joseph B. Foraker* (n.p., [1901?]), 63–64. Anti-imperialist Democrats also claimed that extending free trade to Puerto Rico would mean extending it to the Philippines as well. Foraker anticipated that a test case on the U.S. citizenship of Puerto Ricans would also settle the U.S. citizenship status of Filipinos. I thank Joan Sherer and Evan Duncans for their research insights. For praise of the Foraker bill for inviting judicial review, see 33 Cong. Rec. 1946, discussed in Krishanti Vignarajah, "The Political Roots of Judicial Legitimacy: Explaining the Enduring Validity of the Insular Cases," *University of Chicago Law Review* 77 (2010), 822 and n177.

On the tariff depriving Democrats of that potential campaign issue, see 33 Cong. Rec. 2008. Republican representative Charles Grosvenor of Ohio noted that Democrats planned to argue on the campaign trail that citizenship for Puerto Ricans revealed Republicans' plans to naturalize Filipinos. See ibid., 2080. Powerful sugar interests also weighed in on the tariff question, which despite the relatively small output of Puerto Rico could have had large implications were it a harbinger of policy in the Philippines. S. Rep. No. 249, 56th Cong., 1st sess. (1900), 7–8. The impact of these efforts was blunted, however, by the conflicting interests of sugar growers and processors, the opportunities mainlanders with capital saw in Puerto Rican sugar, and the emergence of antitrust sentiment and tariff policies as partisan U.S. political issues. César J. Ayala, *American Sugar Kingdom: The Plantation Economy of the Spanish Caribbean, 1898–1934* (Chapel Hill, NC, 1999), 48–73, 108–109; Frank R. Rutter, "The Sugar Question in the United States," *Quarterly Journal of Economics* 17 (Nov. 1902): esp. 65–71; "Democratic Platform for 1900," in *The Second Battle; or, The New Declaration of Independence, 1776–1900* (Chicago, 1900), 42.

46. 33 Cong. Rec. 3613, 3616, 1950, 2009, 2199 3282, 3682, 4068, and app. 232–235, including as quoted in Cabranes, "Citizenship," 431–432; Office Director Census of Puerto Rico, War Department, *Report on the Census of Porto Rico, 1899* (Washington, DC, 1900), 57–58. On racialization of Filipinos, see Mae M. Ngai, *Impossible Subjects: Illegal Aliens and the Making of Modern America* (Princeton, NJ, 2004), 96–126, and "The Architecture of Race," 70. Bate was a lawyer. On the colonists' legal understanding of contemporary British legislation, see John Philip Reid, *Constitutional History of the American Revolution*, vols. 1–4 (Madison, WI, 1987–1993). Unfortunately for Puerto Ricans, the logic that Puerto Ricans were too white to be treated like free antebellum African Americans could run in reverse. The denial of rights could be cited as evidence of racial inferiority. A classic text on such legal construction of race is Ian Haney Lopez, *White by Law: The Legal Construction of Race* (New York, 1996).

47. Degetau, "Puerto-Rico ante el Congreso" ("hay en los Estados Unidos ó que puede haber dos clases de ciudadanos; dos condiciones de derecho").

48. Degetau, "Por honor" ("no se atrevió á despojar a esclavizadores y esclavizados de las … garantías y de las inmunidades de la Constitución"); Degetau, "Puerto-Rico ante el Congreso" ("adiós Washington, adiós Padres venerables de la Constitución"); Foraker Act, 31 Stat. 77 (1900); Degetau, "La constitución Americana"; "La constitución de los Estados Unidos," *El País*, 23 Apr. 1900, CIHCAM 12/L2; Cullinane, *Liberty and American Anti-Imperialism*, 45–49, 115–147; Kramer, *Blood*, 87–158; Richard E. Welch Jr., *Response to Imperialism: The United States and the Philippine-American War, 1899–1902* (Chapel Hill, NC, 1979), 17–49; Degetau, "El dilema"; Degetau, "La palabra del Choctaw"; "La convención republicana," newspaper unknown, [Sept. 1900?], CIHCAM 12/L2. On constitutional limits on Congress that Degetau depicted as applicable in the territories, see the *El País* articles "La libertad individual" and "La libertad en la constitución." On ascriptive strands in the history of U.S. citizenship, see Rogers M. Smith, *Civic Ideals: Conflicting Visions of Citizenship in U.S. History* (New Haven, CT, 1997).

49. "Candidatos o candiditos," *El Diario*, 11 Sept. 1900, CIHCAM 22/L2 ("principios básicos de la Constitución de los Estados Unidos"; "Estados Autónomos de la Unión"); "A el 'Diario,'" *El País*, 15 Sept. 1900, CIHCAM 22/L1 ("esgrimiré"); Degetau, *Al País*; "Una prueba más," *La bandera Americana*, 6 Oct. 1900, CIHCAM 12/L2; "Remitido," *La Correspondencia*, 15 Oct. 1900, CIHCAM 12/L2.

50. Iglesias, *Luchas*, 1:59, 104–105, 117–125; "Meeting Republicano en Vieques," *El País*, 27 Oct. 1899, CIHCAM 12/L2; Shaffer, *Black Flag Boricuas*, 42; Carroll, *Report*, 51. The racial edge should not be overstated. In November Iglesias met with Henry Carroll as part of a committee of labor unions in which nine of the eleven representatives were, in Carroll's view, men of color.

51. Iglesias, *Luchas*, 1:94, 113, 119–126, 136–138, 144–150, 155, 162–166; Ileana M. Rodríguez-Silva, *Silencing Race: Disentangling Blackness, Colonialism, and National Identities in Puerto Rico* (New York, 2012), 172–174; Morris Hillquit, *History of Socialism in the United States* (New York, 1903), 326–329; Robert William Iversen, "Morris Hillquit, American Social Democrat: A Study of the American Left from Haymarket to the New Deal," PhD diss., State University of Iowa, 1951, 21–22; Ira Kipnis, *The American Socialist Movement, 1897–1912*

(New York, 1952), 25–106; Howard H. Quint, *The Forging of American Socialism: Origins of the Modern Movement* (Columbia, SC, 1953), 332–388; Eddie Gonzalez and Lois Gray, "Puerto Ricans, Politics, and Labor Activism," in *Puerto Rican Politics in Urban America*, ed. James Jennings and Monte Rivera (Westport, CT, 1984), 117; Bernardo Vega, *Memoirs of Bernardo Vega: A Contribution to the History of the Puerto Rican Community in New York*, ed. César Andreu Iglesias, trans. Juan Flores (New York, 1984 [1977]).

On the Socialist Labor Party leadership's critique of U.S. expansion from the perspective of international Marxism, see, for example, Howard H. Quint, "American Socialists and the Spanish-American War," *American Quarterly* 10 (Summer 1958): 131–141; Philip S. Foner, "Why the United States Went to War with Spain in 1898," *Science & Society* 32 (Winter 1968): 40–41. On the "Hispanic-American self-definition" of Socialist leader Daniel DeLeon, see L. Glen Seretan, *Daniel DeLeon: The Odyssey of an American Marxist* (Cambridge, MA, 1979), 10.

52. El Comité Central, *Manifiesto de la Federación Libre de San Juan: A los trabajadores en general y á los políticos-burgueses en particular* ([San Juan?, PR], 1900), CPMN, Movimiento obrero puertorriqueño: hojas sueltas (1898–1937) ("tener esclavo al pueblo trabajador"); Iglesias, *Luchas*, 1:131–132, 167–169, 173–176, 187–189, 191–193, 196–197; Córdova, *Resident Commissioner*, 79–80; Sen. Doc. No. 79, 57th Cong., 1st sess., *First Annual Report of Charles H. Allen, Governor of Porto Rico* (Washington, DC, 1901), 403–404; "Porto Rican Strikes," *Washington Post*, 22 Aug. 1900, 2; Mariano Negrón-Portillo, *Las turbas republicanas, 1900–1904* (Río Piedras, PR, 1990), 37–38, 73, 80–83, 90, 105, 109, 112–117, 135, 156, 209; Rodríguez-Silva, *Silencing Race*, 171, 175; "Labor Leader Was Jailed"; "De los Estados Unidos," *El porvenir Social*, 11 Apr. 1899, 2, CPMN, roll S-450; El Comité Central, *Federación Libre: Comité Central* ([San Juan, PR], [1900]), CPMN, Movimiento obrero puertorriqueño: hojas sueltas (1898–1937). A former congressional representative from Massachusetts, Allen came to the governorship following a stint as assistant secretary of the Navy. His annual report of May 1901 advocated facilitating investment by stateside sugar corporations. *First Annual Report of Charles H. Allen*, 39–41.

53. "La raza negra en los Estados Unidos," *La Democracia*, 16 Aug. 1900, 2 ("absorción"; "grandes injusticas"); various Republicanos, *¡¡Solo es esclavo quien merece* [sic] *serlo!! ¡¡Los federales infaman; los republicanos dignifican!! ¡¡El hijo del negrero hiere al negro!! ¡¡Malditos sean los que separan á la familia puertorriqueña!!* ([San Juan, PR?], n.d.), CPMN, Movimiento obrero puertorriqueño: hojas sueltas (1898–1937); "El banquete republicano"; Rowe, *United States and Porto Rico*, 247–248; "Meeting Republicano en Vieques"; Iglesias, *Luchas*, 1:125; Findlay, *Imposing Decency*, 142–143; Jiménez Román, "Un hombre."

54. "Mr. Bryan's Speech of Acceptance," *New York Times*, 9 Aug. 1900, 8; "Resolution," *San Juan News*, 1 Oct., 1900, CIHCAM 22/L1, 104; "A la asamblea Federal: los representantes que suscriben," newspaper unknown, 1 Oct. 1900, CIHCAM 22/L2; "Democratic Party Platform of 1900," *The American Presidency Project*, comp. Gerhard Peters and John T. Woolley, www.presidency.ucsb.edu/ws/index.php?pid=29587#axzz1mZkkpGXA; Fred H. Harrington, "The

Anti-Imperialist Movement in the United States, 1898–1900," *Mississippi Valley Historical Review* 22 (Sept. 1935): 226; Rowe, *United States and Porto Rico*, 251–253; Pedro A. Cabán, *Constructing a Colonial People: Puerto Rico and the United States, 1898–1932* (Boulder, CO, 1999), 167; Negrón-Portillo, *Turbas republicanas*, 37–38, 75, 80–90, 95–99, 105–117, 125–139, 156–199, 209.

55. Miles Galvin, *The Organized Labor Movement in Puerto Rico* (London, 1979), 47–48; Iglesias, *Luchas*, 1:198–199; Iglesias de Pagán, *El obrerismo*, 152, 158.

56. Frederic R. Coudert, "The Evolution of the Doctrine of Territorial Incorporation," *Columbia Law Review* 26 (1926), 823–825; Sparrow, *Insular Cases*, 55–56, 111.

"WE ARE NATURALLY AMERICANS": FEDERICO DEGETAU AND SANTIAGO IGLESIAS PURSUE CITIZENSHIP

1. "Porto Rico Delegate," *Indianapolis Journal*, 3 Dec. 1900, CIHCAM 12/L2; "Hawaii and Porto Rico at Washington," *Sunday Pioneer Press*, 10 Feb. 1901, CIHCAM 12/L2; "A Credit to Porto Rico," *Washington Times*, 19 Nov. 1901, CIHCAM 18/L1; "Statehood Their Aim," *Washington Post*, 15 Dec. 1900; "Porto Rico's Delegate," *St. Louis Republic*, 3 Dec. 1900, CIHCAM 12/L2; title unknown, *Detroit News*, 3 Dec. 1900, CIHCAM 12/L2; "Porto Rican Commissioner," *New York Sun*, 3 Dec. 1900, CIHCAM 12/L2. On U.S. willingness in the early twentieth century to admit states with large populations of color so long as "whites" predominated within them, see John Nieto-Phillips, "Citizenship and Empire: Race, Language, and Self-Government in New Mexico and Puerto Rico, 1898–1917," *Journal for the Center for Puerto Rican Studies* (Fall 1999): 57.

2. Cayetano Coll y Cuchi, "Iglesias perdió el socialismo en Loiza disfrazado de mujer," *El Mundo*, 9 Feb. 1947 ("la bandera Americana, que nos proteja en nuestros derechos de ciudadanos"; "ya lo tenemos"; "la ayuda de las organizaciones obreras americanas"; "muy pronto conseguiré lo Segundo"), quoted in Igualdad Iglesias de Pagán, *El obrerismo en Puerto Rico: Época de Santiago Iglesias (1896–1905)* (San Juan, PR, 1973), 152; Santiago Iglesias Pantín, *Luchas emancipadoras: Crónicas de Puerto Rico*, 2nd ed., vol. 1 (San Juan, PR, 1958), 199.

3. Though often overlooked in existing scholarship, administrators were thus among the crucial agents of early twentieth-century constitutional changes concerning U.S. empire. Their responses to claims also created potential test cases, altered stakes on the ground in those and related controversies, and provided models on which other officials might later draw in adjudicating similar disputes. More generally, federal administration before the New Deal played numerous and powerful roles, including undertaking mass adjudications and developing extensive internal administrative law to guide their resolution. See Jerry L. Mashaw, "Federal Administration and Administrative Law in the Gilded Age," *Yale Law Journal* 119 (2010): 1362–1472. For a critical review of perceptions of federal administration as weak and lawless, see, for example, Desmond King and Robert C. Lieberman, "Finding the American State: Transcending the 'Statelessness' Account," *Polity* 40 (July 2008): 370. On administrative responsibility for speech regulation in the first half of the twentieth century, see Reuel E. Schiller, "Free Speech and Expertise: Administrative Censorship and the Birth of the Modern First Amendment," *Virginia Law Review*

86 (2000): 1–102. Anuj C. Desai, in "Wiretapping before the Wires: The Post Office
and the Birth of Communications Privacy," *Stanford Law Review* 60 (2007): 553–
594, suggests that federal legislation and administrative practice lay foundations for
modern Fourth Amendment jurisprudence. In "Race, Sex, and Rulemaking:
Administrative Constitutionalism and the Workplace, 1960 to the Present,"
Virginia Law Review 96 (2010): 806nn14–16, 809n23, and throughout, and in
The Workplace Constitution from the New Deal to the New Right (Cambridge,
2014), Sophia Z. Lee describes active administrative attempts to shape law and
gathers scholarship and sources on how the "president's closest legal advisors"
made constitutional meaning and how agencies have often worked on matters of
potential constitutional import. See also Gillian E. Metzger, "Administrative
Constitutionalism," *Texas Law Review* 91 (2013): 1897–1935; Karen M. Tani,
States of Dependency: Welfare, Rights, and American Governance, 1935–1972
(Cambridge, 2016). On agencies being prodded into constitutional meaning
making, see Sophia Z. Lee's "Hotspots in a Cold War: The NAACP's Postwar
Workplace Constitutionalism, 1948–1964," *Law and History Review* 26 (2008):
327–377, and Lee, *Workplace Constitution*.

4. The view that all Americans were citizens required that noncitizen American Indians
were either not part of the U.S. people or were an exception to the general rule.
Nancy F. Cott explains how citizenship bound people to each other and to the state
and conferred membership and standing, in "Marriage and Women's Citizenship in
the United States, 1830–1934," *American Historical Review* 103 (Dec. 1998):
1440–1474. On the enduring power of rhetorical associations of citizenship with
broad substantive legal benefits, notwithstanding the fact that the reality is often
otherwise, see Frederick Cooper, Thomas C. Holt, and Rebecca J. Scott,
"Introduction," in *Beyond Slavery: Explorations of Race, Labor, and Citizenship
in Postemancipation Societies* (Chapel Hill, NC, 2000), 16.

5. Ileana M. Rodríguez-Silva, *Silencing Race: Disentangling Blackness, Colonialism,
and National Identities in Puerto Rico* (New York, 2012), 152, 179. On the
antilabor orientation of U.S. courts during these years, see William E. Forbath,
Law and the Shaping of the American Labor Movement (Cambridge, MA, 1991);
Christopher L. Tomlins, *The State and the Unions: Labor Relations, Law, and the
Organized Labor Movement in America, 1880–1960* (Cambridge, 1989 [1985]).
On the cultural power of law, see Ariela Gross, "Beyond Black and White: Cultural
Approaches to Race and Slavery," *Columbia Law Review* 101 (2001): 651–654;
Robert W. Gordon, "Critical Legal Histories," *Stanford Law Review* 36 (Jan.
1984): 57–125; Richard Wightman Fox, *Trials of Intimacy: Love and Loss in the
Beecher-Tilton Scandal* (Chicago, 1999); Barbara Young Welke, *Recasting
American Liberty: Gender, Race, Law, and the Railroad Revolution, 1865–1920*
(Cambridge, 2001).

6. The last justice to embark on the practice of law had been Justice Edward Douglass
White in 1868, the same year that the Fourteenth Amendment took effect. Hampton
L. Carson, *The History of the Supreme Court of the United States with Biographies
of all the Chief and Associate Justices*, vol. 2 (Philadelphia, [1904]), 477, 525, 535,
538, 541, 562, 570, 576.

7. The approach to judges laid out here is one answer to Paul Frymer's call for new inquiries into the relationship between an institutional understanding of courts and how "courts play an often central and vital role in enhancing the power of the modern state." Frymer, "Law and American Political Development," *Law & Social Inquiry* 33 (Summer 2008): 794, 782. Reuel E. Schiller describes justices' perceptions that courts lacked the institutional skills to second-guess agencies, in "The Era of Deference: Courts, Expertise, and the Emergence of New Deal Administrative Law," *Michigan Law Review* 106 (2007): 399–441. Keith Whittington observes that judges often work with political allies in a knotty political environment, acting as nation builders and also exercising judicial review to uphold laws against constitutional challenge. See Whittington, "The Politics of Judicial Review," in *Repugnant Laws: Judicial Review of Acts of Congress from the Founding to the Present* (Lawrence, KS, forthcoming).

   On judges as feeling at least somewhat bound by law, see Duncan Kennedy, "Toward an Historical Understanding of Legal Consciousness: The Case of Classical Legal Thought in America, 1850–1940," *Research in Law and Sociology* 3 (1980): 6; Howard Gillman, *The Constitution Besieged: The Rise and Demise of Lochner Era Police Powers Jurisprudence* (Durham, NC, 1993), 16–18; Peter Karsten, *Heart versus Head: Judge-Made Law in Nineteenth-Century America* (Chapel Hill, NC, 1997). On judges as committed to the norms of legal communities, see Lawrence Baum, *Judges and Their Audiences: A Perspective on Judicial Behavior* (Princeton, NJ, 2006); Keith E. Whittington, "Once More unto the Breach: PostBehavioralist Approaches to Judicial Politics," *Law & Social Inquiry* 25 (2000).

8. De Lima v. Bidwell, 182 U.S. 1 (1901); Downes v. Bidwell, 182 U.S. 244 (1901).

9. Tariff Act of 24 July 1897, 30 Stat. 151, 151; Opening Argument of Mr. Coudert for Plaintiff in Error, No. 507, *Downes*, 182 U.S. 244 (8 Jan. 1901), 9; "American Life Split into Parts," *Philadelphia Bulletin*, 19 Dec. 1900, CIHCAM 22/L1; Bartholomew H. Sparrow, *The Insular Cases and the Emergence of American Empire* (Lawrence, KS, 2006), 55, 122–125, 130–132, 140. Though resident commissioners' terms subsequently ran from March to March of odd years, Degetau may have been permitted to occupy his official post as early as December 1900. See Act of 1 July 1902, sec. 3, 32 Stat. 731, 732; "Porto Rico Delegate's Status," *New York Evening Post*, 7 Dec. 1900, CIHCAM 12/L2.

   On the *Insular Cases* of 1901–1904 as authorization of deannexation and noncitizen U.S. nationality, see Christina Duffy Burnett, "'They Say I Am Not an American...': The Noncitizen National and the Law of American Empire," *Virginia Journal of International Law* 48 (Summer 2008): 659–718; Christina Duffy Burnett, "Untied States: American Expansion and Territorial Deannexation," *University of Chicago Law Review* 72 (Summer 2005): 797–879. The *Insular Cases* marked a transformation of political debates over U.S. imperialism into judicial ones. See Krishanti Vignarajah, "The Political Roots of Judicial Legitimacy: Explaining the Enduring Validity of the *Insular Cases*," *University of Chicago Law Review* 77 (2010): 822 and n177; Sparrow, *Insular Cases*, 3–9, 40; Juan R. Torruella, "The *Insular Cases*: The Establishment of a Regime of Political Apartheid," *University of Pennsylvania Journal of International Law* 29 (2007): 284–285. [Federico Degetau], "Manifiesto del Comisionado Señor Degetau," *La Correspondencia*, 6 June 1901, CIHCAM 12/L2.

10. Virginia Kays Veenswijk, *Coudert Brothers: A Legacy in Law: The History of America's First International Law Firm, 1853–1993* (New York, 1994), 94–97, 29–30, 36, 50, 54, 60, 72, 98–170; Frederic R. Coudert, *Certainty and Justice: Studies of the Conflict between Precedent and Progress in the Development of the Law* (New York, 1913). On lawyers and the bar as potentially powerful institutions within the U.S. state, see John D. Skrentny, "Law and the American State," *Annual Review of Sociology* 32 (2006): 231; Whittington, "Once More unto the Breach," 618; Paul Frymer, *Black and Blue: African Americans, the Labor Movement, and the Decline of the Democratic Party* (Princeton, NJ, 2007); John Fabian Witt, "Law and War in American History," *American Historical Review* 115 (2010): 769–770 (noting that four of the most important secretaries of war were lawyers); William J. Novak, "The Myth of the 'Weak' American State," *American Historical Review* 113 (June 2007): 767; Daniel R. Ernst, "The Politics of Administrative Law: New York's Anti-Bureaucracy Clause and the O'Brian-Wagner Campaign of 1938," *Law and History Review* 27 (2009): 331–372; Daniel R. Ernst, "*Morgan* and the New Dealers," *Journal of Policy History* 20 (2008): 447–481.

11. "F. R. Coudert for Taft," *New York Tribune*, 24 Sept. 1908, 3; Veenswijk, *Coudert Brothers*, 26, 36–37, 39–40, 70–71, 80, 84–93; John W. Burgess, *Reconstruction and the Constitution, 1866–1876* (New York, 1905 [1902]), especially 275. J. W. Burgess agreed with Coudert, in "The Relations of the Constitution of the United States to Newly Acquired Territory," *Political Science Quarterly* 15 (Sept. 1900): 381–398, that the Foraker Act tariff was unconstitutional. On the relationship between ideology, judicial decision making, and the partisan makeup of the political branches at the time of judicial appointments, see Lee Epstein, William M. Landes, and Richard A. Posner, *The Behavior of Federal Judges: A Theoretical and Empirical Study of Rational Choice* (Cambridge, MA, 2013).

12. Brief for the United States, No. 340, Goetze v. United States, 182 U.S. 221 ([1900–1901]), 16, 28, 59–60, 69, 105–106, 172–173; Brief for the United States, No. 456, De Lima v. Bidwell, 182 U.S. 1 (7 Jan. 1901), 50, 68.

13. Argument of the Attorney General, No. 340, *Goetze*, 182 U.S. 221 (18 Dec. 1900), 73, 86; *Census Reports Volume I: Twelfth Census of the United States, Taken in the Year 1900* (Washington, DC, 1901), cxiv; Brief for the United States, *Goetze*, 182 U.S. 221, 71; Brief for Appellant, No. 340, *Goetze*, 182 U.S. 221 ([1900–1901]), 59; Table Ad106-120, "Immigrants, by Country of Last Residence – Europe: 1820–1997," contributed by Robert Barde, Susan B. Carter, and Richard Sutch, in *Historical Statistics of the United States, Millennial Edition On Line*, ed. Susan B. Carter et al. (Cambridge, MA, 2006), https://hsus.cambridge.org/; Michael R. Haines, "French Migration to the United States: 1820–1950," *Annales de Démographie Historique* (2000): 84–85; Lanny Thompson, "The Imperial Republic: A Comparison of the Insular Territories under U.S. Dominion after 1898," *Pacific Historical Review* 71 (Nov. 2002): 541–47; Hawaiian Organic Act, 31 Stat. 141 (1900).

14. Brief for the United States, No. 340, *Goetze*, 182 U.S. 221, 72.

15. Opening Argument of Mr. Coudert, *Downes*, 182 U.S. 244, 42–44; "Caffery on the Philippines," *New York Times*, 7 Feb. 1900, 5; Brief for Plaintiffs in Error, No. 507, *Downes*, 182 U.S. 244 (2 Jan. 1901), 78, 79–99. Coudert's argument was stronger than he realized. Contemporary federal Indian policy naturalized Indians as part of allotting away reservations, dissolving tribal governments, and imposing what

increasingly looked like indefinite wardship. It thus demonstrated that subordination and exclusion did not require withholding citizenship. On U.S. policy toward American Indians during the period, see Frederick E. Hoxie, *A Final Promise: The Campaign to Assimilate the Indians, 1880–1920* (Lincoln, NE, 2001 [1984]); Jacqueline Fear-Segal, *White Man's Club: Schools, Race, and the Struggle of Indian Acculturation* (Lincoln, NE, 2007), xiv; Francis Paul Prucha, *The Great Father: The United States Government and the American Indians*, vol. 2 (Lincoln, NE, 1984), 609–916. On American Indians' attempts to resist these processes, including in court, see Frederick E. Hoxie, *This Indian Country: American Indian Political Activists and the Place They Made* (New York, 2012), 183–219; Frederick E. Hoxie, *Talking Back to Civilization* (Boston, 2001), 21–24, 103–104. Were the argument accepted, it would provide grounds that could distinguish Puerto Rico and the Philippines. See Opening Argument of Mr. Coudert, *Downes*, 182 U.S. 244, 42–43.

16. Opening Argument of Mr. Coudert, *Downes*, 182 U.S. 244, 44, 43; Brief for Plaintiffs in Error, *Downes*, 182 U.S. 244, 95, 84, 99. On reenslavement, see Ira Berlin, *Slaves without Masters: The Free Negro in the Antebellum South* (New York, 1974), 370–380; Rebecca J. Scott, "Paper Thin: Freedom and Reenslavement in the Diaspora of the Haitian Revolution," *Law and History Review* 29 (2011): 1061–1087; Rebecca J. Scott, "Under Color of Law: *Siliadin v. France* and the Dynamics of Enslavement in Historical Perspective," in *Understanding Human Dignity*, ed. C. McCrudden (Oxford, 2014), 152–164.

17. Opening Argument of Mr. Coudert, *Downes*, 182 U.S. 244, 41–42, 40; Brief for Plaintiffs in Error, *Downes*, 182 U.S. 244, 92, 82, 85–93. The brief did not mention the Philippines when asserting that it was "very clear that Porto Rico and the Island of Guam have no nationality of their own." Ibid., 86.

18. Opening Argument of Mr. Coudert, *Downes*, 182 U.S. 244, 45; [Degetau], "Manifiesto." See also untitled article, *Detroit News*, 3 Dec. 1900, CIHCAM 12/L2; Draft, [Federico Degetau] to Manuel Rossy, 20 Feb. 1901, CIHCAM 2/VII/47; Brief for Plaintiffs in Error, *Downes*, 182 U.S. 244, 80–99, 102–103. The federal lawmakers who had framed the Foraker Act had thought it worthwhile to stack the stakes of the test suit in ways calculated to curry judicial favor.

19. "Admission of Mr. Degetau," *Washington Post*, 1 May 1901, CIHCAM 12/L2; Draft, [Federico Degetau] to Manuel Rossy, 3 May 1901, CIHCAM 3/I/4 ("Mi admisión … fijaba mi status personal y el de mis representados como ciudadanos americanos"); Un Puertorriqueño, "Importante comunicación," paper unknown, 10 May 1901, CIHCAM 12/L2; José Barbosa to Federico Degetau, May 13, 1901, CIHCAM 3/I/17. "Importante comunicación," newspaper unknown, 10 May 1901, CIHCAM 12/L2 ("La Gran Constitución Nacional Cubre a Puerto-Rico"; "otros territorios como Arizona"; "Ahora si que creo que la Constitución está en Puerto Rico"); "Grata noticia," *El País*, 30 Apr. 1901, CIHCAM 12/L2; "Constitution Follows the Flag," *Minneapolis Tribune*, 1 May 1901, CIHCAM 12/L2.

20. [Degetau], "Manifiesto" ("victoria"); *De Lima*, 182 U.S., at 200 (1901); *Downes*, 182 U.S., at 287; U.S. Const. art. I, sec. 8, cl. 1.

21. [Degetau], "Manifiesto" ("Las decisiones del Tribunal Supremo de los Estados Unidos … han producido una perplejidad"); Charles E. Littlefield, "The *Insular*

Cases," Southern Law Review 1 (1901): 478; Sparrow, *Insular Cases*, 125–126, 129–132, 140.

22. *Downes*, 182 U.S., at 274 (Brown, J.); ibid., 291 (White, J., concurring); Dred Scott v. Sandford, 60 U.S. 393, 447 (1857).

23. *Downes*, 182 U.S., at 311–312, 306, 287, 320–336, 340–341 (White, J., concurring). Tribal lands were also places with limited federal rights and extensive federal oversight that were neither wholly foreign nor wholly domestic. But with such holdings slotted to be allotted out of existence, White made no mention of them. Aziz Rana argues that White sought to circumvent the *Dred Scott* bar on exercising external federal power in internal spaces and thus proposed a major increase in federal power; see *The Two Faces of American Freedom* (Cambridge, MA, 2010), 277–279.

24. Frederic R. Coudert, "The Evolution of the Doctrine of Territorial Incorporation," *Columbia Law Review* 26 (1926): 832; *Downes*, 182 U.S., at 279, 286, 282 (Brown, J).

25. "Porto Rico, Territory," *Buffalo Courier*, 31 July 1901, CIHCAM 18/L1; [Degetau,] "Manifiesto" ("una 'posesión' ó ... una 'colonia'"; "Arizona"); Charles E. Magoon, *Reports on the Law of Civil Government in Territory Subject to Military Occupation by the Military Forces of the United States, Submitted to Hon. Elihu Root, Secretary of War, by Charles E. Magoon, Law Officer, Bureau of Insular Affairs, War Department, Published by Order of the Secretary of War*, 3rd ed. (Washington, DC, 1903), 120. Jerry L. Mashaw, in "Between Facts and Norms: Agency Statutory Interpretation as an Autonomous Enterprise," *University of Toronto Law Journal* 55 (2005): 515–516, observes that agencies more than courts are the institutions to push constitutional limits and be able to shape constitutional settlements by lobbying, testing waters, negotiating, and reaching accommodations.

26. Burnett, "Untied States," 800–801, reviews work taking the traditional position, from which this book departs, that *Downes v. Bidwell* (1901) denied residents of unincorporated territories such as Puerto Rico an array of constitutional rights and eventual statehood. An additional difficulty with the traditional account is that it was far from certain that the Court could require that a territory be offered the privilege of statehood.

27. Federico Degetau to Manuel Rossy, 4 Jan. 1901, CIHCAM 2/VI/2 ("excede con mucho al que los [ideas] más pesimistas entre nosotros haya podido expresar ni suponer"; "La obra magna de rectificar esa errónea apreciación"; "primer deber"); "Porto Rican's Ambition," *Washington Times*, 10 July 1901, CIHCAM 18/L1; [Federico Degetau], Diary, 10 Dec. 1901, CIHCAM 11/L4.

28. Federico Degetau to Manuel Rossy et al., 8 Dec. 1900, CIHCAM 2/V/12 ("cultura y del estado de civilización"); title unknown, *Wheeling* (WV) *Register*, [Dec. 1900?], CIHCAM 12/L2. See also "Porto Rican Lawmaking," *New York Times*, 26 Jan. 1902, 8; John J. Johnson, *Latin America in Caricature* (Austin, TX, 1980); Lanny Thompson, "Representation and Rule in the Imperial Archipelago: Cuba, Puerto Rico, Hawai'i, and the Philippines under U.S. Dominion after 1898," *American Studies Asia* 1 (2002): 32; Lanny Thompson, "Aesthetics and Empire: The Sense of Feminine Beauty in the Making of the U.S. Imperial Archipelago," *Culture & History Digital Journal* 2, no. 2 (2013): e027, http://dx.doi.org/10.3989/chdj.2013.027; Degetau to Rossy, 4 Jan. 1901. On image makers' disparagement

of Cubans and Filipinos, see Bonnie M. Miller, *From Liberation to Conquest: The Visual and Popular Cultures of the Spanish-American War of 1898* (Amherst, MA, 2011); Michael C. Hawkins, *Making Moros: Imperial Historicism and American Military Rule in the Philippines' Muslim South* (Dekalb, IL, 2013); Servand D. Halili Jr., *Iconography of the New Empire: Race and Gender Images and the American Colonization of the Philippines* (Quezon City, the Philippines, 2006).

29. "A Credit to Porto Rico"; "Hawaii and Porto Rico at Washington"; [Degetau], Diary, 18 Nov. 1901 to 18 Feb. 1902; Federico Degetau, "The Porto Ricans as Soldiers and as Legislators," *Philadelphia Record*, 23 May 1901, CIHCAM 12/L2. On making governmental contacts, see Degetau to Rossy, 4 Jan. 1901; [Degetau], Diary. On nongovernmental networks, see, for example, [Degetau], Diary; Geo. Moore to Federico Degetau, Feb. 1903, CIHCAM 3/VII/29; Draft, [Federico Degetau], Toast of Federico Degetau on "The Government of the United States," given at the Banquet at the Battle House, Mobile, AL, 22 Apr. 1903, CIHCAM 18/L1; Henry Cooper to Federico Degetau, 3 May 1903, CIHCAM 4/II/159; Manuel Rojas to Federico Degetau, 6 Jan. 1903, CIHCAM 3/VII/4; Fred Woodward to F. Degetau, 18 Mar. 1903, CIHCAM 4/I/91; E. Harris to Frederico Degetau, 11 Apr. 1903, CIHCAM 4/II/133; John Leathers to Frederico Degetau, 24 Sept. 1903, CIHCAM 4/V/297. On follow-up, see, for example, [Federico Degetau] to Henry Cooper, 15 July 1901, CIHCAM 3/II/33; Henry Hoyt to Federico Degetau, 12 Dec. 1903, CIHCAM 4/VII/16; Draft, Federico Degetau to Ramón B. López, 31 May 1901, CIHCAM 3/I/42; J. Goulden to Federico Degetau, 6 June 1904, CIHCAM 5/II/9; [Illegible] Hughes to Federico Degetau, 1 June 1904, CIHCAM 5/II/1; E. D. Crumpacker to Federico Degetau, 15 Dec. 1902, CIHCAM 3/VI/65; J. B. Foraker to Federico Degetau, 22 Dec. 1902, CIHCAM 3/VI/70; Sereno Payne to Federico Degetau, 21 Apr. 1904, CIHCAM 5/I/14. For academic gatherings, see, for example, "Porto Rico Glad of Our Friendship," *Philadelphia Press*, 19 Dec. 1900, CIHCAM 22/L1

30. Degetau, "Porto Ricans as Soldiers and as Legislators"; Jacob H. Hollander et al., "Discussion," *Publications of the American Economic Association*, 3rd ser., 3 (1902): 342, 347–350; "American Life Split into Parts"; "La American Economic Association y el Comisionado Señor Degetau," *La Correspondencia*, 22 Jan. 1902, CIHCAM 18/L1; Federico Degetau, *The Political Status of Porto Rico* (Washington, DC, 1902), 14; Luis A. Figueroa, *Sugar, Slavery, and Freedom in Nineteenth-Century Puerto Rico* (Chapel Hill, NC, 2005), 79. For less heroic accounts of the historical status and rights of Puerto Ricans, see, for example, José Trías Monge, *Historia constitucional de Puerto Rico* (Río Piedras, PR, 1980–1994); Francisco A. Scarano, *Puerto Rico: Cinco siglos de historia* (New York, 1993).

31. [Federico Degetau], "Something That the American People Must Know about Porto Rico," CIHCAM 7/I/2. Two drafts of this chapter have been preserved. I draw from both. On the failure of Cuban arms to vanquish U.S. imperial aims, see generally Louis A. Pérez Jr., *Cuba between Empires 1878–1902* (Pittsburgh, 1983). On the cross-sectional U.S. linking of manhood, participation in combat, and national membership, from the Civil War through the Spanish American War, see Kristin L. Hoganson, *Fighting for Manhood: How Gender Politics Provoked the Spanish-American and Philippine-American Wars* (New Haven, CT, 1998); Jennifer Rae Greeson, *Our South: Geographic Fantasy and the Rise of National Literature*

(Cambridge, MA, 2010), 251–276; Barbara A. Gannon, *The Won Cause: Black and White Comradeship in the Grand Army of the Republic* (Chapel Hill, NC, 2011), 6–9, 146, 177; John R. Neff, *Honoring the Civil War Dead: Commemoration and the Problem of Reconciliation* (Lawrence, KS, 2005), 221–230; Nina Silber, *The Romance of Reunion: Northerners and the South, 1865–1900* (Chapel Hill, NC, 1993), 178–195.

32. Degetau, "Porto Ricans as Soldiers and as Legislators"; [Degetau], "Something That the American People Must Know."

33. Allison L. Sneider, *Suffragists in an Imperial Age: U.S. Expansion and the Woman Question 1870–1929* (Oxford, 2008), 9–10, 12–13, 67, describes debates over suffrage intertwining with those around empire, American Indians, and the legacy of the Civil War. As she notes, some advocates of women's rights also endorsed racial hierarchy.

34. Degetau, *Political Status of Porto Rico*, 7; [Federico Degetau], Drafts, "The Truth about Porto Rico" and "Puerto-Rico and Its People," n.d., CIHCAM 18/L2.

35. R. B. López to Federico Degetau, 6 Dec. 1903, CIHCAM 4/VII/7 ("Ese país es tan grande, y este tan pequeño, que es preciso estar siempre promoviendo algo, para que se acuerdan de nosotros"); Degetau to López, 31 May 1901. On institution-level differences in approaches to law, see Mark A. Graber, "Looking Off the Ball: Constitutional Law and American Politics," manuscript (2007), 35, http://digitalcommons.law.umaryland.edu/fac_pubs/381/; Keith Whittington, *Political Foundation of Judicial Supremacy* (Princeton, NJ, 2007), 14–18, 22–23, 52, 287; Bradley W. Joondeph, "The Many Meanings of 'Politics' in Judicial Decision Making," *University of Missouri Kansas Law Review* 77 (2008): 347–349; Thomas M. Keck, "Party Politics or Judicial Independence? The Regime Politics Literature Hits the Law Schools," *Law & Social Inquiry* 32 (Spring 2007): 532. Luke M. Milligan collects sources on the topic in "Congressional End-Run: The Ignored Constraint on Judicial Review," *Georgia Law Review* 45 (2010): 245–248, 273.

36. [Degetau], Diary, 10 Dec. 1901 ("no se puede considerar á Puerto Rico en sí, sino que hay que tener en cuenta á Filipinas"); "Porto Rican's Ambition"; Draft, [Federico Degetau] to Manuel Rossy, 18 Jan. 1901, CIHCAM 2/VI/11; House Committee on Insular Affairs, *Committee Reports, Hearings, and Acts of Congress Corresponding Thereto*, 57th Cong. 34–39 (1903) (accompanying H.R. 14083); [Federico Degetau] to William Hunt, 16 May 1902, CIHCAM 3/VI/5. See also Foraker to Degetau, 22 Dec. 1902; J. B. Foraker to Federico Degetau, 25 Apr. 1901, CIHCAM 2/IX/18; [Federico Degetau] to J. B. Foraker, 15 May 1901, CIHCAM 3/I/19; Henry Cooper to Federico Degetau, 8 July 1901, CIHCAM 3/II/33; [Degetau] to Cooper, 15 July 1901.

37. 34 Cong. Rec. 5101; House Comm. on Insular Affairs, *Committee Reports*, 38–39; "Porto Rican Land Bills Passed Senate," [*News*], 26 June 1902, CIHCAM 11/L4.

38. [?] Rossy to Bonifacio Sánchez, 21 Apr. 1902, CIHCAM 4/II/147 ("una camarilla de aventureros continentales ocupando puestos oficiales que son un descrédito para el gobierno americano que nos rije: estos empleados que en su país no serían nunca gente"); J. Sifre to Federico Degetau, 1 July 1902, CIHCAM 3/VI/30 ("Son preferidos los de allá y existe el consiguiente disgusto"); *Eighteenth Report of the United States Civil Service Commission, July 1, 1900, to June 30, 1901* (Washington, DC, 1902), 48, 331; David Ortiz Jr., *Paper Liberals: Press and*

Politics in Restoration Spain (Westport, CT, 2000), 21–22; Astrid Cubano Iguina, "Political Culture and Male Mass-Party Formation in Late-Nineteenth-Century Puerto Rico," *Hispanic American History Review* 78 (1998): 641–642; Scott C. James, "Patronage Regimes and American Party Development from 'The Age of Jackson' to the Progressive Era," *British Journal of Political Science* 36 (2005): 39; Cablegram, Colton to Edwards, 1 Mar. 1910, MD NARA 350/5A/3377–49; Colton to Edwards, 2 Mar. 1910, MD NARA 350/5A/3377–57; Kermit L. Hall, "Hacks and Derelicts Revisited: American Territorial Judiciary, 1789–1959," *Western Historical Quarterly* 12 (July 1981): 284; Kenneth N. Owens, "The Prizes of Statehood," *Montana: The Magazine of Western History* 37 (Autumn 1987): 2–3, 6–7; Roland L. De Lorme, "Westward the Bureaucrats: Government Officials on the Washington and Oregon Frontiers," *Arizona and the West* 22 (Autumn 1980): 223; [Degetau], Diary, 18 Nov. 1901; "Allotment of Clerks," *Washington Post*, 4 Mar. 1902, 2. Two of the three Civil Service commissioners were lawyers. See *Eighteenth Report*, 23; William Dudley Foulke, *A Hoosier Autobiography* (New York, 1922), 13–14. For a constituent who faced exclusion from the civil service, see [?] [Hernanchez?] to President of Civil Service, 18 Nov. 1901, CIHCAM 3/IV/3. See also J. Henna to Federico Degetau, 30 Nov. 1902, CIHCAM 3/IV/11.

39. *Revised Statutes of the United States Passed at the First Session of the Forty-Third Congress, 1873–1874*, 2nd ed. (Washington, DC, 1878), Title 47, § 4076, 786; [Degetau] to Cooper, 15 July 1901; Henry Randall Webb to Federico Degetau, 15 Nov. 1901, CIHCAM 3/III/99; Henry Webb to Federico Degetau, 14 Aug. 1901, CIHCAM 3/III/61; Henry Webb to Federico Degetau, 10 Aug. 1901, CIHCAM 3/III/56; Gaillard Hunt, *The American Passport: Its History and a Digest of Laws, Rulings, and Regulations Governing Its Issuance by the Department of State* (Washington, DC, 1898), 28. On the Supreme Court's early twentieth-century shift toward reviewing agencies for legal error, see Jerry L. Mashaw, *Creating the Administrative Constitution: The Lost One Hundred Years of American Administrative Law* (New Haven, CT, 2012), 245–249.

40. Theodore Roosevelt to Federico Degetau, 24 June 1901, CIHCAM 3/II/22; [Degetau], Diary, 18, 25 Nov. 1901 ("Los puertorriqueños [*sic*] son y desean ser americanos, aunque creen que no se les ha hecho justicia, pero confían"). On Hay's legal training, see Hay, John, www.brown.edu/Administration/News_Bureau/ Databases/Encyclopedia/search.php?serial=H0060 (1993), reprinted from Martha Mitchell, *Encyclopedia Brunoniana* (Providence, 1993). H. W. Brands, *T.R: The Last Romantic* (New York, 1998), 110, notes that Roosevelt was a Columbia Law School alumnus.

41. Federico Degetau to Theodore Roosevelt, 7 Dec. 1901, reprinted in "Federico Degetau González," newspaper unknown, n.d., CIHCAM 18/L1/195 ("*todos los habitantes*"; "habían aceptado la nacionalidad del territorio en que residían"; "un territorio de los Estados Unidos"; "el pueblo de Puerto Rico"; "una entidad o cuerpo político"; "distinta ciudadanía"; "protección como ciudadanos de la Unión Americana"; "La única interpretación constitucional y justa"; "ciudadanía americana"). Degetau's first two arguments became potentially applicable to the Philippines following passage of the Philippine Act of 1902, 32 Stat. 691 (1902), which used similar language to that in the Foraker Act.

42. See "A Letter from Mr. Degetau," *Puerto Rico Herald*, 11 Jan. 1902, 4; "Civil Service in Porto Rico," *Washington Post*, 10 Feb. 1902, 4; H.R. 8129, in H.R. Rep.

No. 57-559 (1902), CIHCAM 3/V/20; Theodore Roosevelt, *Rules Governing the Granting and Issuing of Passports in the Insular Possessions of the United States* (19 July 1902), MD NARA 350/5B/19929; [Degetau], Diary, 25 Nov. 1901, Feb. 1902; Law of 14 June 1902, 32 Stat. 386. See also S. 2298 (7 Jan. 1902), CIHCAM 11/L4; 35 Cong. Rec. 4992–4995, 5697–5699, 6588–6589 (1902).

43. "Porto Rican's Romance," *Pioneer Press*, 3 Aug. 1901, CIHCAM 18/L1; "Casamiento," *La Democracia*, 15 Mar. 1902, 4 ("el ideal de toda su vida"; "spiritual"; "inteligentisima"); "First Delegate from Porto Rico an Author," *St. Louis Post-Dispatch*, 6 July 1902, A12; "Married," *Homeless Children's Advocate*, Mar. 1902, CIHCAM 17/II/2; Notarial Document of Adolfo Molinas witnessed by Albion Tourgée, 25 Mar. 1902, CIHCAM 3/V/36; J. C. Barbosa to Federico Degetau, 9 Jan. [?], CIHCAM 2/VI/3–A; Frederick Van Dyne, *Citizenship of the United States* (Rochester, NY, 1904), 119–127, 227; Clifford Stevens Walton, *The Civil Law in Spain and Spanish America* (Washington, DC, 1900), 126; Draft, [Federico Degetau] to Adolfo Marin Molinas, 16 Dec. 1901, CIHCAM 3/IV/18; Mark Elliott, *Color Blind Justice: Albion Tourgée and the Quest for Racial Equality from the Civil War to* Plessy v. Ferguson (Oxford, 2008).

44. 24 Op. Att'y Gen. 41, 40, 42–44 (1902); "Porto Rican an American Artist," *Washington Post*, 17 May 1902, 11.

45. [Federico Degetau] to Secretary of State, 31 Jan. 1901, CIHCAM 2/VII/65; David Hill to Federico Degetau, 16 Feb. 1901, CIHCAM 2/VII/40; Federico Degetau y González, Memorandum in Relation to the American Citizenship of Porto Ricans, CIHCAM 2/VI/19–A; "Las gestiones de Degetau en defensa de los emigrantes á las islas Hawaii," *La Correspondencia*, 25 Sept. 1901, CIHCAM 12/L2; Norma Carr, "The Puerto Ricans in Hawaii: 1900–1958," PhD diss., University of Hawai'i, 1989, 85–169; Carmelo Rosario Natal, *Exodo puertorriqueño (Las emigraciones al caribe y Hawaii: 1900–1915)* (San Juan, PR, 1983), 21–34, 58, 60–61, 71–79; Ronald D. Arroyo, "Da Borinkees: The Puerto Ricans of Hawaii," PhD diss., Union Graduate School – West, 1977); Nitza C. Medina, "Rebellion in the Bay: California's First Puerto Ricans," *Centro Journal* 13 (Spring 2001): 83–84; Austin Días, "Carlo Mario Fraticelli: A Puerto Rican Poet on the Sugar Plantations of Hawai'i," *Centro Journal* 13 (Spring 2001): 94; Transcription, "Citizenship of Porto Ricans Again Brought Up," *San Francisco Call*, 28 Nov. [1899/1900?], 2–4, Center for Puerto Rican Studies, Hunter College, Archives of the Puerto Rican Migration, Blase Camacho Souza Papers, Box 21; Ernest K. Wakukawa, *A History of the Japanese People in Hawaii* (Honolulu, 1938), 126–135; Dorothy Ochiai Hazama and Jane Okamoto Komeiji, *Okage Sama De: The Japanese in Hawai'i* (Honolulu, 1986), 42; Adam McKeown, *Chinese Migrant Networks and Cultural Change: Peru, Chicago, Hawaii, 1900–1936* (Chicago, 2001); Eileen H. Tamura, *Americanization, Acculturation, and Ethnic Identity: The Nisei Generation in Hawaii* (Urbana, IL, 1994), 5. Aubrey Parkman describes Hill's legal training in *David Jayne Hill and the Problem of World Peace* (Cranbury, NJ, 1975), 65.

46. Kenneth W. Mack, *Representing the Race: The Creation of the Civil Rights Lawyer* (Cambridge, MA, 2012).

47. Ronald Takaki, *Pau Hana: Plantation Life and Labor in Hawaii, 1835–1920* (Honolulu, 1983), 131, 72, 74–75, 83–84; transcription, "It Is Alleged They Were Procured by a New York Emigration Agent," *San Francisco Examiner*, 8 Dec. 1900,

1, Center for Puerto Rican Studies, Hunter College, Archives of the Puerto Rican Migration, Blase Camacho Souza Papers, Box 21; "De Hawaii a Puerto-Rico," *La Democracia*, 27 Dec. 1901 ("al huir nuestros pobres paisanos, refugiándose en los bosques, se les persiguió á tiros y se lanzó contra ellos una jauría de perros de caza"); Alan Takeo Moriyama, *Imingaisha: Japanese Emigration Companies and Hawaii, 1894–1908* (Honolulu, 1985), 106; Yukiko Kimura, *Issei: Japanese Immigrants in Hawaii* (Honolulu, 1988), 89; Gary Y. Okihiro, *Cane Fires: The Anti-Japanese Movement in Hawaii, 1865–1945* (Philadelphia, 1991), 26–27, 35; Eileen H. Tamura, *Americanization, Acculturation, and Ethnic Identity: The Nisei Generation in Hawaii* (Urbana, IL, 1994), 12; Ronald Takaki, *Strangers from a Different Shore: A History of Asian Americans* (New York, 1998 [1989]), 25–26, 134–147, 158; "Looking Backward," *Honolulu Record*, 11 Sept. 1952, 8; extract, "Contract Laborers from Porto Rico," *New York Tribune*, 7 Dec. 1900, CIHCAM 2/VI/19; Draft, [Federico Degetau] to Secretary of State, [30] Jan. 1901, CIHCAM 2/VI/19; "Puerto Ricans Fight for Food," page and newspaper unknown, [Jan. 1901?], CIHCAM 12/L2; "Mutiny in Honolulu Harbor," *Washington Post*, 26 Jan. 1901, CIHCAM 2/VI/19; "Porto-Ricans 'Vagrant,'" *Puerto Rico Herald*, 12 Oct. 1901, CIHCAM 17/III/1; W. O. Smith to Henry Cooper, 22 May 1902, CIHCAM 3/VI/48; Henry Cooper to [State Department?], 27 May 1902, CIHCAM 3/VI/14; L. A. Andrews to A. M. Brown, 27 June 1902, CIHCAM 3/VI/48; A. M. Brown to S. B. Dole, 10 July 1902, CIHCAM 3/VI/48; Sanford Dole to Secretary of the Interior, 4 Sept. 1902, CIHCAM 3/VI/48; Iglesias, *Luchas*, 1:261.

48. In Hawai'i, Sally Engle Merry explains, law functioned as a tool of labor regulation, and individuals from recently arrived ethnic groups faced disproportionate prosecution. See Merry, *Colonizing Hawai'i: The Cultural Power of Law* (Princeton, NJ, 2000).

49. Draft, [Federico Degetau] to Francisco Valls de la Log, 25 Apr. 1902, CIHCAM 3/V/57 ("los emigrantes tuvieran sus derechos de ciudadanos reconocidos, para que pudieran ejercer el derecho electoral en el Hawaii"; "deseaba que yo fuese quien arguyese el caso ..., por entender él que esta era una garantía de éxito"; "no parece verosímil que si los hechos denunciados fueran exactos, los plantadores se manifestaran tan interesados en investir con las garantías constitucionales y de proveer del voto á [ellos]"); [Degetau] to Secretary of State, [30] Jan. 1901; "Las gestiones de Degetau"; [Degetau], Diary, 23 Apr. 1902; John Hay to Federico Degetau, 12 May 1902, CIHCAM 3/VI/4; Copy, "Well Treated Over in Hawaii," *San Juan News*, 8 May 1902, CIHCAM 3/VI/48; Hill to Degetau, 16 Feb. 1901; F. A. Schaefer to Sanford Dole, 6 Mar. 1901, CIHCAM 2/IX/4; [Federico Degetau] to Secretary of State, 13 Apr. 1901, CIHCAM 2/IX/13; "Desde Washington," *La Correspondencia*, n.d., CIHCAM 18/L1; Stanley L. Engerman, "Contract Labor, Sugar, and Technology in the Nineteenth Century," *Journal of Economic History* 43 (Sept. 1983): 635–659; Carr, "The Puerto Ricans in Hawaii," 85–223; Arroyo, "Da Borinkees."

More than a decade later, Puerto Ricans disagreed with Degetau's conclusion. According to the governor of Puerto Rico, the migration "ended so disastrously" that now "you could not get any Porto Ricans to go to Hawaii." *A Civil Government for Porto Rico: Hearings before the Committee on Insular Affairs House of Representatives, 64th Cong., 1st sess., on H.R. 8501, a Bill to Provide a Civil Government for Porto Rico, and for Other Purposes* (Washington, DC, 1916), 33–34. For protests by other Puerto Rican politicians, see Rosario Natal, *Exodo puertorriqueño*, 61; "De Hawaii a Puerto-Rico." Had Degetau wanted to challenge the reports, he could have pointed out that in one of them, islanders made all their statements clearing planters and their allies of wrongdoing in the presence of those very men. See CIHCAM 2/IX.

50. Manuel Rojas et al. to Degetau, 24 June 1903, CIHCAM 4/VII/51 ("siente por sus hijos como una [amanbsonia?] madre por su hijo adorado"; "[suena?] a tiempo para el esclavo y los dueños de plantaciones"); Carmelo Montalvo to [Federico Degetau], [June 1903?], CIHCAM 4/III/233; Carr, "The Puerto Ricans in Hawaii," 170–223. For a letter from a Puerto Rican in Mexico who believed that Degetau should act as a kind of consul for islanders abroad, see [Loren?] [Proscini?] to Federico Degetau, 6 Feb. 1902, CIHCAM 3/V/15; Sotero Rosario to Federico Degetau, 28 Mar. 1902, CIHCAM 3/V/39.

On cultural formation, conceptualization of the homeland, claims making, and the advantages of access to a consul (and disadvantages of its lack) among immigrants who engage in unidirectional or circular migration, see George J. Sánchez, *Becoming Mexican American: Ethnicity, Culture, and Identity in Chicano Los Angeles, 1900–1945* (New York, 1993); Benjamin Heber Johnson, *Revolution in Texas: How a Forgotten Rebellion and Its Bloody Suppression Turned Mexicans into Americans* (New Haven, CT, 2003); Marc C. McLeod, "Undesirable Aliens: Race, Ethnicity, and Nationalism in the Comparison of Haitian and British West Indian Immigrant Workers in Cuba, 1912–1939," *Journal of Social History* 31 (Spring 1998): 599–623; Barry Carr, "Identity, Class, and Nation: Black Immigrant Workers, Cuban Communists, and the Sugar Insurgency, 1915–1934," *Hispanic American Historical Review* 78 (Feb. 1998): 83–116; Winston James, *Holding Aloft the Banner of Ethiopia: Caribbean Radicalism in Early Twentieth-Century America* (New York, 1998); Irma Watkins-Owens, *Blood Relations: Caribbean Immigrants and the Harlem Community, 1900–1930* (Bloomington, IN: 1996); Silvio Torres-Saillant, "The Tribulations of Blackness: Stages in Dominican Racial Identity," *Callaloo* 23 (Summer 2000): 1086–1111; Nina Glick Schiller and Georges Eugene Fouron, *Georges Woke Up Laughing: Long-Distance Nationalism and the Search for Home* (Durham, NC, 2001); Caryn Cossé Bell, *Revolution, Romanticism, and the Afro-Creole Protest Tradition in Louisiana, 1718–1868* (Baton Rouge, LA, 1997); Mary Niall Mitchell, "'A Good and Delicious Country': Free Children of Color and How They Learned to Imagine the Atlantic World in Nineteenth-Century Louisiana," *History of Education Quarterly* 4 (Summer 2000): 123–144.

51. Pablo Navarro-Rivera, "Acculturation under Duress: The Puerto Rican Experience at the Carlisle Indian Industrial School 1898–1918," *Centro Journal* 18, no. 1 (2006): 222–259; R. H. Pratt, "The Advantages of Mingling Indians with Whites," in *Official Report of the National Conference of Charities and Correction*, ed. Isabel C. Barrows (Boston, 1892), 46; José-Manuel Navarro, *Creating Tropical Yankees: Social Science Textbooks and U.S. Ideological Control in Puerto Rico, 1898–1908* (New York, 2002), 120–121, 71, 115–119, 124–125; R. H. Pratt to Federico Degetau, 24 Jan. 1903, CIHCAM 3/VII/17; "Civilizing Indian Youth," *New York Times*, 16 Mar. 1880, 2; "The Indian at School," *Washington Post*, 9 Nov. 1884, 3; David Wallace Adams, *Education for Extinction: American Indians and the Boarding School Experience, 1875–1928* (Lawrence, KS, 1995), 100–112; Hoxie, *A Final Promise*, 54–66; Prucha, *Great Father*, 694–700.

On the Carlisle school and corporal discipline, abuse, high mortality, epidemic disease, the trauma of separation from family, and punishments inflicted on those who attempted to escape, see Fear-Segal, *White Man's Club*, xix, 62–63, 223–224, 232–233; Jacqueline Fear-Segal, "The Man on the Bandstand at Carlisle Indian Industrial School: What He Reveals about the Children's Experiences," in *Boarding School Blues: Revisiting American Indian Boarding School Experiences*, ed. Clifford E. Trafzer, Jean A. Keller, and Lorene Sisquoc (Lincoln, NE, 2006), 115; Scott Riney, "Loosening the Bonds: The Rapid City Indian School in the 1920s," in Frafzer, Keller, and Sisquoc, *Boarding School Blues*, 132; Adams, *Education for Extinction*, 121.

52. C[illegible] de Denton to Federico Degetau, 14 Sept. 1903, CIHCAM 4/V/285; Isabel Gonzalez to Federico Degetau, 10 Apr. 1904, CIHCAM 5/I/5. See also Luis Gonzalez to Federico Degetau, 5 Feb. 1903, CIHCAM 3/VII/35; A. T. Stuart to Federico Degetau, 10 Feb. 1903, CIHCAM 3/VII/45; "Una visita á Carlisle," *La Correspondencia*, 17 Aug. 1901; R. H. Pratt to Federico Degetau, 8 Aug. 1901, CIHCAM 3/III/52; R. H. Pratt to [Federico Degetau], 19 Jan. 1903, CIHCAM 3/VII/13; "Annual Exercises at Carlisle," *Washington Post*, 3 Feb. 1902, 3; R. H. Pratt to Federico Degetau, 20 Dec. 1902, CIHCAM 3/VI/69; Pratt to Degetau, 24 Jan. 1903; Eugenio Lecompte to Federico Degetau, 13 Feb. 1903, CIHCAM 3/VII/47; Booker T. Washington to Ana Moreno Degetau, 16 May 1903, CIHCAM 4/III/182; Antonio Trujillo to Federico Degetau, 19 May 1903, CIHCAM 4/III/186; Booker T. Washington to Federico Degetau, 28 May 1903, CIHCAM 4/III/198; G. W. A. Johnston to Federico Degetau, 20 May 1903, CIHCAM 4/III/187.

53. Booker T. Washington, "Industrial Education for Cuban Negroes," *New York Times*, 16 Aug. 1898, 6; "The Negro's Future," *Los Angeles Times*, 17 Dec. 1899, 16; R. H. Pratt to Federico Degetau, 15 Mar. 1904, CIHCAM 4/IX/14; Angela Rivera-Tudó, "The Puerto Rican Indians," trans. Vilma Irrizary, originally in *La Correspondencia de Puerto Rico*, 3 Jan. 1931, 4, quoted in Sonia M. Rosa, "The Puerto Ricans at Carlisle Indian School," *KACIKE: The Journal of Caribbean Amerindian History and Anthropology*, 28 Dec. 2003, https://archive.org/stream/KacikeJournal_34/soniarosa_djvu.txt; "Porto Ricans Coming Here to Study," *New York Times*, 28 Apr. 1901, 23; "Porto Rican Boys to Study at Carlisle," *New York Times*, 17 May 1901, 5; "Eaton to Take Charge," *Washington Post*, 31 Jan. 1899, 8; Aida Negron de Montilla, *La americanización en Puerto Rico y el sistema de instrucción pública 1900–1930* (San Juan, PR, 1976), 22–23; General Order No. 12, Headquarters Department of Porto Rico, 6 Feb. 1899, MD NARA 350/5A/168–4; Victor S. Clark, "Porto Rico under American School System," *Chicago Daily Tribune*, 13 May 1900, 41; "Porto Rico Nominations," *New York Times*, 5 June 1900, 7; Navarro, *Tropical Yankees*; Navarro-Rivera, "Acculturation"; "Cubans in a Southern Negro School," *New York Times*, 2 Dec. 1898, 3; An Act to Provide for the Education of Certain Young Men and Women in the United States, 1 P.R. Stat. 12, 13 (1901); "A Word from Booker Washington," *Washington Post*, 18 Aug. 1898, 6; 36 Cong. Rec. 1349–1350, 1426; "Indian Bill Is Passed," *Washington Post*, 30 Jan. 1903, 4; "Riverside: Filipinos in Indian School," *Los Angeles Times*, 9 Feb. 1903, 12; Degetau, *Political Status of Porto Rico*; Pratt to Degetau, 20 Dec. 1902; Pratt to Degetau, 24 Jan. 1903; Arturo Schulze to Federico Degetau, 13 Aug. 1901, CIHCAM 3/III/59.
On Washington's efforts to recruit Cubans and on the value that Cubans saw in Tuskegee's training, see Frank Andre Guridy, *Forging Diaspora: Afro-Cubans and*

African Americans in a World of Empire and Jim Crow (Chapel Hill, NC, 2010). On the limited and at times counterproductive efforts by some African American cultural elites to promote racial uplift, see Kevin K. Gaines, *Uplifting the Race: Black Leadership, Politics, and Culture in the Twentieth Century*, 2nd ed. (Chapel Hill, NC, 1996). On tensions in the late nineteenth and early twentieth centuries between established U.S. Jewish communities with ancestral roots in Germany and newer Jewish arrivals from Eastern Europe and Russia, see Gerald Sorin, "Mutual Contempt, Mutual Benefit: The Strained Encounter between German and Eastern European Jews in America, 1880–1920," *American Jewish History* 81 (Fall 1993): 34–59. Scholars studying Puerto Rican students at Carlisle and Tuskegee have focused on the cultural coercion that the students faced. Navarro, *Tropical Yankees*; Navarro-Rivera, "Acculturation"; Rosa, "Puerto Ricans at Carlisle."

54. "Prelate Vexes Porto Ricans," *Detroit Journal*, 2 June 1902, CIHCAM 18/L1; William S. Bryan, ed., *Our Islands and Their People as Seen with Camera and Pencil*, vol. 2 (New York, 1899; repr. 1905), photograph on 408 in 1899 edition; Thompson, "Aesthetics and Empire"; Lanny Thompson, *Imperial Archipelago: Representation and Rule in the Insular Territories under U.S. Dominion after 1898* (Honolulu, 2010), 104, 132, 158, 249–252.

55. David Montgomery, *The Fall of the House of Labor: The Workplace, the State, and American Labor Activism, 1865–1925* (New York, 1987), 5–6; Marc Karson, *American Labor Unions and Politics, 1900–1918* (Boston, 1958), x, 20–21, 132, 135, 137–141, 149; David Montgomery, "Workers' Movements in the United States Confront Imperialism: The Progressive Era Experience," *Journal of the Gilded Age and Progressive Era* 7 (Jan. 2008): 14; *Report of Proceedings of the Twentieth Annual Convention of the American Federation of Labor* (Louisville, KY, [1900]), 19; Philip S. Foner, *History of the Labor Movement in the United States*, vol. 3: *The Policies and Practices of the American Federation of Labor, 1900–1909* (New York, 1973 [1964]), 219, 233–246, 268–270.

56. *Twentieth Annual Convention of the American Federation of Labor*, 64–65; Miles Galvin, *The Organized Labor Movement in Puerto Rico* (London, 1979), 47–48; Iglesias, *Luchas*, 1:200. The previous dozen years had seen the collapse of farmers' alliances, cross-racial labor-farmer political coalitions, radical and utopian groups, and a broad-based working people's organization. See Montgomery, *Fall of the House of Labor*; Herbert G. Gutman, *Power and Culture: Essays on the American Working Class*, ed. Ira Berlin (New York, 1987); Herbert G. Gutman, *Work, Culture, and Society in Industrializing America: Essays in American Working-Class and Social History* (New York, 1976); Matthew Hild, *Greenbackers, Knights of Labor, and Populists: Farmer-Labor Insurgency in the Late-Nineteenth-Century South* (Athens, GA, 2007); Steve Leikin, *The Practical Utopians: American Workers and the Cooperative Movement in the Gilded Age* (Detroit, 2005); Joseph Gerteis, *Class and the Color Line: Interracial Class Coalition in the Knights of Labor and the Populist Movement* (Durham, NC, 2007); Norman J. Ware, *The Labor Movement in the United States, 1860–1895: A Study in Democracy* (Gloucester, MA, 1959 [1929]); Philip S. Foner, *History of the Labor Movement in the United States*, vol. 2: *From the Founding of the A.F. of L. to the Emergence of American Imperialism* (New York, 1975 [1955]), 400–402. Some large industry-specific unions within the AFL organized across race, sex, and skill lines. On the United Mine Workers, see Gutman, *Work, Culture, and*

Society, 122–208. On interracial waterfront labor activism in New Orleans, see Eric Arnesen, *Waterfront Workers of New Orleans: Race, Class, and Politics, 1863–1923* (Oxford, 1991).

57. "Samuel Gompers Is Hissed," *Chicago Daily Tribune*, 19 Oct. 1898, 4; *Report of Proceedings of the 19th Annual Convention of the American Federation of Labor* (1899), 148–150; Samuel Gompers, "For Justice Even in Puerto Rico," *American Federationist*, Feb. 1902, 72–73, quoted in Iglesias de Pagán, *El obrerismo*, 177; Eric T. Love, *Race over Empire: Racism and U.S. Imperialism, 1865–1900* (Chapel Hill, NC, 2004), 183–184; James R. Barrett and David Roediger, "Inbetween Peoples: Race, Nationality and the 'New Immigrant' Working Class," *Journal of American Ethnic History* 16 (Spring 1997): 3–44; Catherine Collomp, "Unions, Civics, and National Identity: Organized Labor's Reaction to Immigration, 1881–1897," *Labor History* 29 (1988): 450–474; Samuel Gompers, *Seventy Years of Life and Labor: An Autobiography*, vol. 2 (New York, 1925), 63–67; Jesse Hoffnung-Garskof, "The Migrations of Arturo Schomburg: On Being *Antillano*, Negro, and Puerto Rican in New York 1891–1938," *Journal of American Ethnic History* 21 (Fall 2001): 9; Juan José Baldrich, "From Handcrafted Tobacco Rolls to Machine-Made Cigarettes: The Transformation and Americanization of Puerto Rican Tobacco, 1847–1903," *Centro Journal* 17, no. 2 (Fall 2005): 145–169; A. G. Quintero-Rivera, "Socialist and Cigarmaker: Artisans' Proletarianization in the Making of the Puerto Rican Working Class," *Latin American Perspectives* 10 (Summer 1983): 19–38. Montgomery, "Workers' Movements," 17, describes the links between expansion and reform politics that led Gompers and the AFL to cease their protests, as here, where they bracketed the Philippines question. On Gompers's reorganization of the Cigarmakers' International Union, see Bernard Mandel, "Gompers and Business Unionism, 1873–1890," *Business History Review* 28 (Sept. 1954): 264–275.

58. Gompers, *Seventy Years*, 2:1–28; Forbath, *Law and the Shaping of Labor*.

59. Iglesias, *Luchas*, 1:202–211, 216–217; *Report of Proceeding of the Twenty-First Annual Convention of the American Federation of Labor, 1901* (Washington, DC, 1901), 160; Samuel Gompers to Santiago Iglesias, 12 Sept. 1901, SGL 46/283; Samuel Gompers to Santiago Iglesias, 1 Oct. 1901, SGL 46/578; William George Whittaker, "The Santiago Iglesias Case, 1901–1902: Origins of American Trade Union Involvement in Puerto Rico," *Americas* 24 (Apr. 1968): 380; "New Governor of Porto Rico," *New York Times*, 31 Aug. 1901, 6; Iglesias de Pagán, *El obrerismo*, 161–162. Hunt came to the governor's post after stints as a justice of the Montana Supreme Court, Montana attorney general, and a member of the Montana legislature and constitutional convention.

60. *San Juan News*, 26 Jan. 1902 ("no habrán de unirse con los puertorriqueños, a muchos de los cuales desprecian porque son negros"), quoted in Iglesias de Pagán, *El obrerismo*, 188; Santiago Iglesias, "Federación del Trabajo Americana," *Puerto Rico Herald*, 2 Nov. 1901, quoted in Bernardo Vega, *Memoirs of Bernardo Vega: A Contribution to the History of the Puerto Rican Community in New York*, ed. César Andreu Iglesias, trans. Juan Flores (New York, 1984 [1977]), 87–88; [Degetau] to Foraker, 15 May 1901; Iglesias, *Luchas*, 1:216, 261.

61. Samuel Gompers to Santiago Iglesias, 20 Nov. 1901, SGL 48/256–257, quoted in Iglesias de Pagán, *El obrerismo*, 169; Whittaker, "The Santiago Iglesias Case," 381–385; Iglesias, *Luchas*, 1:218–219. For articles on related matters where Gompers

was a likely source, see "Iglesias to Be Free To-Day," *Washington Post*, 18 Nov. 1901, 2; "Iglesias Still in Jail," *New York Times*, 20 Nov. 1901, 2.

62. "Después del juicio," *La Democracia*, 16 Dec. 1901 ("Puerto Rico estaba bajo la Constitución Americana"; "la Constitución seguía la bandera"), quoted in Iglesias de Pagán, *El obrerismo*, 172; Santiago Iglesias to Chas. Hartzell, 11 Dec. 1901, reprinted in "Una carta de Santiago Iglesias," *La Democracia*, 12 or 13 Dec. 1901. *La Democracia*, 14 Dec. 1901 ("libertad de asociación, de la Prensa, de la palabra") quoted in Iglesias de Pagán, *El obrerismo*, 186; Iglesias, *Luchas*, 1:220–221, 272–273, 277–278, 282–289; Mariano Negrón Portillo, *Las turbas republicanas 1900–1904* (Río Piedras, PR, 1990), 75, 90, 103, 105, 109, 112–117, 125, 135, 156, 209; Juan Ángel Silén, *Apuntes para la historia del movimiento obrero puertorriqueño* (San Juan, PR, 1978), 61; Whittaker, "The Santiago Iglesias Case," 385, 389.

63. José Barbosa to Federico Degetau, 28 Jan. 1902, CIHCAM 3/V/9 ("se dice con frecuencia que la Constitución de los Estados Unidos rige en Pto Rico en todo aquello que se refiere á los derechos individuales, pero en la práctica no resulta . . . acaba de hacer con Iglesias"); Samuel Gompers, "The Conspiracy to Raise the Price of Labor," *American Federationist* 9 (Jan. 1902): 27–28, and *San Juan News*, 2 Dec. 1901, 2, are quoted in Whittaker, "The Santiago Iglesias Case," 387–390. See also ibid., 385–386; "Appeal of Santiago Iglesias," *New York Times*, 30 Mar. 1902, 10; Iglesias, *Luchas*, 1:221, 227–245; David Ray Papke, *The Pullman Case: The Clash of Labor and Capital in Industrial America* (Lawrence, KS, 1999), 38, 51, 75–76, 98; Tomlins, *The State and the Unions*; Alfonso García Martínez, "El proceso judicial de Santiago Iglesias 1901–1902," *Revista del Colegio de Abogados de Puerto Rico* 40 (Feb. 1979): 125–148; Juan Carreras, *Santiago Iglesias Pantín: Su vida, su obra, su pensamiento (datos biográficos)* (San Juan, PR, 1965), 110–111; Forbath, *Law and the Shaping of Labor*, 61.

64. "Topics of the Times," *New York Times*, 17 Apr. 1902, 8; Gompers quoted the *Post* in "Conspiracy," 27–28, which is quoted in Whittaker, "The Santiago Iglesias Case," 388; "Santiago Iglesias," *La Democracia*, 25 Dec. 1901; "La sentencia contra Iglesias," *La Democracia*, 19 Dec. 1901; "Porto Rico Labor Laws," *Chicago Daily Tribune*, 14 Dec. 1901, 12; Iglesias, *Luchas*, I:243–244; "An Un-American Law," *Washington Post*, 7 Jan. 1902, 5; "Labor Agitator Sent to Prison," *Chicago Tribune*, 13 Dec. 1901, 1; "Jail for Iglesias," *Washington Post*, 13 Dec. 1901, 1; Gervasio L. García and A.G. Quintero Rivera, *Desafío y solidaridad: Breve historia del movimiento obrero puertorriqueño* (San Juan, PR, 1986); Carreras, *Santiago Iglesias*, 111; Santiago Iglesias, "Obreros Puerto-Riqueños ¡Unirse!" *Puerto Rico Herald*, 4 Oct. 1901, 10; Santiago Iglesias, "Federación del Trabajo Americana," *Puerto Rico Herald*, 2 Nov. 1901, 10; "Unionism a Crime in Puerto Rico," *Puerto Rico Herald*, 21 Dec. 1901, 4; "The Discrediting of a Country," *Puerto Rico Herald*, 28 Dec. 1901, 3. Cooperation between Iglesias and Muñoz Rivera was visible by April 1901. "Porto Rican Lies Refuted," *Los Angeles Times*, 11 Apr. 1901, 8; "Reply to Gov. Allen," *New York Times*, 11 Apr. 1901, 8; "Porto Rican Conditions," *New York Times*, 25 Apr. 1901, 5.

65. Samuel Gompers, "For Justice," quoted in Whittaker, "The Santiago Iglesias Case," 391; "The Porto Rico Labor Case," *New York Times*, 11 Apr. 1902, 3; Iglesias, *Luchas*, 1:268–269. See also "Gov. Hunt's Message to the Porto Ricans," *New York Times*, 3 Jan. 1902, 2; *Report of Proceedings of the Twenty-Second Annual Convention of the American Federation of Labor* (Washington, DC, 1902), 15; García Martínez, "El proceso," 145.

66. Iglesias de Pagán, *El obrerismo*, 195, 205; *Twenty-Second Annual Convention of the American Federation of Labor*, 88, 155; Iglesias, *Luchas*, 1:261; Kirwin R. Shaffer, *Black Flag Boricuas: Anarchism, Antiauthoritarianism, and the Left in Puerto Rico, 1897–1921* (Urbana, IL, 2013), 49.

67. Iglesias, *Luchas*, especially 1:268–269, 299–300; Ángel Silén, *Apuntes para la historia*, 61–62; Whittaker, "The Santiago Iglesias Case," especially 383–385, 388–389, 392; *Twenty-Second Annual Convention of the American Federation of Labor*, 226, 15–16, 78–79, 133.

68. Barbara Y. Welke, *Law and the Borders of Belonging in the Long Nineteenth Century United States* (Cambridge, 2010).

69. *Twenty-Second Annual Convention of the American Federation of Labor*, 112, 219.

70. Draft, [Federico Degetau] to Pedro Besosa, 6 Sept. 1902, CIHCAM 3/VI/49 ("compromiso de honor"; "me obligan á solicitar de nuevo de mis correligionarios el honor de ser su candidato, y del cuerpo electoral el de ser reelegido para continuar la labor emprendida [*sic*] en favor de nuestra ciudadanía americana; de la admisión de Puerto-Rico en la Unión como un Territorio organizado para ser en día no lejano uno de tantos Estados"); *Informe de los delegados del Partido Republicano de Puerto Rico ante la Convención Nacional Republicana celebrada en Chicago, en 21 de junio de 1904* ([San Juan?], PR, 1904), CIHCAM 6/L8, 5–6; Copy, [Federico Degetau] to Teodoro Moscoso, 2 Oct. 1903, CIHCAM 4/V/309; Ramón Lebrón to Federico Degetau, 10 Oct. 1902, CIHCAM 3/VI/57; Fernando Bayrón Toro, *Elecciones y partidos políticos de Puerto Rico (1809–1976)* (Mayagüez, PR, 1977), 119–121; Negrón Portillo, *Turbas republicanas*, 149, 151.

"AMERICAN ALIENS": ISABEL GONZALEZ, DOMINGO COLLAZO, FEDERICO DEGETAU, AND THE SUPREME COURT, 1902–1905

1. "Porto Rican Test Case," *New York Times*, 3 Nov. 1903, 6. I thank Christina Ponsa and Veta Schlimgen for sharing helpful research in progress.

2. On the subjective process by which harms may give rise to disputes, see William L. F. Felstiner, Richard L. Abel, and Austin Sarat, "The Emergence and Transformation of Disputes: Naming, Blaming, Claiming," *Law & Society Review* 15, no. 3/4 (1980–1981): 641–654.

3. Federico Degetau to Secretary of Treasury, 5 Oct. 1902, CIHCAM 3/VI/56; Domingo Collazo to Federico Degetau, 27 Aug. 1903, CIHCAM 18/L1; Transcript of Record, No. 225, Gonzales v. Williams, 192 U.S. 1 (27 Feb. 1903), 3–6; Luis Gonzalez to Federico Degetau, 5 Feb. 1903, CIHCAM 3/VII/35; Isabel Gonzalez to Federico Degetau, 10 Apr. 1904, CIHCAM 5/I/5; "Porto Ricans Not Aliens," *New York Times*, 5 Jan. 1904, 8; "Porto Rican Test Case."

4. Philippine Bill of 1902, secs. 4, 1–2, 5, 7, 32, 76–84, 32 Stat. 691, 692, 691, 693–694, 710–711 (1902); 35 Cong. Rec. 2096; Act of March 8, 1902, sec. 2, 32 Stat. 54, 54; J. H. Hollander, "The Finances of Porto Rico," *Political Science Quarterly* 16 (Dec. 1901): 553.

5. Circular No. 97, 2 Aug. 1902, in *Circular Instructions of the Treasury Department Relating to the Tariff, Navigation, and Other Laws for the Year Ended December 31, 1902* (Washington, DC, 1903); Transcript of Record, *Gonzales*, 3–6.

6. Erika Lee, *At America's Gates: Chinese Immigration during the Exclusion Era,*
   1882–1943 (Chapel Hill, NC, 2003); Louis Anthes, "The Island of Duty: The
   Practice of Immigration Law on Ellis Island," *New York University Review of*
   Law and Social Change 24 (1998): 563–600; Lucy E. Salyer, *Laws Harsh as*
   Tigers: Chinese Immigrants and the Shaping of Modern Immigration Law
   (Chapel Hill, NC, 1995), 141, 144–148, 184, 196–197; Secretary to the President
   to William Williams, 1 Apr. 1902, William Williams Papers, New York Public
   Library, box 1; "Williams Regains Immigration Office," *New York Times*, 19
   May 1909, 2.
7. William Williams, Outline of Address Delivered to the Senior Class of Princeton in
   November, 1904, William Williams Papers, New York Public Library, box 6, folder
   4; Immigration Act of 1891, 26 Stat. 1084, 1084 (1891); Salyer, *Laws Harsh as*
   Tigers, 147, 141–148, 154, 184, 196–197; John Higham, *Strangers in the Land:*
   Patterns of American Nativism, 1860–1925 (New Brunswick, NJ, 1955); Matthew
   Frye Jacobson, *Whiteness of a Different Color: European Immigrants and the*
   Alchemy of Race (Cambridge, MA, 1999); Alan M. Kraut, *Silent Travelers:*
   Germs, Genes, and the Immigrant Menace (Baltimore, MD, 1995), 57; Margot
   Canaday, *The Straight State: Sexuality and Citizenship in Twentieth-Century*
   America (Princeton, NJ, 2009); Anthes, "Island of Duty," 565–566, 581–582,
   587–589; Stephen Skowronek, *Building a New American State: The Expansion of*
   National Administrative Capacities, 1877–1920 (New York, 1982); Lee, *At*
   America's Gates; Secretary to the President to Williams, 1 Apr. 1902; Linda
   Gordon, "Social Insurance and Public Assistance: The Influence of Gender in
   Welfare Thought in the United States, 1890–1935," *American Historical Review*
   97 (Feb. 1992): 19–54; Joanne L. Goodwin, "'Employable Mothers' and 'Suitable
   Work': A Re-Evaluation of Welfare and Wage-Earning for Women in the
   Twentieth-Century United States," *Journal of Social History* 29 (Winter 1995):
   253–274. Like Roosevelt, Williams was a Republican.
      Kunal M. Parker explores the relationship between migration, dependence, and
   status in the context of state law in *Making Foreigners: Immigration and Citizenship*
   Law in America, 1600–2000 (Cambridge, 2015).
8. Salyer, *Laws Harsh as Tigers*, 147, included the italics in the first quotation, which
   Salyer took from the "Rules for Registry Division." The other quotations are from
   Transcript of Record, *Gonzales*, 192 U.S. 1, 4–5. See also Manifest for the S.S.
   Ponce, Arrival at Port of New York, 18 May 1903, 78, Ellis Island Archives.
      A history of how U.S. empire building transformed, combined, and was itself
   shaped by island and mainland notions of honor could be a book in itself. By
   identifying such overlapping dynamics here, I hope to encourage legal historians to
   take up the project and incorporate the United States more fully into the transnational
   history of honor. On diverse notions of honor among Puerto Ricans subject to U.S.
   rule, see Eileen J. Suárez Findlay, *Imposing Decency: The Politics of Sexuality and*
   Race in Puerto Rico, 1870–1920 (Durham, NC, 1999). Aside from Findlay, modern
   scholarship has largely overlooked the similarities that contemporary U.S. officials
   denied between Latin American honor dynamics and mainland realities. To the extent
   that historians of the United States once emphasized honor, they did so in relation to
   the antebellum South. The classic account is Bertram Wyatt-Brown's *Southern*
   Honor: Ethics and Behavior in the Old South (New York, 1982). It proposed an
   opposition between honor and law that did not withstand scrutiny from cultural legal

historians. See Ariela Gross, "Beyond Black and White: Cultural Approaches to Race and Slavery," *Columbia Law Review* 101 (2001): 688. Today, honor figures little in most histories of the United States, notwithstanding the examples discussed in Angela M. Hornsby-Gutting, "Manning the Region: New Approaches to Gender in the South," *Journal of Southern History* 75 (Aug. 2009): 667–669. By contrast, myriad works on Latin America describe pervasive honor-infused clientelism. See Emanuel Pfoh, "La formación del Estado Nacional en América Latina y la cuestión del clientelismo político," *Revista de Historia de América* 136 (Jan.–Dec. 2005): 129–148; Barbara Schröter, "Clientelismo político: ¿Existe el fantasma y cómo se viste?" *Revista Mexicana de Sociología* 72 (Jan.–Mar. 2010): 141–175; Manuel Marín, "El cacique protector," *Historia Social* 36 (2000): 21–34. Other, at times overlapping work identifies class-differentiated conceptions of honor and delineates the roles of law and legal institutions in constructing and contesting honor. See Sueann Caulfield, Sarah C. Chambers, and Lara Putnam, eds., *Honor, Status and Law in Modern Latin America* (Durham, NC, 2005); Lyman L. Johnson and Sonya Lipsett-Rivera, eds., *The Faces of Honor: Sex, Shame, and Violence in Colonial Latin America* (Albuquerque, NM, 1998); Karl Monsma, "Words Spoken and Written: Divergent Meanings of Honor among Elites in Nineteenth-Century Rio Grande do Sul," *Hispanic American Historical Review* 92 (2012): 269–302.

9. Transcript of Record, *Gonzales*, 192 U.S. 1, 5–6.

10. Ibid., 2, 5–6. Findlay, *Imposing Decency*, 9–10, 20, 24–25, 40–47, 55, 74, 81, 85–86, 91–100, 120–121; Eileen J. Findlay, "Courtroom Tales of Sex and Honor: *Rapto* and Rape in Late Nineteenth-Century Puerto Rico," in Caulfield, Chambers, and Putnam, *Honor, Status and Law*, 205; Jesse Hoffnung-Garskof, *Racial Migrations: New York City and the Revolutionary Politics of the Spanish Caribbean, 1850–1902* (Princeton, NJ, forthcoming), chs. 2, 5; Rosa E. Carrasquillo, *Our Landless Patria: Marginal Citizenship and Race in Caguas, Puerto Rico, 1880–1910* (Lincoln, NE, 2006), 99–100. Puerto Rican women were sometimes able to use a seduction and the need for an honor-restoring marriage to overcome parents' disapproval of a proposed marriage. Despite such bounded opportunities for women's autonomy, honor norms were more often instruments of women's discipline and subordination. Given that many Puerto Rican couples entered into long-term consensual unions without formally marrying, Domingo Collazo's account of Isabel Gonzalez's "husband" may be better understood as translation than deception. Astrid Cubano Iguina has observed how gendered concepts and legal categories that have different implications for men and women developed in tandem in late nineteenth-century Puerto Rico; see "Legal Constructions of Gender and Violence against Women in Puerto Rico under Spanish Rule, 1860–1895," *Law and History Review* 22 (2004): 531–564.

11. William Williams to Henry Burnett, 26 Aug. 1903, DC NARA 85/151/4~340/394/19045; In re Gonzalez, 118 F. 941, 941 (C.C.S.D.N.Y. 1902); Secretary of Treasury to Secretary of War, 13 Oct. 1902, MD NARA 350/5A/1444-6; "Porto Ricans Not Aliens," 5 Jan. 1904; Transcript of Record, *Gonzales*, 192 U.S. 1, 1–8; William Williams to Commissioner General of Immigration, 24 Aug. 1903, DC NARA 85/151/4~340/268/19045.

12. William Williams to William Anderson, 2 Sept. 1903, DC NARA 85/151/5~340/97/19045; Transcript of Record, *Gonzales*, 192 U.S. 1, 7, 1–2, 8–14; Domingo Collazo to José Pérez Losada, 19 Dec. 1928, in "Debemos los puertorriqueños tener un poco

de mas cuidado con la verdad histórica de nuestras cosas regionales – dice Domingo Collazo," *El Imparcial,* 24 Dec. 1928, CIHCAM 18/L1 ("expresa solicitud"); Appellant's Brief, No. 225, *Gonzales,* 192 U.S. 1 (30 Nov. 1902), 3; Williams to Commissioner General, 24 Aug. 1903; D. Collazo, "Desde Nueva York," *La Correspondencia de Puerto Rico,* 19 Dec. 1903, 1; Petition of Federico Degetau, Resident Commissioner from Porto Rico, *Gonzales,* 192 U.S. 1 (n.d.); Brief Filed by Leave of the Court by Federico Degetau, Resident Commissioner from Porto Rico, as Amicus Curiæ, No. 225, *Gonzales,* 192 U.S. 1 (Nov. 1903); Frederic Coudert to Federico Degetau, 20 Apr. 1903, CIHCAM 4/II/144.

13. Manuel Rossy to Federico Degetau, 12 May 1903, CIHCAM 4/II/176 ("no es tan libre la acción legislativa del influjo de la acción ejecutiva como nos habíamos figurado leyendo lo que dicen los libros"); Draft, [Federico Degetau] to Manuel Rossy, 20 Feb. 1901, CIHCAM 2/VII/47 ("el respeto profundo"; "instituciones judiciales"); Charles E. Le Barbier and Orrel A. Parker to Federico Degetau, 12 Jan. 1903, CIHCAM 3/VII/6; Coudert to Degetau, 20 Apr. 1903; Brief Filed by ... Federico Degetau, *Gonzales,* 192 U.S. 1, 2; Argument of Frederic R. Coudert Jr., Esq., on Behalf of the Petitioner-Appellant, *Gonzales,* 192 U.S. 1 (7 Dec. 1903), 73; Herminio Diaz to Federico Degetau, 5 Jan. 1904, CIHCAM 4/VIII/3; Petition of Federico Degetau, *Gonzales,* 192 U.S. 1; Hamilton Holt to Federico Degetau, 5 Nov. 1903, CIHCAM 4/VI/342; Hamilton Holt to Federico Degetau, 12 Nov. 1903, CIHCAM 4/VI/354; Hamilton Holt to Federico Degetau, 19 Nov. 1903, CIHCAM 4/VI/364; [Hamilton Holt] to Federico Degetau, 27 Nov. 1903, CIHCAM 4/VI/379.

14. Robert B. Armstrong to Collector of Customs, 9 Dec. 1903, CIHCAM 4/VII/11; Brief Filed by ... Federico Degetau, *Gonzales,* 192 U.S. 1, 25–26; Copy, [Federico Degetau] to Teodoro Moscoso, 2 Oct. 1903, CIHCAM 4/V/309; "El Sr. Degetau: Su conferencia de anoche," newspaper unknown, 5 Aug. 1903, CIHCAM 18/L1; H.R. 3540 [Rep. No. 8], 58th Cong., 2d sess., 14 Dec. 1903, CIHCAM 4/VI/358; C. H. Keep to Federico Degetau, 11 Nov. 1903, CIHCAM 4/VI/352; R. B. Armstrong to Federico Degetau, 9 Dec. 1903, CIHCAM 4/VII/9; C. H. Keep to Melchior et al., 10 Nov. 1903, CIHCAM 4/VI/351; Manifest for the S.S. *Lorraine,* Port of New York, 24 Oct. 1903, PCLVANY M237/La Lorraine. My account of this dispute builds on Christina Duffy Burnett, "'They Say I Am Not an American ...': The Noncitizen National and the Law of American Empire," *Virginia Journal of International Law* 48 (2008): 691–692.

Seeking confirmation of what he had earlier told President Roosevelt was a civil service decision classifying Puerto Ricans as citizens, Degetau also reached out to the recent chief of the Civil Service Record Division, George Leadley. Leadley responded that no such opinion had been published. Geo. Leadley to Federico Degetau, 29 Mar. 1904, CIHCAM 4/IX/26; Geo. Leadley to Bonifacio Sánchez, 7 Apr. 1903, CIHCAM 4/II/124; Draft Petition for Mandamus, no. 1504, Rodriguez v. Bowyer, 25 App. D.C. 121 (n.d.), CIHCAM 6/III/56; Transcript of Record, No. 1504, *Rodriguez,* 25 App. D. C. 121 (31 Dec. 1904), 1–2, CIHCAM 6/V/32. For Degetau's inquiries to the Census and the Bureau of Navigation, see Translation of Extract from "Special Instruction for the Enumerators of Department Number 2," n.d., CIHCAM 2/IV/15; Draft, Federico Degetau to Clarence Edwards, 20 June 1903, CIHCAM 4/III/222; Edgard Mc[?] to Federico Degetau, 27 June 1903, CIHCAM 4/III/230; Charles Magoon to Federico Degetau, 8 July 1903, CIHCAM 4/IV/239; Brief Filed by ... Federico Degetau, *Gonzales,* 192 U.S. 1, 38; E. Cha[?] to Federico Degetau, 15 June 1903, CIHCAM 4/

III/217. On an Ellis Island inquiry, see [Illegible] to Frederico Degetau, 14 Dec. 1903, CIHCAM 4/VII/23.

15. Gonzalez to Degetau, 5 Feb. 1903 ("estudiar … en algo"; "en muy mala posición"; "deseo de su buen corazón me allude [sic]"); Manifest for the S.S. *Ponce*, 18 May 1903, 78.

16. "Porto Ricans Not Aliens," 5 Jan. 1904; Frederic R. Coudert Jr., "Our New Peoples: Citizens, Subjects, Nationals or Aliens," *Columbia Law Review* 3 (Jan. 1903): 13–32; Porto Rican Vote Pledged to Bryan," *New York Times*, 1 Aug. 1908, 2; Veta R. Schlimgen, "Neither Citizens nor Aliens: Filipino 'American Nationals' in the U.S. Empire, 1900–1946," PhD diss., University of Oregon, 2010, and Christina Duffy Burnett, "Empire and the Transformation of Citizenship," in *Colonial Crucible: Empire in the Making of the Modern American States*, ed. Alfred W. McCoy and Francisco A. Scarano (Madison, WI, 2009), 332–341. Appellant's Brief, Gonzales v. Williams, 192 U.S. 1. On naturalization by marriage, see Act of Feb. 10, 1855, 10 Stat. 604, reenacted in *Revised Statutes of the U.S.* (1878), sec. 1994; Candice Lewis Bredbenner, *A Nationality of Her Own: Women, Marriage, and the Law of Citizenship* (Los Angeles, 1998), 15–44 and n1.

17. On the legal stories about Gonzalez that judges, lawyers, and inspectors crafted from the testimonies witnesses strategically provided them, see Burnett, "'They Say I Am Not an American'"; Éfren Rivera Ramos, *The Legal Construction of Identity: The Judicial and Social Legacy of American Colonialism in Puerto Rico* (Washington, DC, 2001). On legal stories more generally, see Barbara Young Welke, *Recasting American Liberty: Gender, Race, Law, and the Railroad Revolution, 1865–1920* (Cambridge, 2001), 234–245.

18. Collazo to Degetau, 27 Aug. 1903 ("de una serie que me propongo publicar, y que tomarán carácter político"); Mariano Negrón Portillo, *Cuadrillas anexionistas y revueltas campesinas en Puerto Rico, 1898–1899* (Río Piedras, PR, 1987), 27–28; James H. McLeary, *First Annual Register of Porto Rico* (San Juan, PR, 1901), 59, 67; D. Collazo to Federico Degetau, 21 Nov. [1903], CIHCAM 6/I/42; D. Collazo, "Cosas Literarias de Puerto Rico: 'Tropicales,'" newspaper unknown, n.d., CIHCAM 18/L1; [Matter?] to Federico Degetau, 21 Oct. 1903, CIHCAM 4/V/327; B. Díaz to Federico Degetau, 6 Oct. 1903, CIHCAM 4/V/312.

19. Collazo, "Desde Nueva York," 19 Dec. 1903 ("posesión de 'dependencias'"; "instituciones"; "espíritu … democrático"; "se les niega … los derechos personales protegidos por la Constitución"; "podemos acariciar la esperanza"); Collazo to Degetau, 21 Nov. [1903] ("nos dirá *once again* la Corte Suprema que no somos americanos"); Porto Rican Exile, "Correo de Nueva York," *La Democracia*, 6 Aug. 1910, 1.

20. Racial analogies and comparisons integrated and reintegrated communities into racial hierarchies whose changeability underlay their resilience. Law reinforced and altered racial hierarchies by defining racial groups and enforcing their subordination or elevation. Las was also centripetal, privileging analogies and comparison and widely understood to form a unified, rational whole. Such traits encouraged fitting new racialized communities into one or another doctrinal form already applicable to another community. Law and race thus operated as potential exceptions to what Karen Barkey describes as the general structure of empire as a hub connected by spokes to distinct peripheries, few of which have substantial connections to each other or are subject to common forms of governance. See *Empire of Difference: The*

Ottomans in Comparative Perspective (Cambridge, 2008), 1, 9. On classical legal thought, including its depiction of law as a rational whole, see Morton J. Horwitz, *The Transformation of American Law 1870–1960: The Crisis of Legal Orthodoxy* (New York, 1992); Thomas C. Grey, "Langdell's Orthodoxy," *University of Pittsburgh Law Review* 45 (1983): 1–53; Duncan Kennedy, "Toward an Historical Understanding of Legal Consciousness: The Case of Classical Legal Thought in America, 1850–1940," *Research in Law and Sociology* 3 (1980): 3–24; Stephen A. Siegel, "Francis Wharton's Orthodoxy: God, Historical Jurisprudence, and Classical Legal Thought," *American Journal of Legal History* 46 (2004): 422–446. On race as relational, alterable, resilient, consequential, and shaped and enforced by law with respect to late nineteenth- and, especially, early twentieth-century U.S. residents of Mexican descent, see Natalia Molina, *Fit to Be Citizens? Public Health and Race in Los Angeles, 1879–1939* (Berkeley, CA, 2006); Julie M. Weise, *Corazón de Dixie: Mexicanos in the U.S. South since 1910* (Chapel Hill, NC, 2015).

21. Brief for the United States, No. 225, *Gonzales*, 192 U.S. 1 (n.d.), 37–38, 41, 57–58, 55–60.

22. Appellant's Brief, *Gonzales*, 192 U.S. 1, 32, 3–4.

23. Ibid., 4–5, 3, 6–7, 13–21, 28, 32; Brief for Plaintiffs in Error, No. 507, *Downes*, 182 U.S. 244 (2 Jan. 1901), 84, 82, 85–91, 93; Opening Argument of Mr. Coudert, *Downes*, 182 U.S. 244 (8 Jan. 1901), 9, 41–42. On the changing substance and prominence of international law and its relationship to U.S. empire, see Benjamin Allen Coates, *Legalist Empire: International Law and American Foreign Relations in the Early Twentieth Century* (Oxford, 2016).

24. Appellant's Brief, *Gonzales*, 192 U.S. 1, 12, 15, 10, 13–27, 36–39. On judicial paternalism, see Michael Grossberg, *Governing the Hearth: Law and Family in Nineteenth-Century America* (Chapel Hill, NC, 1985). *Rapto* was not part of U.S. law, but as Grossberg recounts, U.S. justices had come of age in a legal culture that enforced a civil action for breach of contract to marry.

25. Appellant's Brief, *Gonzales*, 192 U.S. 1, 18–28; Slaughter-House Cases, 83 U.S. 36 (1873); Minor v. Happersett, 88 U.S. 162 (1875); Civil Rights Cases, 109 U.S. 3 (1883); Wong Wing v. United States, 163 U.S. 228 (1896); United States v. Wong Kim Ark, 169 U.S. 649 (1898); Plessy v. Ferguson, 163 U.S. 537 (1896); Giles v. Harris, 189 U.S. 475 (1903); Rebecca J. Scott, "Public Rights, Social Equality, and the Conceptual Roots of the *Plessy* Challenge," *Michigan Law Review* 106 (Mar. 2008): 777–804; Richard H. Pildes, "Democracy, Anti-Democracy, and the Canon," *Constitutional Commentary* 17 (Summer 2000): 295–319; Pamela Brandwein, *Rethinking the Judicial Settlement of Reconstruction* (Cambridge, 2011).

26. Appellant's Brief, *Gonzales*, 192 U.S. 1, 6, 35–36, 33–34, 1–7, 22–24, 27–28, 37. See also Argument of Coudert, *Gonzales*, 51–53, 62–65; Brandwein, *Rethinking the Judicial Settlement* .

27. Appellant's Brief, *Gonzales*, 192 U.S. 1, 6, 38–39, 25, 28–32; Scott v. Sanford, 60 U.S. 393 (1857); Elk v. Wilkins, 112 U.S. 94 (1884); Dawes Act, 24 Stat. 388 (1887); Patrick Weil, *How to Be French: Nationality in the Making*, trans. Catherine Porter (Durham, NC, 2008).

28. Brief Filed by … Federico Degetau, *Gonzales*, 192 U.S. 1, 33. In "Evaluating Legality: Toward a Cultural Approach to the Study of Law and Social Change,"

Law & Society Review 37 (June 2003): 323–368, Idit Kostiner observes that the activists she studied initially saw law as an instrumental means both to achieve particular material ends and to empower marginalized people; most attempted to alter societal views more broadly only after discovering the limits of the former strategies. By contrast, in following his vision of paternalistic leadership, Degetau focused on instrumentalism and changing the views of the U.S. public but did not seek to empower marginalized people by bringing them to law.

29. Treaty of Peace between the United States of America and the Kingdom of Spain, 10 Dec. 1898, 30 Stat. 1754, 1759; Brief Filed by . . . Federico Degetau, *Gonzales*, 192 U.S. 1, 30, 18, 19–22, 27–29, 36. Degetau's brief gives the source of the nested quotation as "Zamora y Coronado, 'Legislación Ultramarina,' Tomo I, p. 255–257."

30. Brief Filed by . . . Federico Degetau, *Gonzales*, 192 U.S. 1, 28, 19–20, 33–36. Degetau's brief gives the source of the quotation as "Foreign Relations of the United States, 1898. Correspondence with the United States Peace Commissioners, p. 961."

31. Brief Filed by . . . Federico Degetau, *Gonzales*, 192 U.S. 1, 25–26. The source of the nested quotation is Degetau's own certificate.

32. Ibid., 21–22, 33–34, 37–41; Foraker Act, sec. 14, 31 Stat. 77, 80 (1900).

33. U.S. Constitution, am. XIV, sec. 1; Brief Filed by . . . Federico Degetau, *Gonzales*, 192 U.S. 1, 13, 12, 34. The source of the nested quotations is the *Slaughter-House Cases*, 83 U.S. 36, 77 (1873).

34. Brief Filed by . . . Federico Degetau, *Gonzales*, 192 U.S. 1, 39, 43.

35. Pedro García Olivieri, Letter to Editor, "Puerto Rico en la Corte Suprema Nacional," *Puerto Rico Herald*, 12 Dec. 1903, 1127 ("por cortesía"; "por su derecho"). According to War Department law officer Charles Magoon, insular residents could not be considered aliens following the decision to preempt Degetau's passport test case by providing them consular protection. See MD NARA 350/5A/5507-1.

36. Argument of Coudert, *Gonzales*, 192 U.S. 1, 54–55, 49–56.

37. Ibid.; Annex 1 to Protocol No. 22, 10 Dec. 1898, in *A Treaty of Peace between the United States and Spain: Message from the President of the United States, Transmitting a Treaty of Peace between the United States and Spain, Signed at the City of Paris, on December 10, 1898*, S. Doc. No. 62, pt. 2, 55th Cong., 3d sess. (1899), 261–262.

38. *Gonzales*, 192 U.S., at 12, 10, 8–15; "Porto Ricans as 'Aliens,'" *Chautauquan* 36 (Dec. 1902): 233. Multiple factors that the Court cited as indicating integration of Puerto Rico into the United States did not apply to U.S.–Philippines relations. Philippines Organic Act of 1902, 32 Stat. 691.

39. *Gonzales*, 192 U.S., at 12.

40. On courts and constitutional outliers, see Thomas M. Keck, "Party Politics or Judicial Independence? The Regime Politics Literature Hits the Law Schools," *Law & Social Inquiry* 32 (2007): 528; Keith E. Whittington, "Once More unto the Breach: PostBehavioralist Approaches to Judicial Politics," *Law & Social Inquiry* 25 (2000): 613; Michael J. Klarman, *From the Closet to the Altar: Courts, Backlash, and the Struggle for Same-Sex Marriage* (Oxford, 2012), 205.

41. F. R. Coudert to Clarence Edwards, 14 Dec. 1909, MD NARA 350/5A/2333-3; "The Week," *Nation*, 7 Jan. 1904, 2; D. Collazo, Letter to Editor, "Nationality of Porto Ricans," *New York Times*, 13 Sept. 1904, 8. I thank Christina Ponsa for

alerting me to Collazo's letter. See Burnett, "'They Say I Am Not an American,'" 660, 670, 710.

Neal Kumar Katyal and Thomas P. Schmidt use the term "generative avoidance" to describe the phenomenon of reserving constitutional questions in ways that create new constitutional norms, in "Active Avoidance: The Modern Supreme Court and Legal Change," *Harvard Law Review* 128 (2015): 2109–2165. Keith Whittington, *Political Foundation of Judicial Supremacy* (Princeton, NJ, 2007), 72, suggests that general articulations of constitutional visions by the Supreme Court may at times be of more moment than the specific judgments the Court issues. William J. Novak, "The Myth of the 'Weak' American State," *American Historical Review* 113 (June 2007): 767–768, observes that law is a creative source of power that operates both within and beyond courts. But Cass Sunstein, "Beyond Judicial Minimalism," *Tulsa Law Review* 43 (2008): 839, implicitly places judicially minimalistic reasoning and holdings in opposition to judicial activism.

Some early twentieth-century legal scholars included *Gonzales* among the *Insular Cases*: Pedro Capó Rodríguez, "The Relations between the United States and Porto Rico," *American Journal of International Law* 13 (1919): 483–525; Quincy Wright, "Treaties and the Constitutional Separation of Powers in the United States," *American Journal of International Law* 12 (1918): 64–95. Many modern scholars would agree that it belongs there. See Bartholomew H. Sparrow, *The* Insular Cases *and the Emergence of American Empire* (Lawrence, KS, 2006); Rivera Ramos, *Legal Construction of Identity*; Christina Duffy Burnett, "A Note on the *Insular Cases*," in *Foreign in a Domestic Sense: Puerto Rico, American Expansion, and the Constitution*, ed. Christine Duffy Burnett and Burke Marshall (Durham, NC, 2001), 389–392.

On women, dependency, and citizenship, see Adam Winkler, "A Revolution Too Soon: Woman Suffragists and the 'Living Constitution,'" *New York University Law Review* 76 (Nov. 2001): 1456–1526; Linda Kerber, *No Constitutional Right to Be Ladies: Women and the Obligations of Citizenship* (New York, 1998); Nancy F. Cott, *Public Vows: A History of Marriage and the Nation* (Cambridge, MA, 2000); Nancy F. Cott, "Marriage and Women's Citizenship in the United States, 1830–1934," *American Historical Review* 103 (Dec. 1998): 1440–1474; Linda K. Kerber, "Toward a History of Statelessness in America," *American Quarterly* 57 (2005): 728–749; Martha S. Jones, *"All Bound Up Together": The Woman Question in African-American Public Culture, 1830–1900* (Chapel Hill, NC, 2007).

42. See, for example, Paul Charlton, Memorandum Regarding Naturalization of Residents of the Philippine Islands, with draft of proposed bill, 13 Feb. 1906, MD NARA 350/5A/5507-6. The challenge to individual honor mattered because honor was a measure of conformity with associated codes of conduct and a measure of hierarchical social standing capable of influencing other criteria, such as race, wealth, femininity, manliness, and authority. The failed attempt to secure citizenship for all Puerto Ricans mattered for a similar reason. Loyalty to one's people and principles as well as to one's associates demonstrated honor and was required by it. On these aspects of honor in the United States, see Wyatt-Brown, *Southern Honor*; Nicole Etcheson, "Manliness and the Political Culture of the Old Northwest, 1790–1860," *Journal of the Early Republic* 15 (Spring 1995): 59–77; Kenneth S. Greenberg, *Honor and Slavery: Lies, Duels, Noses, Masks, Dressing as a Woman, Gifts, Strangers, Humanitarianism, Death, Slave Rebellions, the Proslavery Argument, Baseball, Hunting, and Gambling in the Old South*

(Princeton, NJ, 1996); Ariela J. Gross, *Double Character: Slavery and Mastery in the Antebellum Southern Courtroom* (Princeton, NJ, 2000). On honor in Latin America, see Johnson and Lipsett-Rivera, *Faces of Honor*; Caulfield, Chambers, and Putnam, *Honor, Status and Law*.

43. "Porto Ricans Not Aliens," 5 Jan. 1904; "Are Not Citizens," *Star* (Reynoldsville, PA), 15 Oct. 1902, 6; Collazo, "Nationality of Porto Ricans"; "The Forgotten Island,"*Commoner* (Lincoln, NE), 23 June 1905, 14; "Every Encroachment Important," *Commoner* (Lincoln, NE), 30 Sept. 1904, 3; State of New York Certificate and Record of Birth of Eva Gonzalez Vinals, 8 Sept. 1902, No. 35785, NYCMA; Transcript of Record, *Gonzales*, 192 U.S. 1, 4. A search of the New York Municipal records has not revealed a marriage certificate. The birth certificate used the anglicized "Vinals."

44. Adolfo Vinals, Letter to Editor, "Commerce with Latin America," *New York Tribune*, 19 Feb. 1905, 7; N. *Bolet-Peraza, Memoratissimus* (n.p., 1907?), 52–53; *Trow's General Directory of the Boroughs of Manhattan and Bronx City of New York for the Year Ending August 1, 1910*, vol. 123 (New York, 1909), 1513, Ancestry.com; *The Trow (Formerly Wilson's) Copartnership and Corporation Directory of the Boroughs of Manhattan and the Bronx City of New York* (New York, Mar. 1909), 634; 1910 Census I/12/619/13A/Manhattan, NY.

45. Isabel Gonzalez, Letter to Editor, "'Citizenship for Porto Ricans,'" *New-York Daily Tribune*, 25 Nov. 1906, 13; Luis Sánchez Morales, "El famoso caso de ciudadanía de Isabel Gonzalez," *Almanaque puertorriqueño asenjo* (San Juan, PR, 1937), 97 ("conejillo de Indios"); 1915 Census 8/15/New York, NY/48; 1904 Census 34/19; 1904 Census 35/55; Death Certificate of Maria Vinal, 29 May 1905, NYCMA Richmond/rn 573/1322798, https://familysearch.org/ark:/61903/1:1:2W59-YSF; 1910 Census 1/619/12/13A/Manhattan, NY; 1915 Census 8/19/New York/48; Acta de Matrimonio de Adolfo Viñals Jiminez y Maria Luisa Pacheco Santiago; List 2 of Manifest for SS *Caracas*, 21 Mar. 1910, PCLVANY T715/1433; 1910 Census 1/1638/35/9A/Bronx, NY; Juan F. Torres Hinkson, Registration of Puerto Rican Citinez [*sic*], American Consulate, Puerto Plata, DR, 8 Jan. 1908, DC NARA, RG 59, U.S. Consular Registration Certificates, 1907–1918, Certificate Number: 4001-4500, no. 4126, Ancestry.com; Manifest of SS *Montserrat*, 11 Dec. 1902, PCLVANY T715/1387; Birth Record of Jose Torres y Davila, 17 Dec. 1902, Registro Civil, 1805–2001, Departamento de Salud de Puerto Rico, municipio de Bayamón, volumen de nacimientos abr. 1894–feb. 1904/398, https://familysearch.org/pal:/MM9.3.1/TH-1-159372-85925 5-83?cc=1682798; Acta de Nacimiento de Sabina Concepción Feliciano Davila, 29 Mar. 1908, Registro Civil, 1805–2001, Departamento de Salud de Puerto Rico, municipio de Bayamón, volumen de nacimientos 1907–1908, 272, https://familysearch.org/ark:/61903/1:1:QV1Y-2JYZ; 1920 Census PR/San Juan/Santurce/24/28; Marriage Certificate of Juan Frank Torres and Isabel Gonzalez, NYCMA Manhattan/cn 28024/1614231, https://familysearch.org/ark:/61903/1:1:24QZ-6FH; 1915 Census 18/23/New York/11.

46. Gonzalez to Degetau, 10 Apr. 1904 ("Una de las cosas por que vine yo á los Estados Unidos fue por la educación de una hermanita que hoy tengo á mi lado, y que desearía poner en uno de esos Colegios de pobres en los que están poniendo muchos de nuestros paisanos"); Gonzalez to Degetau, 5 Feb. 1903.

47. Isabel Gonzales, "What Porto Rico Demands," *New York Times*, 20 Dec. 1905, 10; Isabel Gonzalez, "Sauce for Goose and Gander," *New York Times*, 5 Aug. 1905, 6.

Like Coudert, Gonzalez drew lessons from other colonial experiences, and like
Degetau she complained that the United States treated civilized Puerto Ricans
with less dignity than other empires treated their natives. Isabel Gonzalez, "Where
England Shows Tact," *New York Times*, 3 Sept. 1905. When lobbying for a Puerto
Rican naturalization bill in 1906, secretary of war and future president William
Howard Taft characterized the Court as classifying Puerto Ricans as "neither
citizens ... nor aliens." See correspondence collected at MD NARA 350/5A/5507-
11. Although Collazo later wrote that "'Isabel Gonzales' was only a penname" for
himself, the same article quoted a letter from the secretary of Boston's Anti-
Imperialist League that investigated the matter and labeled Gonzalez a separate
and "valuable correspondent." Porto Rican Exile, "Correo." For a discussion of
narratives of Puerto Rican women's rescue as justification for colonial projects, see,
for example, Laura Briggs, *Reproducing Empire: Race, Sex, Science, and U.S.
Imperialism in Puerto Rico* (Berkeley, CA, 2002), 15.

48. Collazo, "Nationality of Porto Ricans"; D. Collazo, Letter to Editor, "The Plight of
Porto Rico," *New York Times*, 24 Oct. 1904, 8.

49. Manuel Rossy to Federico Degetau, 26 Jan. 1904, CIHCAM 4/VIII/14 ("Si el
Tribunal Supremo pudiera declarar ciudadanos americanos á los habitantes de un
país por el mero hecho de la ... anexión"; "tendrían que conceder la ciudadanía [a]
cualquier advenedizo ó enemigo que por azares de la vida hubiese necesidad de
anexar ó conquistar"; "no formarían una verdadera nación, porque llevarían dentro
de sí los gérmenes destructores de su propia soberanía"); *Informe de los delegados
del Partido Republicano de Puerto Rico ante la Convención Nacional Republicana
celebrada en Chicago, en 21 de junio de 1904* ([San Juan?], PR, 1904), CIHCAM 6/
L8; [Federico Degetau] to Joseph Babcock, 30 May 1904, CIHCAM 5/I/35. For
examples of Puerto Rican media coverage of *Gonzales*, see "Puerto Ricans
Admitted," *Puerto Rico Herald*, 9 Jan. 1904, 1188; "Puerto Rico ante la Corte
Suprema," *Puerto Rico Herald*, 9 Jan. 1904, 1191; "Porto Ricans Not Aliens," *San
Juan News*, 6 Jan. 1904, 1. On Federales' agreement that Congress and not the
courts was the only way to gain citizenship, see "El señor Degetau dio una
conferencia en Ponce," *La Democracia*, 1 Aug. 1904, 2; "Conferencia del Sr.
Degetau," *La Democracia*, 8 July 1904, 1.

50. Degetau to Moscoso, 2 Oct. 1903 ("mantenernos como una dependencia
indefinidamente"; "el Tribunál [sic] Supremo nos declara ciudadanos
americanos"); "Puerto Ricans Admitted"; W. Wheelock to Federico Degetau, 14
Jan. 1904, CIHCAM 4/VIII/11; Federico Degetau, *The Constitution and the Flag in
Porto Rico: Why the Porto Ricans Are Proud of Their Regiment: Speech of Hon.
Federico Degetau of Porto Rico in the House of Representatives, Thursday, January
19, 1905* (Washington, DC, 1905), CIHCAM 6/L10; *Informe de los delegados*, 4–
12; Manuel Rossy to Federico Degetau, 2 Dec. 1903, CIHCAM 4/VII/3; title
unknown, *Evening Star*, 11 Dec. 1903, CIHCAM 18/L1; José de [?]man
[Semilez?] to Federico Degetau, 7 Jan. 190[4], CIHCAM 3/V/4; "Recognition of
Porto Rico," *Washington Post*, 12 Dec. 1903, 3; "Chicago Secures Big
Convention," *Chicago Daily*, 13 Dec. 1903, 1; Draft, [Federico Degetau] to Mr.
Henry, [June 1904], CIHCAM 5/II/8; Franklin Mooney to Federico Degetau, 2 June
1904, CIHCAM 5/II/5; Hamilton Holt to Federico Degetau, 25 Feb. 1904,
CIHCAM 4/VIII/40; W. W. Wheelock to Federico Degetau, 26 Feb. 1904,

CIHCAM 4/VIII/41; "Delegate from Porto Rico," *New York Times*, 3 Feb. 1904, 6; H.R. 11592 (2 Feb. 1904); 38 Cong. Rec. 1543, [Bills] 307; 39 Cong. Rec. [Bills], 87.

51. "Habla Degetau," *La Democracia*, 24 Aug. 1904, 5 ("colocó á Puerto Rico … *on the colonial basis*"; "Territorio indio"; "incluyendo … indios"); platform of National Republican Party, quoted in "Párrafos del Manifiesto del señor Degetau," *La Democracia*, 2 Sept. 1904, 4 ("Hemos organizado el gobierno de Puerto-Rico y sus habitantes ahora gozan de paz, libertad, orden y prosperidad"); *Informe de los delegados*, 19–21; "D. Federico Degetau y González," *La Democracia*, 24 June 1904, 2; "Platform of Republican Party, 1904," in *Republican Campaign Text-Book* (Milwaukee, 1904), 485–488.

52. "Párrafos" ("que 'antes de gobernarnos debemos probar que sabemos hacerlo'"; "luchando por nuestra ciudadanía"); A. Navarrete to Federico Degetau, 30 Sept. 1904, CIHCAM 5/II/17; Negrón Portillo, *Cuadrillas anexionistas*, 16–17; "Puerto Rican Commissioners Accompanying General Miles's Army" (photograph), *Harper's Weekly*, 13 Aug. 1898, 800; *Second Annual Report of the Governor of Porto Rico, Covering the Period from May 1, 1901, to July 1, 1902* (Washington, DC, 1902), 86; Harold J. Lidin, *History of the Puerto Rican Independence Movement*, vol. 1 (Hato Rey, PR, 1981); "Candidatura republicana," *La Democracia*, 19 Sept. 1904, 1; "Porto Rico Nominations," *Washington Post*, 11 Oct. 1904, 4.

53. "Candiditos [*sic*] á Washington," *La Democracia*, 6 July 1904, 1; Pedro A. Cabán, *Constructing a Colonial People: Puerto Rico and the United States, 1898–1932* (Boulder, CO, 1999), 182–187; "Asamblea para constituir la Unión de Puerto Rico," *Puerto Rico Herald*, 5 Mar. 1904, 1317; "De cómo puede hacerse la unión," *Puerto Rico Herald*, 9 Jan. 1904, 1191; "Ponce viene á 'la Unión,'" *La Democracia*, 1 Aug. 1904, 1.

54. Fernando Bayrón Toro, *Elecciones y partidos políticos de Puerto Rico* (1809–1976) (Mayagüez, PR, 1977), 125–126; L. David Roper, "Composition of Congress since 1867" (2009?), www.roperld.com/personal/politics/congress.htm.

55. Brief for Appellant, No. 1504, *Rodriguez*, 25 App. D.C. 121 (n.d.), CIHCAM 6/VI/33; Transcript of Record, No. 1504, *Rodriguez*, 25 App. D.C. 121, 7, 3–11; Degetau, *The Constitution and the Flag in Porto Rico*; Brief for Appellees, No. 1504, *Rodriguez*, 25 App. D.C. 121 (4 Feb. 1905), 11–13, CIHCAM 6/VI/34. The secretary of state was a lawyer. Merrill E. Gates, ed., *Men of Mark in America*, vol. 1 (n.p., 1905), 274.

56. Brief for Appellant, *Rodriguez*, 25 App. D.C. 121; Rule 5 of the Civil Service Commission, quoted in "Porto Rican Eligible," *Washington Post*, 8 Mar. 1905, 6; "The Legal Record," *Washington Post*, 8 Feb. 1905, 9; *Rodriguez*, 25 App. D.C. 121 (1905). The brief gives as the respective sources of the nested quotations the Constitution's preamble and "Monsieur de Cogordan, in his book on French Nationality." Degetau's vision of universal U.S. citizenship seemingly encompassed Filipinos as well as Puerto Ricans.

57. Passport Application of Ana Moreno Viuda de Degetau, 29 Apr. 1914, PAHIPRP 1913–1914/14/1103; William Jennings Bryan et al., *El paso de Mr. Bryan por San Juan* (n.p., 1910), 24–25 ("la alta distinción recibida del Tribunal Supremo de los Estados Unidos"; "la definición de nuestro *status* como ciudadanos americanos"); [Federico Degetau] to Pedro Salazar, 16 June 1909, CIHCAM 10/II/26; Draft, Federico Degetau to Julio Gonzalez Pola, 6 Dec. 1910, CIHCAM 5/IV/15. Degetau initially succeeded but ultimately failed to use

litigation to expand his political movement, garner support for it, and leverage his other political tactics. See John D. Skrentny, "Law and the American State," *Annual Review of Sociology* 32 (2006): 231, suggesting the possibility of these benefits of litigation.

RECONSTRUCTING PUERTO RICO, 1904–1909

1. William R. Merriam, *Census Reports*, vol. 1 (Washington, DC, 1901), xxii; *Thirteenth Census of the United States Taken in the Year 1910: Abstract of the Census* (Washington, DC, 1913), 21; S. N. D. North, *Population of Oklahoma and Indian Territory 1907* (Washington, DC, 1907), 7. In 1907 Oklahoma became a state, with a census-recorded population that was by then somewhat larger than that of Puerto Rico.
2. For work describing and theorizing the slow emergence of powerful, autonomous agencies from a U.S. state largely constituted by political parties and courts, see Stephen Skowronek, *Building a New American State: The Expansion of National Administrative Capacities, 1877–1920* (New York, 1982). See also Theda Skocpol, *Protecting Soldiers and Mothers: The Political Origins of Social Policy in the United States* (Cambridge, MA, 1993); Peter H. Argersinger, "The Transformation of American Politics: Political Institutions and Public Policy, 1865–1910," in *Contesting Democracy: Substance and Structure in American Political* History, *1775–2000*, ed. Byrn E. Shafer and Anthony J. Badger (Lawrence, KS, 2001).
3. Samuel Gompers, "President Gompers in Porto Rico," *American Federationist*, Apr. 1904, 293–294; David Montgomery, "Workers' Movements in the United States Confront Imperialism: The Progressive Era Experience," *Journal of the Gilded Age and Progressive Era* 7 (Jan. 2008): 14; Carlos Sanabria, "Samuel Gompers and the American Federation of Labor in Puerto Rico," *Centro Journal* 17 (Spring 2005): 140–161.
4. Samuel Gompers, "President Gompers in Porto Rico," *American Federationist*, Apr. 1904, 293–294; Elihu Root to Lyman Abbott, n.d., quoted in Dana G. Munro, *Intervention and Dollar Diplomacy in the Caribbean 1900–1921* (Princeton, NJ, 1964), 113, 54–63, 101–106; Montgomery, "Workers' Movements," 14; David Montgomery, *The Fall of the House of Labor: The Workplace, the State, and American Labor Activism, 1865–1925* (New York, 1987), 5–6; Rebecca J. Scott, *Degrees of Freedom: Louisiana and Cuba after Slavery* (Cambridge, MA, 2005), 213–214. On the long history of U.S. involvement in trans-Panama transportation projects, including "the creation of the Panama Canal Zone – a colony in everything but name," see also Aims McGuinness, *Path of Empire: Panama and the California Gold Rush* (Ithaca, NY, 2008), 195.
5. *Report of Proceedings of the Twenty-Fifth Annual Convention of the American Federation of Labor* (Washington, DC, 1905), 17, quoted in Montgomery, "Workers' Movements," 20–21; Joseph Bedford, "Samuel Gompers and the Caribbean: The AFL, Cuba, and Puerto Rico," *Labor's Heritage* 6, no. 4 (1995): 10–11, 22–23; Samuel Gompers to Santiago Iglesias, 16 Oct. 1907, CDO:1; [Samuel Gompers?], [title unknown], *American Federationist* 15 (Dec. 1908): 1070, CDO:1.

6. Preamble, IWW Constitution, *Constitution and By-Law of Industrial Workers of the World Adopted Chicago 1905* (Chicago, 1905), 3; Montgomery, "Workers' Movements," 8, 15, 26; Marc Karson, *American Labor Unions and Politics, 1900–1918* (Boston, 1958), 153–159, 174; Philip S. Foner, *History of the Labor Movement in the United States*, vol. 4: *The Industrial Workers of the World, 1905–1917* (New York, 1973 [1965]), 13–39, 133–134; Montgomery, "Workers' Movements," 26; Copy, Samuel Gompers to Santiago Iglesias, 11 Jan. 1906, CDO:1; Montgomery, *Fall of the House of Labor*, 6.

7. Miles Galvin, *The Organized Labor Movement in Puerto Rico* (London, 1979), 51–52, 72–74; Kelvin A. Santiago-Valles, *"Subject People" and Colonial Discourses: Economic Transformation and Social Disorder in Puerto Rico, 1898–1947* (Albany, NY, 1994), 53–56, 61; Miles Galvin, "II: The Organized Labor Movement and Nationalism," *Latin American Perspectives* 3 (Summer 1976): 25; Robert C. McGreevey, "Borderline Citizens: Puerto Ricans and the Politics of Migration, Race, and Empire, 1898–1948, PhD diss., Brandeis University, 2008, 124–127; Ileana M. Rodríguez-Silva, *Silencing Race: Disentangling Blackness, Colonialism, and National Identities in Puerto Rico* (New York, 2012), 7, 84, 192–193, 218–219, 221; Luis A Figueroa, *Sugar, Slavery, and Freedom in Nineteenth-Century Puerto Rico* (Chapel Hill, NC, 2005), 41–42; Sen. Doc. No. 79, 57th Cong., 1st sess., *First Annual Report of Charles H. Allen, Governor of Porto Rico* (1901), 39–41. After resigning the governorship in 1901, Allen joined the Morgan banking empire and became president of the American Sugar Refining Company, known as the Sugar Trust because of its industry dominance. See "Dictation," *Cincinnati Enquirer*, 31 Mar. 1914; César J. Ayala, *American Sugar Kingdom: The Plantation Economy of the Spanish Caribbean, 1898–1934* (Chapel Hill, NC, 1999), 37–39.
   Female wage labor expanded in early twentieth-century Puerto Rico. Women's participation in organized labor would swell the union ranks, while their exclusion would expand the pool of unorganized workers to whom employers could turn during strikes. See Juan Ángel Silén, *Apuntes para la historia del movimiento obrero puertorriqueño* (San Juan, PR, 1978), 63; Yamila Azize, *La mujer en la lucha* (Río Piedras, PR, 1985), 56–58, 62.

8. Santiago-Valles, *"Subject People,"* 28–29; Laird W. Bergard, *Coffee and the Growth of Agrarian Capitalism in Nineteenth-Century Puerto Rico* (Princeton, NJ, 1983), 204–211; Teresita A. Levy, "The History of Tobacco Cultivation in Puerto Rico, 1899–1940," PhD diss., City University of New York, 2007, 54; Galvin, *Organized Labor Movement*, 32; Miles Galvin, "The Early Development of the Organized Labor Movement in Puerto Rico," *Latin American Perspectives* 3 (Summer 1976): 18, 24; Ayala, *American Sugar Kingdom*, 148–182. James L. Dietz, *Economic History of Puerto Rico: Institutional Change and Capitalist Development* (Princeton, NJ, 1986), 99–100; Pedro A. Cabán, *Constructing a Colonial People: Puerto Rico and the United States, 1898–1932* (Boulder, CO, 1999), 19; Santiago-Valles, *"Subject People,"* 29; Galvin, "Organized Labor Movement and Nationalism," 25; Leo S. Rowe, *The United States and Porto Rico* (New York, 1904), 259.

9. Samuel Gompers, "President Gompers Speaks to Workingmen," *American Federationist*, Apr. 1904, 304–305; Samuel Gompers, "The Negro in the AF of L," *American Federationist*, Jan. 1911, 34–36, quoted in McGreevey, "Borderline Citizens," 119–120; Montgomery, "Workers' Movements," 14; Samuel Gompers,

"President Gompers in Porto Rico," *American Federationist*, Apr. 1904, 295; William H. Hunt, *Third Annual Report of the Governor of Porto Rico, Covering the Period from July 1, 1902, to June 30, 1903* (Washington, DC, 1903), 9–15, 27, 31, 41–42; Juan Carreras, *Santiago Iglesias Pantín: Su vida, su obra, su pensamiento (datos biográficos)* (San Juan, PR, 1965), 122–123; Rodríguez-Silva, *Silencing Race*, 181–182; Samuel Gompers, "Talks on Labor," *American Federationist*, May 1904, 412–417; Samuel Gompers, Address, "Talks on Labor," *American Federationist*, Apr. 1904, 415; Sanabria, "Samuel Gompers," 151–152.

10. Gompers, "Talks on Labor," May 1904, 413, quoted in McGreevey, "Borderline Citizens," 117; *Report of Proceedings of the Twenty-Fourth Annual Convention of the American Federation of Labor* (Washington, DC, 1904), 229–230, 140, 183; Gompers, "Talks on Labor," 412–417; Santiago-Valles, *"Subject People,"* 53–56; ; *Report of Proceedings of the Twenty-Sixth Annual Convention of the American Federation of Labor* (Washington, DC, 1906), 92; *Report of Proceedings of the Twenty-Ninth Annual Convention of the American Federation of Labor* (Washington, DC, 1909), 186, 218; Bedford, "Gompers and the Caribbean"; Samuel Gompers, "Report of President Samuel Gompers to the Twenty-Fifth Annual Convent[i]on of the American Federation of Labor, at Pittsburg, Pennsylvania," *American Federationist* 12 (Dec. 1905): 935; Santiago Iglesias, "Las emigraciones de trabajadores: La huelga general," *Unión Obrera*, 1 Oct. 1907, 2, CDO:1; Ayala, *American Sugar Kingdom*, 148–182; Copy, "Visita al Hon. Governador R. H. Post," *Boletín Mercantil*, 8 Jan. 1909, CDO:1. The massive hurricane of 1899 and soil deterioration also contributed to the decline in the Puerto Rican coffee industry. See Bergard, *Coffee*, 204–211. On the chupacabra and empire, see Lauren Derby, "Imperial Secrets: Vampires and Nationhood in Puerto Rico," *Past and Present* 199, supplement 3 (Aug. 2008): 290–312.

11. Sanabria, "Samuel Gompers," 149–150; Galvin, *Organized Labor Movement*, 61, 72–73; Galvin, "Organized Labor Movement and Nationalism," 24; *Twenty-Fourth Annual Convention of the American Federation of Labor*, 21.

12. *Report of Proceedings of the Twenty-Seventh Annual Convention of the American Federation of Labor* (Washington, DC, 1907), 92, 26; Gompers, "Talks on Labor," May 1904, 412–417; *Twenty-Fourth Annual Convention of the American Federation of Labor*, 21, 129, 229–230; *Twenty-Fifth Annual Convention of the American Federation of Labor*, 17, 187; Federación Libre to Theodore Roosevelt, 21 Nov. 1906, CDO:1; Galvin, "Early Development," 28; *Twenty-Sixth Annual Convention of the American Federation of Labor*, 92, 205–206, 208; Copy, Samuel Gompers to Henry Allen Cooper, 22 Jan. 1906, CDO:1; *Hearing before the Committee on Pacific Islands and Porto Rico, United States Senate*, 6 Feb. 1906; Ángel Silén, *Apuntes para la historia*, 65. The AFL soon reaffirmed its support for citizenship for Puerto Ricans. See *Twenty-Sixth Annual Convention of the American Federation of Labor*, 206.

13. *Inhabitants of Porto Rico to Be Citizens of the United States*, S. Rep. No. 2746, 20 Apr. 1906, 2, 6; *Message from the President of the United States Relative to His Recent Visit to the Island of Porto Rico*, S. Doc. No. 135, 59th Cong., 2d sess. (1906), 5; *American Citizenship for Inhabitants of Porto Rico*, H.R. Rep. No. 4215, 59th Cong., 1st sess., 16 May 1906.

14. *Inhabitants of Porto Rico to Be Citizens of the United States*, 2, 6; *American Citizenship for Inhabitants of Porto Rico*, 2; *War Department Annual Reports*, *1911*, vol. 1 (Washington, DC, 1912), 44; Edward E. Hale, "The Man without a Country," *Atlantic Monthly* 12 (Dec. 1863): 665–680; *Message from the President Relative to Porto Rico*, 5. Even as the literary reference obscured the extent to which U.S. officials recognized that rights alone did not exhaust the consequentiality of citizenship, its dislocation into the past, the sentimental, and the fictional also masked the denial of rights and racial disparagement behind Puerto Ricans' current position. But to mask was not to eliminate. Both mechanisms are present in Hale's story, for those inclined to look. Though the pro-expansion story insists on the essential goodness, hence innocence, of the United States, it is the coercive federal denial of freedom of movement that sustains the plot. Conversely, the poignancy of the story rests on the exiled protagonist's being in all other ways a full citizen. His whiteness is thus presumed, which is to say, invisible, except when expressly contrasted with Africans who have never set foot in the Americas. So too is his manhood. Nancy F. Cott captures the identity-bestowing aspect of citizenship by noting that both it and marriage confer "an identity that may have deep personal and psychological dimensions at the same time that it expresses belonging." See Cott, "Marriage and Women's Citizenship in the United States, 1830–1934," *American Historical Review* 103 (Dec. 1998): 1440. To adapt Robert W. Gordon's terms, citizenship is here "constitutive of consciousness." Gordon, "Critical Legal Histories," *Stanford Law Review* 36 (1984): 109.

    Peggy McIntosh's "White Privilege and Male Privilege: A Personal Account of Coming to See Correspondences through Work in Women's Studies," Working Paper 189, Wellesley Center for Research on Women, 1988, is a foundational statement on unacknowledged white privilege. See also David R. Roediger, "Critical Studies of Whiteness, USA: Origins and Arguments," *Theoria: A Journal of Social and Political Theory*, no. 98 (Dec. 2001): 72–98. On the relative unimportance of the slavery theme to Hale's "The Man Without a Country," see Brooke Thomas, *Civic Myths: A Law-and-Literature Approach to Citizenship* (Chapel Hill, NC, 2007), 100.

15. *Hearing*, 6 Feb. 1906, 4–8; *Inhabitants of Porto Rico to Be Citizens of the United States; American Citizenship for Inhabitants of Porto Rico*; "A Porto Rican Plea against Uncle Joseph," *Arizona Republican*, 18 Apr. 1907, 1; "The Speaker and the Porto Ricans," *Baltimore Sun*, 21 Dec. 1906, 4; "Cannon Answers Porto Rico Plea," *Chicago Daily Tribune*, 12 Mar. 1907, 5; "Porto Rico Demand Sentimental," *New York Times*, 18 Apr. 1907, 6.

16. *Twenty-Fourth Annual Convention of the American Federation of Labor*, 229–230; Immigration Act of 1906, secs. 3, 4, 30, 34 Stat. 596, 596, 598, 606–607 (1906); Judge Bernard Shandon Rodey's August and September 1906 correspondence, in DC NARA 46/91/62A-F17/Olmstead Bill (2/2); Richard Campbell to K. N. Harper, 17 Apr. 1909, MD NARA 350/5A/1286-9; NY NARA 29/Porto Rico/San Juan/3. Contrary to colonial administrators' prior interpretation, the statute declared residence in Puerto Rico to be the residence in the United States that naturalization required.

17. McGreevey, "Borderline Citizens," 124–127; Rodríguez-Silva, *Silencing Race*, 183; Ángel Silén, *Apuntes para la historia*, 66; *Twenty-Fifth Annual Convention of the American Federation of Labor*, 16.

18. "El presidente y la huelga de Arecibo," *Unión Obrera*, 29 Aug. 1906, CDO:1; Copy, Samuel Gompers to Santiago Iglesias, 25 May 1906, CDO:1; Copy, Samuel Gompers to Santiago Iglesias, 16 June 1906, CDO:1; Bedford, "Gompers and the Caribbean," 20–22; Laura Weinrib, *The Taming of Free Speech: America's Civil Liberties Compromise* (Cambridge, MA, 2016), 4, 7, 32–35; Rowe, *United States and Porto Rico*, 259; *Twenty-Sixth Annual Convention of the American Federation of Labor*, 16. The AFL endorsed the work stoppage and then contributed thousands of dollars to the cause.

19. "Santiago Iglesias y el Gobierno," [*Unión Obrera*], 9 Oct. 1906, 22, 24 Sept. 1906 CDO:1. On mainland socialists citing the Constitution as their authority to speak in public, see Weinrib, *Taming of Free Speech*, 25.

20. Copy, Samuel Gompers to Eugenio Sanchez Lopez, 26 Nov. 1909, CDO:1; Rodríguez-Silva, *Silencing Race*, 153, 154; Samuel Gompers to Santiago Iglesias, 22 June 1906, SGL 112/879; *Twenty-Ninth Annual Convention of the American Federation of Labor*, 41; *Report of Proceedings of the Twenty-Eighth Annual Convention of the American Federation of Labor* (Washington, DC, 1908), 13; Galvin, *Organized Labor Movement*, 41, 46, 73; Bedford, "Gompers and the Caribbean," 22; Santiago-Valles, "*Subject People,*" 88–89, 107–109; José Trías Monge, *Puerto Rico: The Trials of the Oldest Colony in the World* (New Haven, CT, 1997), 54; Cabán, *Constructing a Colonial People*, 155–159; "Santiago Iglesias y el Gobierno," [*Unión Obrera*], 7, 10, 11, 20, 22, 24 Sept. and 11, 12, 19 Oct. 1906, CDO:1; "El presidente y la huelga"; Samuel Gompers to Santiago Iglesias, 13 July 1906, SGL 113/529; *Boletín Mercantil*, 5 Aug. 1906 and 5 [?] 1906, CDO:1; Ángel Silén, *Apuntes para la historia*, 67–68; Copy, *Boletín Mercantil*, 5, 10, 11, 14, 22 May 1906, CDO:1; Sanabria, "Samuel Gompers," 154–156; "El presidente y la huelga"; Dionicio Nodín Valdés, *Organized Agriculture and the Labor Movement before the UFW: Puerto Rico, Hawai'i, California* (Austin, TX, 2011), 44; Kirwin R. Shaffer, *Black Flag Boricuas: Anarchism, Antiauthoritarianism, and the Left in Puerto Rico, 1897–1921* (Urbana, IL, 2013), 51, 71. For excerpts of primary sources on the relationship between Gompers and Roosevelt, see Janice A. Petterchak, "Conflict of Ideals: Samuel Gompers v. 'Uncle Joe' Cannon," *Journal of the Illinois State Historical Society* 74 (Spring 1981): 31–40.

21. "Santiago Iglesias y Gobierno," 11 Oct. 1906; "Santiago Iglesias y el Gobierno," [*Unión Obrera*], 27 Oct. 1906, CDO:1; Prueba testificial, No. 16, El pueblo de Puerto Rico vs. Aybar, Corte Distrito del Distrito Judicial de Arecibo, PR, 30 Mar. 1908, CDO:1; Samuel Gompers to Santiago Iglesias, 22 June 1906, SGL 112/881; Gompers to Iglesias, 13 July 1906; "Santiago Iglesias y el Gobierno," [*Unión Obrera*], 7, 11, 20, 22, 24 Sept. and 4, 8, 9, 11, 12, 19 Oct. 1906; Samuel Gompers, [title unknown], *American Federationist* 13 (Dec. 1906): 976, CDO:1; "Cuarto congreso obrero," [publication unknown], n.d., CDO:1; "Appel de Los Trabajadores Puertorriqueños," [*Unión Obrera*], 30 Aug. 1906, CDO:1; Bedford, "Gompers and the Caribbean," 22; Copy, *Boletín Mercantil*, 7, 9 Apr., 27, 28 May, 24, 29 Oct., and 22 Nov. 1908, CDO:1; [Congresos Obreros?], ch. "Resoluciones Generales" (1910): 138–139, CDO:1; *Twenty-Eighth Annual Convention of the American Federation of Labor*, 230; Aybar v. People of Porto Rico, 218 U.S. 669 (1910); Santiago Iglesias, Letter to Editor, "Iglesias Explains," *Porto Rico Review*, 16 June 1909, 16, CDO:1; George Ward to Clarence Edwards, 20 Oct. 1909, MD NARA 350/5A/7937-72.

22. Rodríguez-Silva, *Silencing Race*, 182–183, 153, 184; McGreevy, "Borderline Citizens," 130; Bedford, "Gompers and the Caribbean," 19–21; Rodríguez-Silva, *Silencing Race*, 183–184; Shaffer, *Black Flag*, 65–66; Ángel Silén, *Apuntes para la historia*, 67–69; Fernando Bayrón Toro, *Elecciones y partidos políticos de Puerto Rico (1809–1976)* (Mayagüez, PR, 1977), 148–152.

23. Resolution No. 25, in *Twenty-Seventh Annual Convention of the American Federation of Labor*; ibid., 105–106; "Federación Libre de trabajadores de P.R. afiliada a la American Federation of Labor: Exposición hecha al presidente de los Estados Unidos por la delegación obrera de Puerto-Rico," *Unión Obrera*, 17 Dec. 1907, 2, CDO:1; Copy, Santiago Iglesias to Beekman Winthrop, 1908, CDO:1; "A Suggestion to Labor Unions," *Porto Rico Review/Revista de Puerto Rico*, 30 May 1908, 1–2, CDO:1; Santiago Iglesias, "Lo que será Puerto Rico cuando la Federación Libre triunfe: Los trabajadores organizados son los únicos que pueden salvar al país," *Unión Obrera*, 28, 29 Oct. and 2 Nov. 1906, CDO:1; Gervasio L. García and A. G. Quintero Rivera, *Desafío y solidaridad: Breve historia del movimiento obrero puertorriqueño* (San Juan, PR, 1986), 45–47; Ángel Silén, *Apuntes para la historia*, 71; Galvin, *Organized Labor Movement*, 60, 63; "[illegible] convención: El informe de Gompers sobre Pto Rico es muy importante: Pide la ciudadanía," *Unión Obrera*, 23 Nov. 1907, 2, CDO:1; *Twenty-Eighth Annual Convention of the American Federation of Labor*, 12–13; Galvin, "Early Development," 28–29; "Oppose Porto Rico Change," *New York Times*, 28 Mar. 1909, C4; Copy, "Movimiento obrero," *Boletín Mercantil*, 8 Jan. 1909, CDO:1.

24. Collazo, "Metropolitanas," *La Democracia*, 17 Aug. 1908, 2 ("sin nombre y humillada ante el mundo"); D. Collazo, Letter to Editor, "Status of Island Colonies: Denial of Self-Government Would Endanger the Nation," *New York Times*, 12 Aug. 1904, 6; "Collazo en Denver," *La Democracia*, 25 July 1908, 3; D. Collazo, "Metropolitanas," *La Democracia*, 12 Feb. 1909, 2. For Collazo citing his military service in a bid for a post at the customs receivership in the Dominican Republic, see Domingo Collazo to Francis Loomis, 29 Jan. 1905, MD NARA 350/21/Collazo, Domingo.

25. Collazo, "Metropolitanas," *La Democracia*, 18 June 1909 ("sabuesos del imperialismo"); Collazo, "Status of Island Colonies"; D. Collazo, "El mensaje del presidente sobre el conflicto en Puerto-Rico," *La Democracia*, 20 May 1909, 1; Bernardo Vega, *Memoirs of Bernardo Vega: A Contribution to the History of the Puerto Rican Community in New York*, ed. César Andreu Iglesias, trans. Juan Flores (New York, 1984 [1977]), 72–73. Jesse Hoffnung-Garskof, *Racial Migrations: New York City and the Revolutionary Politics of the Spanish Caribbean, 1850–1902* (Princeton, NJ, forthcoming), ch. 4, reminds us that some Antillean *independistas* of color had stronger ties to the Republican Party.

26. D. Collazo, Letter to Editor, "Justice for Porto Rico," *Brooklyn Daily Eagle*, 30 Aug. 1904, 7; Nélida Pérez and Amilcar Tirado, *Boricuas en el norte* (New York, 1987), 7; "Un club de puertorriqueños en Nueva York," *La Democracia*, 3 June 1904, 1; "Sailed for Porto Rico," *Brooklyn Daily Eagle*, 25 Feb. 1906, 40; Corresponsal [Domingo Collazo?], "Desde Nueva York," *La Democracia*, 2, 5, 7, 19 Jan. and 4, 6 Feb. and 23 Mar. and 4, 6 Apr. 1907; D. Collazo, "Desde Nueva York," *La Democracia*, 4 Jan., 25 Feb. and 2 Mar. 1907, 2; D. Collazo, "Carta de New York," *La Democracia*, 11 Mar. 1907, 2; D. Collazo, "Un anónimo y la dignidad humana: Al 'Puertorriqueño-Americano' de 'El Tiempo,'" *La*

Democracia, 20 Jan. 1908, 2; D. Collazo, "Give the Devil His Due," *La Democracia,* 2 May 1908, 1; D. Collazo, "Metropolitanas," *La Democracia,* 5 June, 29 Aug., and 17 Oct. 1908, 27 Sept. 1909, 2; Antonio Blanco Fernández, *Memorias de un indiano* (San Juan, PR, 1922), 70; "Porto Rican Vote Pledged to Bryan," *New York Times,* 1 Aug. 1908, 2. For a sample of the coverage Collazo received as a delegate, see also "No Alliance at Denver," *Times-Picayune,* 2 July 1908, 1 (New Orleans); "Extol Virtues of Cleveland," *Salt Lake Herald,* 2 July 1908, 3; "Collazo en Denver."

27. Collazo, "Un anónimo y la dignidad humana"; D. Collazo, Letter to Editor, "Nationality of Porto Ricans," *New York Times,* 13 Sept. 1904, 8; Lone Wolf v. Hitchcock, 187 U.S. 553, 567 (1903); Giles v. Harris 189 U.S. 475, 488 (1903); "Recent Views of the Fifteenth Amendment," *Harper's Weekly,* 23 May 1903, 873–874; Bartholomew H. Sparrow, *The* Insular Cases *and the Emergence of American Empire* (Lawrence, KS, 2006), 142–211; 1867 Treaty of Cession, 15 Stat. 539, 542 (1867). In *James v. Bowman,* 190 U.S. 127 (1903), the Court declared that the Fifteenth Amendment did not empower Congress to bar private racial discrimination in voting. The decision definitively ended the Court's prior adherence to the contrary rule. *Hodges v. United States,* 203 U.S. 1 (1906), definitively foreclosed the Court's one-time view that the Fourteenth Amendment empowered Congress to bar private racial discrimination when states failed to act. See Pamela Brandwein, *Rethinking the Judicial Settlement of Reconstruction* (Cambridge, 2011), 18, 192–193.

The Court's post-1901 *Insular Cases* decisions brought it closer to an unequivocal embrace of Justice White's proposed doctrine of territorial nonincorporation. Scholars diverge as to when the nonincorporation doctrine became binding constitutional law. Sarah H. Cleveland, "Our International Constitution," *Yale Journal of International Law* 31 (2006): 47, cites *Dorr v. United States,* 195 U.S. 138 (1904), as the key moment. Andrew Kent, in *"Boumediene, Munaf,* and the Supreme Court's Misreading of the Insular Cases," *Iowa Law Review* 97 (2011): 160, chooses *Rasmussen v. United States,* 197 U.S. 516 (1905). Alan Tauber, "The Empire Forgotten: The Application of the Bill of Rights to U.S. Territories," *Case Western Reserve Law Review* 57 (2006): 155, 163, elects *Balzac v. Porto Rico,* 258 U.S. 298 (1922), as does Sparrow, in *Insular Cases,* 5. The case for *Dorr* is too subtle by half, for Justice Henry Brown joined the opinion of the Court despite strongly opposing nonincorporation before and again later in *Rasmussen v. United States,* 197 U.S. 516, 531 (1905) (Brown, J., concurring). While *Rasmussen* was a substantial step toward unequivocal embrace, doubts remained. As Sparrow, *Insular Cases,* 189–190, notes, Justice White sought to ensure his view of the decision by telling the Court reporter, "Now *Downes vs. Bidwell* is the opinion of the Court and I want you to make it so appear." James Bradley Thayer, in *Legal Essays* (Boston, 1908), 171, wrote, notwithstanding *Rasmussen,* that no existing decision "has thoroughly dealt with the matter, or can be regarded as at all final." I join those, such as Sparrow, in *Insular Cases,* 189, for whom *Balzac* culminates the long process by which nonincorporation became legal orthodoxy. Tribal governments were not bound by constitutional jury requirements, per *Talton v. Mayes,* 163 U.S. 376 (1896).

28. D. Collazo, "Metropolitanas," *La Democracia,* 4 Sept. 1908, 2 ("servidumbre colonial"; "en los Territorios se goza"); "Porto Rican Vote Pledged to Bryan"; "Collazo en Denver"; D. Collazo, "Correspondencia de New York," *La*

Democracia, 26 June 1908, 2; Isabel Gonzalez, Letter to Editor, "A Tribute to Governor Winthrop," *New-York Daily Tribune*, 4 Oct. 1906, 6.

29. D. Collazo, "Metropolitanas," *La Democracia*, 29 July 1909 ("horrendo espantajo"), 2 Jan. 1909 ("hegemonía continental"; "Hispano América"), 29 Aug. 1908 ("bajo el protectorado republicano"; "herida de muerte por sus pseudo queredores de Washington"), 9 Jan., 27 Sept., 2 Nov., 2, 3 Dec. 1909; Collazo, "Carta de New York" ("poder portentoso"). Cyrus Veeser argues in *A World Safe for Capitalism: Dollar Diplomacy and America's Rise to Global Power* (New York, 2002) that informal U.S. empire in Santo Domingo dated to the large-scale late nineteenth-century extension of credit to Santo Domingo by U.S. financial institutions.

30. D. Collazo, Letter to Editor, "Porto Rico's Hope," *New York Times*, 17 July 1904, 6; 1904 Democratic Party Platform, quoted in Collazo, "Give the Devil His Due" ("política de explotación colonial"); Collazo, "Status of Island Colonies." Collazo attributed the lack of accompanying demand for citizenship to Democrats' faith that citizenship was a prerequisite to territorial status and hence implicitly included in that demand. See D. Collazo, "Metropolitanas," *La Democracia*, 27 July 1909. Though nobody questioned the idea that Congress could avoid customs problems by passing funds through the U.S. treasury on their way to Puerto Rico, U.S. officials continued to treat as disastrous the prospect of losing the ability to deposit funds directly into the island's treasury. See Copy, Civil Government for Porto Rico, 21 Dec. 1914, 1–3, MD NARA 350/5B/3377-232; Ana Georgina Sagardia de Alvarado, "United States–Puerto Rican Relations: The Changing Citizenship Status of the Puerto Rican People under the United States Sovereignty (1898–1917)," PhD diss., University of California, Berkeley, 1983, 350–353.

31. Collazo, "Metropolitanas," 17 Aug. 1908 ("exótico"; "saliéndose de la Constitución"); Gonzalez, "A Tribute"; Gabel Gonzalez, Letter to Editor, "Porto Rico's Complaints," *New York Times*, 13 Oct. 1905, 8; D. Collazo, "Metropolitanas," *La Democracia*, 2, 15 Jan. and 1 Feb. 1909; José A. Cabranes, "Citizenship and American Empire: Notes on the Legislative History of the United States Citizenship of Puerto Ricans," *University of Pennsylvania Law Review* 127 (Dec. 1978): 415–435. On Republican political dominance after 1900, see Gerard N. Magliocca, *The Tragedy of William Jennings Bryan: Constitutional Law and the Politics of Backlash* (New Haven, CT, 2011), especially 6.

32. John W. Burgess, *Reconstruction and the Constitution, 1866–1876* (New York, 1905 [1902]); Mark Elliott, *Color-Blind Justice: Albion Tourgée and the Quest for Racial Equality from the Civil War to* Plessy v. Ferguson (Oxford, 2006), 181, 306–307; Eric Foner, *Reconstruction: America's Unfinished Revolution, 1863–1877* (New York, 1988), xix–xx; C. Vann Woodward, *Origins of the New South, 1877–1913*, rev. ed. (Baton Rouge, LA, 1999 [1951]), 431–433, 441–443; C. Vann Woodward, *The Strange Career of Jim Crow* (Oxford, 2001 [1955]), 54–56, 77–81; Michael Perman, *Struggle for Mastery: Disfranchisement in the South, 1898–1908* (Chapel Hill, NC, 2001), 224–328.

33. "American Politicians," *Puerto Rico Herald*, 1 Nov. 1902, 243; "A Complete Farce," *Puerto Rico Herald*, 8 Nov. 1902, 257; *Puerto Rico Herald*, 27 Aug. 1901, 2; *Puerto Rico Herald*, 7 Sept. 1901, 1; Mariano Negrón-Portillo, *Las turbas republicanas, 1900–1904* (Río Piedras, PR, 1990), 144–149, 151–153, 193; "The Porto Rican Elections," *New York Times*, 6 Nov. 1902, 8; 53 Cong.

Rec. 7471. On the phrase "sweeping away," see Scott, *Degrees of Freedom*, 69. The *Herald* aspired to reach journalists, clubs, hotels, congressmen, important public figures, and interested readers "in Porto Rico, Cuba, South America and the United States." Advertisers anticipated a more modest reach and primarily targeted Puerto Ricans on the island and in New York with Spanish-language ads for room, board, luxury goods, transportation, communications, and professional services. As measured by its performance, the focus of the newspaper was politics, not profit. Like *La Democracia*, the Federales' organ on the island, the *Herald* did not become self-supporting. For details, see "Porto Rican Editor Coming Here," *New York Times*, 21 Mar. 1901, 1; *Puerto Rico Herald*, 27 Aug. 1901, 2; *Puerto Rico Herald*, 7 Sept. 1901; "Al público y á las agencias de 'The *Puerto Rico Herald*,'" *Puerto Rico Herald*, 3 Aug. 1901, 13; B. Díaz to Federico Degetau, 6 Oct. 1903, CIHCAM 4/V/ 312; "Sobre 'The *Puerto Rico Herald*,'" *La Democracia*, 26 July 1904. To determine the content of advertisements in 1901 I looked at all the ads on fifteen pages chosen from eleven issues published between 27 August and 28 December 1901.

34. Eileen J. Suárez Findlay, *Imposing Decency: The Politics of Sexuality and Race in Puerto Rico, 1870–1920* (Durham, NC, 1999), 142–143, 57; "Llegan los esclavos," *La Democracia*, 21 Nov. 1900, 2; Mariano Abril, "Crónica," *La Democracia*, 21 Nov. 1900, 2 ("raza degenerada y servil"; "contra los que quitaron el látigo de sus espaldas"; "libertades y derechos"; "por los que se sacrificó toda una generación de patriotas"); Henry Gannett, U.S. War Department, Puerto Rico Census Office, *Report on the Census of Porto Rico, 1899* (Washington, DC, 1900), 56; Cabán, *Constructing a Colonial People*, 180–182; Miriam Jiménez Román, "Un hombre (negro) del pueblo: José Barbosa and the Puerto Rican 'Race' toward Whiteness," *Centro* 8 (Spring 1996): 17. Passage of the Republicanos' voting law, which had reversed Elihu Root's implementation of a limited franchise consonant with white-supremacist disfranchisement strategies, had required the consent of high Republican U.S. officials on the island. Gervasio Luis García, in "I Am the Other: Puerto Rico in the Eyes of North Americans, 1898," *Journal of American History* 87 (June 2000): 53–54, 56–57, describes Muñoz Rivera's disparagement of the island's masses.

35. Emilio Sánchez Pastor, "La grandeza de Japón," *La Democracia*, 25 Feb. 1904, 1 ("las naciones civilizadas"); "Los blancos contra los amarillos," *La Democracia*, 27 July 1904, 5 ("conflicto de razas"); "La guerra entre Rusia y Japón," *La Democracia*, 18 Mar. 1904, 1 ("conceptuosamente los calificaban de monos"); "Resume de la historia del Japón," *La Democracia*, 22 Apr. 1904, 1 ("Dos siglos de letargo"; "Restauración del poder del Mikado"); "Poder y propósitos del Japón," *La Democracia*, 20 July 1904, 4 ("como pueblo de combatientes solamente"); Sarah Barringer Gordon, *The Mormon Question: Polygamy and Constitutional Conflict in Nineteenth-Century America* (Chapel Hill, NC, 2002); Cardell K. Jacobson, "Black Mormons in the 1980s: Pioneers in a White Church," *Review of Religious Research* 33 (Dec. 1991): 146–152; Scott, *Degrees of Freedom*; Ada Ferrer, *Insurgent Cuba: Race, Nation, and Revolution, 1868–1898* (Chapel Hill, NC, 1999); Louis A. Pérez Jr., *Cuba between Empires 1878–1902* (Pittsburgh, 1983); "La nueva república Bóer," *La Democracia*, 11 Mar. 1904, 3; "Los mormones y el Senado," *La Democracia*, 7 Apr. 1904, 5.

36. D. Collazo, "Metropolitanas," *La Democracia*, 20 Feb. 1909 ("redentor verdadero"), 8, and 17 Aug. 1908. For examples of Collazo's use of the term "carpetbaggers," see "Metropolitanas," *La Democracia*, 12 June, 27 July, and 23 Oct. 1909; D. Collazo, Letter to Editor, "Porto Rico and 'Overaspiring' Officials," *New York Times*, 1 Oct. 1907, 10.

37. Collazo, "Desde Nueva York," 25 Feb. 1907 ("solamente á los negros y á los chinos los sientan en escuelas separadas"; "italianos, alemanes, y judíos"; "caer"; "bajezas en los puertos de los Estados Unidos"); D. Collazo, "Metropolitanas," *La Democracia*, 24 Apr. 1909, 2 ("escupitina"; "'raza hibrida'"; "la humanidad es igual en todas partes"; "acaso no anduvieron muy descaminados los californianos al oponerse a la irrupción de tanto mono amarillo"); Roger Daniels, *The Politics of Prejudice: The Anti-Japanese Movement in California and the Struggle for Japanese Exclusion* (New York, 1977), 31–45. The nested quotation is from another correspondent.

38. D. Collazo, Letter to Editor, "Porto Ricans for Panama? Suggested Relief for a Congested Population and Labor Supply for the Canal," *New York Sun*, 20 May 1904; Joaquín Colón López, *Pioneros puertorriqueños en Nueva York 1917–1947* (Houston, TX, 2002), 87–88, 183; Vega, *Memoirs*, 128, 139; "All Around the Horizon," *Christian Work and the Evangelist*, 14 Sept. 1907, 334; D. Collazo, Letter to Editor, "Gov. Post as a Reformer," *New York Sun*, 22 Aug. 1907, 4; D. Collazo, Letter to Editor, "Porto Rican Jibaros," *New York Times*, 25 Aug. 1907, 6; "'La Correspondencia' ha inquirido datos de interés general," *La Correspondencia*, 16 Sept. 1905, 1; Samuel Gompers and Herman Gutstadt, *Meat vs. Rice: American Manhood against Asiatic Coolieism: Which Shall Survive?* (San Francisco, 1908 [1902]); *Inhabitants of Porto Rico to Be Citizens of the United States*, 5; D. Collazo, Frank Martinez, and W. McK. Jones, Ponce Branch of the Chamber of Commerce of Porto Rico to Committee on Ways and Means, 30 Nov. 1908, in H.R. Doc. No. 1505, 60th Cong. 2d sess., *Tariff Hearings . . . Schedule G Agricultural Products and Provisions* (1909), 4187, 4176–4186; Collazo, "Justice for Porto Rico"; D. Collazo, Letter to Editor, "Porto Rico and the Tariff," *New-York Tribune*, 10 Mar. 1909, 10; "Puerto Rico y su café," *La Democracia*, 2 Jan. 1909; D. Collazo, "Metropolitanas," *La Democracia*, 27 July, 26 Sept., 14 Nov. 1908 and 2, 15 Jan., 1 Feb. 1909; *The Campaign Textbook of the Democratic Party of the United States* (Chicago, 1908).

39. D. Collazo, Letter to Editor, "Bryan Porto Rico's Moses," *New York Times*, 4 Sep. 1908, 6; Julie Greene, *Pure and Simple Politics: The American Federation of Labor and Political Activism, 1881–1917* (Cambridge, 2004 [1999]), 71–180; William E. Forbath, *Law and the Shaping of the American Labor Movement* (Cambridge, MA, 1991); Collazo, "Desde Nueva York," 2 Mar. 1907; D. Collazo, "Metropolitanas," *La Democracia*, 5 June, 21 Sept., and 2 Nov. 1908. The AFL had earlier shied away from politics. It was poorly positioned to swing federal elections, and courts could and did overturn its legislative gains. A partisan commitment could divide its politically diverse membership.

40. "Porto Rican Vote Pledged to Bryan"; Collazo, "Desde Nueva York," 2 Mar. 1907 ("ignorantes"); D. Collazo, "Metropolitanas," *La Democracia*, 13 June 1908, 1 May 1909, 2 ("preocupados imbéciles"), 2 Nov. 1908; Tulio Larrinaga, "Porto Rico's Attitude Toward the United States," Address before the Lake Mohonk Conference, Lake Mohonk, NY, 25 Oct. 1907, *Proceedings of the Twenty-Fifth*

Annual Meeting of the Lake Mohonk Conference of Friends of the Indian and Other Dependent Peoples 1907 (New York, 1907), 159–164; Corresponsal [Collazo?], "Desde Nueva York," 4 Apr. 1907; Collazo, "Carta de New York"; Collazo, "Un anónimo y la dignidad humana"; D. Collazo, "Castigando a Puerto Rico," *La Democracia*, 7 June 1909, 2; Ann J. Lane, *The Brownsville Affair: National Crisis and Black Reaction* (London, 1971); John D. Weaver, *The Senator and the Sharecropper's Son: Exoneration of the Brownsville Soldiers* (College Station, TX, 1997); John D. Weaver, *The Brownsville Raid* (New York, 1970).

41. Corresponsal [Collazo?], "Desde Nueva York," 23 Mar. 1907 ("Sísifo rodando constantemente la piedra de nuestros azarosos destinos"; "vuelve á recaer pesadamente de la cumbre al abismo"); L. Muñoz Rivera, C. Coll Cuchi, and Eugenio Benítez, untitled pamphlet, [Mar.–May?] [1909], MD NARA 350/5A/ 3377-0.5, 12; Collazo, "Castigando a Puerto Rico"; 44 Cong. Rec. 4344–4345; Chauncey M. Depew, "Porto Rico: Speech on the Effort of the Porto Rican House of Delegates to Coerce Congress by Refusing to Pass Appropriation Bills, July 9, 1909," *Orations, Addresses and Speeches of Chauncey M. Depew*, vol. 7 (New York, 1910); *Amending Act to Provide Revenues, etc., for Porto Rico*, Sen. Rep. No. 10, 61st Cong., 1st sess. (3 July 1909), 9–11; 44 Cong. Rec. 4344–4345; "Hacía la metrópoli," *La Democracia*, 18 Mar. 1909, 2; Luis Muñoz Rivera and Cay. Coll Cuchi, "Regreso de la comisión," *La Democracia*, 5 May 1909, 1; "La comisión de la Cámara," *La Democracia*, 22 Apr. and 6 May 1909; "Noticias de Washington," *La Democracia*, 3 Apr. 1909, 1; "El mensaje del presidente," *La Democracia*, 13 May 1909, 1; Sagardia de Alvarado, "United States–Puerto Rican Relations," 262–269.

42. "Comisión de la cámara en Washington," *La Democracia*, 1 or 2 Apr. 1909, 1; "La comisión," *La Democracia*, 23 Mar. 1909, 1; "Ante el presidente," *La Democracia*, 26 Mar. 1909, 1; "La comisión de la Cámara," *La Democracia*, 8, 16 Apr. 1909, 1; Domingo Collazo to Chauncey Depew, 5 May 1909, DC NARA 46/91/Sen 62A-F17/Army Vetinary Bill to Citizenship Granting of to Porto Rico; Depew, "Porto Rico"; Frank McIntyre to William Willoughby, 15 May 1909, MD NARA 350/5A/ 186-47; D. Collazo, "Metropolitanas," *La Democracia*, 18 June, 29 July, and 13 Aug. 1909; Collazo, "El mensaje del presidente"; "Con el gobernador," *La Democracia*, 21 May 1909, 1; "Carta de Collazo," *La Democracia*, 5 June 1909, 3.

43. *Amending Act to Provide Revenues for Porto Rico*, 1–5; Muñoz Rivera, Coll Cuchi, and Benítez, untitled pamphlet; "La comisión de la Cámara," 6 May 1909.

44. "A Gold Letter," *La Democracia*, 16 July 1909, 1; 44 Cong. Rec. 2469, 2466–2472, 2927–2928, 4343; "La comisión de la Cámara," 22 Apr. 1909.

45. Collazo, "Metropolitanas," 23 Oct. 1909 ("no es lo mismo ser presidente de una república que amo y señor de colonos"), 29 July 1909; "Con el gobernador"; Olmsted Amendment, 36 Stat. 11; "El mensaje del presidente," 13 May 1909.

46. *Five Years of the War Department following the War with Spain, 1899–1903, as Shown in the Annual Reports of the Secretary of War* ([Washington, DC?], [1904?]), 237; "A Promotion," *Austin Daily Statesman*, 21 Feb. 1900, 8; 32 Stat. 691 (1902). On exports, see "Exports from the Philippine Islands," *Official Gazette* (Manila, the Philippines), 27 Jan. 1904, 74; *Third Annual Report of the Governor of Porto Rico, Covering the Period from July 1, 1902, to June 30, 1903*, S. Doc. No. 26, 58th Cong., 1st sess. (1903), 23; *Annual Reports of the Department of the Interior for the Fiscal Year Ended June 30, 1902, Miscellaneous Reports*, part II

(Washington, DC, 1903), 337. Daniel P. Carpenter describes the importance of such bureau chiefs to the growth and maintenance of agency autonomy, in *The Forging of Bureaucratic Autonomy: Reputations, Networks, and Policy Innovation in Executive Agencies, 1862–1928* (Princeton, NJ, 2001).

47. Michael E. Shay, *Revered Commander, Maligned General: The Life of Clarence Ransom Edwards, 1859–1931* (Columbia, MO, 2011), 1–57; Edward M. Coffman, Review, *Journal of Military History* 75 (July 2011): 945–946; Walter L. Williams, "United States Indian Policy and the Debate over Philippine Annexation: Implications for the Origins of American Imperialism," *Journal of American History* 66 (Mar. 1980): 829; "Gen. Edwards Dies; Led 26th Division," *New York Times*, 15 Feb. 1931, 28.

48. Paul Charlton to Herbert Parsons, 10 Apr. 1907, MD NARA 350/5A/9003-7; Herbert Parsons, "A Bureau of Information and Report for the Insular Possessions," *Annals of the American Academy of Political and Social Science* 30 (July 1907): 123–129; "Our Insular Affairs," *Washington Evening Star*, 29 Oct. 1903, 1, MD NARA 350/5A/9003; "A Seeker after Light," *Washington Post*, 15 Apr. 1907, MD NARA 350/5A/9003-6; H.R. Rep. No. 8118, 59th Cong., 2d sess., 27 Feb. 1907, MD NARA 350/5A/168-43; "Bureau for 'Colonies,'" *Boston Evening Transcript*, 24 Apr. 1907, last ed., 1, MD NARA 350/5A/9003; "Chats of Visitors to the Capital," *Washington Post*, 22 July 1909, 6; U.S. National Archives and Records Administration, *Statistical Summary of Holdings: Record Group 301–Record Group 400*, http://www.archives.gov/research/guide-fed-records/index-numeric/301-to-400.html. For a lawmaker who sought information from the bureau, see Parsons, "A Bureau of Information." For administrators, see Bureau of Insular Affairs, Memo: for Gen. Edwards, 2 July 1908, MD NARA 350/5A/9003-11; Bureau of Insular Affairs, Memorandum, Reports of Insular Possessions, Oct. 1908, MD NARA 350/5A/9003-10.

49. Walter L. Williams, "United States Indian Policy and the Debate over Philippine Annexation: Implications for the Origins of American Imperialism," *Journal of American History* 66 (Mar. 1980), 814–815; *Message from the President Relative to Porto Rico*; Charlton to Parsons, 10 Apr. 1907; Bureau of Insular Affairs, Memorandum, Reports of Insular Possessions; Geo. R. Colton, "Inaugural Address of Governor Geo. R. Colton Delivered at San Juan, Porto Rico, November, 1909" ([1909]), 5, MD NARA 350/5A/7937-78; correspondence collected at MD NARA 350/5A/14840-1 to -3, -5, -10 to -11, and 12604-43.

50. Charlton to Parsons, 10 Apr. 1907; Bureau of Insular Affairs, Memorandum, Reports of Insular Possessions; Parsons, "A Bureau of Information"; "Our Insular Affairs"; "To Protect Porto Rico," *New York Tribune*, 17 Nov. 1906, MD NARA 350/5A/9003-2; "Bureau for 'Colonies.'"

51. Paul Charlton to Franklin Lane, 4 June 1909, MD NARA 350/5A/186-48; Paul Charlton, Memorandum Regarding Naturalization of Residents of the Philippine Islands, with draft of proposed bill, 13 Feb. 1906, MD NARA 350/5A/5507-6; Paul Charlton to Herbert Parsons, 26 Mar. 1908, MD NARA 350/5A/9003-9; Franklin Lane to Paul Charlton, 2 June 1909, MD NARA 350/5A/186-48; Charlton to Lane, 4 June 1909; "C. E. Magoon Dies; Once Ruled Cuba," *New York Times*, 15 Jan. 1920, 11; "Ex-Judge Charlton Dies in Porto Rico," *New York Times*, 5 June 1917, 11; Fred [P?]arker, *Insular Cases*, 28 Aug. 1906, MD NARA 350/5A/8550-5; Sparrow, *Insular Cases*, 257–263; Paul Charlton, Note, 14 Mar. 1906, MD

NARA 350/5A/5507-10; "The Forgotten Island," *Commoner* (Lincoln, NE), 23 June 1905, 14; Paul Charlton to Redfield Proctor, 15 Feb. 1907, MD NARA 350/5A/1444-10; Francis McIntyre to Ernst Freund, 1 July 1909, MD NARA 350/5A/9003-15; Ernst Freund to Clarence Edwards, 28 June 1909, MD NARA 350/5A/9003-15; Daniel R. Ernst, *Tocqueville's Nightmare: The Administrative State Emerges in America, 1900–1940* (Oxford, 2014), 10–15; MD NARA 350/5A/5507-1 to -12; Charlton to Parsons, 10 Apr. 1907; Herbert Parsons to Paul Charlton, 14 Mar. 1908, MD NARA 350/5A/9003-9; Naturalization Law of 1906, sec. 30, 34 Stat. 596, 606–607 (1906).

52. Prior to 1900 the United States had exercised authority in American Samoa without extending U.S. sovereignty there. See, generally, Nicholas Thomas, *Islanders: The Pacific in the Age of Empire* (New Haven, CT, 2010), 272–281; George Herbert Ryden, *The Foreign Policy of the United States in Relation to Samoa* (New Haven, CT, 1933). In *The Forging of Bureaucratic Autonomy*, Carpenter observes that agencies are most autonomous when they offer a unique and useful service, communicate that fact broadly, and develop a friendly coalition that cannot be reduced to lines of party, class, or parochial interest. Edwards achieved the first two conditions, but not the third. Carpenter also observes the importance of policy innovation to agency success.

53. Walter J. Ballard, "Wanted – A Colonial Department," *Troy Times*, 29 Sept. 1905, MD NARA 350/5A/9003-1; "Our Insular Affairs"; Collazo, "Metropolitanas," 12 June 1909 ("Imperio universal de Estados Unidos"); "Plans Colonial Office," *Washington Post*, 5 June 1909, MD NARA 350/5A/9003-13; *Five Years of the War Department*, 237; "To Protect Porto Rico"; *Message from the President Relative to Porto Rico*; H.R. 23568 (7 Jan. 1909), MD NARA 350/5A/168-43; H.R. Rep. No. 8118; Parsons, "A Bureau of Information"; Parsons to Charlton, 14 Mar. 1908; Walter J. Ballard, "The Emergency and the Issue," *Park County (CO) Bulletin*, 15 July 1904, 4; "Bureau for 'Colonies'"; Robert C. Kennedy, "Cartoon of the Day: '1907,'" *HarpWeek* (2008), www.harpweek.com/09Cartoon/BrowseByDateCartoon.asp?Month=November&Date=16.

54. "To Protect Porto Rico"; Colton, "Inaugural Address," 4–5; " William E. Pulliam, Receiver General of Dominican Customs," *Bulletin of the Pan American Union* 57 (July 1913), 86; "Shonts Canal Chief," *Washington Post*, 2 Apr. 1905, 6; Shay, *Revered Commander*, 71; "Taft Praises Magoon," *Washington Post*, 6 June 1909, 12; Scott, *Degrees of Freedom*, 213–214; Cable, McCoy to McIntyre, 29 Sept. 1906, MD NARA 350/5A/12604-9; Cable, McIntyre to Taft, 29 Sept. 1906, MD NARA 350/5A/12604-9; Parsons, "A Bureau of Information"; Clarence Edwards to Albert Smiley, 9 July 1908, MD NARA 350/5A/14840-5; Charlton to Proctor, 15 Feb. 1907; [P?]arker, *Insular Cases*; Colin D. Moore, "State Building through Partnership: Delegation, Public-Private Partnerships, and the Political Development of American Imperialism, 1898–1916," *Studies in American Political Development* 25 (Apr. 2011): 29, 32, 42–43, 46, 51–53.

55. S[illegible], Memorandum for Mr. Wilcox, 2 July 1908, MD NARA 350/5A/9003-11; Executive Order of 11 May 1907, MD NARA 350/5A/9003-9; Executive Order, 25 May 1909, MD NARA 350/5A/9003-12; Department of Commerce and Labor, Bureau of Statistics, *The Commerce and Navigation of the United States for the Year Ending June 30, 1911* (Washington, DC, 1912), 24–25; Mara Loveman and Jeronimo O. Muniz, "How Puerto Rico Became White: Boundary Dynamics and

Intercensus Racial Reclassification," *American Sociological Review* 27 (Dec. 2007): 921; Bureau of the Census, Department of Commerce, *Fourteenth Census of the United States Taken in the Year 1920*, vol. 3 (Washington, DC, 1923), 11; *Census of the Philippine Islands Taken under the Direction of the Philippine Commission in the Year 1903*, vol. 2 (Washington, DC, 1905), 14. Guam and American Samoa also fell outside the bureau's jurisdiction. See McIntyre to Freund, 1 July 1909; Freund to Edwards, 28 June 1909. The lack of interest at the Department of the Interior meant that there would not be a repeat of the War Department's long-resented mid-nineteenth-century loss of American Indian Affairs to the Department of the Interior. See Jeffrey Ostler, "Conquest and the State: Why the United States Employed Massive Military Force to Suppress the Lakota Ghost Dance," *Pacific Historical Review* 65 (May 1996): 217–248.

56. Depew, "Porto Rico"; M. E. Olmsted to Clarence Edwards, 2 Nov. 1909, MD NARA 350/5A/3377-1; D. Collazo, "Metropolitanas," *La Democracia*, 28 Jan. 1910 ("franca hostilidad"); Frank H. Richmond to Senate Committee on Judicial Affairs, 7 Jan. 1910, quoted in Domingo Collazo, "Metropolitanas," *La Democracia*, 21 Jan. 1910, 2 ("vana, cobarde, hipócrita"; "corrupción"), 12 June 1909; Fred W. Carpenter to C. R. Edwards, 11 May 1909, MD NARA 350/5A/168-46; C. R. Edwards to Chauncey Depew, 13 May 1909, MD NARA 350/5A/186-46; Olmsted Amendment, 36 Stat. 11; Executive Order No. 1110, 15 July 1909, MD NARA 350/5A/168-50. For the view that white Southerners were less oppressed by military occupation than by the civil government that followed, see Burgess, *Reconstruction and Constitution*, 247–248.

57. *Report of the Governor of Porto Rico to the Secretary of War* (Washington, DC, 1910), 13; Clarence Edwards to Marlin Olmsted, 30 Oct. 1909, MD NARA 350/5A/3377, 9–10; "George R. Colton Dead," *New York Times*, 8 Apr. 1916; [Illegible] to Clarence Edwards, 15 Dec. 1904, MD NARA 350/5A/7937-5; George Colton to Captain McIntyre, 8 Dec. 1906, MD NARA 350/5A/7937-12; George Colton to General Edwards, 8 Dec. 1909, MD NARA 350/5A/858-14; Frank McIntyre, Memorandum for the Secretary of War, 18 Mar. 1913, MD NARA 350/8/C239-5; Memorandum, Apr. 1913, MD NARA 350/21/George Colton; *Hearings upon the Bill Proposing to Amend the Present Organic Law of Porto Rico* (Washington, DC, 1910), 2–7, 21–22, 193–199; Clarence Edwards to Finis Garrett, 8 Mar. 1910, MD NARA 350/5A/3377-57; Cablegram, Edwards to Colton, 16 Apr. 1910, MD NARA 350/5A/3377-82; Clarence Edwards to George Colton, 1 Dec. 1910, MD NARA 350/5A/3377-99; C. R. Edwards to George Colton, 20 Jan. 1911, MD NARA 350/5A/3377-103; Frank McIntyre to M. E. Olmsted, 12 Nov. 1909, MD NARA 350/5A/3377-1; M. E. Olmsted to Frank McIntyre, 13 Nov. 1909, MD NARA 350/5A/3377-1; M. E. Olmsted to E. C. Edwards 20 Dec. 1909, MD NARA 350/5A/3377-6; Clarence Edwards to M. Olmsted, 4 Mar. 1910, MD NARA 350/5A/3377-51; Olmsted to Edwards, 2 Nov. 1909; "The Day in Washington," *New-York Daily Tribune*, 24 Jan. 1910, 3; 45 Cong. Rec. 1244, 2932, 3223; Clarence Edwards to George Colton, 9 Mar. 1910, MD NARA 350/5A/3377-60; *Amending Act Relating to Revenues of Civil Government of Porto Rico*, H.R. Rep. No. 750, 61st Cong., 2d sess., 15 Mar. 1910; McIntyre to Colton, 16 June 1910, MD NARA 350/5A/3377-88; MD NARA 350/5A/3377-0 to -28; MD 350/5A, especially file numbers beginning 3377.

Old colonial hands other than Colton also soon occupied top Puerto Rico posts. Chief of Police George Shanton had previously served in Cuba and the Canal Zone. See Memorandum re Services of George R. Shanton, 5 Oct. 1915, MD NARA 350/ 21/George Shanton. Secretary M. Drew Carrel had been chief clerk in the bureau of customs and immigration in the Philippines and served in Cuba and Santo Domingo as well. See *The Directory & Chronicle for China, Japan, Corea, ... the Philippines, &c.* ([Hong Kong], 1910), 1452; *Report of the Governor of Porto Rico to the Secretary of War*, 21–22; Frank McIntyre, Memorandum for the Secretary of War, 16 Sept. 1913, MD NARA 350/21/George Colton.

58. Henry Hoyt to Harry, 22 Dec. 1909, MD NARA 350/5A/1286-15; George Colton to Clarence Edwards, 15 Dec. 1909, MD NARA 350/5A/1286-13; "Republican Party Platforms: Republican Party Platform of 1908," *The American Presidency Project*, comp. Gerhard Peters and John T. Woolley, www.presidency.ucsb.edu/ws/ ?pid=29632 (2016); William Willoughby to William Taft, 6 Dec. 1909, MD NARA 350/5A/3377-4; *Hearings to Amend the Present Organic Law*, 241.

59. *Kopel*, 211 U.S. 468, 476 (1909); Henry Hoyt to Secretary of State, 3 Jan. 1910, MD NARA 350/5A/1286-14; Paul Charlton, Memorandum for General Edwards: In the Matter of Citizenship for Porto Ricans, 21 Dec. 1909, MD NARA 350/5A/1286-11; Henry Hoyt to George Colton, 14 Dec. 1909, MD NARA 350/5A/1286-12; *Civil Government for Porto Rico: Speech of Hon. Marlin E. Olmsted of Pennsylvania in the House of Representatives, Wednesday, May 25, 1910* (Washington, DC, 1910), 10–14, MD NARA 350/5A/3377-89; F. R. Coudert to Clarence Edwards, 14 Dec. 1909, MD NARA 350/5A/2333-3; *Hearings to Amend the Present Organic Law*, 131, 221, 236.

60. Hoyt to Secretary of State, 3 Jan. 1910; H.R. Rep. No. 750, 2; Colton to Edwards, 15 Dec. 1909; George Colton to Clarence Edwards, 12 Jan. 1910, MD NARA 350/ 5A/19929-9; *Hearings to Amend the Present Organic Law*, 242; Hoyt to Secretary of State, 3 Jan. 1910; Hoyt to Harry, 22 Dec. 1909.

61. Benjamin B. Hampton, "The Vast Riches of Alaska: Will the Morgan-Guggenheim Combination Acquire Them, or Will They Benefit the Whole People?" *Hampton's Magazine*, 1 Apr. 1910, 462, 460; 45 Cong. Rec. 1838, 8177–8210, [S. Bills] 46, 47, ibid., 4285–4286; *Amending Act Relating to Revenues*, 5–6; Perman, *Struggle for Mastery*, 196–204; William H. Taft, "Address at the Alaska-Yukon-Pacific Exposition, Seattle, Wash., 29 Sept. 1909," in *William Howard Taft, Presidential Addresses and State Papers of William Howard Taft from March 4, 1909, to March 4, 1910*, vol. 1 (New York, 1910), 282–285; "Annual Message of the President to Congress," 7 Dec. 1909, in *The Abridgment 1909 Containing the Annual Message of the President of the United States to the Two Houses of Congress, 61st Congress, 2d Session, with Reports of Departments and Selections from Accompanying Papers*, vol. 1 (Washington, DC, 1910), 40–41; "His Own Reputation," *New-York Tribune*, 13 July 1910, 6; David Sarasohn, "The Insurgent Republicans: Insurgent Image and Republican Reality," *Social Science History* 3 (1979), 246; "Taft Forwards Bill," *Washington Post*, 29 Jan. 1910, 4; H.R. Rep. No. 750, 5–6; National Archives and Records Administration, *Guide to Federal Records: Records of the Bureau of Insular Affairs*, www.archives.gov/research/guide-fed-records/groups/350.html.

On involvement of bureau officials in attempts to improve policing in Nicaragua, see Jeremy Kuzmarov, *Modernizing Repression: Police Training and Nation Building in the American Century* (Amherst, MA, 2012), 47; William Kamman,

"Carter, Calvin Brooks (1887?–)," in *The War of 1898 and U.S. Interventions 1898–1934*, ed. Benjamin R. Beede (New York, 1994), 94. On bureau involvement in a 1910–1911 attempt to establish a customs receivership in Honduras, see Munro, *Intervention and Dollar Diplomacy*, 223. On bureau supervision of the customs receivership in Haiti after 1920, see *Report of the Third Fiscal Period Haitian Customs Receivership, 1919, Fiscal Year October 1, 1918, to September 30, 1919* (Washington, DC, 1921), 3–4. On its role during the early years of the receivership, see Richard L. Millett, "Searching for Stability: The U.S. Development of Constabulary Forces in Latin America and the Philippines," Occasional Paper 30 (Fort Leavenworth, KS, 2010), 59. For an overview of the bureau's failure to emerge as a colonial office, see Earl S. Pomeroy, "The American Colonial Office," *Mississippi Valley Historical Review* 30 (Mar. 1944): 521–532.

THE JONES ACT AND THE LONG PATH TO COLLECTIVE
NATURALIZATION

1. Copy, Santiago Iglesias and Abraham Peña to William Taft, 27 Nov. 1909, CDO:1.
2. *Report of Proceedings of the Twenty-Ninth Annual Convention of the American Federation of Labor* (Washington, DC, 1909), 40–42, 185, 204, 263, 300; Extract, Report of the Federación Libre de Los Trabajadores to the American Federation of Labor, Nov. 1911, MD NARA 350/5B/1286-22; Free Federation of Laborers of Porto Rico, *The Tyranny of the House of Delegates of Porto Rico* (1913), CDO:2; La Unión Obrera Central, Los Obreros Contra Herminio Díaz Navarro, San Juan, PR, 2 Sept. 1912, CDO:2; Santiago Iglesias, "The People and Their Civil and Political Rights – Period of Autonomous Government. Electoral Campaign," 1912, CDO:2; copies, letters of Santiago Iglesias and Abraham Peña to William Taft, 27 Nov. 1909, CDO:1; Shelton Stromquist, *Reinventing "The People": The Progressive Movement, the Class Problem, and the Origins of Modern Liberalism* (Urbana, IL, 2006); Ramón Grosfoguel, *Colonial Subjects: Puerto Ricans in a Global Perspective* (Los Angeles, 2003), 54–55.
3. *Report of Proceedings of the Thirty-Third Annual Convention of the American Federation of Labor* (Washington, DC, 1913), 125; *Twenty-Ninth Annual Convention of the American Federation of Labor*, 41, 40, 42, 87, 217–218, 220; Iglesias and Peña to Taft, 27 Nov. 1909; James R. Barrett and David Roediger, "Inbetween Peoples: Race, Nationality and the 'New Immigrant' Working Class," *Journal of American Ethnic History* 16 (Spring 1997): 4–9; Stromquist, *Reinventing "The People,"* 162; Laura Briggs, *Reproducing Empire: Race, Sex, Science, and U.S. Imperialism in Puerto Rico* (Berkeley, CA, 2002), 2; Free Federation of Laborers of Porto Rico, *Tyranny*. In "The Constitution of Aspiration and 'The Rights that Belong to Us All,'" *Journal of American History* 74 (Dec. 1987): 1016–1020, Hendrik Hartog observes the tension between claims to the right to be free from official relations of dependency and the numerous occasions when people need support.
4. George Colton to Clarence Edwards, 2 Mar. 1910, MD NARA 350/5A/3377-57; Cablegram, Colton to Edwards, 1 Mar. 1910, MD NARA 350/5A/3377-49; Copy, Cablegram Excerpt, Colton to Secretary, 2[5?] Mar. 1910, CDO:1; George Colton

to Lindley Garrison, 5 Apr. 1913, MD NARA 350/5A/3377-130.5; Colton to SecWar, 23 Feb. 1910, MD NARA 350/5A/3377-40.

5. Geo. R. Colton, "Inaugural Address of Governor Geo. R. Colton Delivered at San Juan, Porto Rico, November, 1909" ([1909]), MD NARA 350/5A/7937-78; Clarence Edwards to Marlin Olmsted, 30 Oct. 1909, MD NARA 350/5A/3377; Cable, Colton to SecWar, 5 Dec. 1909, MD NARA 350/5A/858-14; Memorandum of Proposed Changes in the Organic Act of Porto Rico, [27] Jan. 1910, MD NARA 350/5A/3377-27; J. M. Dickinson to President, 20 Jan. 1910, in *House Documents*, vol. 131 (Washington, DC, 1910), no. 615, 2–10; Colton to Secretary, 2[5?] Mar. 1910; W. H. Taft to Mr. Iglesias, 15 Apr. 1912, CDO:2; William Willoughby to William Taft, 6 Dec. 1909, MD NARA 350/5A/3377-4; *War Department Annual Reports, 1911*, vol. 1 (Washington, DC, 1912); William Taft to Henry Stimson, 30 July 1912, MD NARA 350/5B/1286-69; George Colton to Clarence Edwards, 15 Nov. 1911, MD NARA 350/5B/1286-27.

6. Frank McIntyre to Drew Carrell, 14 June 1912, MD NARA 350/5B/1286-60; Samuel Gompers to John Lennon, 12 Mar. 1915, CDO:2; "The A. F. of L. in Porto Rico," *American Federationist*, Mar. 1911, 207; Colton to Secretary, 2[5?] Mar. 1910; Copy, Santiago Iglesias to Frank McIntyre, 23 Feb. 1910, CDO:1; *Citizens of Porto Rico to Be Citizens of the United States*, H.R. Rep. 341 (1912); *A People without a Country* (Washington, DC, 1912); Marc Karson, *American Labor Unions and Politics, 1900–1918* (Boston, 1958), 57–64, 71–73, 132.

7. Geo. Colton to Santiago Iglesias, 30 Oct. 1911, DC NARA 46/91/Sen 62A-F17/ Citizenship Granting of to Porto Ricans; "Gran oración parlamentaria: Discurso del Presidente de la Cámara, Don José de Diego, sobre las cuestiones obreras," *La Democracia*, 12 Feb. 1913, 1; *Thirty-Third Annual Convention of the American Federation of Labor*, 122–123, 124; Samuel Gompers, "For Porto Rican Uplift," *American Federationist*, Apr. 1913, 312–314; J. C. Bills to Felix Frankfurter, 19 Sept. 1913, MD NARA 350/5A/25142-14; Samuel Gompers, "Editorial," *American Federationist*, Dec. 1910, 1085–1087; Copy, Santiago Iglesias, "Franca contestación," *Unión Obrera*, 22 Aug. 1910, 2, CDO:1; Juan Ángel Silén, *Apuntes para la historia del movimiento obrero puertorriqueño* (San Juan, PR, 1978), 72–73; César J. Ayala and Rafael Bernabe, *Puerto Rico in the American Century: A History since 1898* (Chapel Hill, NC, 2007), 64; Lawrence B. Glickman, *A Living Wage: American Workers and the Making of Consumer Society* (Ithaca, NY, 1997), xiv.

As Richard A. Greenwald explains in *The Triangle Fire, the Protocols of Peace, and Industrial Democracy in Progressive Era New York* (Philadelphia, 2005), 10–14, 215–216, the signal event in the emergence of the movement for industrial democracy was the successful negotiation by future Supreme Court justice Louis Brandeis of the "Protocol of Peace" in 1910. After a bitter strike in the New York garment industry, the Protocol of Peace laid the foundation for years of growth and stability. Key provisions included sanitation and arbitration committees on which unions, manufacturers, and the public would have representation. On progressives' embrace of "the people" as an undivided whole and their antipathy for "interests" such as political bosses and monopolies that exploited workers, see Stromquist, *Reinventing "The People."*

8. *¡Tierra!*, 4 Apr. 1909, 2, quoted with alteration in Kirk Shaffer, "Tropical Libertarians: Anarchist Movement and Networks in the Caribbean, Southern United States, and Mexico, 1890s–1920s," in *Anarchism and Syndicalism in the*

Colonial and Postcolonial World, 1870–1940, ed. Steven Hirsch and Lucien van der Walt (Boston, 2010), 296; Kirwin R. Shaffer, *Black Flag Boricuas: Anarchism, Antiauthoritarianism, and the Left in Puerto Rico, 1897–1921* (Urbana, IL, 2013), 2–5, 27; Ángel Silén, *Apuntes para la historia*, 69–70; A. G. Quintero-Rivera, "Socialist and Cigarmaker: Artisans' Proletarianization in the Making of the Puerto Rican Working Class," *Latin American Perspectives* 10 (Summer 1983): 19, 24–26, 35; Yamila Azize, *La mujer en la lucha* (Río Piedras, PR, 1985), 56–58, 62, 93.

9. Colton to Edwards, 15 Nov. 1911; Ileana M. Rodríguez-Silva, *Silencing Race: Disentangling Blackness, Colonialism, and National Identities in Puerto Rico* (New York, 2012), 160; Frank McIntyre to George Colton, 11 Feb. 1913, MD NARA 350/5B/1286-98; *Twenty-Ninth Annual Convention of the American Federation of Labor*, 40–41; *Thirty-Third Annual Convention of the American Federation of Labor*, 122–126; "Advance Has Come to Porto Rico, Justice Must," *American Federationist*, Apr. 1914, 320–324; "A. F. of L. in Porto Rico"; DC NARA, 233/626/HR 62A-H13.1.

10. *Hearings upon the Bill Proposing to Amend the Present Organic Law of Porto Rico* (Washington, DC, 1910), 241; *61st Congress, 2d Session, 1909–1910, House Reports (Public)*, vol. 2 (Washington, DC, 1912), no. 750; *62d Congress, 2d Session, December 4, 1911–August 26, 1912, House Reports (Public)*, vol. 2 (Washington, DC, 1912), no. 341; D. Collazo, "Metropolitanas," *La Democracia*, 13 Aug. and 15 Oct. 1909, 2; Un Nativo, "Desde Nueva York," *La Democracia*, 1 Mar. 1910; "Desde Washington," *La Democracia*, 1 Apr. 1910, 1; Porto Rican Exile, "Correo de Nueva York," *La Democracia*, 13 Oct. 1910, 1.

11. "Root against Vote for Porto Ricans," *New York Times*, 15 Feb. 1912, 10; "Habla el Sr. Collazo," *La Democracia*, 26 July 1912, 1 ("gobierno propio"); "En Washington," *La Democracia*, 26 Apr. 1912, 1; "Porto Ricans Here Organize a Club," *New York Times*, 26 June 1911, 4; "Clubhouse for Porto Ricans," *New-York Tribune*, 23 July 1911, 7; "Porto Rican Alliance to Give a Ball," *New York Times*, 27 Dec. 1911, 11; "Porto Ricans Want Self-Government," *Dubuque Telegraph Herald*, 30 Dec. 1911, 4; "Porto Ricans Have a Dance," *New York Times*, 31 Dec. 1911, 8; Edwardo J. L. Raldires, "Citizenship and Self-Government for Puerto Rico," *Report of the Twenty-Ninth Annual Lake Mohonk Conference of Friends of the Indian and Other Dependent Peoples* (Mohonk Lake, NY, 1911), 196–202; "Patriotas en acción," *La Democracia*, 6 Dec. 1911, 1; "A Resolution," 8 Aug. 1911, MD NARA 350/5A/7937-165; Nicolás Kanelos, ed., *Herencia: The Anthology of Hispanic Literature of the United States* (Oxford, 2002), 389; New York State Medical Association, *The Medical Directory of New York, New Jersey and Connecticut*, vol. 6 (New York, [1905]), 35; *The Trow Copartnership and Corporation Directory of the Boroughs of Manhattan and the Bronx, City of New York* (New York, 1914), 1004; Fernando Gaudier, "Crónica de Nueva York," *América*, Oct. 1909, 334; "Spanish Phonographic Records," *American Exporter* 63 (June 1909): 104; "Porto Rican Democrats," *Louisville (KY) Courier-Journal*, 3 June 1908, 1; *Official Report of the Proceedings of the Democratic National Convention Held in Denver, Colorado, July 7, 8, 9 and 10, 1908* (Chicago, 1908), 98, 244; Urey Woodson, comp., *Official Report of the Proceedings of the Democratic National Convention, Held in Baltimore, Maryland, June 25, 26, 27, 28, 29 and July 1 and 2, 1912* (Chicago,

1912), 36–38, 119; Corresponsal, "Desde Nueva York," *La Democracia*, 19 Oct. 1912, 2; "Bryan in New York," *Brooklyn Eagle*, 18 Apr. 1910, 2; "'Tainted' Cash Bogus," *Washington Post*, 24 Aug. 1912, 3; Woodson, *Proceedings of the Democratic National Convention*, 1912, 36–38; "Democrat for Protection," *New York Times*, 5 Aug. 1912, 2.

12. "Patriotas en acción" ("abusos"); Resolution, 8 Aug. 1911; Cablegram, Edwards to Colton, 4 Oct. 1911, MD NARA 350/5A/7937-169; Secretary of War to Domingo Collazo, 19 Aug. 1911, MD NARA 350/5A/7937-164; Domingo Collazo to William Taft, 8 Aug. 1911, MD NARA 350/5A/7937-164; George Colton to Clarence Edwards, 23 Aug. 1911, MD NARA 350/5A/7937-167; Oct. 1911 correspondence between Frankfurter and Flynn in MD NARA 350/21/121/ Collazo, Domingo; and Clarence Edwards to George Colton, 29 Aug. 1911, MD NARA 350/5A/7937-167. Flynn would later head the Federal Bureau of Investigation.

13. Luis Muñoz Rivera, Address, "Political Conditions in Porto Rico," in *Report of the Twenty-Ninth Annual Lake Mohonk Conference*, 195, 196; Luis Muñoz Rivera to Fernandez Vanga, 2 Aug. 1912, CDO:2 ("es un ideal puramente abstracto"; "no puede realizarse"); D. Collazo, "Alienating Porto Rico," *New York Sun*, 28 May 1909, 8; Gonzalo F. Córdova, *Resident Commissioner, Santiago Iglesias and His Times* (Río Piedras, PR, 1993), 113, 117; Translation of an Article Published in the San Juan "Times," February 22d, with Extract from Speech of Speaker de Diego, MD NARA 350/5A/3377-58; María del Pilar Argüelles, *Morality and Power: The U.S. Colonial Experience in Puerto Rico from 1898 to 1948* (New York, 1996), 37, 42; "Root against Vote for Porto Ricans"; *A Civil Government for Porto Rico: Hearings before the Committee on Insular Affairs House of Representatives, 64th Cong., 1st sess., on H.R. 8501, A Bill to Provide a Civil Government for Porto Rico, and for Other Purposes* (Washington, DC, 1916), 10, 98–100 (hereinafter cited as H.R. 8501 Hearings); Jose de Diego, "The Problem of Porto Rico," *Report of the Thirty-First Annual Lake Mohonk Conference of Friends of the Indian and Other Dependent Peoples* (1913), 154–161; George Cabot Ward to Secretary of Interior, 8 June 1909, CDO:1.

14. Elihu Root to Henry Stimson, 7 Dec. 1911, MD NARA 350/5B/1286-36.5; "An Interview with Senator Root," *Observer*, 27 Jan. 1912, 28, MD NARA 350/5B/ 1286-39. Root advocated similar outcomes for Hawai'i and the Philippines.

15. Corresponsal, "Desde Nueva York," 19 Oct. 1912 ("nuevo sistema colonial"; "hemisferio"); D[omingo] Collazo, "Metropolitanas," *La Democracia*, 20 Aug., 2 Nov., and 2, 9 Dec. 1909; Porto Rican Exile, "Correo de Nueva York," *La Democracia*, 22–23 Sept. 1910, 1; Dana G. Munro, *Intervention and Dollar Diplomacy in the Caribbean 1900–1921* (Princeton, NJ, 1964). U.S. colonial officials reinterpreted Caribbean nations' difficulties not as symptoms of oppressive U.S. foreign policy but as native failures that only U.S. occupation would remedy. See George Colton to Clarence Edwards, 20 Jan. 1912, MD NARA 350/5A/3377-121.

16. Root to Stimson, 7 Dec. 1911; "Root against Vote for Porto Ricans"; "Comment," *Harper's Weekly*, 24 Feb. 1912, 5; "Interview with Senator Root"; Clarence Edwards to George Colton, 7 Mar. 1911, MD NARA 350/5A/3377-111; R. H. Todd to Clarence Edwards, 31 Jan. 1912, MD NARA 350/5B/1286-40; "The

Harper's Weekly," *La Democracia*, 12 Mar. 1912, 1; "Porto Rico May Be Independent," *Fairfield Daily Journal*, 15 Feb. 1912, 1.

17. "The Harper's Weekly"; D. Collazo, Letter to Editor, "The Restless Porto Ricans," *New York Times*, 24 Mar. 1912, C11; Ana Georgina Sagardia de Alvarado, "United States–Puerto Rican Relations: The Changing Citizenship Status of the Puerto Rican People under the United States Sovereignty (1898–1917)," PhD diss., University of California, Berkeley, 1983, 304; "1908 Democratic Party Platform,"*The American Presidency Project*, comp. John Woolley and Gerhard Peter (2016), www.presidency.ucsb.edu/ws/?pid=29589; "Republican Party Platform of 1908," in ibid., www.presidency.ucsb.edu/ws/? pid=29632; "1912 Democratic Party Platform," ibid., www.presidency.ucsb.edu/ ws/index.php?pid=29590; "Republican Party Platform of 1912," ibid., www .presidency.ucsb.edu/ws/index.php?pid=29633; Córdova, *Resident Commissioner*, 114–121.

18. Felix Frankfurter to Judge Brown, 29 Dec. 1911, MD NARA 350/5A/23436 4.5; Colton to Edwards, 20 Jan. 1912; *House Documents*, vol. 131, no. 615, 1, 5; [Frank McIntyre?] to George Colton, 22 Nov. 1911, MD NARA 350/5B/1286-22.

19. *Hearings to Amend the Present Organic Law*, 46–47, 128–131, 145; A. Navarrete, "Cuestión de Raza," *La Democracia*, 29 Nov. 1909, 1.

20. *Hearings to Amend the Present Organic Law*, 123, 136–137, 145; Colton to President, 20 Apr. 1910, MD NARA 350/5A/3377-85; Copy, Santiago Iglesias, [Title unknown], *Unión Obrera*, 29 Apr. 1910, CDO:1; Copy, Santiago Iglesias to William Taft, 11 May 1910, CDO:1.

21. Roland P. Falkner, "Citizenship for the Porto Ricans," *American Political Science Review* 4 (May 1910): 180–195; 49 Cong. Rec. 208; *War Department Annual Reports, 1911*, 44–45; H.R. 23000 (16 June 1910); Colton to Edwards, 15 Nov. 1911; Frankfurter to Brown, 29 Dec. 1911.

22. *Hearings to Amend the Present Organic Law*, 128; *1909–1910, House Reports*, no. 750; Frank McIntyre, Memorandum for Secretary of War, 4 May 1912, MD NARA 350/5A/25142-9; Edith Wood to Clarence Edwards, 4 Nov. 1909, MD NARA 350/ 5A/50-8.

23. Colton to Edwards, 2 Mar. 1910; "Views of the Minority," *1909–1910, House Reports*, no. 750, pt. 2; Clarence Edwards to Finis Garrett, 8 Mar. 1910, MD NARA 350/5A/3377-57; Edwards to Colton, 7 Mar. 1911; H.R. 24961 (29 May 1912).

24. Root to Stimson, 7 Dec. 1911; Cablegram, Colton to Clarence Edwards, 24 Jan. 1910, MD NARA 350/5A/3377-23; Clarence Edwards to George Colton, 1 Dec. 1910, MD NARA 350/5A/3377-99; McIntyre to Carrell, 14 June 1912; John Arthur Tarr, *A Study in Boss Politics: William Lorimer of Chicago* (Urbana, IL, 1971), 264–301; *61st Cong., 3d Session, December 5, 1910–March 4, 1911, Senate Reports (Public)*, vol. 1 (Washington, DC, 1911), no. 920; H.R. 23000 (20 Jan. 1911); *62d Cong., 3d session, December 12, 1912–March 4, 1913, Senate Reports (Public)*, vol. 1 (Washington, DC, 1913), no. 1300; H.R. 20048 (24 Feb. 1913); Memorandum for the Secretary of War, 6 Oct. 1913, MD NARA 350/5A/1286-115; "Interview with Senator Root"; Elihu Root to Luis Muñoz Rivera, 10 Feb. 1912, MD NARA 350/5B/1286-44; [Frank McIntyre?] to George Colton, 23 Dec. 1912, MD NARA 350/5B/1286-85; James P. Clarke to Duncan U. Fletcher, 6 Aug. 1912, DC NARA 46/91/Sen 62A-F17/Army Vetinary Bill to Citizenship Granting of

to Porto Rico; Cablegram, McIntyre to Colton, 28 Dec. 1912, MD NARA 350/5B/1286-86; Frank McIntyre to James Clarke, 17 Jan. 1913, MD NARA 350/5B/1286-91; Secretary of War to James Clarke, 27 Jan. 1913, MD NARA 350/5B/1286-93; Frank McIntyre to James Clarke, 28 Feb. 1913, MD NARA 350/5B/1286-104; Santiago Iglesias to Governor Wilson, 25 Feb. 1913, MD NARA 350/5B/1286-104; Samuel Gompers to James P. Clark, 9 Aug. 1912, DC NARA 46/91/Sen 62A-F17/Army Vetinary Bill to Citizenship Granting of to Porto Rico.

25. "Patriotas en acción."
26. "Chief of Bureau of Insular Affairs," *Boston Daily Globe*, 4 Feb. 1912, SM4; Cecilia Elizabeth O'Leary, *To Die For: The Paradox of American Patriotism* (Princeton, NJ, 1999), 195; George Colton to Clarence Edwards, 31 Jan. 1911, MD NARA 350/5A/3377-107; H.R. 24961, sec. 12; Frank McIntyre to Newton Gilbert, 23 July 1912, MD NARA 350/5A/10418-6. On Wilson's early support among Southern whites, his professed support for segregation, his condonation of those who demoted and fired African American workers in the South, and his break with traditions reserving certain federal posts for African Americans, see Nell Irvin Painter, *Standing at Armageddon: The United States 1877–1919* (New York, 1987), 278–279, and Michael McGerr, *A Fierce Discontent: The Rise and Fall of the Progressive Movement in America, 1870–1920* (New York, 2003), 195–196.
27. D. Collazo, Letter to Editor, "Porto-Rican Conditions," *New York Evening Post*, 14 Aug. 1916, MD NARA 350/21/Collazo, Domingo; McIntyre to Gilbert, 23 July 1912; Memorandum for the Secretary of War, 6 Oct. 1913.
28. McIntyre to Clarke, 17 Jan. 1913; McIntyre to Gilbert, 23 July 1912; H.R. 8501 Hearings, 55; Felix Frankfurter to John Gray, 2[9/7?] Nov. 1911, MD NARA 350/5A/12603-12; *Government for Porto Rico: Hearings before the Committee on Pacific Islands and Porto Rico United States Senate, 64th Cong., 1st sess., on S. 1217, a Bill to Provide a Civil Government for Porto Rico and for Other Purposes* (Washington, DC, 1916), 92, 16 [hereinafter cited as S. 1217 Hearings]; *A Civil Government for Porto Rico: Hearings before the Committee on Insular Affairs, House of Representatives, 63d Cong., 2d sess., on H.R. 13818, a Bill to Provide a Civil Government for Porto Rico, and for Other Purposes* (Washington, DC, 1914), 26 [hereinafter cited as H.R. 13818 Hearings); Emily S. Rosenberg, *Financial Missionaries to the World: The Politics and Culture of Dollar Diplomacy, 1900–1930* (Cambridge, MA, 1999); Frederick E. Hoxie: *A Final Promise: The Campaign to Assimilate the Indians, 1880–1920* (Lincoln, NE, 2001 [1984]), 152–168, 191–234; Arthur Yager to Frank McIntyre, 4 July 1914, MD NARA 350/5B/3377-214. On the failure of the bureau to convince other departments to cede it responsibilities in deference to Puerto Rican autonomy, see Lindley Garrison to Secretary of Treasury, 19 May 1914, MD NARA 350/5B/3377-197, and Frank McIntyre, "The Pending Organic Act for Porto Rico," 7 July 1916, MD NARA 350/5B/3377-284.
29. David W. Blight, *Race and Reunion: The Civil War in American Memory* (Cambridge, MA, 2001), 394 and n20, 111–112, 148–149, 263, 295–296, 358, 394–397; Eric Foner, *Reconstruction: America's Unfinished Revolution, 1863–1877* (New York, 1988), xix–xx and nn1–2, 609–610; Michael Perman, *Struggle for Mastery: Disfranchisement in the South 1888–1908* (Chapel Hill, NC, 2001); John Tweedy, *A History of the Republican National Conventions from 1856 to 1908* (Danbury, CT, 1910); "Republican Party Platform of 1912"; C. Vann

Woodward, *The Strange Career of Jim Crow* (Oxford, 2001 [1955]), 98; C. Vann
Woodward, *Origins of the New South, 1877–1913,* rev. ed. (Baton Rouge, LA,
1999 [1951]), 431–434, 440–443, 456–468; Maxwell Bloomfield, "Dixon's 'The
Leopard's Spots': A Study in Popular Racism," *American Quarterly* 16 (1964): 392;
Nina Silber, *The Romance of Reunion: Northerners and the South, 1865–1900*
(Chapel Hill, NC, 1993), 185–186; O'Leary, *To Die For,* 133, 206–208, 132, 194–
205; Mark Elliott, *Color-Blind Justice: Albion Tourgée and the Quest for Racial
Equality from the Civil War to* Plessy v. Ferguson (Oxford, 2006), 308; Justin
Behrend, "Facts and Memories: John R. Lynch and the Revising of
Reconstruction History in the Era of Jim Crow," *Journal of African American
History* 97 (2012): 427–448.
   On the glorification during the period of the Confederacy and the society from
which it sprang, see W. Fitzhugh Brundage, *The Southern Past: A Clash of Race and
Memory* (Cambridge, MA, 2005), 33, 49–50, 106, 136; O'Leary, *To Die For,* 194–
195, 198–199; John. M. Coski, *The Confederate Battle Flag: America's Most
Embattled Emblem* (Cambridge, MA, 2005), 50; Blight, *Race and Reunion,* 394–
395; Cynthia Mills, "Introduction," in *Monuments to the Lost Cause: Women, Art,
and the Landscapes of Southern Memory,* ed. Cynthia Mills and Pamela H. Simpson
(Knoxville, TN, 2003), xvii; Karen L. Cox, *Dixie's Daughters: The United
Daughters of the Confederacy and the Preservation of Confederate Culture*
(Gainesville, FL, 2003), 49–72; John R. Neff, *Honoring the Civil War Dead:
Commemoration and the Problem of Reconciliation* (Lawrence, KS, 2005), 209–
210, 213, 222–230. Frequency of the use of variants of the term "carpetbagger" in
book print increased 240 percent across 1897–1916, according to my 23 April 2013
Culturomics analysis, www.culturomics.org/home. On fights over history-textbook
treatments of the Civil War, see Stuart McConnell, *Glorious Contentment: The
Grand Army of the Republic, 1865–1900* (Chapel Hill, NC, 1992); and James M.
McPherson, "Long-Legged Yankee Lies," in *The Memory of the Civil War in
American Culture,* ed. Alice Fahs and Joan Waugh (Chapel Hill, NC, 2004), 64–78.
30. D. Collazo, Letter to Editor, "Our Rule in Porto Rico," *Evening Post,* 4 Feb. 1920,
MD NARA 350/5B/50-74; H.R. 13818 (24 Feb. 1914); H.R. 14694 (17 Mar. 1914);
S. 4604 (25 Feb. 1914); S. 5845 (13 Jun 1914); S. 1217 (10 Dec. 1915); H.R. 8501
(10 Jan. 1916); Frank McIntyre to Arthur Yager, 6 Mar. 1914, MD NARA 350/5A/
3377-156; "All Porto Rico for Jones Bill," *Porto Rico Progress,* 8 July 1914, MD
NARA 350/5B/3377A; Sagardia de Alvarado, "United States–Puerto Rican
Relations," 358; *Report of Proceedings of the Thirty-Fourth Annual Convention
of the American Federation of Labor* (Washington, DC, 1914), 89.
31. Memorandum for the Secretary of War, 6 Oct. 1913, 15; H.R. 13818 Hearings, 69,
7–8, 26, 34–36; *Civil Government for Porto Rico: Hearings before the Committee
on Pacific Islands and Porto Rico United States Senate, 63d Cong., 2d sess., on S.
4604 a Bill to Provide a Civil Government for Porto Rico, and for Other Purposes*
(Washington, DC, 1914), 6, 1–4 [hereinafter S. 4604 Hearings, 25 Feb. 1914];
Sagardia de Alvarado, "United States–Puerto Rican Relations," 318; Charlotte
Jean Shelton, "William Atkinson Jones, 1848–1918: Independent Democracy in
Gilded Age Virginia," PhD diss., University of Virginia, 1980; *1909–1910, House
Reports,* no. 750; *Hearings to Amend the Present Organic Law,* 128, 130, 241;
H.R. 8501 Hearings, 7, 11; Arthur Yager to Lindley Garrison, 19 Feb. 1914, MD
NARA 350/5A/1286-128; Regis Post, "Report and Tally on Interrogatories Sent

Out by Governor Post to Various Citizens of Porto Rico, in September, 1909," 1 Oct. 1909, MD NARA 350/5A/168-58; Tomás Pérez Varela, "Conversación en torno a la ciudadanía: Los cuestionarios de 1909," master's thesis, Universidad de Puerto Rico, Recinto de Río Piedras, 2007, especially 2, 30–31; Falkner, "Citizenship for the Porto Ricans"; Frank McIntyre, Memorandum for the Secretary of War, 20 July 1916, MD NARA 350/5B/3377-285; Frank McIntyre to Senator Shafroth, 25 July 1916, MD NARA 350/5B/1286-134 and accompanying correspondence.

McIntyre and Jones also worried that, because extending the Constitution to Puerto Rico could trigger the requirement of equal taxation, "there would be some constitutional question" as to whether the island could continue to retain its customs receipts. See Sagardia de Alvarado, "United States–Puerto Rican Relations," 352; McIntyre, "Pending Organic Act." But as one former attorney general of Puerto Rico commented, "nothing" in the Constitution "binds the Congress in any way as to the disposition of the money received" as duties. See Sagardia de Alvarado, "United States–Puerto Rican Relations," 352–353. In any case, the solution chosen for this problem was the same as that chosen when seeking to avoid constitutional jury guarantees. Congress did not include that constitutional language in bills extending rights to Puerto Rico. See S. 4604; H.R. 13818. Both McIntyre and Yager stressed that citizenship "has nothing whatever to do with the franchise of [*sic*] power to vote." See Copy, Statement of Hon. Arthur Yager before the Senate Committee on Pacific Islands and Porto Rico, 21 Dec. 1914, MD NARA 350/5A/3377-232, 1–3 [hereinafter S. 4604 Hearings, 21 Dec. 1914]; Frank McIntyre to Hugh Healy, 28 May 1912, MD NARA 350/5B/ 1286-59. Jones also worried that congressional extension of the formal label of "territory" could trigger eventual statehood. See H.R. 13818 Hearings, 69. But the demand for territorial status was not as insistent as that for citizenship. As Felix Frankfurter wrote in his memorandum of 6 October 1913 to the Secretary of War, MD NARA 350/5A/1286-115, good nonlegal reasons also existed to withhold the moniker. On the rare Democrat still demanding citizenship for all Americans and "State government" for every "qualified" "territory," and on incredulous reactions from both parties, see H.R. 13818 Hearings, 69–71.

32. Felix Frankfurter to Secretary of War, 11 Mar. 1914, quoted in S. 4604 Hearings, 25 Feb. 1914, 21–24; H.R. 13818 Hearings, 49–50. The absence of existing or planned tariffs on United States–Puerto Rico trade insulated debate over the bill from fights over protectionism. As Frankfurter's citations to both Justice Brown's opinion for himself and Justice White's concurrence in *Downes v. Bidwell* (1901) reflected, the Supreme Court had yet to embrace White's nonincorporation doctrine unequivocally. In a letter to Foster Brown on 6 January 1912, MD NARA 350/ 5B/1286-39, Frankfurter predicted that U.S. citizenship was even consistent with Elihu Root's aim of establishing U.S. protectorates throughout the Caribbean. On debates over whether women should demand or reject dependence as a basis for labor protections such as maximum-hours laws, see Adam Winkler, "A Revolution Too Soon: Woman Suffragists and the 'Living Constitution,'" *New York University Law Review* 76 (2001): 1456–1526, and Karen Pastorello, *A Power among Them: Bessie Abramowitz Hillman and the Making of the Amalgamated Clothing Workers of America* (Urbana, IL, 2008), 60–61.

33. Jones Act (the Philippines), 39 Stat. 545 (1916); H.R. 13818; S. 4604; H.R. 14694; S. 1217; H.R. 8501; H.R. 18459 (20 Aug. 1914).
34. Luis Muñoz Rivera to Woodrow Wilson, 18 Nov. 1913, MD NARA 350/5A/ 26429-33; Beckwith, 10 Dec. 1913 translation of "Attitude Defined," *La Democracia,* 18 Nov. 1913, MD NARA 350/5A/26429-35; Translation, "Interview with Mr. Texidor," *El Tiempo,* 24 Mar. 1913, MD NARA 350/5A/ 20808-22; "Democrats for Protection"; Luis Muñoz Rivera to Lindley Garrison, 6 Mar. 1913, MD NARA 350/21/Luis Muñoz Rivera; Beckwith translation of "Important Statements," *Heraldo Español,* 23 Oct. 1913, MD NARA 350/5A/ 26429-28; Porto Rican Exile, "Correo de Nueva York," *La Democracia,* 22 July 1910, 1.
35. Memorandum, 8 Oct. 1913, MD NARA 350/21/Luis Muñoz Rivera; Domingo Collazo to Lindley M. Garrison, 22 Mar. 1913, MD NARA 350/21/Collazo, Domingo; Henry Molina to Woodrow Wilson, 22 Nov. 1913, MD NARA 350/ 5A/26522-1; Woodson, *Proceedings of the Democratic National Convention, 1912,* 119, 230; MD NARA 350/21/Collazo, Domingo.
36. Copy, Sam Gompers to Prudencia Rivera Martinez, n.d., CDO:2; Sagardia de Alvarado, "United States–Puerto Rican Relations," 317, 341–342; *Thirty-Fourth Annual Convention of the American Federation of Labor,* 53; D. Collazo, "Porto Rican Autonomy," *New York Times,* 7 July 1914, 8; President's Wilson's First Annual Message, 2 Dec. 1913, in *The State of the Union Messages of the Presidents (1790–1966),* ed. Fred L. Israel, vol. 3 (New York, 1969), 2548; *Yearbook of Association Sugar Producers of Porto Rico* (San Juan, PR, 1911), MD NARA 350/5A/24066-4; "Democrats for Protection"; Corresponsal, "Desde Nueva York," 19 Oct. 1912; *Schedule E: Duties on Sugar, Molasses, Sirups, Etc.* (Washington, DC, 1912), 113–117, 136, 248–249; Porto Rico Official Economic Commission, *Porto Rico's Case and the Tariff Bill* (Washington, DC, 1913), MD NARA 350/5A/422-90; [illegible], Acting Secretary of Porto Rico to Chief of Bureau of Insular Affairs, 2 Apr. 1912, CDO:2; Cablegram Wrapper, del Valle to Colton, 6 Apr. 1912, CDO:2; C. P. Edwards to Rafael del Valle, 1[?] Apr. 1912, CDO:2; Cablegram, McIntyre to R. Del Valle, 22 Apr. 1912, CDO:2; Cablegram, Rodríguez to Col. McIntyre, 22 Apr. 1912, CDO:2; Santiago Iglesias to Woodrow Wilson, 8 Apr. 1913, MD NARA 350/5A/422-76; Clarence Edwards, Memorandum, 25 Mar. 1912, MD NARA 350/5A/422-44; "Protection and Sugar," *American Economist,* 7 Dec. 1917, 270; "Tariff and Retail Price," *Facts about Sugar* 2 (Dec. 1915): 4; Jorge Perez-Lopez Jr., *The Economics of Cuban Sugar* (Pittsburgh, 1991), 130; "Sugar Prices in 1915," *Facts about Sugar* 2 (Jan. 1916): 1; "Free Sugar Repeal Bill," *Facts about Sugar* 2 (Mar. 1916): 1, 4.
37. Porto Rican Exile, "Correo de Nueva York," *La Democracia,* 20 Aug. 1910, 1 ("la gran familia latino americana"), 26 Aug. and 2–3 Sept. 1910, 1; "Una Carta Curiosa," *La Democracia,* 20 Sept. 1910, 1; Joaquín Colón López, *Pioneros puertorriqueños en Nueva York 1917–1947* (Houston, TX, 2002), 87–88, 183; Nélida Pérez and Amilcar Tirado, *Boricuas en el norte* (New York, 1987), 7; Bernardo Vega, *Memoirs of Bernardo Vega: A Contribution to the History of the Puerto Rican Community in New York,* ed. César Andreu Iglesias, trans. Juan Flores (New York, 1984 [1977]), 99; "Personalities at the Lake Mohonk Conference," *African Times and Orient Review* 1, no. 5 (Nov. 1912): 161; "Don Domingo Collazo recibirá hoy el postrer homenaje de sus compatriotas," *La Prensa*

(New York), 26 Sept. 1929, 3; Emilio Yaselli to Newton D. Baker, 17 Feb. 1917, MD NARA 350/21/Collazo, Domingo; D. Collazo to Hugh Wallace, 2 Feb. 1917, MD NARA 350/21/Collazo, Domingo; Memorandum, 8 Oct. 1913; Muñoz Rivera to Wilson, 18 Nov. 1913.

38. D. Collazo, Letter to Editor, "Porto Rico's Decision," *New York Sun*, 2 Nov. 1915, 6; H.R. 13818 Hearings, 53–60; Frank Otto Gatell, "The Art of the Possible: Luis Muñoz Rivera and the Puerto Rican Jones Bill," *Americas* 17 (July 1960): 1–20; Sagardia de Alvarado, "United States–Puerto Rican Relations," 342, 358; McIntyre to Yager, 6 Mar. 1914; Martin Travieso Jr. et al., Draft Platform of the Partido Unionista, trans. Beckwith, 22 Nov. 1913, MD NARA 350/5A/26429-34, 54; 53 Cong. Rec. 7469; José de Diego to Prudencio Rivera Martinez, 14 June [1913?], CDO:2; Falkner, "Citizenship for the Porto Ricans"; George Colton to Clarence Edwards, 17 Jan. 1912, MD NARA 350/5B/1286-38; Jones Act (the Philippines), 39 Stat. 545 (1916); José A. Cabranes, "Citizenship and the American Empire: Notes on the Legislative History of the United States Citizenship of Puerto Ricans," *University of Pennsylvania Law Review* 127 (1978): 480; "Porto Ricans Hope for U.S. Citizenship," *Washington Star*, 9 Jan. 1916, MD NARA 350/5B/3377A-4; Gompers to Rivera Martinez; correspondence collected at MD NARA 350/5A/ 3377-152 and 5B/3377-187, -200, -207, -222 to -224, -247, -250, -300. Even as posturing, Unionistas' pro-independence demand was misguided. It divided Unionistas from potential Republicano and colonial allies without constituting a credible threat. Puerto Rico was too small to go it alone, and neither Cuban nor Dominican authorities had encouraged de Diego's plans for a Spanish "Antillean Confederation."

39. 54 Cong. Rec. 2250; S. 1217 Hearings, 62, ii, 94; Woodward, *Origins of the New South*, 375; O'Leary, *To Die For*, 195, 203–205, 242–243. Vardaman sat on the Committee on Pacific Islands and Porto Rico. For an account of a prominent House member who doubted Puerto Ricans' racial fitness for self-government, see, Cabranes, "Citizenship," 481. Implicit in Vardaman's account was a point that Governor Yager expressly conceded. Democrats had "fully accepted" a federal power of a sort at the heart of the Civil War: "the dictum of the constitution that Congress alone can alienate territory of the United States." See "Porto Rico Versus Philippines," paper unknown, [Nov.? 1913], MD NARA 350/21/Arthur Yager. On metaphors and realities of disease and contagiousness in the construction of race, governance, and polity, see Nayan Shah, *Contagious Divides: Epidemics and Race in San Francisco's Chinatown* (Berkeley, CA, 2001).

40. 53 Cong. Rec. 7470–7473; S. 1217 Hearings, 55; *Hearings to Amend the Present Organic Law*, 146; H.R. 8501 Hearings, 10. Cabranes, "Citizenship," 473–482, presents Muñoz Rivera's opposition as more half-hearted. Hilda Sabato describes a gap between ideals and practices of citizenship, in "On Political Citizenship in Nineteenth-Century Latin America," *American Historical Review* 106 (Oct. 2001): 9. Historical examples of broadly distributed national citizenship that carried civil and political rights existed in countries near Puerto Rico and the United States. For examples, see Laurent Dubois, *A Colony of Citizens: Revolution and Slave Emancipation in the French Caribbean, 1787–1804* (Chapel Hill, NC, 2004); C. L. R. James, *The Black Jacobins* (London, 1938); Thomas Holt, *The Problem of Freedom: Race, Labor, and Politics in Jamaica and Britain, 1832– 1938* (Baltimore, 1991); Myriam Cottias, "Gender and Republican Citizenship in

the French West Indies, 1848–1945," *Slavery and Abolition* 26 (Aug. 2005): 233–245. While the legal content of citizenship never matched ideals of full national membership and complete civil and political rights, the Unionista leaders had once hoped that the gap would be modest enough to render the status a waystation to self-government.

41. Collazo, "Porto-Rican Conditions"; *Civil Government for Porto Rico*, H.R. Rep. 77 (25 Jan. 1916); H.R. 9533 (20 Jan. 1916, 20 Feb. 1917); Jones Act, 39 Stat. 951 (1917); *House Documents*, vol. 131, no. 615; Pedro A. Cabán, *Constructing a Colonial People: Puerto Rico and the United States, 1898–1932* (Boulder, CO, 1999), 209; "El Bill Jones," *La Democracia*, 28 July 1916, 1; Copy, Beckwith translation of ["Interview with the Governor"], *La Democracia*, 5 Feb. 1916, MD NARA 350/5B/3377A-7; "Porto Ricans Hope for U.S. Citizenship"; "El Bill Jones," *La Democracia*, 27 Jan. 1916, 4; "El Bill Jones es superior a la ley Foraker," *La Democracia*, 11 Feb. 1916, 2; correspondence at MD NARA 350/5B/3377-269, -275, and -305 to -308.

Elihu Root, who had pressed the alternative of formal independence tempered by dollar diplomacy, had left the Senate in 1915. Republican Representative Wesley Jones of Washington, not William A. Jones, was the author of the Jones Act of 1920, 41 Stat. 988 (1920), 46 U.S.C.A. § 55102 (2018). That law still requires that maritime trade between Puerto Rico and other parts of the United States be conducted by vessels sailing under the flag of the United States. Without citizenship, island migrants to the mainland could find themselves barred from voting, at least initially. On the state-by-state end of alien voting from 1874 to 1926, see Aziz Rana, *The Two Faces of American Freedom* (Cambridge, MA, 2010), 237.

42. For a review of work establishing the importance of grounding groups' present struggles in their hopes of achieving longer-term goals and in the role of jurisgenesis (the creation of legal meaning through storytelling) in creating doctrine, see James Gray Pope, "Labor's Constitution of Freedom," *Yale Law Journal* (1997): 941–1031, and "The Thirteenth Amendment versus the Commerce Clause: Labor and the Shaping of American Constitutional Law," *Columbia Law Review* 102 (2002): 1–122. Francesca Polletta describes a dynamic during the Civil Rights movement that, similar to the dynamic envisioned by Iglesias, involved legalistic claims making. See Polletta, "The Structural Context of Novel Rights Claims: Southern Civil Rights Organizing, 1961–1966," *Law & Society Review* 34 (2000): 385–388.

43. Statement of Frank McIntyre, Assistant to the Chief of the Bureau of Insular Affairs, *Hearings before the Committee on Insular Affairs, U.S. Senate, 2–4 May 1912*, quoted in Robert C. McGreevey, "Borderline Citizens: Puerto Ricans and the Politics of Migration, Race, and Empire, 1898–1948," PhD diss., Brandeis University, 2008, 132–133, 131; Samuel Gompers, "Porto Rico," *American Federationist*, May 1914, 377–389; *Final Report of the Commission on Industrial Relations* (Washington, DC, and Chicago, 1915), 240, 239; J. C. Bills Jr., *Report on the Housing Conditions of Laborers in Porto Rico* (San Juan, PR, 1914), 84, MD NARA 350/5B/975-58; Ayala and Bernabe, *Puerto Rico*, 39; Kelvin A. Santiago-Valles, *"Subject People" and Colonial Discourses: Economic Transformation and Social Disorder in Puerto Rico, 1898–1947* (Albany, NY, 1994), 28, 56–57, 61, 88–89; James L. Dietz, *Economic History of Puerto Rico: Institutional Change and Capitalist Development* (Princeton, NJ, 1986), 117; Shaffer, *Black Flag Boricuas*, 27; *Thirty-Third Annual Convention of the American Federation of Labor*, 123,

376; César J. Ayala, *American Sugar Kingdom: The Plantation Economy of the Spanish Caribbean, 1898–1934* (Chapel Hill, NC, 1999), ch. 4; Cesar J. Ayala and Laird W. Bergad, "Rural Puerto Rico in the Early Twentieth Century Reconsidered: Land and Society, 1899–1915," *Latin American Research Review* 37 (2002): 65–97; Angel G. Quintero Rivera, *Patricios y plebeyos: Burgueses, hacendados, artesanos y obreros: Las relaciones de clase en el Puerto Rico de cambio siglo* (San Juan, PR, 1988), 151–153; Miles Galvin, "II: The Organized Labor Movement and Nationalism," *Latin American Perspectives* 3 (Summer 1976): 25; D. Collazo, Letter to Editor, "Porto Rican Politics," *New York Evening Post*, 25 Aug. 1919, MD NARA 350/21/Domingo Collazo; C. B. Hode[?], Memorandum for General Walcutt, 26 Apr. 1920, MD NARA 350/5B/975-281; Miles Galvin, "The Early Development of the Organized Labor Movement in Puerto Rico," *Latin American Perspectives* 3 (Summer 1976): 25; Miles Galvin, *The Organized Labor Movement in Puerto Rico* (London, 1979), 32, 57–58, 74; Galvin, "Organized Labor Movement and Nationalism," 24–25; McGreevey, "Borderline Citizens," 127. Seasonally adjusted unemployment ran around 18 percent.

44. David Montgomery, *The Fall of the House of Labor: The Workplace, the State, and American Labor Activism, 1865–1925* (New York, 1987), 6; Josiah Bartlett Lambert, *"If the Workers Took a Notion": The Right to Strike and American Political Development* (Ithaca, NY, 2005), 69; Stromquist, *Reinventing "The People,"* 169; Karson, *American Labor,* 73–112, 174, 193, 198; Philip S. Foner, *History of the Labor Movement in the United States,* vol. 4: *The Industrial Workers of the World, 1905–1917* (New York, 1973 [1965]), 175, 183–185, 191, 198–201, 320, 325, 368–371; William E. Forbath, *Law and the Shaping of the American Labor Movement* (Cambridge, MA, 1991), 156–157; Letter to Editor, "Should the Bureau of Labor of Porto Rico Be a Dependency of Iglesias's Federation?" *San Juan Times,* 13 Oct. 1915, MD NARA 350/5B/975-103; Philip S. Foner, *History of the Labor Movement in the United States,* vol. 6: *On the Eve of America's Entrance into World War I, 1915–1916* (New York, 1982), 222–223; Philip S. Foner, *History of the Labor Movement in the United States,* vol. 7: *Labor and World War I, 1914–1918* (New York, 1987), 159; W. B. Wilson to the Secretary of War, 27 Mar. 1913, CDO:2; Samuel Gompers to Santiago Iglesias, 29 Jan. 1916, SGL 214/877; MD NARA 350/21/Flournoy Roberts.

    On conflict between the AFL and the Amalgamated Clothing Workers of America, which aimed to organize the needle trade across race and sex lines, see Pastorello, *A Power among Them*; Steven Fraser, *Labor Will Rule: Sidney Hillman and the Rise of American Labor* (New York, 1991). United Mine Workers locals were racially integrated at mines that hired African American and white workers. For the foundational account, see Herbert G. Gutman, "The Negro and the United Mine Workers of America: The Career and Letters of Richard L. Davis and Something of Their Meaning: 1890–1900," in *The Negro and the American Labor Movement,* ed. Jacobson Julius (Garden City, NY, 1968), 49 et seq.

45. *Report of Proceedings of the Thirty-Sixth Annual Convention of the American Federation of Labor* (Washington, DC, 1916), 166; *Thirty-Fourth Annual Convention of the American Federation of Labor,* 54; Santiago Iglesias to Woodrow Wilson, 14 June 1915, CDO:2; *Report of Proceedings of the Thirty-Fifth Annual Convention of the American Federation of Labor* (Washington, DC, 1915), 181; Dionicio Nodín Valdés, *Organized Agriculture and the Labor*

Movement before the UFW: Puerto Rico, Hawai'i, California (Austin, TX, 2011), 45–46; Arthur Yager to Woodrow Wilson, 19 Apr. 1915, MD NARA 350/5B/975-66; F. C. Roberts, Fourth Annual Report of the Bureau of Labor to the Legislature of Porto Rico (San Juan, PR), 6–7, MD NARA 350/5B/25142-33; McGreevey, "Borderline Citizens," 157–158, 168; Gervasio L. García and A. G. Quintero Rivera, Desafío y solidaridad: Breve historia del movimiento obrero puertorriqueño (San Juan, PR, 1986), 64–71; Shaffer, Black Flag Boricuas, 108; Santiago-Valles, "Subject People," 113; Galvin, "Early Development," 25; Santiago Iglesias to Samuel Gompers, 22 Feb. 1915, CDO:2.

46. Government of Porto Rico, Administrative Bulletin No. 89, San Juan, PR, 20 Feb. 1915, MD NARA 350/5B/975-66; Arthur Yager to the Fiscals, the Alcaldes, and the District Chiefs of Police of Porto Rico, 20 Feb. 1915, MD NARA 350/5B/975-66; Iglesias to Gompers, 22 Feb. 1915; S. 1217 Hearings, 110–111, 118–119, 141–142; Nodín Valdés, Organized Agriculture, 45–46; Yager to Wilson, 19 Apr. 1915; Thirty-Sixth Annual Convention of the American Federation of Labor, 166; Santiago Iglesias to Frank McIntyre, 20 May 1914, MD NARA 350/5B/975-43; Santiago Iglesias to Arthur Yager, 5 May 1914, MD NARA 350/5B/975-44; Santiago Iglesias to Arthur Yager, 9 May 1914, MD NARA 350/5B/975-41; Thirty-Fourth Annual Convention of the American Federation of Labor, 198–199; Final Report and Testimony Submitted to Congress by the Commission on Industrial Relations (Washington, DC, 1916), 11153–11154; J. Hernandez Users to Attorney General, 19 Apr. 1915, CDO:2; Santiago Iglesias, "Strike of Porto Rican Agricultural Workers," American Federationist, Apr. 1915, 264–267; Iglesias to Wilson, 14 June 1915.

47. Copy, Woodrow Wilson to Samuel Gompers, 20 Mar. 1916, SGL 217/321; H.R. 8501 Hearings, 17; McGreevey, "Borderline Citizens," 33; Beekman Winthrop, "Industrial Progress in Porto Rico," North American Review, Jan. 1906, 105; "Dr. Arthur Yager," New York Times, 25 Dec. 1941, 25; Truman R. Clark, Puerto Rico and the United States, 1917–1933 (Pittsburgh, 1975), 22, 57.

48. Iglesias, "Strike"; Pope, "Labor's Constitution of Freedom"; Pope, "The Thirteenth Amendment"; See William E. Forbath, Law and the Shaping of the American Labor Movement (Cambridge, MA, 1991), 136–137; Santiago Iglesias Pantín, ¿Quiénes somos? (Organizaciones obreras) (San Juan, PR, 1914), especially 32–33, 80; Santiago Iglesias, "Fundamental Economic Questions," trans. Macias, 1915, MD NARA 350/5B/975-102; Iglesias to Gompers, 22 Feb. 1915; S. 1217 Hearings, 116, 140; Ruth O'Brien, Workers' Paradox: The Republican Origins of New Deal Labor Policy, 1886–1935 (Chapel Hill, NC, 1998), 19; W. Pitkin to Santiago Iglesias, 21 May 1914, CDO:2; Santiago Iglesias to Arthur Yager, May [23, 1914?], CDO:2; Iglesias to Wilson, 14 June 1915; Laura Weinrib, The Taming of Free Speech: America's Civil Liberties Compromise (Cambridge, MA, 2016), 8, 32–35; Thirty-Fourth Annual Convention of the American Federation of Labor, 195; Nodín Valdés, Organized Agriculture, 45–46; Galvin, "Organized Labor Movement and Nationalism," 17–33, 24; A. G. Quintero Rivera, Conflictos de clase y política en Puerto Rico (Río Piedras, PR, 1977), 103; Samuel Gompers to Woodrow Wilson, 29 July 1915, CDO:2; Thirty-Fifth Annual Convention of the American Federation of Labor, 181. The American Federationist includes many examples of contemporary Thirteenth Amendment arguments. For an early argument along such lines by Gompers, see "Wrongs of the Sailors," New York Times, 26 Mar. 1897, 1.

Karson, Lambert, and Daniel Katz each describe similar benefits from strikes on the mainland. See Karson, *American Labor*, 187, 193; Lambert, *"If the Workers Took a Notion,"* 10–11; and Daniel Katz, *All Together Different: Yiddish Socialists, Garment Workers, and the Labor Roots of Multiculturalism* (New York, 2011), 51.

49. Abstract of Arthur Yager, "Fundamental Social and Political Problems of Porto Rico," Address Given at Lake Mohonk Conference, 22 Oct. 1915, MD NARA 350/5B/975-101A; Arthur Yager to Frank McIntyre, 24 Jan. 1917, MD NARA 350/5B/975-122; *Final Report and Testimony on Industrial Relations*, 11151–11154; Arthur Yager to Joseph Tumulty, 28 June 1915, MD NARA 350/5B/975-93B; Greenwald, *Triangle Fire*, 9–13; Stromquist, *Reinventing "The People,"* 71; Gompers, "Porto Rico"; Arthur Yager to Frank McIntyre, 10 June 1914, MD NARA 350/5B/3377-207; Yager to Iglesias, 5 Oct. 1914, CDO:2.

On U.S. judges' equation of strikes with violent extortion, see Melvyn Dubofsky, "The Federal Judiciary, Free Labor, and Equal Rights," in *The Pullman Strike and the Crisis of the 1890s: Essays on Labor and Politics*, ed. Richard Schneirov, Shelton Stromquist, and Nick Salvatore (Urbana, IL, 1999), 165–166. Puerto Rico joined much of the United States in lacking governmental institutions capable of addressing causes of industrial unrest. Just as stateside presidents, governors, and mayors deployed armed forces to contain conflicts that arose, so too was this done in Puerto Rico, where police clashed with strikers and Yager warned against removing a military regiment amid labor tensions. See Lambert, *"If the Workers Took a Notion,"* 10, 13, 44, 58, 65; Arthur Yager to Frank McIntyre, 14 Apr. 1914, MD NARA 350/5B/3377-189; Arthur Yager to Frank McIntyre, 22 Apr. 1914, MD NARA 350/5B/3377-194; Yager to McIntyre, 10 June 1914; Arthur Yager to Walcutt, 10 Aug. 1915, MD NARA 350/21/Flourney Roberts. On free labor and strikes, see Dubofsky, "The Federal Judiciary." On liberty of contract, see Lochner v. New York, 198 U.S. 45 (1905); Forbath, *Law and Labor*, 37–58; and Gary D. Rowe, "The Legacy of *Lochner*: *Lochner* Revisionism Revisited," *Law & Social Inquiry* 24 (1999): 221–252. For an overview of U.S. thought on free speech, see David M. Rabban, *Free Speech in Its Forgotten Years, 1870–1920* (Cambridge, 1997); Weinrib, *Taming of Free Speech*, 4, 32.

50. Samuel Gompers, *Seventy Years of Life and Labor: An Autobiography*, vol. 2 (New York, 1925), 222–223, 203; "Letter of Mr. Samuel Gompers," *Justicia*, [Aug.?] 1915, 1, MD NARA 350/5B/975-93; [Santiago Iglesias] to Samuel Gompers, [Apr. or May, 1915], CDO:2; Assistant to Chief of Bureau to Arthur Yager, 29 June 1915, MD NARA 350/5A/14840-100; *Final Report and Testimony on Industrial Relations*, 11194, 11197–11198; Chester Wright to President, 5 Apr. 1915, MD NARA 350/5B/975-61; Samuel Gompers to Santiago Iglesias, 14 Mar. 1916, SGL 217/2. In pursuing his claims-making strategy, Iglesias benefited from workers' personal and family memories of bringing complaints concerning illegal and immoral labor conditions before island authorities. In "Freedom in the Making: The Slaves of Hacienda La Esperanza, Manatí, Puerto Rico, on the Eve of Abolition, 1868–76," *Social History* 36 (Aug. 2011): 280–293, Astrid Cubano Iguina reports how slaves during the last year of slavery brought complaints to authorities about mistreatment by masters.

For more on Gompers's understanding and deployment of inherent rights, see Weinrib, *Taming of Free Speech*, 15–16, 25–26, 32, 34–35; Daniel R. Ernst, *Lawyers against Labor: From Individual Rights to Corporate Liberalism* (Urbana,

IL, 1995), 1, 130–135. On understandings of rights that sweep more broadly than existing laws among late twentieth-century, working-class disputants in eastern Massachusetts, see Sally Engle Merry, *Getting Justice and Getting Even: Legal Consciousness among Working-Class Americans* (Chicago, 1990). On similar dynamics along the overland trail, see John Phillip Reid, *Law for the Elephant: Property and Social Behavior on the Overland Trail* (San Marino, CA, 1980). Naomi Mezey and Hendrik Hartog imply that approaches to law such as that of Iglesias and Gompers are less common than those in which people engage in legalistic social practices that only subtly, relatively unintentionally, and slowly change legal meanings. See, respectively, Mezey, "Out of the Ordinary: Law, Power, Culture, and the Commonplace," *Law & Social Inquiry* 26 (2001): 149–150; and Hartog, *Man and Wife in America: A History* (Cambridge, MA, 2000). On expressive and constitutional claims-making as a glue that bound ethnically diverse workers, see James R. Barrett, "Americanization from the Bottom Up: Immigration and the Remaking of the Working Class in the United States, 1880–1930," *Journal of American History* 79 (Dec. 1992): 996–1020. On seeking to turn one arm of the state against another while in a position of relative electoral weakness, see, for example, Polletta, "Structural." On perpetuating inequality and subordination through legal processes that offer procedural but not substantive fairness, see Rebecca L. Sandefur, "Access to Civil Justice and Race, Class, and Gender Inequality," *Annual Review of Sociology* 34 (2008): 16.1 to 16.20. In "Legal Consciousness: Some Observations," *Modern Law Review* 67 (2004): 939, Dave Cowans observes that presenting claims in legal terms often causes those called on to respond to feel bound by the result.

51. *Final Report and Testimony on Industrial Relations*, 11168–11170, 11043, 11063, 11046, 11053, 11055, 11059, 11064, 11066–11071, 11171, 11173, 11181–11183, 11187–11190, 11194; *Thirty-Fourth Annual Convention of the American Federation of Labor*, 198; S. 1217 Hearings, 110–111, 118–119, 142; Copy, Samuel Gompers to Woodrow Wilson, 16 Mar. 1916, SGL 217/321; Copy, Telegram, Martinez to Federationist, 13 Mar. 1916, SGL 216/929; Carlos Sanabria, "Samuel Gompers and the American Federation of Labor in Puerto Rico," *Centro Journal* 17 (Spring 2005): 156.

52. Arthur Yager to Frank McIntyre, 21 Apr. 1915, MD NARA 350/5B/975-66; Frank McIntyre to Arthur Yager, 22 Mar. 1917, MD MARA 350/5B/975-131; Memorandum for General McIntyre, 10 June 1915, MD NARA 350/5B/975-83; Yager to Tumulty, 28 June 1915; Memorandum, 19 Mar. 1917, MD NARA 350/ 5B/25142-30; *Thirty-Fourth Annual Convention of the American Federation of Labor*, 53, 195, 198–199; *Final Report and Testimony on Industrial Relations*, 11170–11173, 11195–11198; Arthur Yager to Frank McIntyre, 8 May 1915, MD NARA 350/5B/975-71; Memo. for Colonel Walcutt, n.d. [mid-July 1915?], MD NARA 350/21/Flourney Roberts; Samuel Gompers to Joseph Tumulty, 11 June 1915, CDO:2; Bernogenes Vargas to House of Delegates, 13 Apr. 1916, CDO:2; *Thirty-Fifth Annual Convention of the American Federation of Labor*, 185; *Thirty-Sixth Annual Convention of the American Federation of Labor*, 164, 170; J. P. Tumulty to Samuel Gompers, 4 June 1915, CDO:2; Samuel Gompers to Woodrow Wilson, 5 June 1915, CDO:2; Samuel Gompers to Woodrow Wilson, 22 Nov. 1914, CDO:2; Samuel Gompers to Santiago Iglesias 1, 19 Mar. 1915, CDO:2; Samuel Gompers to Santiago Iglesias, [?] Mar. 1915, CDO:2; [Frank McIntyre],

Memorandum for the Secretary of War, n.d., CDO:2; Gompers to Wilson, 29 July
1915; Samuel Gompers to Santiago Iglesias, 10 Mar. 1916, CDO:2; Samuel
Gompers to Santiago Iglesias, 23 Mar. 1916, CDO:2; Frank McIntyre to Arthur
Yager, 22 Dec. 1916, MD NARA 350/21/Flourney Roberts; Santiago Iglesias to
Frank McIntyre, 6 June 1914, MD NARA 350/5B/1286-132; Frank McIntyre to
Santiago Iglesias, 18 June 1914, MD NARA 350/5B/1286-132; [Frank McIntyre] to
Arthur Yager, 23 June 1915, CDO:2; Wilson to Gompers, 20 Mar. 1916; Samuel
Gompers to Woodrow Wilson, 29 Apr. 1916, SGL 219/305; Frank Morrison to
Woodrow Wilson, 30 Mar. 1915, CDO:2; J. Tumulty to Lindley Garrison, 1 Apr.
1915, MD NARA 350/5B/975-60; Samuel Gompers to Santiago Iglesias, [?] Apr.
1915, CDO:2; Joseph Tumulty to L. Garrison, 4 Aug. 1915, MD NARA 350/5B/
975-94; correspondence at MD NARA 350/5B/975-94 to -98.

Austin Sarat, who describes how the law backed by state power "catches" people
in its rules, also observes that appeals to the higher ideals of those in power can
sometimes provide bases for successful claims. "'The Law Is All Over': Power,
Resistance and the Legal Consciousness of the Welfare Poor," _Yale Journal of
Law and the Humanities_ 2 (1990): 343–379. As Laura Weinrib has observed was
true of the coalition between the AFL and progressives at the time, Iglesias did not
express great optimism that courts would soon embrace his constitutional vision.
See Weinrib, _Taming of Free Speech_, 4, 15–16, 25–28, 31–32, 36–40, 47, 104, 126.

53. Dante Barton, "Frank P. Walsh," _Harper's Weekly_, 27 Sept. 1913, 24, quoted in
Weinrib, _Taming of Free Speech_, 24; _Final Report and Testimony on Industrial
Relations_, especially 145–147, 11029–11224; Weinrib, _Taming of Free Speech_, 24–
25; Frank Walsh to Lindley Garrison, 20 Apr. 1915, CDO:2; Samuel Gompers to
Santiago Iglesias, 15 Apr. 1915, CDO:2; Gompers to Lennon, 12 Mar. 1915; Samuel
Gompers to John Lennon, 17 Mar. 1915, CDO:2; Robin L. Einhorn, "Industrial
Relations in the Progressive Era: The United States and Great Britain," _Social Service
Review_ 58 (Mar. 1984): 106–107. Commissioners ultimately fractured over how to
understand and improve industrial relations. A four-person plurality friendly to labor
supported the director's report, the radical recommendations of which included an
end to judicial declarations that legislation was unconstitutional and an end to
privately owned mines. Three members friendly to business presented separate
justifications for employers' hostility toward labor. The final two members took a
middle road, dedicating substantial attention to the creation of state and federal
industrial commissions. Only the director's report addressed Puerto Rico directly.
See "Report of the Commission on Industrial Relations," _Monthly Review of the U.S.
Bureau of Labor Statistics_, 1 (Nov. 1915): 48–76; David Montgomery, Review,
Technology and Culture 8 (Apr. 1967): 234–237.

Karen Orren and Stephen Skowronek, in _The Search for American Political
Development_ (New York, 2004), describe a government of competing
institutions, each shaped by the distinct moment at which it was created. Sandefur
explains, in "Access to Civil Justice," 16.14, how money, information, social
networks, faith in the legitimacy and efficacy of legal institutions, and the
availability of a legal institution willing to hear one's claim can each increase the
likelihood that a person will make use of legalistic institutions.

54. _Final Report and Testimony on Industrial Relations_, 18, 1–4; "The Delegation of
the Free Federation before the Washington Authorities," _Justicia_, [June?] 1915, MD
NARA 350/5B/975-93; Graham Adams Jr., _Age of Industrial Violence 1910–1915_:

The Activities and Findings of the United States Commission on Industrial Relations
(New York, 1966), 204; Alan Dawley, Struggles for Justice: Social Responsibility
and the Liberal State (Cambridge, MA, 1991), 155; Montgomery, Fall of the House
of Labor, 365; Stromquist, Reinventing "The People," 186.

Gompers gained political returns on receiving a prison sentence (later reversed on
appeal) for contempt of court in a dispute with Buck's Stove Company concerning
the line between protected expression and enjoined incitement to boycott. In
Lawyers against Labor, 109–146, Ernst describes the Buck's Stove case as a
"crucible of interest-group formation." Iglesias's free-speech activism also had
potential to steal thunder from the IWW, whose free-speech protests across 1909–
1914 put it at the vanguard of free-speech activism. See Foner, History of the Labor
Movement, 6:172–212, on how IWW members stepped forward to be arrested
when municipalities suppressed labor speech in streets. Their strategy of flooding
jails, demanding individual trials, and overtaxing city resources sometimes
succeeded and other times brought brutal antilabor repression that won members
sympathy and reputations for bravery and delegitimized their opponents as lawless
despots. On growth in the United States of state power to mediate labor disputes as
the Democrats rose to national power, see David Montgomery, Workers' Control in
America: Studies in the History of Work, Technology, and Labor Struggles
(Cambridge, 1979), 82–83. On how Iglesias benefited from and circulated reports
of his interactions with government officials, see, for example, Yager to Tumulty, 28
June 1915. On how the creation and receipt of legal texts can influence people's
sense of themselves and their relationships to law, see Mezey, "Out of the
Ordinary," 159. For more on the symbolic power of securing a gesture from a
legal body, see Merry, Getting Justice, 86–87. Idit Kostiner provides a framework
for categorizing Iglesias's progress in "Evaluating Legality: Toward a Cultural
Approach to the Study of Law and Social Change," Law & Society Review 37
(June 2003): 323–368.

55. Thirty-Sixth Annual Convention of the American Federation of Labor, 172–173.
For Gompers using citizenship as Iglesias envisioned, see Gompers to Wilson, 29
Apr. 1916. On key mainland labor organizers and their allies whose visions of rights
creation tracked Iglesias's, see Weinrib, Taming of Free Speech, 88, 129. For a
similar approach among Mexican American activists in Texas after World War I,
see Benjamin Heber Johnson, Revolution in Texas: How a Forgotten Rebellion and
Its Bloody Suppression Turned Mexicans into Americans (New Haven, CT, 2003),
5, 160–189.

56. Santiago Iglesias to Samuel Gompers, 29 Apr. 1914, MD NARA 350/5B/1286-132;
Frankfurter to Secretary of War, 11 Mar. 1914; Secretary of War to John Shafroth, 2
Mar. 1914, MD NARA 350/5A/3377-152.

57. McIntyre to Yager, 22 Mar. 1917; Iglesias to Gompers, 29 Apr. 1914; Frankfurter
to Secretary of War, 11 Mar. 1914; Secretary of War to Shafroth, 2 Mar. 1914;
Charles Walcutt to Arthur Yager, 28 July 1915, MD NARA 350/21/Flourney
Roberts; [McIntyre] to Yager, 23 June 1915; W. B. Wilson to Lindley Garrison,
15 July 1915, MD NARA 350/21/Flourney Roberts; Chas Walcutt Jr. to Secretary
of War, 10 Aug. 1915, CDO:2; Samuel Gompers to Santiago Iglesias, 15 Sept. 1915,
CDO:2; F. C. Roberts to Walcutt, 8 Oct. 1915, MD NARA 350/21/Flourney
Roberts; Roberts, Fourth Annual Report; Santiago Iglesias to Samuel Gompers, 5
July 1915, CDO:2.

Roberts's ad hoc approach to governmental intervention in strikes was in tension
with notions of voluntarism and part of a broader pattern. Lambert describes the
interventions of presidents, the Department of Labor, the Federal Conciliation and
Mediation Service, and the Commission on Industrial Relations in similar terms. See
Lambert, *"If the Workers Took a Notion."* In *Triangle Fire*, Greenwald describes
how the New York Factory Investigation Committee transformed from a fact-
finding body into a lawmaking body. Foner relates how, after the Public Service
Commission reported that strikers were prepared to arbitrate and that transit
companies were stubbornly refusing, the Merchants' Association of New York
demanded that the companies meet with the mayor and labor representatives.
Foner, *History of the Labor Movement*, 6:80–81.

58. Santiago Iglesias to P. River Martínez, 5 Jan. 1917, MD NARA 350/5B/3377-320A;
    Santiago Iglesias to H. B. Wilson, 22 Nov. 1916, CDO:2; S. 1217 Hearings, 145–
    146, 136–138; Copy, Agricultural Workers Union No. 14861 to Senate of the
    United States, 14 Jan. 1917, CDO:2; Iglesias to P. Rivera Martínez, 2 Feb. 1917,
    MD NARA 350/5B/975-127C; García and Quintero Rivera, *Desafío y solidaridad*,
    63–64.
    Gompers initially disapproved of Iglesias's new Socialist Party. The AFL's
    nonpartisan policy evaluated candidates by their support for workers' rights and
    welfare. But a strategy that worked for skilled workers in a trade union backed by a
    powerful labor federation made little sense for largely unorganized agricultural
    workers whose primary weapon, strikes, could be easily broken. Only by
    recruiting and nominating political allies could workers have candidates, a reality
    Gompers soon accepted. See Samuel Gompers to Santiago Iglesias, 19 May 1916,
    SGL 220/296; Montgomery, *Workers' Control*, 73–74; Karson, *American Labor*,
    30; Galvin, *Organized Labor Movement*, 65–66; Gompers to Iglesias, 14 Mar.
    1917.
59. Iglesias to River Martínez, 5 Jan. 1917; 54 Cong. Rec. 4170; H.R. 8501 Hearings,
    12, 15–16; 53 Cong. Rec. 8511; H.R. 9533 (18, 24 May 1916), sec. 35; *Civil
    Government for Porto Rico*, S. Rep. 579 (1916), 5–6.
60. Iglesias to Martínez, 2 Feb. 1917 ("espléndida batalla"); Samuel Gompers to Robert
    LaFollette, 19 Feb. 1917, SGL 230/50; Prudencio Rivera Martinez to Santiago Iglesias,
    6 Dec. 1916, CDO:2; Frank McIntyre to Arthur Yager, 5 Dec. 1916, MD NARA 350/
    5B/3377-300; Iglesias to River Martínez, 5 Jan. 1917; Letter of Santiago Iglesias, 10
    Jan. 1917, CDO:3; G. F. Bell to Santiago Iglesias, 4 Feb. 1917, CDO:3; Agricultural
    Workers Union to Senate, 14 Jan. 1917; 54 Cong. Rec. 3007–3010, 3468–3479, 3666;
    Frank McIntyre to Arthur Yager, 21 Feb. 1917, MD NARA 350/5B/3377-329.
61. Erez Manela, *The Wilsonian Moment: Self-Determination and the International
    Origins of Anticolonial Nationalism* (Oxford, 2007), 16, 22–24; Israel, *Messages of
    the Presidents*, 2568–2569; Samuel Gompers, "Keep Faith with Porto Rico,"
    American Federationist, Feb. 1917, 127; Sagardia de Alvarado, "United States–
    Puerto Rican Relations," 345–346; María Eugenia Estades Font, *La presencia
    military de Estados Unidos en Puerto Rico 1898–1918: Intereses estratégicos y
    dominación colonial* (San Juan, PR, 1998), 213–214. On the importance of
    foreign relations to domestic legal change, see Mary Dudziak, *Cold War Civil
    Rights: Race and the Image of American Democracy* (Princeton, NJ, 2000); Rana,
    Two Faces, 7. For interrelationships between U.S. domestic issues and U.S.
    imperialism, see Shelley Fisher Fishkin, "Crossroads of Cultures: The

Transnational Turn in American Studies," *American Quarterly* 57 (Mar. 2005): 17–57.

62. Newton Baker to John Shafroth, 16 Feb. 1917, MD NARA 350/5B/489/3377-327; Gompers, "Keep Faith"; Jackson Lears, *Rebirth of a Nation: The Making of Modern America, 1877–1920* (New York, 2009), 324–325; McGreevey, "Borderline Citizens," 142n10; McIntyre, Memorandum, 20 July 1916; Secretary of War to James Vardaman, 5 Aug. 1916, MD NARA 350/5B/1175-32.

63. Newton Baker to Woodrow Wilson, 21 July 1916, MD NARA 350/5B/3377-286; "Senate Rushes Its Legislation," *New York Times*, 21 Feb. 1917, 6; Baker to Shafroth, 16 Feb. 1917; Cabán, *Constructing a Colonial People*, 199; Shaffer, *Black Flag Boricuas*, 155; 53 Cong. Rec. 7473; McIntyre, Memorandum, 20 July 1916; Grosfoguel, *Colonial Subjects*, 55; Estades Font, *Presencia militar*, 213–214.

64. Frank McIntyre to Arthur Yager, 23 Feb. 1917, MD NARA 350/5B/3377-331; McIntyre to Yager, 21 Feb. 1917; Baker to Shafroth, 16 Feb. 1917; MD NARA 350/5B/3377-300, -320, -331, -335; 54 Cong. Rec. 3666–3667, 4171; Jones Act, 39 Stat. 951 (1917). On how meanings and impacts of legislation emerge and change following enactment, see Nancy MacLean, *Freedom Is Not Enough: The Opening of the American Workplace* (Cambridge, MA, 2006); Karen M. Tani, *States of Dependency: Welfare, Rights, and American Governance, 1935–1972* (Cambridge, 2016). For a broader argument that legal change favorable to those with limited power often results from a temporary convergence of their interests with more powerful actors, see Derrick A. Bell Jr., "*Brown v. Board of Education* and the Interest-Convergence Dilemma," *Harvard Law Review* 93 (1980): 518–533.

65. For recent work dispelling heroic visions of courts protecting individual rights in the face of the strong, persistent, uniform opposition from other powerful institutions, see, for example, Michael J. Klarman, *From Jim Crow to Civil Rights: The Supreme Court and the Struggle for Racial Equality* (Oxford, 2004); Gerald N. Rosenberg, *The Hollow Hope: Can Courts Bring About Social Change?* (Chicago, 1991); Mark Tushnet, *A Court Divided: The Rehnquist Court and the Future of Constitutional Law* (New York, 2005). Thomas M. Keck, "Party Politics or Judicial Independence? The Regime Politics Literature Hits the Law Schools," *Law & Social Inquiry* 32 (Spring 2007): 511–544, argues that Klarman, Tushnet, and Rosenberg overstate judicial impotence. Barry Friedman, in *The Will of the People: How Public Opinion Has Influenced the Supreme Court and Shaped the Meaning of the Constitution* (New York, 2009), relates that courts have come to track public opinion closely while acknowledging exceptions that include the stickiness of precedents. Michael J. Klarman, *From the Closet to the Altar: Courts, Backlash, and the Struggle for Same-Sex Marriage* (Oxford, 2012), describes how judges both advanced gay rights and provoked backlashes against them during the two decades preceding 2012. Nonjudicial officials' freedom to set federal policy brought with it potential responsibility for those policies. Conversely, consider Keith Whittington's description, in *Political Foundation of Judicial Supremacy* (Princeton, NJ, 2007), 113, 124–126, of benefits to regimes of using the Court to avoid deciding issues that threaten to unravel their coalitions, and Howard Gillman's aptly named, "How Political Parties Can Use the Courts to Advance Their Agendas: Federal Courts in the United States, 1875–1891," *American Political Science Review* 96 (2002): 513. Official actors and private individuals produced constitutional change through diverse means and for differing reasons that often varied by their institutional

roles. Acting in concert in this way did not necessarily require active cooperation, however. See Gordon Silverstein, "Law's Allure in American Politics and Policy: What It Is, What It Is Not, and What It Might Yet Be," *Law & Social Inquiry* 35 (2010): 1080, 1089. Seeking patterns within the Court's colonial jurisprudence, Bartholomew H. Sparrow observes greater deference to Congress than to the executive branch and greater protection of commerce than of criminal-procedure rights. See Sparrow, *The Insular Cases and the Emergence of American Empire* (Lawrence, KS, 2006), 160, 167–168, 207–208.

CONCLUSION

1. For an introduction to scholarship on the decline of civil liberties during World War I, see the sources Laura M. Weinrib collected in "Freedom of Conscience in War Time: World War I and the Limits of Civil Liberties," *Emory Law Journal* 65 (2016): 1052–1056. Eric Hobsbawm argues, in *The Age of Empire: 1875–1914* (New York, 1987), 8–12, that World War I ended what he terms the "long nineteenth century" of imperial rivalries in Europe.

2. In AG/OG/Justicia, Ciudadanía, dic. 1917–1918, 1390: Frank McIntyre to Arthur Yager, 2 May 1917; Yager to SecWar, 30 Apr. 1917; Frank McIntyre, Memorandum on Application of Pending Army Bill to Porto Rico, 1 May 1917; Cablegram of 18 Oct. 1917; Memorandum, 1 Oct. 1917. See also Translation, "Our Interview with the Governor of Porto Rico," *El Mundo*, 3 Apr. 1919, MD NARA 350/21/Arthur Yager; Arthur Yager to Frank McIntyre, 10 July 1917, MD NARA 350/5B/723-47; Pub. L. 65-12, sec. 2, 40 Stat. 76, 78 (1917); H.R. 3545 (19 Apr. 1917); "States' Quotas for Draft Army," *Nashville Tennessean and the Nashville American*, 14 July 1917, 1; MD NARA 350/5B/26490-42 to -43; José Trías Monge, *Puerto Rico: The Trials of the Oldest Colony in the World* (New Haven, CT, 1997), 79. McIntyre did not implement the draft in the Philippines. The provost marshal general confirmed McIntyre's analysis, as Yager learned on 18 October 1917. As Russel Lawrence Barsh explains, in "American Indians in the Great War," *Ethnohistory* 38 (Summer 1991): 276–303, U.S. officials initially sought to avoid controversy with American Indians by decoupling actual citizenship from the citizenship required for conscription. All cases of doubt as to citizenship, of which there were many, were to be resolved in favor of noncitizenship, hence exemption from conscription. See also *Report of the Commissioner of Indian Affairs to the Secretary of the Interior for the Fiscal Year Ended June 30, 1918* (Washington, DC, 1918), 8–9.

3. María de Fátima Barceló Miller, *La lucha del sufragio femenino en Puerto Rico 1896–1935* (Río Piedras, PR, 1997), 102–104, 160–162, 225.

4. Translation, "Americans but Strangers," *El Mundo*, 8 Apr. 1926, MD NARA 350/5B/26954-2; Robert C. McGreevey, "Borderline Citizens: Puerto Ricans and the Politics of Migration, Race, and Empire, 1898–1948," PhD diss., Brandeis University, 2008, 183, 195, 197–198, 202, 219; Memo, stamped 4 May 1918, MD NARA 350/5B/19929-92; Secretary of State to SecWar, 13 May 1921, MD NARA 350/5B/19929-172; newspaper articles collected in BCSP/X/21/1; Joseph P. Pagan to Chief of the Bureau of Insular Affairs, 3 May 1919, MD NARA 350/5B/26490-56; correspondence collected at MD NARA 350/5B/26490-56, -57, -68 to

-72, and at AG/OG/CG/180/Justicia, Ciudadanía, 1919–1921, Exp. 1390; *The Records of the Offices of the Government of Puerto Rico in the United States, 1930-1993: Finding Aid* (New York, n.d.), https://centropr.hunter.cuny.edu/sites/default/files/faids/pdf/OGPRUS.pdf, 8–12, 18–28. The bureau's broadside is quoted in McGreevey, "Borderline Citizens," 202. Bureau files also included "Where Does Porto Rico Stand in U.S.?" *Journal of Commerce and Commercial Bulletin* (New York), 29 Jan. 1919, available at MD NARA 350/5B/1444-33, which reported U.S. officials listing Puerto Rican casualties among "men of foreign countries" and treating Puerto Rico as "foreign" for censorship and some trade purposes. On a similar problem to that in Hawai'i arising in California, see Arcadio Santiago to Commissioner for Porto Rico in Washington, 19 Mar. 1919, AG/OG/CG/180/Expediente: Justicia, Ciudadanía, 1919–1921, Exp. 1390.

5. "South Carolina Objects to Negro Encampment," *Louisville (KY) Courier-Journal,* 22 Aug. 1917, 4; Translation, J. W. Hernández et al. to Hon. Sen., Mar. 1919, MD NARA 350/5B/26954-1; Joaquín Colón López, *Pioneros puertorriqueños en Nueva York 1917–1947* (Houston, TX, 2002), 31, 59; Arthur Yager to Frank McIntyre, 5 Sept. 1917, MD NARA 350/5B/723-56; collected correspondence, MD NARA 350/5B/723-56, -67, -79, -91, -101A; Translation, "Very Important," *El Tiempo,* 17 Nov. 1917, MD NARA 350/5B/26691-3.

6. Erez Manela, *The Wilsonian Moment: Self-Determination and the International Origins of Anticolonial Nationalism* (Oxford, 2007), especially 40–44, 56–62; Translation, "The Entertainment at Yaguez," *Diario del Oeste* (Mayagüez), 20 Jan. 1916, MD NARA 350/5B/1175-33; María del Pilar Argüelles, *Morality and Power: The U.S. Colonial Experience in Puerto Rico from 1898 to 1948* (New York, 1996), 45.

7. The quotations appear in Nelson Denis, *War against All Puerto Ricans: Revolution and Terror in America's Colony* (New York, 2015), 59–61. See also Dana G. Munro, *Intervention and Dollar Diplomacy in the Caribbean 1900–1921* (Princeton, NJ, 1964), 210, 228–240, 269, 325, 425, 427, 505–511; Hans Schmidt, *The United States Occupation of Haiti, 1915–1934* (New Brunswick, NJ, 1971); Mary A. Renda, *Taking Haiti: Military Occupation and the Culture of U.S. Imperialism, 1915–1940* (Chapel Hill, NC, 2001); *Annual Reports of the Navy Department for the Fiscal Year 1919* (Washington, DC, 1920), 140–141; William A. DuPuy, "Larger American Territories Now All under One Director," *New York Times,* 4 Nov. 1934, XX5; Frank McIntyre, "Memorandum: The Bureau of Insular Affairs," 8 Feb. 1921, MD NARA 350/5B/24983-64; documents collected at MD NARA 350/5B/975-280 and -288, MD NARA 350/5B/975A-19, -33, and -79. The transfer to the Department of the Interior occurred in 1934.

8. Frank McIntyre to Felix Frankfurter, 20 Sept. 1917, MD NARA 350/21/Manuel Matienzo; Frank McIntyre to Antonio Barceló, 30 July 1921, MD NARA 350/5B/26429-75.

9. Secretary of War to President, 5 July 1923, MD NARA 350/5B/1175-63.

10. For a more honest recollection of congressional responses to Puerto Rican demands for collective naturalization, see Paul Charlton, "Naturalization and Citizenship in the Insular Possessions of the United States," *Annals of the American Academy of Political and Social Science* 30 (July 1907): 111.

11. John Weeks to Montgomery Reily, 27 June 1921, MD NARA 350/5B/1175-53.

12. 203 U.S. 1, 19–20 (1906); Ariz. Const. art. 7, § 2, quoted in Porter v. Hall, 34 Ariz. 308, 271 P. 411 (1928), quoted in Frederick E. Hoxie, *A Final Promise: The Campaign to Assimilate the Indians, 1880–1920* (Lincoln, NE, 2001 [1984]), 234. In 1911 Dudley O. McGovney was already advancing the view that the territorial nonincorporation doctrine should be recognized as the basis for United States–American Indian relations. "American Citizenship: Part II: Unincorporated Peoples and Peoples Incorporated with Less Than Full Privileges," *Columbia Law Review* 11 (Apr. 1911): 326–347.

13. *Celestine*, 215 U.S. 278 (1909); *Nice*, 241 U.S. 591 (1916); Hoxie, *Final Promise*, 233–234, 213, 215, 231, 236; Frederick E. Hoxie, *This Indian Country: American Indian Political Activists and the Place They Made* (New York, 2012), 227, 244, 273–275.

14. Brief for the People of Porto Rico, No. 534, People v. Tapia, 245 U.S. 639 (n.d.), 46 and throughout, MD NARA 350/5B/27188-12; *Muratti*, 25 D.P.R. 568 (1917); The Conferring of Citizenship on Porto Ricans as Affecting the Territorial Status of Porto Rico under the Constitution, 1 Sept. 1917, MD NARA 350/5B/1444-25; Chief of Bureau, Memorandum for the Law Officer, Bureau of Insular Affairs, 21 Aug. 1917, MD NARA 350/5B/1444-24. *Tapia* appears in *Porto Rico Federal Reports*, vol. 9 (Rochester, NY, 1918), 455–497.

15. Secretary of War to President, 5 July 1923; People v. Tapia, 245 U.S. 639; People v. Muratti, 245 U.S. 639; T. H. J. L., Memorandum for Mr. Marmack, 25 Feb. 1920, MD NARA 350/5B/50-75; Antonio Barceló to Frank McIntyre, 13 July 1921, MD NARA 350/5B/26429-75.

16. Frederic Dean, "Porto Rico Asks Statehood or Freedom," *New York Tribune*, 29 May 1921, 12. Dean's mention of "Mahomet's coffin" was a reference to a legend that Muhammad's coffin was suspended in midair in his tomb without any means of support. For an account of the legend, see *Curiosities for the Ingenious: Selected from the Most Authentic Treasures of Nature, Science and Art, Biography, History, and Literature*, 2nd ed. (London, 1822), 73–74. The metaphor was in wide use in the years preceding Dean's remark. See, for example, Park Benjamin, *The Intellectual Rise of Electricity: A History* (London, 1895), 46.

17. *Report of Proceedings of the Fortieth Annual Convention of the American Federation of Labor* (Washington, DC, 1920), 235. Gordon Silverstein argues that "to fully appreciate and understand how law shapes and constrains politics and policy, we have to consider the iterated *interaction* between and among these institutions." Silverstein, "Law's Allure in American Politics and Policy: What It Is, What It Is Not, and What It Might Yet Be," *Law & Social Inquiry* 35 (Fall 2010): 1080. Variations on this question are long-standing in legal history: Robert W. Gordon, "Critical Legal Histories," *Stanford Law Review* 36 (Jan. 1984): 57–125; Robert W. Gordon, "Introduction: J. Willard Hurst and the Common Law Tradition in American Legal Historiography," *Law & Society Review* 10 (Fall 1975): 9–12. Recognizing this dynamic helps solve the puzzle of dramatic shifts in constitutional doctrine that do not produce unambiguous, far-reaching Supreme Court holdings. Key pathways by which the law of empire developed have largely escaped prior notice, in part because no single Supreme Court decision marked the doctrinal shift. Instead, generative avoidance and productive inaction did the greater part of the work. On legal change unmarked by holdings, see Keith E.

Whittington, "Once More Unto the Breach: PostBehavioralist Approaches to Judicial Politics," *Law & Social Inquiry* 25 (Apr. 2000): 621.

18. Frank McIntyre, Memorandum, 14 Aug. 1918, MD NARA 350/5B/975-214; correspondence from February through August 1917 at MD NARA 350/21/ Domingo Collazo; Manifest of SS *Coamo*, Port of San Juan, 23 June 1917, Passenger Lists of Vessels Arriving at San Juan, Puerto Rico, 10/07/1901–06/30/ 1948, DC NARA 85, NAI#: 2945834, Microfilm Roll 52, Ancestry.com; D. Collazo, Letter to Editor, "Porto Rican Politics," *New York Evening Post*, 25 Aug. 1919, MD NARA 350/21/Domingo Collazo; "Report of the Governor of Porto Rico," in *War Department Annual Reports, 1918*, vol. 3 (Washington, DC, 1918), 43; Excerpt, D. C., Letter to Editor, *San Juan (PR) Times*, 28 Feb. 1918, MD NARA 350/5B/750-17; Note re: letter of 14 Apr. 1918, MD NARA 350/21/ Domingo Collazo; Translation, "Santiago Iglesias in Washington," *La Correspondencia de Puerto Rico*, 30 July 1918, MD NARA 350/5B/975-209; "Ibero Society Indorses Wilson Mexican Policy," *New York Tribune*, 12 Jan. 1920, 3; "Mexico Defended in Jenkins Case by Latin-Americans," *New York Tribune*, 15 Dec. 1919, 3; Samuel Gompers to Woodrow Wilson, 30 July 1918, in *The Papers of Woodrow Wilson*, ed. Arthur S. Link et al., vol. 49 (Princeton, NJ, 1985), 135–136; [Frank McIntyre], Memorandum, 1 July 1918, MD NARA 350/ 21/Domingo Collazo; Translation, "General Report of the President of the Free Federation to the Delegates of the Tenth Labor Congress," *Justicia*, 22 Mar. 1920, available at MD NARA 350/5B/975-280.

19. Domingo Collazo, Letter to Editor, "Porto Rico's Government," *New York Times*, 3 June 1923, XX8; Domingo Collazo, "Porto Rico's Aspiration," *New York Herald Tribune*, 2 Feb. 1925, 12; D. Collazo, Letter to Editor, "Our Rule in Porto Rico," 4 Feb. 1920, *Evening Post*, MD NARA 350/5B/50-74; Domingo Collazo, Letter to Editor, "The Governor of Porto Rico," *New York Times*, 14 Dec. 1924, XX20.

20. Bernardo Vega, *Memoirs of Bernardo Vega: A Contribution to the History of the Puerto Rican Community in New York*, ed. César Andreu Iglesias, trans. Juan Flores (New York, 1984 [1977]), 128, 85–86, 112, 121, 140–141; "Se designa una comisión que redacte una constitución aceptable para todos," *La Prensa* (New York), 20 Aug. 1923; Lorrin Thomas, *Puerto Rican Citizen: History and Political Identity in Twentieth-Century New York City* (Chicago, 2010), 41, 44, 39–54; "Un núcleo borinqueño trata de organizar políticamente a los electores hispanos," *La Prensa* (New York), 22 Oct. 1925, 1; "Notas hispanas de 'up town,'" *La Prensa* (New York), 7 Mar. 1928, 2; Liborio Boricua, "Rumores políticos," *Grafico* (New York), 4 May 1929, 6; Liborio Boricua, "Del ambiente político," *Grafico* (New York), 29 June 1929, 4; Virginia E. Sánchez Korrol, *From Colonia to Community: The History of Puerto Ricans in New York City, 1917–1948* (Westport, CT, 1983), 58; Colón López, *Pioneros*, 149; Jesse Hoffnung-Garskof, "The Migrations of Arturo Schomburg: On Being *Antillano*, Negro, and Puerto Rican in New York 1891–1938," *Journal of American Ethnic History* 21 (Fall 2001): 20–29; Domingo Collazo, "Carta Prologo," in Gonzalo O'Neill, *La indiana borinqueña: Diálogo en verso* (New York, 1922), 3–4; "Sociededades Hispanas," *La Prensa* (New York), 20 July 1927, 6. One result of Collazo's disengagement from island politics was his increased willingness to criticize Unionistas, Iglesias, Gompers, and their allies: Collazo, "Porto Rican Politics"; D. Collazo, "Advertising in Spanish," *New York Times*, 14 May 1922, 107. On

attempts by leading Puerto Ricans on the mainland to draw a line between African Americans and Puerto Ricans, see Hoffnung-Garskof, "Migrations of Arturo Schomburg," 28; Thomas, *Puerto Rican Citizen*, 26–28, 39, 50–53.

21. Isabel Gonzalez, "Porto Rico's Plight," *New York Times*, 21 May 1927, 18; 1930 Census, Manhattan/New York/NY/1087/21A; photos, tombstone of Eva C. de Delgado Chalbaud, and Isabel and Juan Torres, on file with Belinda Torres-Mary; emails from Belinda Torres-Mary to Sam Erman, 4, 24 Mar. 2010, on file with author. One clue that the letter was ghostwritten is that it purports to come from New York and Gonzalez had relocated to New Jersey several years earlier. See 1930 Census Crawford/Union/NJ/8/12B; Manifest SS *Philadelphia*, 18 May 1922, PCLVANY T715/3112.

Collazo was not alone in appropriating Isabel Gonzalez while also seeking to honor her and the truth. After Gonzalez died in June 1971, representations of her remained in her descendants' memories and stories. See Transcription, Social Security Administration, Social Security Death Index, Master File, Isabel Torres, June 1971, SSN 146-22-7652 (issued NJ before 1951), Ancestry.com. More recently, imperial, legal, transnational, and microhistorical turns in history have brought academic attention to Gonzalez, including from me. Gonzalez's great-granddaughter, Belinda Torres-Mary, has also uncovered new information about Gonzalez and sought to disseminate it. My collaboration with Torres-Mary has produced further representations of Gonzalez. This book is one example. See also "Isabel González," Wikipedia, https://en.wikipedia.org/wiki/Isabel_Gonz%C3%A1lez. Consumers of these representations (you, gentle reader) add further interpretations. We all (you and I, judges and lawyers, Collazo and his media contacts, census and immigration officials, and Torres-Mary and her and Gonzalez's family) confront versions of what Nolan Porterfield describes as the biographer's challenge. "Like the novelist," we each "find and 'create' a story, ... create the voice which tells it, ... orchestrate [our] characters and bring them to life." Porterfield, "Telling the Whole Story: Biography and Representation," *Journal of Folklore Research* 37 (May–Dec. 2000): 181.

22. Domingo Collazo," "Mujeres notables de Hispanoamérica," *La Prensa* (San Antonio, TX), 18 Sept. 1929, 9 ("los derechos ciudadanos"); "Want Mont Reilly [*sic*] Recalled," *Arkansas City (KS) Daily Traveler*, 3 Sept. 1921, 2; Memorandum, Sept. 1921, MD NARA 350/5B/50-81; "Porto Ricans Seek Removal of Governor," *Wilmington (NC) Morning Star*, 5 Dec. 1921, 1; "Ship Arrives Afire; Blaze Seen as Plot against Gov. Reily," *New York Times*, 21 Nov. 1921, 1; Collazo, "Porto Rico's Government"; Domingo Collazo, "Philippines and Porto Rico," *New York Times*, 20 Dec. 1923, 16; "El Comité de Defensa de Pto. Rico y la candidatura de comisionado residente," *La Prensa* (New York), 26 July 1924, 1; Collazo, "Governor of Porto Rico"; Collazo, "Porto Rico's Aspiration"; "Notas hispanas"; Boricua, "Del ambiente político"; "Citizenship Again," *Porto Rico Progress*, 22 Oct. 1920, 4, MD NARA 350/5B/719-55; Vega, *Memoirs*, 111, 120–121, 128, 139. For the definitive telling of the *colonia*'s turn to citizenship in the 1920s and afterward, see Thomas, *Puerto Rico Citizen*.

23. "Don Domingo Collazo recibirá hoy el postrer homenaje de sus compatriotas," *La Prensa* (New York), 26 Sept. 1929, 3. Collazo witnessed an early instance of the shift from petitioning the resident commissioner to petitioning one's stateside representative when Democratic congressman Sol Bloom of New York sought the

Puerto Rico vote by introducing a bill to create an elected governorship for Puerto Rico. For a fuller recounting, see Thomas, *Puerto Rico Citizen*, 47–48; Vega, *Memoirs*, 140–141. Confirming the shift in how Puerto Ricans gained influence in Congress, a member of the staff of the resident commissioner could not help but smile in 2013 at the notion of stateside residents of Puerto Rican descent seeking help from his boss rather than from their own representatives.

24. Philip S. Foner, *History of the Labor Movement in the United States*, vol. 7: *Labor and World War I, 1914–1918* (New York, 1987), 159, 174–175, 253, 257, 273, 276–279, 305–318, 337; Kirwin R. Shaffer, *Black Flag Boricuas: Anarchism, Antiauthoritarianism, and the Left in Puerto Rico, 1897–1921* (Urbana, IL, 2013), 146; Marc Karson, *American Labor Unions and Politics, 1900–1918* (Boston, 1958), 85, 88, 92–100, 108, 112, 200–209; Alan Dawley, *Struggles for Justice: Social Responsibility and the Liberal State* (Cambridge, MA, 1991), 197; Josiah Bartlett Lambert, *"If the Workers Took a Notion": The Right to Strike and American Political Development* (Ithaca, NY, 2005), 76–78; David Montgomery, "Workers' Movements in the United States Confront Imperialism: The Progressive Era Experience," *Journal of the Gilded Age and Progressive Era* 7 (Jan. 2008): 34–37; Samuel Gompers, *Preparedness for National Defense* (Washington, DC, 1916), 9.

25. "Report of the Governor of Porto Rico," 47–53, in *War Department Annual Reports, 1919* (Washington, DC, 1919); Richard B. Gregg, "The National War Labor Board," *Harvard Law Review* 33 (Nov. 1919): 39–63; Brief of Documents, Porto Rican Agricultural Workers v. Employers, 46–47, MD NARA 2/Case Files Apr. 1918 to Aug. 1919; [H.?] Humkins, National War Labor Board, Brief of 10 June 1918, Porto Rican Agricultural Workers v. Employers, 10 et seq., MD NARA 2/Case Files Apr. 1918 to Aug. 1919/7; "Remove Governor of Porto Rico, Is Gompers's Demand," *New York Tribune*, 10 May 1918, MD NARA 350/5B/975-170; Lawrence B. Glickman, *A Living Wage: American Workers and the Making of Consumer Society* (Ithaca, NY, 1997), pt. 4 and 83, 96–98, 116, 119.

26. Newton Baker to William Wilson, 19 Aug. 1918, MD NARA 350/5B/975-223; [W. B.?] Wilson to Newton Baker, 3 Sept. 1918, MD NARA 350/21/Flourney Roberts; Frank McIntyre to Arthur Yager, 16 May 1918, MD NARA 350/5B/975-176; Humkins, Brief of 10 June 1918, Porto Rican Agricultural Workers v. Employers, 16 et seq.; Dionicio Nodín Valdés, *Organized Agriculture and the Labor Movement before the UFW: Puerto Rico, Hawai'i, California* (Austin, TX, 2011), 47; *Proceedings of the Fortieth Convention of the American Federation of Labor*, 236–245.

27. Brief of Documents, Porto Rican Agricultural Workers v. Employers, 24; Humkins, Brief of 10 June 1918, Porto Rican Agricultural Workers v. Employers, 16 et seq.; Samuel Gompers to Santiago Iglesias, 17 Jan. 1918, SGL 242/[?]; Samuel Gompers, Brief of Memorandum, Porto Rican Agricultural Workers v. Employers, 48, MD NARA 2/Case Files Apr. 1918 to Aug. 1919/7; Nodín Valdés, *Organized Agriculture*, 47; Note, Porto Rican Agricultural Workers v. Employers, 3, MD NARA 2/Case Files Apr. 1918 to Aug. 1919/7; "Remove Governor"; Summary of Santiago Iglesias Charges, Porto Rican Agricultural Workers v. Employers, 7, MD NARA 2/Case Files Apr. 1918 to Aug. 1919/7.

28. Summary of Charges by Samuel Gompers, Porto Rican Agricultural Workers v. Employers, 8, MD NARA 2/Case Files Apr. 1918 to Aug. 1919/7; Press Release, 3

Apr. 1917, MD NARA 350/5B/975-132; Charges, 30 Apr. 1918, MD NARA 350/
5B/975-196; P. Rivera Martinez and Rafael Alonso to Woodrow Wilson, 9 Nov.
1918, MD NARA 350/5B/975-210; Santiago Iglesias, Complaint, Porto Rican
Agricultural Workers v. Employers, 4, MD NARA 2/Case Files Apr. 1918 to Aug.
1919/7; Summary of Santiago Iglesias Charges, Porto Rican Agricultural Workers v.
Employers, 7; Pilar Argüelles, *Morality and Power*; Samuel Gompers to Frank
McIntyre, 3 Jan. 1918, MD NARA 350/5B/975-145.

In bringing their complaint, the men hoped that the board's reluctance to protect
African American workers' rights would not extend to Puerto Ricans. As they knew,
racism against African Americans could be worse than that against Puerto Ricans,
and Southern senators were more concerned about federal "interference" with race
and labor relations within state lines than with such activity in the colonies. See
Robert H. Zieger, *For Jobs and Freedom: Race and Labor in America since 1865*
(Lexington, KY, 2007), 98–100.

29. Frank McIntyre to Arthur Yager, 5 Apr. 1917, MD NARA 350/5B/1175-38;
    McIntyre to Yager, 16 May 1918; Newton Baker to Arthur Yager, 8 July 1918,
    MD NARA 350/5B/975-197A; correspondence collected at MD NARA 350/5B/
    975-228; Memorandum, 3 Feb. 1919, MD NARA 350/5B/975-229.

30. Montgomery, "Workers' Movements," 33–34; *First Pan American Financial
    Conference* (Washington, DC, 1915), 7; Sinclair Snow, *The Pan-American
    Federation of Labor* (Durham, NC, 1964), 4–6, 9–11, 16–18, 28–29, 37–46, 52,
    56–57; Nell Irvin Painter, *Standing at Armageddon: The United States 1877–1919*
    (New York, 1987), 292, 310–313; John Mason Hart, *Revolutionary Mexico: The
    Coming and Process of the Mexican Revolution* (Berkeley, CA, 1987), 283; *Pan-
    American Labor Press*, various dates, 1918. Following the outbreak of the Mexican
    Revolution in 1910, U.S. officials had raised the specter of threats to U.S. property
    and interests in Mexico and twice sent troops there.

31. "Unrest in Porto Rico Stirs Washington," *Baltimore Sun*, 27 Nov. 1925, MD
    NARA 350/5B/975A-79; Samuel Gompers to W. D. Mahon, 19 Dec. 1916, SGL;
    William Green to William E. Borah, 30 Dec. 1924, SGL 305/223; Snow, *Pan-
    American Federation of Labor*, 53, 46, 48–49, 60–61, 129–130; Santiago Iglesias
    to Samuel Gompers, 5 July 1916, CDO:2; correspondence in SGL 286/460, 287/
    416, 288/67, 289/278, 289/279, 289/281, 297/894, 297/985, 297/987, 312/913,
    335/874.

32. "Labor's 'Monroe Doctrine,'" *New York Herald Tribune*, 18 Oct. 1925, A6;
    "American Federation of Labor Denounces Communist Philosophy – Declares
    against 'Red Internationale of Autocratic Moscow' in Declining to Join Alliance,"
    Commercial and Financial Chronicle, 24 Oct. 1925, 1997; Karson, *American Labor
    Unions*, 136–137; Snow, *Pan-American Federation of Labor*, 59, 149; Shaffer,
    Black Flag Boricuas, 146; McGreevey, "Borderline Citizens," 186–187;
    Montgomery, "Workers' Movements," 26, 40; United States Immigration Act of
    1918, secs. 2–3, 40 Stat. 1012, 1012 (1918); *Exclusion and Expulsion of Anarchists
    from the United States* (Washington, DC, 1918), 2; *Report of the Proceedings of the
    Second Congress of the Pan-American Federation of Labor* ([1919?]), especially 8–
    9; Gonzalo F. Córdova, *Resident Commissioner: Santiago Iglesias and His Times*
    (Río Piedras, PR, 1993); Painter, *Standing at Armageddon*, 381; Philip S. Foner,
    History of the Labor Movement in the United States, vol. 8: *Postwar Struggles,
    1918–1920* (New York, 1988), 13, 20–21, 25–26, 50; Translation, "Disturbing

Propaganda," *La Democracia*, 30 Jan. 1920, MD NARA 350/5B/975A-58; correspondence in SGL 284/16, 285/593, 288/486, 306/405, 306/979, 306/1003, 307/19, 307/52, 307/113–115, 307/165–169, 307/205. Gompers's views on immigration dovetailed with those of the congressionally created Dillingham Commission. In an influential forty-one-volume 1911 report, the commission had recommended tilting the balance of U.S. immigration toward northern and western European peoples.

33. Mae M. Ngai, *Impossible Subjects: Illegal Aliens and the Making of Modern America* (Princeton, NJ, 2004), 20–27, 50; Immigration Act of 1924, 43 Stat. 153 (1924); Snow, *Pan-American Federation of Labor*, 53, 59, 66; *Second Congress of the Pan-American Federation*, 54. Kunal M. Parker elucidates citizenship as a system and strategy of exclusion; see Parker, "State, Citizenship, and Territory: The Legal Construction of Immigrants in Antebellum Massachusetts," *Law and History Review* 19 (Autumn 2001): 583–643, and *Making Foreigners: Immigration and Citizenship Law in America, 1600–2000* (Cambridge, 2015). The new immigration restrictions grew out of the Dillingham Commission's findings. See Robert E. Zeidel, *Immigrants, Progressives, and Exclusion Politics: The Dillingham Commission, 1900–1927* (DeKalb, IL, 2004), and, from Katherine Benton-Cohen's in-progress research, "The Rude Birth of Immigration Reform: As America Debates Immigration Reform, It Is in Danger of Repeating the Mistakes Made a Century Ago When the Flawed Foundations of Today's Policies Were Established," *Wilson Quarterly* 34 (2010): 16–22. On the rise of the modern passport regime, see John Torpey, "The Great War and the Birth of the Modern Passport System," in *Documenting Individual Identity: The Development of State Practices in the Modern World*, ed. Jane Caplan and John Torpey (Princeton, NJ, 2001), 256–270; Mark B. Salter, *Rights of Passage: The Passport in International Relations* (Boulder, CO, 2003), 77; Craig Robertson, *The Passport in America: The History of a Document* (Oxford, 2010), 13, 101–103, 184–185, 193, 201, 217.

34. *Report of the Proceedings of the Fifth Congress of the Pan-American Federation of Labor* (1927), 107; Colón López, *Pioneros*, 89 ("tan mal compensado, tan ignorado, tan sufrido y abandonado"), 305–306 ("tan grande! Era nada menos que ciudadano de los Estados Unidos de América"; "infierno donde la lucha por la vida es un perenne"); McGreevey, "Borderline Citizens," 182–195, 203–221; correspondence collected at MD NARA 350/5B/1493; Arthur Yager to Frank McIntyre, 20 July 1917, MD NARA 350/5B/1493-22; James R. Barrett, "Americanization from the Bottom Up: Immigration and the Remaking of the Working Class in the United States, 1880–1930," *Journal of American History* 79 (Dec. 1992): 996–1020; Painter, *Standing at Armageddon*, 337, 365–366; Stanley Coben, "A Study in Nativism: The American Red Scare of 1919–20," *Political Science Quarterly* 79 (Mar. 1964): 52–75; James R. Barrett and David Roediger, "Inbetween Peoples: Race, Nationality and the 'New Immigrant' Working Class," *Journal of American Ethnic History* 16 (Spring 1997): 16; Translation, *Extraordinary Convention*, stamped 18 Nov. 1918, MD NARA 350/5B/975A-26; Frank McIntyre, Memorandum for the Secretary of War, 13 Jan. 1922, MD NARA 350/5B/975-316.

For examples of correspondence concerning migrant family members' loss of contact or mistreatment while away, see MD NARA 350/5B/2876-4 to -12. For one demand for an official response, see *Memorial of the Porto Rican Federation of Labor to the*

House of Representatives (San Juan, PR, 1919). For legislation authorizing a response, see Copy, An Act to Regulate Emigration from Porto Rico, and for Other Purposes, 29 May 1919, MD NARA 350/5B/2876-24.

35. *Proceedings of the Fifth Congress of the Pan-American Federation*, 107; Lambert, *"If the Workers Took a Notion,"* 65–66, 79–83; Montgomery, "Workers' Movements," 38; Laura Weinrib, *The Taming of Free Speech: America's Civil Liberties Compromise* (Cambridge, MA, 2016), 115–116, 120–121; David Montgomery, *Workers' Control in America: Studies in the History of Work, Technology, and Labor Struggles* (Cambridge, 1979), 100; David Montgomery, *The Fall of the House of Labor: The Workplace, the State, and American Labor Activism, 1865–1925* (New York, 1987), 6–7; Foner, *History of the Labor Movement*, 8:203; Kelvin A. Santiago-Valles, *"Subject People" and Colonial Discourses: Economic Transformation and Social Disorder in Puerto Rico, 1898–1947* (Albany, NY, 1994), 119, 147–151; Angel G. Quintero Rivera, *Patricios y plebeyos: Burgueses, hacendados, artesanos y obreros: Las relaciones de clase en el Puerto Rico de cambio siglo* (San Juan, PR, 1988), 131, 151–153, 177–179; Cesar J. Ayala and Rafael Bernabe, *Puerto Rico in the American Century: A History since 1898* (Chapel Hill, NC, 2007), 39, 63; Fernando Bayrón Toro, *Elecciones y partidos políticos de Puerto Rico (1809–1976)* (Mayagüez, PR, 1977), 153–190.

Córdova contends in *Resident Commissioner* that Iglesias remained faithful to the workers he represented. The more common interpretation is that Iglesias abandoned militancy for accommodation and corruption as he gained access to electoral power. For examples, see Miles Galvin, *The Organized Labor Movement in Puerto Rico* (London, 1979), 81; Colón López, *Pioneros*, 118–119; Montgomery, "Workers' Movements," 27.

36. Bolivar Pagán, "Memorial Addresses: Remarks by Commissioner Pagán of Puerto Rico," in *Memorial Services Held in the House of Representatives of the United States Together with Remarks Presented in Eulogy of Santiago Iglesias, Late a Resident Commissioner from Puerto Rico* (Washington, DC, 1940), 29, 32; Córdova, *Resident Commissioner*, 98–99.

37. Iglesias named other daughters Luz (Light), Victoria (Victory), and Paz (Peace). América Iglesias Thatcher shared her father's commitment to labor activism and the importance of governmental power. She worked for Samuel Gompers's successor, the next president of the American Federation of Labor, organized garment workers in Los Angeles, and worked for the republican side in the Spanish Civil War. See Rose Pesotta, *Bread upon the Waters* (Ithaca, NY, 1987 [1944]), 358. Like Iglesias but in a different locale, V. C. Bird followed a trajectory from colonial trade union leader to political leader of an increasingly independent insular land. See Paget Henry, *Shouldering Antigua and Barbuda: The Life of V. C. Bird* (Hertford, UK, 2010). On a call for similar work on other Caribbean islands, see Jessica Byron, Book Review, *Social and Economic Studies* 60 (Sept./Dec. 2011): 230–231.

38. Transcript of Record, No. 179, Balzac v. Porto Rico, 258 U.S. 298 (20 Dec. 1920), 1–2, 5, 11–17, 25, 29; Bartholomew H. Sparrow, *The* Insular Cases *and the Emergence of American Empire* (Lawrence, KS, 2006), 197; Shaffer, *Black Flag Boricuas*, 59–60; Brief for Appellant, No. 179, *Balzac* (2[0/9?] Nov. 1921); Caldwell v. Hayden, 42 App. DC 166 (1914); Gompers v. United States, 233 U.S. 604 (1914); Gompers v. Buck's Stove & Range Co., 215 U.S. 605 (1909); Truax v. Corrigan, 257 U.S. 312 (1921); Samuel Gompers to Jackson Ralston, 22 Dec. 1921, SGL 275/474.

39. For an example of noncitizen nationality as a mainstream legal idea, see Charlton, "Naturalization and Citizenship," 106–107.
40. *Balzac*, 258 U.S., 306, 304–305, 309, 313–314.
41. Modern doctrine specifies no constitutional rights that turn on incorporated status, beyond the jury rights and revenue rules identified more than a century ago. See Granville-Smith v. Granville-Smith, 349 U.S. 1 (1955); Reid v. Covert, 354 U.S. 1 (1957); Examining Board v. Flores de Otero, 426 U.S. 572 (1976); Torres v. Commonwealth, 442 U.S. 465 (1979); United States v. Verdugo-Urquidez, 494 U.S. 259 (1990); Boumediene v. Bush, 553 U.S. 723 (2008).

    Taken together, the scholarship agrees that little beyond jury rights and tariff rules has ever been held to turn on unincorporated status. See Christina Duffy Burnett, "Untied States: American Expansion and Territorial Deannexation," *University of Chicago Law Review* 72 (Summer 2005): 834–853; Sparrow, *Insular Cases*, 142–211; Sarah H. Cleveland, "Our International Constitution," *Yale Journal of International Law* 31 (2006): 46–48; Gary Lawson and Robert D. Sloane, "The Constitutionality of Decolonization by Associated Statehood: Puerto Rico's Legal Status Reconsidered," *Boston College Law Review* 50 (2009): 1146. Later recognized as overruled on other grounds in *Limbach v. Hooven and Allison Company*, 466 U.S. 35 (1984), *Hooven and Allison Company v. Evatt*, 324 U.S. 652 (1945), held that shipments from unincorporated territories to states of the Union were "imports" constitutionally unreachable by state taxes. See U.S. Const., art. I, sec. 10, cl. 2. It also read into *Downes* a finding of nonapplicability to unincorporated territories of the constitutional rule that direct federal taxes be proportionate among the states; see ibid., sec. 9, cl. 4. *Evatt* reserved the question whether shipments from incorporated territories to states of the Union were also imports and made no comment on the rule for direct taxes in incorporated territories. *Cross v. Harrison*, 57 U.S. 164, 174 (1853), had nearly a century before stated that the Constitution permitted Congress to exempt territories from direct taxation even when imposing such taxes in states. Though *Board of Public Utility Commissioners v. Ynchausti and Company*, 251 U.S. 401, 404 (1920), strongly suggested that neither Due Process Clause was applicable in unincorporated territory, *Calero-Toledo v. Pearson Yacht Leasing Company*, 416 U.S. 663, 668 n.5 (1974), subsequently held otherwise.
42. *Balzac*, 258 U.S., 311; Pfizer, Inc. v. Government of India, 434 U.S. 308, 313 (1978); 48 Stat. 456 (1934); Treaty of Manila, in *United Nation Treaty Series: Treaties and International Agreements Registered or Filed and Recorded with the Secretariat of the United Nations*, vol. 7 (4 July 1946), 3–39; Commonwealth v. Sanchez Valle, 579 U.S. ___, ___ (2016); U.S. Const., art. IV, sec. 3, cl. 1; Zivotofsky v. Kerry, ___ U.S. ___, ___ (2015).

    For other decisions seeming to state, but perhaps not quite holding, that unincorporated territories may be perpetually denied statehood, see *United States v. Verdugo-Urquidez*, 494 U.S. 259, 268 (1990); *Granville-Smith v. Granville-Smith*, 349 U.S. 1, 5 (1955). *Sanchez Valle* reviews the legal documents that culminated in commonwealth status for Puerto Rico. In "The Basis of Puerto Rico's Constitutional Status: Colony, Compact, or 'Federacy'?" *Political Science Quarterly* 122 (Spring 2007): 115–140, David A. Rezvani describes how elected Puerto Ricans turned to the relationship between Great Britain and its dominions in articulating commonwealth status.

AFTERWORD

1. Sonia G. Collazo, Camille L. Ryan, and Kurt J. Bauman, "Profile of the Puerto Rican Population in the United States and Puerto Rico: 2008," paper presented at the annual meeting of the Population Association of America, Dallas, 15–17 Apr. 2010, 1–2; Sharon R. Ennis, Merarys Ríos-Vargas, and Nora G. Albert, *The Hispanic Population: 2010* (2011), 14; United States Census Bureau, 2010 Population Finder, 2010 Demographic Profile, Puerto Rico, https://www .census.gov/popfinder/.

   Among the large literature investigating Puerto Ricans' participation in mainland politics and the barriers they have faced, see, for example, Lorrin Thomas, *Puerto Rican Citizen: History and Political Identity in Twentieth-Century New York City* (Chicago, 2010); Lilia Fernandez, *Brown in the Windy City: Mexicans and Puerto Ricans in Postwar Chicago* (Chicago, 2012); José Ramon Sánchez, *Boricua Power: A Political History of Puerto Ricans in the United States* (New York, 2007). On racial discrimination, Puerto Ricans, and the census, see Carmen Teresa Whalen, *From Puerto Rico to Philadelphia: Puerto Rican Workers and Postwar Economies* (Philadelphia, 2001); Jorge Duany, *Puerto Rican Nation on the Move: Identities on the Island and in the United States* (Chapel Hill, NC, 2002), chs. 10–11; Carlos Vargas-Ramos, "Some Social Differences on the Basis of Race among Puerto Ricans," Research Brief, Center for Puerto Rican Studies, Hunter College, New York, 2016, https:// centropr.hunter.cuny.edu/sites/default/files/data_briefs/RB2016-10_RACE.pdf.

2. Kinsella v. Krueger, 351 U.S. 470, 475–476 (1956); *Covert*, 354 U.S. 1, 5–6; ibid., 67 (Harlan, J., concurring); United States v. Verdugo-Urquidez, 494 U.S. 259, 275 (1990); Brittany Warren, "The Case of the Murdering Wives: *Reid v. Covert* and the Complicated Question of Civilians and Courts-Martial," *Military Law Review* 212 (2012); Frederick Bernays Wiener, "Persuading the Supreme Court to Reverse Itself: *Reid v. Covert*," *Litigation* 14 (Summer 1988): 6–10. Justice Kennedy provided the fifth vote in *Verdugo-Urquidez* for the proposition that the Fourth Amendment requirement that searches be by warrant did not protect aliens with no significant voluntary connection to the United States from searches abroad. In his opinion for the Court in *Boumediene v. Bush*, 553 U.S. 723, 766 (2008), Justice Kennedy declared that the existence of a constitutional right to challenge overseas confinement through a writ of habeas corpus depended in part on the citizenship of the detainee.

3. Frederic R. Coudert, "The Evolution of the Doctrine of Territorial Incorporation," *Columbia Law Review* 26 (1926): 850, 828. On the impossibility of reconciling republican ideals with colonial racism, and on the productive and contingent interplay that results from the attempt, see Gary Wilder, *The French Imperial Nation-State: Negritude and Colonial Humanism between the Two World Wars* (Chicago, 2005), 6, 8, 13, 20, 301–302.

4. José Trías Monge, *Puerto Rico: The Trials of the Oldest Colony in the World* (New Haven, CT, 1997); *Boumediene*, 553 U.S. 723 (2008); Christina Duffy Burnett, "A Convenient Constitution? Extraterritoriality after *Boumediene*," *Columbia Law Review* 109 (2009): 994–996; Gary Lawson and Robert D. Sloane, "The Constitutionality of Decolonization by Associated Statehood: Puerto Rico's Legal Status Reconsidered," *Boston College Law Review* 50 (2009): 1146; Raymond Carr, *Puerto Rico: A Colonial Experiment* (New York, 1984). For an overview of competing interpretations of the current status of Puerto Rico, see David A.

Rezvani, "The Basis of Puerto Rico's Constitutional Status: Colony, Compact, or 'Federacy'?" *Political Science Quarterly* 122 (Spring 2007): 115–140. The Court has strongly signaled and yet never expressly held that birth in unincorporated territory is not birth within the United States for purposes of the Fourteenth Amendment guarantee of jus soli citizenship. See Toyota v. United States, 268 U.S. 402 (1925); Barber v. Gonzales, 347 U.S. 637, 639 n.1 (1954); Rabang v. Boyd, 353 U.S. 427, 430–431 (1957); Sean Morrison, "Foreign in a Domestic Sense: American Samoa and the Last U.S. Nationals," *Hastings Constitutional Law Quarterly* 71 (2013): 71–150; Brief of Citizenship Scholars as Amici Curiae in Support of Appellants and Urging Reversal, No. 13-5272, Tuaua v. United States, 788 F.3d 300 (12 May 2014).

Index

Adams, Lewis, 65

administrative law. *See* Constitution; law; nonjudicial officials (as Constitution's interpreters); race and racialization; Reconstruction Constitution

AFL (American Federation of Labor): electoral politics and, 110–111; Iglesias and, 7, 47–48, 66–71, 97–98, 135–141; labor protectionism and, 155; Puerto Rican citizenship demands and, 71, 98–105, 121–123, 135–141; race and, 71–72, 99, 110–111, 154–156, 251n52; World War I and, 152–155

African Americans: AFL's hostility toward, 67–69, 71–72, 100; citizenship and, 11, 26, 81, 120, 131, 169n11, 191n46; disfranchisement of, 1, 10, 35, 82–83, 108, 119, 148–149; Dred Scott decision and, 11, 15, 29–30, 51–54, 81–87, 169n11, 180n11, 198n23; educational opportunities for, 65; Great Migration and, 156; labor activism and, 44, 49, 71–72, 99, 110–111, 154–156, 206n56, 247n44, 251n52, 260n28

Alaska, 12, 28, 31, 106, 114–115, 119, 147

Alianza Puertorriqueña, 124–125

alien status (of Puerto Rico/ans), 1, 15–16, 42, 74–87, 96, 98, 146, 218n47

Allen, Charles, 45, 99, 221n7

ambiguity, 3–5, 56, 86–98, 114–120, 122–129, 142–146, 158–159, 257n17

American Indians, 1, 9, 14–15, 26–29, 43, 52, 59, 65, 81, 93–94, 106, 148–149, 178n2, 194n4, 196n15, 233n55, 255n2

American Political Development (APD), 166n16

American Samoa, 1, 14, 98, 115, 147, 233n55

American Tobacco Company, 136

anarcho-syndicalists, 99

annexation: ambiguity and, 3–5, 56, 86–98, 114–120, 122–129, 142–146, 158–159, 257n17; border-extension question and, 40; citizenship status and, 1–2, 12–13, 27–28, 33–34, 39–41, 47, 53–55, 74–76, 81–87, 91–92, 97–98, 114–115, 126, 142–143, 179n7, 257n17; Dred Scott v. Sandford and, 11, 40; Puerto Ricans' disagreements over, 21–26; racial considerations and, 3–4, 6, 8–9, 15–16, 29–30, 45–46, 77–78, 80–87, 112–119, 168n9; Reconstruction Constitution and, 2, 8–16, 26–27, 40–41, 51–53, 181n17; statehood and, 5, 27–30, 40–41, 142–143, 149–150, 158–159, 180n11. *See also* citizenship status; Puerto Rico; race and racialization; Reconstruction Constitution; statehood

Anti-Imperialist League, 29

Arizona, 30–31, 53, 148–149, 156

assimilationism (in Puerto Rico), 18–19

Australia, 151

Autonomistas. *See* Partido Autonomista

Bacon, Augustus, 31

Baker, Newton, 141–142

Baldorioty de Castro, Román, 17, 19–23

Ballinger, Richard, 111

Balzac, José, 158–159

Barbados, 40

Barbosa, José Celso, 23–24, 36, 44–45, 69–70, 183n26

Barkey, Karen, 214n20

Barsh, Russel Lawrence, 255n2